Agrarian Studies Series
Series Editor: V. K. Ramachandran

Agrarian Studies 1
Essays on Agrarian Relations in Less-Developed Countries
edited by V. K. Ramachandran and Madhura Swaminathan

Agrarian Studies 2
Financial Liberalization and Rural Credit in India
edited by V. K. Ramachandran and Madhura Swaminathan

Agrarian Studies 3
Dalit Households in Village Economies
edited by V. K. Ramachandran and Madhura Swaminathan

Agrarian Studies 4
A New Statistical Domain in India: An Enquiry into Village Panchayat Databases
Jun-ichi Okabe and Aparajita Bakshi

Agrarian Studies 5
How Do Small Farmers Fare? Evidence from Village Studies in India
edited by Madhura Swaminathan and Sandipan Baksi

Agrarian Studies 6
Women and Work in Rural India
edited by Madhura Swaminathan, Shruti Nagbhushan, V. K. Ramachandran

Agrarian Studies 7
Economic Change in the Lower Cauvery Delta: A Study of Palakurichi and Venmani
edited by Madhura Swaminathan, V. Surjit, V. K. Ramachandran

Agrarian Studies 7

ECONOMIC CHANGE IN THE LOWER CAUVERY DELTA

A Study of Palakurichi and Venmani

Edited by
Madhura Swaminathan
V. Surjit
V. K. Ramachandran

Tulika Books

Published by
Tulika Books
44, first floor, Shahpur Jat, New Delhi 110 049, India
www.tulikabooks.in

First edition (hardback) 2023

ISBN: 978-81-950559-5-1

Printed at Chaman Offset, Delhi 110 002

In memory of

Abhijit Sen (1950–2022) and Okabe Jun-ichi (1959–2021)

Contents

Tables, Figures, and Boxes

2 Palakurichi, 1916–2019

3 Venmani, 2019

8 Livestock

9 Assets

11 Farm Business Incomes

14 Education

16 Cyclone Gaja

Foreword

This book is an enquiry into social and economic change in the lower Cauvery delta.

Historically, the lower Cauvery delta was one of the most important sites of lowland-irrigated rice cultivation in South India. It was known for extreme concentration of the ownership and control of land in the hands of landlords, who, despite the establishment of the *ryotwari* system, continued to exercise *mirasi* rights. It was also known for the large mass of landless Scheduled Caste workers who actually worked the land, and for the brutal economic and extra-economic coercion to which they were subject.

The book discusses the enormous changes in production and the forces of production in the region, the decline of rice cultivation, and the effects of the sharp decline in the volume of water available to the region from the Cauvery irrigation system. The book also examines the relations of production, employment and incomes, and standards of living in the region. While there have been important changes in these spheres, unemployment, income-poverty, and inequality in living conditions persist.

The major sources of data for the book are detailed surveys of two villages in the region. The surveys were conducted in 2019, with follow-up visits made after pandemic restrictions were lifted. The first village, Palakurichi, was first studied in 1917 and subsequently in 1942, 1963, 1983, and 2005. The second village, Venmani, is a place of great significance in the history of the lower Cauvery delta. It encompasses the hamlet of Keelavenmani, in which landlord-murderers and their henchmen burned 44 Dalit people – men, women, children – to death on December 25, 1968. (A separate volume on the atrocity is being written as part of this project.)

I am happy to write that this is the seventh book in the Agrarian Studies Series published by the Foundation for Agrarian Studies.

Bengaluru
October 23, 2023

V. K. Ramachandran
General Editor
Agrarian Studies Series

Acknowledgements

In 2018, the Foundation for Agrarian Studies (FAS) initiated a project to study agrarian relations in the lower Cauvery delta with a special focus on Venmani and Palakurichi villages. We are very grateful to Krishna Kumar and Saraswathi Menon for their support to the research for this book.

The primary data for the book come from fieldwork undertaken in May–June 2019 in Venmani and Palakurichi villages of Nagapattinam district, under the guidance of V. Surjit. The fieldwork was coordinated by C. A. Sethu and Tapas Singh Modak from FAS. Members of the FAS staff who participated in the survey include Sanjukta Chakraborty, Divya Devadiga, Rakesh Mahato, and N. Sudha. We thank Arindam Das, Pinki Ghosh, Deepak Johnson, Tapas Singh Modak, and T. Sivamurugan for training the investigators and overseeing the survey. T. P. Harshan, Parvathi Menon, V. Sridhar, and Aardra Surendran also participated in the field study.

The survey team included Arun Bharathy, A. Durgadevi, Denver Harrison, O. Kalpanadevi, M. Karuppasamy, A. Logeshwari, B. Monica, M. Muthuneela, Nandhini Nanjappan, S. Nithya, V. Preethi, K. P. Prithviraj, R. Jancy Rani, Sai Rishik, M. Sabarisakthi, R. Sangeetha, M. Sankaran, G. Saranya, K. Sankara Pandi, F. Suresh Kumar, and R. Vignesh. Dr V. Gajendran and Dr N. Arivukkarasi from the Madras School of Social Work helped identify students for the survey.

Data entry and processing were led by Sanjukta Chakraborty, Ritam Dutta, Rakesh Mahato, Subhajit Patra, and C. A. Sethu. R. Goutham, Denver Harrison, M. Muthuneela, R. Jancy Rani, M. Sabarisakthi, R. Sangeetha, and Hanok assisted the process. The data analysis team, led by Arindam Das, comprised Sanjukta Chakraborty, Ritam Dutta, R. Goutham, R. Roshith Krishnan, Rakesh Mahato, Subhajit Patra, R. Jancy Rani, R. Sangeetha, and C. A. Sethu. R. Ashwath translated Tamil documents to English..

Two workshops were conducted while the book was being written. We are grateful to all the participants, in particular to K. Balakrishnan, G. Ramakrishnan, and P. Shanmugam, for their comments and suggestions. We also thank R. Ashwath, Narmadha Devi, and R. Sindhan for preparing the Tamil versions of all the presentations.

Judith Heyer and Venkatesh Athreya read the first draft of the entire manuscript, and provided invaluable comments. We are grateful to John Harriss for his comments. Sandipan Baksi, Director of the Foundation for Agrarian Studies, has helped this project over the last four years.

C. A. Sethu was the overall coordinator of the project that resulted in this volume. He was in charge of the village surveys and played a critical role at every stage thereafter, from participating in data entry, processing, and follow-up data collection, corresponding with various authors, commenting on the chapters, and preparing this manuscript for publication. We are very grateful to Sethu for his manifold contributions to the volume.

Without the support of Krishna Kumar and Saraswathi Menon, and the Kilvenmani Foundation, the research for this book would not have begun. We thank the Rosa Luxembourg Stiftung (RLS) for their support to the fieldwork and follow-up workshops. We are also grateful to the National Institute of Rural Development and Panchayati Raj for supporting the fieldwork. We are grateful to the people of Venmani and Palakurichi villages, and various officials of the district for their cooperation and support.

We thank Indira Chandrasekhar and the team at Tulika Books for preparing the final manuscript, and TNQ books for designing the cover.

Judith Heyer, Barbara Harriss-White, and John Harriss, who have done field-based research in rural Tamil Nadu for more than four decades, have supported the work of the Foundation for Agrarian Studies, and particularly its village studies programme, in different ways. Our special thanks to them.

October 5, 2023

Madhura Swaminathan
V. Surjit
V. K. Ramachandran

1

Introduction

V. K. Ramachandran and Madhura Swaminathan

This book is a study of economic change in the lower Cauvery delta. It draws on socio-economic surveys of two villages in Nagapattinam district, Tamil Nadu.

Palakurichi, in Kilvelur taluk, is a village first studied by economists in 1917, surveyed by K. Soundara Rajalu as part of the famous "Slater studies" supervised by Gilbert Slater, Professor of Economics at the University of Madras. The village was studied subsequently by P. J. Thomas and K. C. Ramakrishnan in 1942, Margaret Haswell in the early 1960s, S. Guhan in 1983, and V. Surjit in 2005.[1] Venmani village encompasses the hamlet of Keelavenmani, the location of the great atrocity of December 25, 1968, when 44 Dalit men, women, and children were forced into a hut and burned to death by caste Hindu landlord-criminals and their henchmen. (As part of the study of the lower Cauvery delta, a history of the Keelavenmani atrocity will also be published by the Foundation for Agrarian Studies.) The study conducted by the Foundation for Agrarian Studies is the first census-type socio-economic survey of households of the two villages.

Our study of Palakurichi and Venmani is different from any other recent study of rural Tamil Nadu in two ways. First, the subject matter and detail of our database are unique. The primary database comes from census-type, schedule-based surveys of all households in the two villages, from interviews with selected respondents, and from discussions with local officials, political workers, agricultural workers' and farmers' union activists, and other local informants. The secondary database draws on extensive and diverse sources of official data from State and Central statistical organisations.

Secondly, the study of the villages is based on a detailed analysis of classes in the two villages. The scientific study of agrarian relations is impossible without a detailed analysis of the classes in rural society. The categorisation of households into socio-economic classes is based on data on the ownership of

[1]Rajalu (1918), Thomas and Ramakrishnan (1940), Haswell (1967), Guhan (1983), and Surjit (2008).

the means of production, the employment and expenditure of labour power, and on the agricultural and non-agricultural incomes of each household in the two villages. Our study of agrarian relations – and class, caste, and gender differentials – in the two villages is based on more detailed information than any other recent study of rural Tamil Nadu.

Palakurichi and Venmani are "tail-end" villages, that is, they are located at the end of the Cauvery irrigation system, and thus among the villages in the deltaic region most affected by the sharp decline in the supply of Cauvery water over the previous two decades.

The lower Cauvery delta is an area that was known for its cultivation of rice and agricultural surplus, and for the particularly harsh and cruel – and often inhuman – forms of exploitation and oppression forced on the working people by feudal landlords and the state. The systems of class exploitation and of caste oppression, exclusion, and separation, and the criminal practice of untouchability were inseparable. "The deeper the oppression, the greater the revolt": the first unions of peasants and agricultural workers to be organised under the red flag in Tamil Nadu were in the lower Cauvery delta (the eastern part of what was then a single Thanjavur district).[2] Today the old crop regime and cultivation have changed, and changed irreversibly, as have the relations of production and the brutal forms of direct discrimination that were the mainstay of the old agrarian regime.

The core data for this book come from a census-type survey of households in the two villages: 390 households in Palakurichi and 415 households in Venmani. The questionnaire was long and wide-ranging, and the chapters describe some of the major findings from the survey, and in most chapters, also from important sources of official secondary statistical data.[3] The reference year for cultivation is 2018–19.[4]

This Introduction does not deal with the findings of each chapter in any detail (these are available in an abstract at the beginning of each chapter). Our attempt here is to introduce the reader to the general state of agrarian relations in the two villages as it emerges from the survey data.

[2] See the account by P. Ramamurti in Ramachandran (2015).

[3] In December 2020, Mayiladuthurai district was formed by separating two revenue divisions of Nagapattinam district. In this book, all data refer to the old Nagapattinam district.

[4] There was drought in the delta in 2000, 2001, 2002, 2008, 2012, and 2016, and flooding occurred in the region in 2008. In 2018, during our reference year, there was a breach in the Upper Anicut in August and Cyclone Gaja hit the region in November.

Production Conditions and Agrarian Relations

The main feature of change in the state of the productive forces in the lower Cauvery delta since the survey conducted in Palakurichi in 2005 is the decline of the delta as a hub of rice cultivation in the State. The annual discharge of water from the Mettur dam, whose reservoir is the main repository of water for the region, declined from around 250 thousand million cubic feet (tmcft) in the 1960s and 1970s to 103 tmcft in the last decade (2010–19). The aridification of land in the lower Cauvery delta is an emerging threat, driven, perhaps, more by changes in the water regime than by changes in rainfall.[5]

The decline in the availability of water, caused mainly by changes in water-sharing arrangements between the States of Karnataka and Tamil Nadu, has made it impossible to continue rice cultivation on the same basis as before. During the "green revolution" years of the 1970s and 1980s the region changed from a single-crop region to a double-cropped region. By the time of our survey, it had reverted to being a single rice-crop region, and rice yields had declined from the levels recorded in earlier surveys in Palakurichi village.

In brief, agriculture and irrigation policy did not successfully address the challenges that came with the decline in Cauvery water supply. Agriculture in the region did not change to crops (and crop varieties and farming practices) and sidelines that were suitable to the new water regime. The State has also not adequately modernised micro-level irrigation systems in the villages – to line channels adequately, for instance, and ensure the conservation of water in other ways. The lower Cauvery delta needs crop regimes and agricultural policy that are suited to a region of intermittent drought and cyclonic activity. These are not easy tasks, but need to be dealt with if the productive forces in agriculture are to recover and grow.

It is noteworthy that many of the foregoing agricultural themes were raised in the 1980s by the late S. Guhan, distinguished administrator and Professor at the Madras Institute of Development Studies.[6] Guhan was clear that, given the demands of inter-State water-sharing, there would be a secular decline in the share of Cauvery water available to Tamil Nadu in general and the tail-end of the delta in particular. He recommended making the irrigation system more efficient (and lining canals), and changing cropping patterns to crops that needed less water than was being used for flood irrigation in low-land rice cultivation at the time. His advice was far-sighted, and the difficult

[5] Aridification is the process of a region becoming increasingly arid or dry. It refers to long-term change, rather than seasonal variation (https://en.wikipedia.org/wiki/Aridification).
[6] Guhan (1983, 1993).

consequences of these observations not having been given full practical form are evident today.

A further and important feature of the villages is that while the gains of the green revolution achieved by the 1980s tended to wither, no major new sources of economic activity or production other than crop (particularly rice) production developed concurrently in the two villages.

As we have written, and as the chapters that follow record, there has been qualitative change over the last century in the forces of production. These have been accompanied by profound changes in the relations of production in the region. Chapter 4 discusses the deeply unequal agrarian relations that were prevalent historically in the lower Cauvery delta. By the seventeenth century the region was characterised by the concentration of ownership and control of land in the hands of a small group of caste Hindu landlords, brought together by a complex system of unfreedom and brutal extra-economic coercion.

With regard to agrarian relations, the main change over historical time is that the old form of tyranny of landlordism, the grip of mainly pre-capitalist forms of exploitation on the economic, social, and personal lives – and even the bodies – of workers, has been broken. It was broken, in the first place, by decades of struggle by the peasants and the agricultural workers of the region led by the Communist Party of India and, after the mid-1960s, by the Communist Party of India (Marxist). State policy had to respond to these struggles, particularly after the atrocity in Keelavenmani and the exposure by the mass movement of the collusion between the institutions of state and the landlords. While tenancy remains a significant feature of agrarian relations, the terms of tenancy have changed, particularly in respect of temple land.

Extra-economic oppression of agricultural workers, long-term farm workers, and Dalits of the forms that existed till the 1970s and early 1980s do not exist today. Landlord-enforced exclusion of Dalits from common public spaces such as schools, eating places, or eating spaces at weddings or funerals is no longer possible. The social gains of the working people and Dalits of the villages have been made possible because of struggle.

Nevertheless it must be understood that the change that has occurred is not the consequence of a policy of land reform given legal basis by legislation from above. The personnel of the richest families in the village today, that is, the capitalist landlord households that are economically dominant in both villages, are *all* drawn from the old landlord families. Although their land has been subdivided over the years, and incomes from cultivation are no longer the major sources of their incomes, landlords sit atop a hierarchy where acute inequality persists. The top landlord families, which constitute 2 per cent of households in Palakurichi, own 38 per cent of the agricultural land held by all households. In Venmani, 1 per cent of landlord households own 18 per cent of all land. Even excluding holdings of gold and financial assets, they own 22 per cent of all assets in Palakurichi and 24 per cent of all assets in Venmani. Of the total number of person-days of daily wage work in Palakurichi in the reference year, landlords employed 33 per cent. The corresponding share of daily labour time employed by landlords in Venmani was 12 per cent. Landlords owned the most and the best land in the villages, and did not work at any of the major agricultural operations. They dominate the villages in respect of ownership of means of non-agricultural income in the village, and in rural and urban areas outside the village. They have been able to take greater advantage of the means of higher education than other households, and thus have greater access to sources of non-agricultural employment and modern salaried incomes.

In Palakurichi and Venmani, landlessness is still high: 46 per cent of households in Palakurichi and 56 per cent in Venmani do not own land. Nevertheless landlessness has actually declined in Palakurichi. Amidst increased proletarianisation, a section of workers has gained ownership of some small plots of land. A significant feature of landholding in the present day is that in both villages, Dalit households own land. Single-acre plots were sold to Dalit households (and registered in the name of women) at Rs 33,000 an acre with a 50 per cent subsidy from the government, in an arrangement mediated by a local social work organisation called Land for Tillers Freedom (LAFTI). One hundred and fifty Dalit households in Palakurichi or 66 per cent of all Dalit households in the village and 95 Dalit households or 36 per cent of all Dalit households in Venmani village now own land. These transactions took place from 2000 to 2019. While the incomes from these plots are wholly inadequate for a satisfactory income, the very fact of Dalit land ownership represents a historic change in the land ownership structure of lower Cauvery delta villages. LAFTI has been active, even within the limits that it has set, in the two villages (and the Nagapattinam–Thiruvarur region) because of the agrarian movement of the poor in the lower Cauvery delta.

Wage workers constitute the major section of workers in the villages. Crop production is no longer the major source of wage labour, and we no longer have separate classes of agricultural and non-agricultural workers in the villages. We have classified wage-worker households into households whose major incomes come from unskilled or semi-skilled work (24 per cent of all households in Palakurichi and 28 per cent in Venmani), and those whose major income is from skilled and formal-sector wage work (12 per cent of all households in Palakurichi and 11 per cent in Venmani). Taken together, poor peasants and wage workers constitute about 70 per cent of all households in Palakurichi and 60 per cent of all households in Venmani.

In general, the majority of wage workers – from 80 per cent in one village to more than 90 per cent in the other – who were employed in unskilled and semi-skilled manual work, and in skilled and formal-sector wage work, were from the Scheduled Caste and Most Backward Class groups.

Scheduled Caste households are disproportionately concentrated – 50 per cent in Venmani and 73 per cent in Palakurichi – in the poor peasant and unskilled and semi-skilled manual worker class categories. Only 5 to 6 per cent fell in the middle and rich peasant categories, and none in the landlord or rich capitalist farmer category.

Employment and Incomes

Unemployment among the poor is the great scourge of the two villages. Agricultural employment and non-agricultural wage employment did not provide adequate incomes for households in the villages. On average, even among persons from households whose major incomes were from unskilled and semi-skilled wage work, the average number of days of work available in agriculture to a woman worker was 23 days a year in Palakurichi and Venmani. The corresponding figure for men was 16 days a year in Palakurichi and 17 days a year in Venmani.

In the two villages, although the number of days of employment per household gained through the Mahatma Gandhi National Rural Employment Guarantee Scheme (MGNREGS) was less than the 100 days promised by the Government of India, it was still the largest source of wage employment, generating 45 days of employment per woman worker and 18 days of employment per male worker from wage-worker households in Palakurichi, and 49 days per woman worker and 22 days per male worker from wage-worker households in Venmani.

Non-agricultural employment was thus central to households in the two villages. A major part of household income was generated from secondary and tertiary sector activities (81 per cent in Palakurichi and 87 per cent in Venmani), and about 42 to 45 per cent of this income was generated in urban and semi-urban areas. While the village remains a unit of residence and economic activity, the village economy is no longer circumscribed by the geography of the village.

Tamil Nadu is distinctive among the States of India for the high rate of urbanisation, for the pattern of diffused urbanisation that prevails, and for a good transport network. The shift in employment and incomes from agriculture to the secondary and tertiary sectors began earlier in Tamil Nadu than elsewhere. C. T. Kurien noted as early as 1980 that "a quiet transformation" was occurring as small farmers joined the rural proletariat and rural workers moved into non-agricultural jobs.[7] In 2021–22, 37 per cent of Tamil Nadu's gross value added (GVA) was contributed by the secondary sector (28 per cent at the national level), and 30 per cent of the rural workforce was in manufacturing and construction in the State (19 per cent nationally).

The movement of employment outside the village implies a diversification of occupations among households. Diversification has occurred across classes and castes. Diversification nevertheless is marked by inequality in the *quality* of jobs available to workers from different caste and class positions. In Palakurichi, two-thirds of wage workers worked in unskilled tasks; the corresponding proportion for Venmani was 71 per cent.[8]

For women, opportunities for employment are extremely limited. While more and more women are coming into the non-agricultural labour force, the gender gap in access to non-agricultural employment and levels of non-agricultural earnings is huge.

Daily wage rates for manual work in the villages follow a familiar pattern with respect to a range of development, particularly human development, indicators: they are substantially higher than the all-India level, lower than the levels reported in official publications for Tamil Nadu as a whole, and substantially lower than the levels reported for Kerala. In both villages, agricultural wages were paid in cash along with some tea and small items of food. The average daily wage paid to men for agricultural work was Rs 496 in Palakurichi and Rs 433 in Venmani. The average daily wage paid to women for agricultural work was Rs 220 in Palakurichi and Rs 233 in Venmani.[9] The average daily wage paid to men for unskilled and semi-skilled work in construction was Rs 463 a day in Palakurichi, and approximately the same in Venmani.[10]

Even with diversification of employment out of agriculture, average absolute levels of household income remain low. No less than a quarter of households in both villages had incomes below the extreme poverty line of two dollars a day, and 50 per cent were unable to afford a healthy diet.

One of the effects of the concentration of Scheduled Caste farmers among

[7] Kurien (1980).

[8] The major categories of unskilled and semi-skilled work included agricultural work, brick-kiln work, head-load work, construction, building fences on agricultural land, MGNREGS, quarrying, cutting wood, and sanitary and cleaning work.

[9] According to the official publication *Wage Rates in Rural India* (WRRI), money-wage rates for sowing and transplanting work in Kerala in 2021–22 were Rs 825 a day for men and Rs 570 a day for women (GoI 2022).

[10] According to WRRI, the money wage in 2020–21 for construction work for men was Rs 483 in Tamil Nadu and Rs 841 a day in Kerala (GoI 2022).

the poor peasantry is that average agricultural incomes earned by Scheduled Caste farmer households are substantially lower than agricultural incomes earned by other sections. The reference year, as mentioned, was a year affected by a cyclone. The data show that the impact of the natural disaster on Dalit farms was much worse than on the farms of all others. The average farm business income from operational holdings in rupees per hectare in Venmani was Rs 280 for Dalit households and Rs 6,456 for all other non-Dalit farming households. In Palakurichi, the numbers showed negative incomes for Dalit farming households, (–)Rs 2,437 per hectare, and Rs 311 per hectare for non-Dalit households. Considering only rice cultivation, the farm business income from cultivation in rupees per hectare in Venmani was Rs 1,229 for Dalit households and Rs 5,336 for non-Dalit households; the corresponding figures for Palakurichi were (–)Rs 1,749 for Dalit households and Rs 5,880 for non-Dalit households.

Credit

In the late 1970s and early 1980s, during the period when social and development banking was official policy, and rural bank branches began to be established all over India (Tamil Nadu was an important site of the growth of rural banking), it was believed that the public sector of banking would serve as a countervailing force to the informal sector, and one that would, in time, overcome and replace it. This expectation has not been realised. Although the formal sector of banking has grown and now encompasses all households, the burden of debt at high rates of interest is a burden that has not gone away. Consumption credit for the poor, particularly for education, health, and housing, is obtained from what we call the "new private formal sector," that is, the microfinance sector, which puts out loans at interest higher than 20 per cent per annum. Microfinance companies also involve low-income borrowers in what can be seen as semi-coercive group activity, where a group monitors and punishes its women members when they do not fulfil the conditions imposed by the microfinance company. Rural finance, particularly in respect of bulky consumption credit needs, continues to be a pathway to a debt trap for the rural poor.

Education

There has been comprehensive change in school and tertiary education in Tamil Nadu over the last four decades. The most important feature of school education in the village is that enrolment is, effectively, universal. The gender gap in educational achievement, however, persists.

With respect to education, the caste gap has narrowed. There was a distinct gender gap between Scheduled Caste men and women above the age of 16. An interesting feature of the Venmani data is that the proportion of women above 16 years with more than 10 completed years of education was higher among women of the Scheduled Caste than other women.

About 20 per cent of children aged 10–14 years in Venmani now attend private schools (it is 36 per cent among those aged 17 years and above). When the private sector in school education expands, educational expenses rise, and households are open to indebtedness in order to achieve schooling. Tamil Nadu must now aim for high quality public education that is completely free and does not create or exacerbate indebtedness for parents.

Some issues in the sphere of education in the villages are thus clear from our data. First, the task of ensuring 100 per cent enrolment and retention of school pupils, first for ten years, then for twelve, remains to be completed, particularly in respect of retention. Secondly, special efforts have to be made to ensure the universal retention of girls. Beyond these, questions of the quality of school education and issues of access to tertiary education of high quality for the poor and the underprivileged must be addressed. Long-term progress in education, especially in school education, will depend on the part played by the public sector in education.

Housing

The study of the quality of housing has been an important component of village studies conducted by the Foundation for Agrarian Studies. The method has been to study housing in terms of whether or not a house meets the following criteria: it is made of *pucca* construction materials (i.e. it has a *pucca* roof, *pucca* walls and *pucca* floors); it has at least two rooms; it has a separate kitchen; it has a source of water for domestic use inside the homestead (we also note whether or not there is a water source within 200 metres of the homestead); it has at least one electricity outlet; and it has a functioning toilet that is used by the residents of the house.

The record here is problematic. To mention a few salient features of our findings, only 22 per cent of the houses in Palakurichi and 19 per cent in Venmani satisfied all six criteria. The criterion on which houses performed best was electricity – almost all households had a functioning electricity connection at the time of the survey. On all other counts – *pucca* housing, living space, the availability of a source of water for domestic use within the house, and functioning toilets – much remains to be done.

Caste differences were marked in the sphere of housing: only 9 per cent of

Scheduled Caste households in Palakurichi and 15 per cent of Scheduled Caste households in Venmani fulfilled all the criteria. The absence of functioning toilets is of serious note – for all households, particularly for Dalit households. The villages are very far from being open defecation-free, and Dalit residences are particularly underprovided with toilets.

Dalit Households

Many decades of fierce struggle have ended the old forms of untouchability, caste-based exclusion from public spaces, and day-to-day anti-Dalit violence.[11] The trajectory from agrestic servitude to land ownership and wage labour represents a profound transformation. Our data also show that, while the struggle of the Dalit masses of the Lower Cauvery delta has won many important victories, institutional barriers to change have obstructed the progress of the war against cumulative deprivation. After many years of struggle and social change, the rural Dalit masses remain separate in many respects – both socially and with respect to physical living spaces.

Dalit households have more landless among them, and those among Dalits who own land, own holdings that are much smaller than the ownership holdings of caste Hindus. Since Dalit households that operate land are concentrated among the poor peasantry, the average incomes they earn are much lower than incomes earned by non-Dalit households. While there have been substantial improvements in formal education, caste differences persist. In the sphere of housing, water supply, and sanitary infrastructure in homes, Dalits are far behind the rest (in an overall situation of inadequate achievement).

Decades of fierce struggle by and the continuing vigilance of unions of the Left today have been the most important locomotives of social change among the Dalit masses of the two villages. Even the achievements of LAFTI were possible only because of the role that the political organisations of the Left played in that region. The consequences of the absence of such organisation can be seen time and again in contemporary Tamil Nadu, where barbaric acts of discrimination and violence against people of the Scheduled Castes have, appallingly, continued to occur in different parts of the State. The title of a recent article in *Economic and Political Weekly*, "Elusive Justice to Dalits in the 'Land of Social Justice'," describes an important aspect of reality in Tamil Nadu today.[12]

[11] Although, as recent events in Vengaivayal in Pudukottai district, Chidambaram in Cuddalore district, Uthapuram in Madurai district, and elsewhere show, these are far from having disappeared in the State. See Rajasekaran (2023), *The Hindu* (2021), and Viswanathan (2008).

[12] Lakshmanan and Sethuraman (2023).

One clear implication of our study is the need for a large-scale economic and sociological study of the position of the Dalit masses in rural Tamil Nadu – of achievement and change, but more importantly for future policy and public action from below, of discrimination and persistent cumulative deprivation.

* * *

In summary, the path of economic change in rural Tamil Nadu has placed the State substantially ahead of the poor performers among Indian States, and, indeed, substantially ahead of the national average with respect to key indicators of economic performance and human development. In the lower Cauvery delta, there have been historic changes with respect to the growth of the productive forces. The main features of this have been changes in the technology of rice production, changes in the crop calendar and land use, a secular decline in the volume of surface water available to the region from the Cauvery system, and urbanisation and the growth of occupations outside crop production. There has been historic change in the relations of production, summarised in this chapter and described in the book, in which decades of class and anti-caste struggle by Dalit working people and the Communist Party have played a decisive role. At the same time, data from our two villages show the limits to the success that the path of "growth without structural change" (in C. T. Kurien's words) has had with respect to economic development, employment, and the reduction of social and economic inequality.[13] Because the countryside has not seen the upheaval in production relations that comes from land reform, acute inequalities of class, caste, and gender persist. These take new forms in new circumstances, but are nevertheless deeply embedded in society.

[13] An argument that has gained recent publicity is that Tamil Nadu has followed a unique inclusive path of development, ensuring "economic growth with social justice," and driven by policies that directly addressed caste-based inequalities and discrimination (Kalaiyarasan and Vijaybhaskar 2021). The claim that economic growth has been inclusive, particularly with respect to people of the Scheduled Castes, has been questioned by scholars. Judith Heyer (2022), for example, points to the relatively low quality of employment received by people of the Scheduled Castes, the low ownership of enterprises among Dalits, and continuing caste atrocities (the book does not refer to the Keelavenmani atrocity). She points also to the lack of gender inclusivity, and to continuing discrimination against women and girls. John Harriss asks if the failure to address the problems of agrarian reforms has not been counterproductive to social justice, arguing that caste–class differentiation and subordination of the Dalits persist (Harriss 2022). The book seems unaware of Kurien's argument on growth and the absence of structural change; indeed, it does not refer to his work on the Tamil Nadu economy at all.

I

The Villages: Setting the Scene

2

Palakurichi, 1916–2019

V. Surjit

HIGHLIGHTS

Palakurichi village, located in the lower Cauvery delta in Nagapattinam district, Tamil Nadu, is unique in having been the site of scholarly study for more than a century. First studied by students of Gilbert Slater, Professor of Economics at the University of Madras in 1916, Palakurichi was re-surveyed in 1938 by P. J. Thomas and K. C. Ramakrishnan, in 1964 by Margaret Haswell, in 1983 by S. Guhan and his colleagues at the Madras Institute of Development Studies (MIDS), in 2004 by V. Surjit, and in the summer of 2019 by the Foundation for Agrarian Studies.

The population of the village grew sharply in the decades of the 1930s and 1940s, after the construction of the Mettur dam, reaching 1,425 persons in 1951; it fluctuated in the decades that followed, but was almost the same in 2019 as in 1951. Sixty per cent of this population is constituted by people of the Scheduled Castes; the proportion was 50 per cent in 1917. There was a sharp fall in the number of Naidu and other upper caste families resident in the village in recent years.

A remarkable feature of cultivation in the village is the dominance of rice in the cropping pattern over the century. At the same time, there were major changes in the yield and production of rice after the introduction of green revolution technologies. From the 1990s, with less water from the Cauvery river coming to Palakurichi, rice yields and incomes declined.

Agrarian relations changed, too. Communist Party workers organised against oppressive forms of discrimination; Naidu owners left the village to seek higher, non-agricultural incomes. The political mobilisation of agricultural workers and release from old forms of landlord oppression, access to land, education, and better housing and other amenities from public programmes, have together improved the living conditions and livelihoods of Dalit families.

The Slater Village Studies

In 1913, Professor Gilbert Slater took charge as Professor of Economics at the Madras University. Slater recognised the disconnect between the economic theory taught in the university, based largely on western text books on economics, and the socio-economic conditions that existed in India at the time. Slater wanted his students to understand rural realities in Indian villages and the causes and remedies of Indian poverty. He gathered his students at the university and decided to do a socio-economic enquiry in rural areas to understand the socio-economic problems of rural India and study the causes and remedies for them. The plan of the study was for each student to undertake a survey of their native village. Each student canvassed a questionnaire designed by the group to facilitate an understanding and analysis of socio-economic conditions of rural households. Slater's students carried out the surveys during 1916 and the results and analysis from 11 villages in the Madras Presidency were published as a book edited by Slater and titled *Some South Indian Villages*. This was the beginning of one the most remarkable series of village studies in India, and these villages have come to be known as the Slater villages (Rajalu 1918; Tirumalai 1940; Haswell 1967; Guhan 1983; Surjit 2008).

The Slater villages were resurveyed in 1938 by his students Thomas and Ramakrishnan. In 1964, some Slater villages were studied by Margarat Haswell, an agricultural economist from the University of Oxford. In 1983, S. Guhan and his colleagues at the MIDS undertook a detailed resurvey of the Slater villages. In 2004, I surveyed one of the Slater villages, Palakurichi in Nagapattinam district. After nearly two decades, in 2019, Palakurichi was surveyed by the Foundation for Agrarian Studies, Bengaluru.

A century has passed since the first study of Palakurichi, and there have been six studies of Palakurichi village between 1916 and 2019. We thus have a unique database on social and economic change in an Indian village over an entire century.

Palakurichi: Location and Geography

Marshall Bouton (1985) classified the Thanjavur region into five different zones. Bouton's classification was based on two major criteria: the nature of irrigation facilities, and the nature and composition of the agricultural workforce. To characterise the nature of irrigation facilities, Bouton examined (a) whether there was irrigation at all, (b) the spread of canal irrigation facilities, and (c) the quality and dependability of water delivered through the irrigation system. For characterising differences in the composition of the agricultural workforce, Bouton looked at the share of agricultural labourers and cultivators in the agricultural work force and in total population, as well as agrarian density, defined as the number of agricultural workers per unit area of land.

In terms of Bouton's classification, Palakurichi falls in the Old Delta Coastal Zone. The soil of the Old Delta Coastal Zone was sandy and often suffered from problems of salinity. The region suffered from low levels of water availability, poor drainage facilities, floods, and uncertainty in availability of water through canals. The only source of irrigation was the water from the network of canals branching out of the Cauvery irrigation system. This zone had a bipolar agro-economic structure with the agricultural work force sharply divided between large landowning cultivators belonging to non-Brahmin upper castes and Dalit agricultural labourers.[1]

Palakurichi village is located in Keelaiyur block of Kilvelur taluk in Nagapattinam district (see Appendix Figure 2.1). The village is located at the tail end of the Cauvery irrigation system, where the network of canals in the Cauvery irrigation system drains into the sea.

A significant share of Palakurichi's population is dependent on agriculture for livelihood. The village is located at a distance of 12 kilometers from the district headquarters of Nagapattinam, and 14 kilometers from Velankanni, a major pilgrimage centre. In recent times, many youth of the working age population have gone for employment in a wide range of non-agricultural activities in the towns of Nagapattinam and Velankanni. This has led to a diversification of incomes in the contemporary period. In earlier periods, agriculture was the sole provider of livelihoods for households in the village.

Key Phases of Transformation

Palakurichi village has the distinction of being the subject of at least six scholarly studies during the last century. These six studies were each conducted at an interval of approximately two decades. Some major phases of agriculture and rural development in the village emerge from these studies.

The first study was conducted in 1916, and the results were published in 1918. The study provides us a picture of socio-economic conditions of a village in a traditional rural setting in pre-Independence India, a village marked by

[1] In this zone, agricultural labourers were organised and mobilised against the large land owners. There was an "isomorphism of caste and class relations" in this region and the bond was much stronger than in any other region (Bouton 1985). This peculiar agro-economic structure resulted in a high degree of agrarian radicalism in this region than any other part of Thanjavur (Bouton 1985; Gough 1981, 1989; Beteille 1974).

extreme poverty, inequality, mass illiteracy, dominance of landlords, extreme forms of caste oppression, and inhuman living conditions of Dalits in the village. The second study, undertaken in 1938 and published in 1940, is also a picture of pre-Independence rural living conditions, but by then, Palakurichi village was slowly beginning to experience changes on account of improvement in irrigation infrastructure in the region with the construction of the Mettur dam in 1934. The new dam brought in improvements in the irrigation system through better flood control mechanisms in the delta and this was reflected in improved agricultural production in the village.

The study of Palakurichi village in 1964 by Margaret Haswell discussed characteristics of agricultural production, and also examined the role of caste and gender relations in the village. The study was conducted in a period when agricultural production systems in the region were being transformed through the introduction of green revolution technologies, and the village was witnessing improvements in production and productivity with the introduction of short-duration varieties and two crops of rice, taking advantage of the improved irrigation infrastructure.

The results of the next study of the village by Guhan in 1983 clearly brought out the transformation in agricultural production and gains made by the introduction of green revolution technologies as well as significant social changes in the lives of Dalit households, largely because of Left political movements that protected their rights and enhanced their dignity. The Guhan study is more comprehensive than the earlier ones as it gives quantitative estimates of crop incomes and data on the extent of inequality in land ownership and other assets.

The fifth study by Surjit in 2003 is of a period when deterioration in the Cauvery irrigation system had severely affected agriculture in the region, and a period in which droughts and intermittent floods had adversely affected crop production and the livelihoods of cultivators in the village. The picture revealed by this study was one of declining prosperity in a village that was once part of the "rice bowl" of south India. The study showed the beginning of a slow transition from dependence on agriculture to dependence on the non-agriculture sector.

The sixth and most recent study, conducted in 2019, is also the most detailed study of the village with respect to economic data. The findings of this survey give a clear picture of the shift from household dependence on agriculture to the non-agriculture sector, of the importance of the MGNREGA programme as a support to vulnerable households during periods of crisis in the agriculture sector, of changes in caste relations, and of the beginnings of access to land among Dalits through various interventions.

Figure 2.1 *Timeline of studies and phases of transformation in Palakurichi village, 1916–2019*

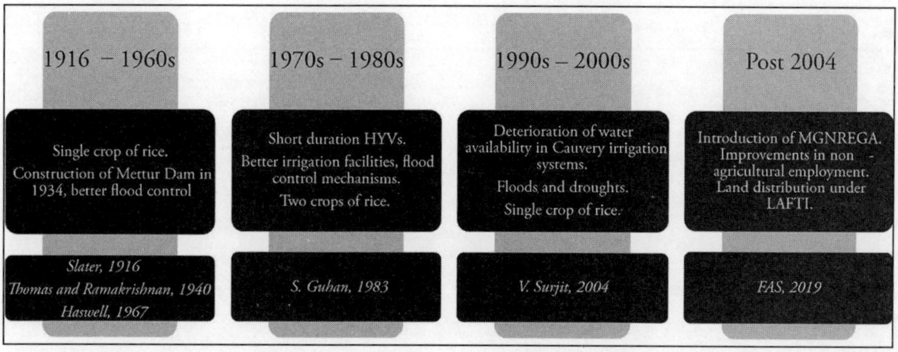

Based on these six studies, I have sketched the major phases of socio-economic transformation of the village in Figure 2.1.

Demographic Structure in Palakurichi

Population Size

At the time of the 2019 survey, Palakurichi village had 390 households with a population of 1,448 persons. There has been a slow but consistent decline in the number of persons in the village since 2004. In the Census of 2011, Palakurichi reported 455 households with a population of 1,624 persons. In 2004, there were 427 households in Palakurichi with a population of 1,647 persons.[2]

Guhan's analysis of the long-term trend of population in the village since 1901 shows that changes in population size were largely dependent on prospects in agriculture (Table 2.1 and Table 2.2). He points out three major features of long-term population growth of Palakurichi (Guhan 1983, pp. 8–13).

(1) The population increased steadily during the period from 1901 to 1911, but declined sharply between 1911 and 1921 because of emigration of a large number of poor peasants and tenants to cities like Colombo, Rangoon, Singapore, and Penang to work as labourers in plantations (*ibid.*, p. 8).[3]

[2] The total number of households according to 2001 Census was 424, with a population of 1,649 (PCA, Census 2001).

[3] Gough (1981, p. 130) notes: "In addition to its paddy, Thanjavur exported perhaps a million people in the last century of British rule. . . . A total of 6,22,543 emigrated by sea between 1881 and 1931, the peak year being 1900." During the 1917 survey, Rajalu (1918, p. 82) writes: "Emigration to Indian cities [from Palakurichi] seldom occurs, but emigration of *padials* or poor tenants or peasant proprietors to foreign cities, such as Colombo, Rangoon, Singapore, and Penang, is common."

Table 2.1 *Population structure by sex, Palakurichi village, 1901 to 2019* in number

Year	Male	Female	Total
1901	349	420	769
1911	406	463	869
1917	NA	NA	851
1921	366	383	749
1931	364	406	770
1937	426	443	869
1951	693	732	1,425
1961	781	801	1,582
1971	668	631	1,299
1981	722	689	1,411
1983	710	713	1,423
1991	762	754	1,516
2001	846	803	1,649
2004	846	801	1,647
2011	837	787	1,624
2019	728	720	1,448

Note: NA – not applicable.
Sources: Guhan (1983), Table 2, p. 9 for data up to 1983; Primary Census Abstract (PCA), Census of India (1991, 2001, 2011); Surjit (2008); Survey data, 2019.

(2) The population growth during the next decade (1921 to 1931) was positive but low. Improvement in irrigation infrastructure after completion of the Cauvery–Mettur Project (CMP) in 1934 resulted in substantial immigration, and thus, a huge increase in the population growth in Palakurichi (85.1 per cent) between 1931 and 1951.[4]
(3) The population growth, which almost stabilised during 1951 to 1961 (compared to very high growth rates during 1931–51), again declined steeply over the 1960s. A major factor contributing to this decline was the large scale out-migration of labourers due to an increased demand for agricultural labour in the region because of introduction of

Guhan further observes that the decline was steep during 1917–21 because of an influenza epidemic and successive drought years resulting in higher rates of mortality and emigration.

[4] They did not have population figures for Palakurichi at the 1941 Census. Guhan (1983) also notes that the irrigation infrastructure of the village which was prone to floods and droughts has improved considerably with the completion of the Mettur project and this has resulted in "steady growth" in output. This increased the scope of employment for hired labour and hence the large scale immigration resulted in higher population growth rates during this decade (*ibid.*, pp. 11–13).

Table 2.2 *Population growth rates, Palakurichi village, 1901 to 2019* in per cent

Period	Decadal growth rate
1901–11	13.01
1911–21	-13.7
1921–31	2.8
1931–51	85.1
1951–61	11.0
1961–71	-17.8
1971–81	8.6
1981–91	7.4
1991–2001	8.8
2001–2011	-1.39
2011–2019	-5.6

Sources: Guhan (1983); Primary Census Abstract, Census of India (1991; 2001, 2011); Survey data, 2019.

> Intensive Agricultural Development Programme (IADP) programme in the early 1960s (*ibid.*, p. 13).

Over the three decades from 1981 to 2001, there has been no big fluctuation in growth of population, rather a steady growth of population at 7–9 per cent. However, from 2001 onwards, the population has shown a declining trend, with a fall of –1.39 per cent per annum during 2001–11 and –5.6 per cent per annum from 2011 to 2019. The declining trend in population in Palakurichi during the post-2000 period is largely due to declining returns from agriculture production and movement of people out of the village in search of employment and livelihood opportunities in non-agriculture sectors.

Caste Composition

In 2019, Scheduled Caste households constituted nearly 60 per cent of total households in the village. This has historically been the case since 1916. The next largest group is of Padayachi caste, constituting 17 per cent of total households in the village. Over the years, there has been a decline in the number of Naidu households in the village, from 18 in 2004 to 11 households during 2019. Naidu households remain the dominant caste group in the village in terms of ownership of land and control over agricultural production and other economic activities in the village.

In 2019, a majority of households (226 out of a total of 390 households, or 58 per cent) were Dalit households. Of the 226 Dalit households in the village, 102 belonged to the Paraiyar caste and 124 belonged to the Pallar caste (Appendix Table 2.1). Among caste Hindus, Padayachis were the largest caste group and constituted about 20 per cent of total households. They were followed by Vellalar, Yadhava, Naidu, Pillai, Kammalar, Chettiyar, Konars and Thevar households, each constituting less than 5 per cent of all households. Naidu households, which constituted only 2.8 per cent of all households, were historically the largest landowners in the village.

One of the most interesting features of demographic change in Palakurichi has been a sharp decline in the population and number of households belonging to the Naidu caste and an increase in the population of Dalits. The decline in the Naidu population was on account of the migration of educated persons for salaried jobs in urban areas. In Palakurichi, the population of persons belonging to the Naidu caste declined from 147 persons in 1917 to 59 persons in 2004 and further to 40 during 2019 (Table 2.3). The number of Naidu households in the village declined from 28 in 1917 to 18 in 2004 and to 11 in 2019. At the same time, there was a marked increase in the absolute number and proportion of Scheduled Caste households. Another notable feature is

Table 2.3 *Caste-wise changes in population, Palakurichi village, 1917 to 2019* in number and per cent

Caste	1917	1937	1983	2004	% age change between 1983 and 2004	2019	% age change between 2004 and 2019
Naidus	147	128	91	59	-35	40	-32
Brahmins	17	13	26	8	-69	3	-63
Chettiars	12	6	18	20	11	19	-5
Pillais	9	2	108	74	-31	88	19
Padayachis	83	181	252	273	8	279	2
Asaris	44	41	56	16	-71	0	NA
Konar	29	31	87	63	-28	0	NA
Thevar	0	6	46	51	11	4	-92
Other caste Hindus	64	25	40	133	233	138	4
Dalits	430	432	692	946	37	877	-7
Christians	4	0	0	4	NA	0	NA
Muslims	12	4	7	0	NA	0	NA
All	851	869	1,423	1,647	16	1,448	-12

Note: NA – not applicable.
Sources: Guhan (1983), Table 4, p. 12; Survey data, 2004 and 2019.

the increase in the number of Padayachi households, the second largest caste group in the village, from 67 households in 2004 to 77 households in 2019. Their population has been steadily increasing since 1917.

Occupational Structure in Palakurichi

The occupational structure of the population in Palakurichi village during 2004 and 2018–19 is given in Table 2.4. In 2018, cultivators and agricultural labourers constituted around 44 per cent of the total work force in the village. The Census of 2011 reports that 9.5 per cent of workers in the population were cultivators and 76.1 per cent were agricultural labourers. At the same time, the share of non-agricultural labourers in the work force has increased significantly from one per cent in 2004 to 33 per cent in 2018–19. In 2004, agricultural labourers and cultivators together constituted 78 per cent of the total work force in Palakurichi. At the Census of 2001, 78 per cent of workers in population were agricultural labourers and 10 per cent were cultivators; together 88 per cent were engaged in agriculture. During the study by Surjit in 2004, 64 per cent were agricultural labourers and 14 per cent were cultivators. Eight per cent of workers were engaged in work of different types, for example, in small shops, hotels in Nagapattinam and as casual workers in

Table 2.4 *Occupational structure of Palakurichi village, 2004 and 2018–19* in number and per cent

Category	2004		2018–19	
	Total	Share	Total	Share
Cultivators	*107*	*14*	*194*	*22*
Agricultural labourers	476	*64*	196	*22*
Fisherman	4	1	–	–
Non-agricultural labourers	*5*	*1*	*296*	*33*
Artisans	12	2	1	0.1
Other manual work	60	8	54	6
Government servants	20	3	22	2
Business	9	1	37	4
Professionals	44	6	61	7
Others	5	1	31	3
Total	742	100	900	100

Note: This classification is based on primary occupations self-identified by respondents above the age of 14. Domestic work is excluded.
Source: Survey data, 2004 and 2019.

private or government offices. A smaller share of the workforce (6 per cent) were professionals, who worked in the cities of Chennai, Coimbatore, and Thanjavur. The latter spent a substantial, though not the major, part of the year outside the village and brought a part of their incomes to support their families in Palakurichi. This process gained momentum during the subsequent period, indicated by the nature of work force composition in 2019. There was thus a decline in the share of work force engaged in agriculture sector in the village over the last two decades, and there was a flow of the work force towards the non-agriculture sector. The shift in livelihoods towards the non-agricultural sector is supported by improvements in literacy and skill levels among the population.

Data in Table 2.5 show a big increase in the number of agricultural labourers between 1937 and 1961. There is also a rise in the number of agricultural labourers between 1991 and 2001. However, data from Surjit (2008) show a substantially lower number of agricultural labourers. These data are consistent with the explanation that in a drought year such as 2003–04, lack of employment in agriculture in the village led to migration of workers. Surjit (2008) noted the migration of agricultural labourers from the village to nearby districts and even to Chennai and Kerala. The decline continued thereafter and the pace of decline intensified by 2018, when the population of agricultural labourers declined to almost half the number counted in the

Table 2.5 *Number of agricultural labourers, by gender, Palakurichi village, 1917–2019* in number

Year (Source)	Male	Female	Total
1917 (Rajalu 1918)	NA	NA	120
1937 (Thomas and Ramakrishnan, eds. 1940)	103	95	198
1961 (Census 1961)	312	236	548
1971 (Census 1971)	211	172	383
1981 (Census 1981)	251	229	480
1983 (Guhan 1983)	249	227	476
1991 (Census 1991)	296	248	544
2001 (Census 2001)	328	282	610
2004 (Surjit 2008)	261	215	476
2011 (Census 2011)	358	342	700
2018 (Survey data 2019)	150	224	374

Note: NA – not available.

Sources: Guhan (1983); Census of India (1961, 1971, 1981) cited in Guhan (1983); Census of India (1991, 2001); Survey data, 2004 and 2019.

Census of 2011. This decline is also substantiated by the fact that combine harvesters for mechanised harvesting were introduced in the village. This reduced the demand for agricultural labourers even further, and workers began to seek non-agriculture labour opportunities in nearby towns of Nagapattinam and Velankanni. The new jobs were not very highly paid jobs, but when compared to the drudgery and uncertainty of employment in agriculture, non-agricultural jobs offered workers a better livelihood opportunity.

Literacy Levels in Palakurichi Village

Literacy rates in the village were very low at the time of the first estimates of literacy in 1937 made by Thomas and Ramakrishnan (1940), and were lower than district and taluk level literacy rates. According to Thomas and Ramakrishnan (1940), the average overall literacy ratio was 13.3 per cent. Data on caste-wise and gender-wise literacy rates in the village during 2001, 2004, 2011, and 2019 showed that Dalits and females had very low levels of literacy (Tables 2.6 and 2.7). There was sharp gender discrimination with female literacy rates substantially lower than male literacy rates during 2004, 2011, and 2019, and even lower than at the district and taluk levels.

The level of literacy of a population reflects the socio-economic conditions of the village. As discussed earlier, the majority of households were Scheduled

Table 2.6 *Literacy rate among persons of age seven years and above, by sex and social group, Palakurichi village, 2004 and 2019* in per cent

Year	All Persons			Dalit			Non-Dalit		
	Male	Female	Persons	Male	Female	Persons	Male	Female	Persons
2004	42	29	36	27	19	23	60	45	53
2019	81	65	73	76	58	67	89	76	83

Source: Survey data, 2004 and 2019.

Table 2.7 *Literacy rate among persons of age seven years and above, by gender, in Nagapattinam district, Kilvelur taluk, and Palakurichi village, 2001 and 2011* in per cent

Item	Literacy rate (2001)			Literacy rate (2011)		
	Male	Female	Persons	Male	Female	Persons
Nagapattinam (rural)	83	65	74	79	74	68
Kilvelur taluk (rural)	84	64	74	80	68	74
Palakurichi village	63	48	56	81	65	73

Source: Primary Census Abstract, Census of India (2001, 2011).

Caste households that were landless and depended on agricultural labour for their livelihoods. They were *pannaiyals* of large land-owning Naidu households in the village and their life has been described as a type of agrestic servitude (Menon 1983). They were subjected to extreme forms of economic and extra-economic coercion by the land-owning Naidu households who kept the village under their control. Hence, they could not afford to lead a normal life, let alone gain the opportunity to access educational facilities.[5] Only a few Naidu households in the village could afford to travel to nearby places so as to access educational facilities. During the next decades, there was slow progress in overall literacy levels of the population, but the low level of literacy among Dalits and the gender bias in literacy continued.

This disparity in literacy levels continued till the early 1970s, when as a result of the intervention of progressive political forces, Dalits started mobilising and improved their socio-economic status in terms of freedom from extreme forms of caste discrimination and bondage. At that time, public institutions providing education were absent in the village and students had to travel far, at least to Nagapattinam town, to gain access to educational facilities. The majority of Dalit households could not afford to send their children to school in the nearby town for education. Social discrimination against Dalits prevented them from access to educational facilities. Thus, it took nearly a century for half of the population in the village to become literate. It was in 2001 that the overall literacy rate in the village reached 56 per cent. But this was still much lower than the literacy rate at the taluk and district levels. Only 27 per cent of Dalit households were then literate, half the village average.

The census data on literacy rates in the village show that there was hardly any progress in overall literacy rates between 2001 and 2011. However, there was a sharp increase in literacy in the following decade, as we see from the most recent study of the village in 2019. The overall literacy ratio increased from 56 per cent to 73 per cent. There was a notable improvement in the literacy levels of Dalits and women by 2019. Nearly 67 per cent of the Dalit population and 65 per cent of Dalit females were literate in 2019. The most important factor in these improvements in literacy is the improvement in educational facilities in and around Palakurichi village (see chapter 14 in this volume). Further, Dalits were not subject to the same forms of caste discrimination as earlier, and were able to enrol their children in educational institutions in Palakurichi and nearby places. All these factors contributed to an improvement in the literacy levels of the population in Palakurichi by the time of the survey of 2019.

[5] Tirumalai (1940) observes that Paraiyar and Pulayar children were not admitted to school till 1937.

Land Ownership and Access to Land in Palakurichi Village

In an agrarian economy, access to land plays a key role in determining livelihoods as well as the position of households in the social and economic structure of the village.

Historically, inequality in distribution of ownership holdings has been high in Palakurichi. In his study in 1917, Rajalu (1918, p. 81) observed, "evidence from tradition shows that the whole village was for generations in the hands of large landlords." The resurvey in 1983 by Guhan showed that inequality in ownership of landholdings increased over time. According to Guhan (1983), inequality in ownership of landholdings (excluding landless households), estimated in terms of the Gini coefficient increased from 0.69 in 1896 to 0.71 in 1980 (Table 2.8). Data collected in 2003–04 show that inequality in the distribution of ownership holdings of land among landed households declined marginally between 1983 and 2004. This decline of inequality in distribution of ownership holdings among landed households was accompanied by an increase in the proportion of landless households. The proportion of landless households increased from 72.5 per cent in 1983 to 80 per cent in 2004. The Gini coefficient of the distribution of land ownership declined from 0.61 during 2004 to 0.56 in 2019. Also, the share of landless households has declined from 80 per cent in 2004 to 45 per cent in 2019.

This decline in the share of landless households is largely because of the Land for Tillers' Freedom (LAFTI), and not a programme of land reform. The survey of 2019 shows that 118 Dalit households in Palakurichi village received up to one acre of land each in Palakurichi through LAFTI. This has significantly influenced land distribution among Dalit households in the village. LAFTI was founded by Krishnammal Jagannathan and S. Jagannathan in 1981. In the years that followed the Keelavenmani atrocity in 1968, they came to the view that the way to end such atrocities was to empower Dalits with ownership of the most important productive asset in the village, i.e. land.

Table 2.8 *Gini coefficient for the distribution of ownership holdings, Palakurichi village, 1896 to 2019*

Year	Gini coefficient
1896	0.69
1980	0.71
2004	0.61
2019	0.56

Sources: Guhan (1983); Survey data, 2004, 2019.

They were also influenced by Gandhian ideas and Vinoba Bhave's Bhoodan movement. Their intention was to provide ownership of land they gathered through donations from various individuals and organisations, purchased from landlords through negotiations, to Dalit families in the region. Dalit households also were given support to receive formal credit from cooperatives to partially support the purchase of such land. This credit was repaid by the families in instalments. LAFTI conducted negotiations with landowners for the donation or sale of land, helped gain access to formal credit sources, helped with legal processes for transfer of ownership, managed contributions, and generally helped implement the programme. LAFTI has an ongoing programme at various stages of implementation in different villages in the Thanjavur region and other parts of Tamil Nadu.[6]

The disparity in ownership and operational holdings of households belonging to different caste groups is striking. For the period up to the study of 2004, Dalit households had little access to either ownership holdings of land or operational holdings of land. About 93.1 per cent of Dalit households (57.5 per cent of all households in the village) and 61.7 of non-Dalit households did not own any land in 2004 (Table 2.9). Further, 83 per cent of Dalit households and 48.9 per cent of non-Dalit households did not possess any operational holdings of land. However, by the study of 2019, the period after the intervention through the programme undertaken by LAFTI and the State Government, there was a significant improvement in access to ownership of land among Dalit households. The share of households without any ownership holdings declined from 93.1 per cent in 2004 to 36.2 per cent in 2019. Similarly, the share of Dalit households without any operational holding declined from 83 per cent in 2004 to 44.3 per cent in 2019. Overall, the incidence of landlessness among households declined from 80 per cent in 2004 to 45.6 per cent in 2019. Although there was an improvement in the access to land ownership among Dalit households in the village, whether the land provided them with adequate returns for a decent standard of living remains an open question. This issue is addressed in chapter 11, where the returns from farming among Dalit and non-Dalit cultivators are analysed.

The disparity in access to land among Dalits and non-Dalit households in Palakurichi during this period is reflected in the index of access to land (Table 2.10).[7] A higher value of access index indicates better access to land (Nagaraj

[6] Interview with Krishnammal Jagannathan, June 2019. More details on LAFTI are in the Appendix.

[7] Access index for the social group j, denoted as Aj can be represented as:

$$Aj = \frac{\text{percentage of total extent of landholding owned or operated by group j}}{\text{percentage of households in group j among total households}}$$

Table 2.9 *Landless households as a proportion of all households, by caste, Palakurichi village, 2004 and 2018* in per cent

Year	Percentage of households with no ownership holdings			Percentage of households with no operational holdings		
	Dalits	non-Dalits	All	Dalits	non-Dalits	All
2004	93.1	61.7	80.0	83.0	48.9	68.6
2019	36.2	60	45.6	44.3	63.9	52.1

Source: Survey data, 2004 and 2019.

Table 2.10 *Access to land, by caste, Palakurichi village, 2004 and 2019* in per cent

Year	Access to ownership of land			Access to operational holding of land		
	Access index for Dalits	Access index for non-Dalits	Relative access index*	Access index for Dalits	Access index for non-Dalits	Relative access index
2004	12.2	220.5	18.1	20.1	209.6	10.4
2019	56.2	166.4	3.0	46.0	181.9	4.0

Note: * Relative access index is the ratio of access index for non-Dalits to that of Dalits.
Source: Survey data, 2004 and 2019.

2007). The access index for ownership holdings of land in 2004 for Dalit households was 12.2, while the corresponding figure for non-Dalits was 220.5. The access index for ownership of land for Dalit households in 2019 rose to 56.2 in 2019. Over the same period, the access index of operational holdings improved from 20.1 to 46.0, indicating improved access to ownership and operational holdings of land among Dalit households over the last decade and a half. Similarly, the relative access index for non-Dalit households declined (from 18.1 to 3.0 for ownership holdings and 10.4 to 4.0 for operational holdings). This is largely due to increased access to ownership holdings of land among Dalit households through the LAFTI programme.

Cropping Pattern in Palakurichi Village

As we have written, Palakurichi lies in the Coastal Zone of the lower Cauvery delta, where the river empties into the Bay of Bengal. Since this is the tail end of the delta and near the sea, the soil type is largely sandy with problems of salinity. Nearness to the sea also prevents cultivators from drawing groundwater because of a low water table and salinity. The only source of water for cultivation and domestic use is thus from the Cauvery irrigation system, which reaches the village through a network of canals that originates from the Grand Anicut near Thanjavur. Being a tail-end delta village, Palakurichi often faces problems of saline water intrusion, which damages crops and soil. In addition, the village is often affected by floods and drought, which hit cultivation and returns from crop production.

Historically, Thanjavur was known for its prosperous rice production system. The agro-ecological conditions of Palakurichi are suitable for rice cultivation, but in the early twentieth century, because of constraints in the availability of irrigation water and the geographic location of the region, cultivators could grow only one crop of rice, that is, in the *samba* season (September–October to February–March). Although some of cultivators grew a short-duration *kuruvai* crop, this was limited to the very few households that could afford to irrigate the crop using water from small ponds or tanks. In general, there was only one crop of rice in an agricultural year (July–June) and the livelihoods of the people, cultivators and workers, were completely dependent on that crop. The cropping pattern of Palakurichi village from 1922 to 2019 is in Table 2.11.

Three major points emerge. First, rice is the dominant crop and accounted for more than 95 per cent of the gross cropped area in the village for most of a century. The survey of 2019 shows that this has continued.

Secondly, the area under rice cultivation increased slowly from 1922 to 1974–78 and slowly declined afterwards. The increase in area is largely explained by the development of irrigation infrastructure after the construction of the Mettur dam in 1934. A qualitative change in rice cultivation occurred in the 1960s and 1970s after the introduction of high-yielding short-duration varieties of rice. As a result of the introduction of short-duration rice varieties, and improved irrigation facilities and the availability of irrigation water, cultivators began to grow a short-duration second crop of rice. The cultivation

Table 2.11 *Cropping pattern, Palakurichi village, 1922–23 to 2018–19* in acres

Crop	1922–23	1935–37*	1974–78**	2003–04	2004–05	2005–06	2018–19
Rice	879	942	995	957	968	948	964
Pulses	2	4	11	0	244	244	150
Oil seeds	2	0.1	0	0	0	0	50
Other crops and trees	7	13	0	4	4	4	2
Total	890	959	1,006	961	1,215	1,195	1,115

Notes: * Average value for the period 1935–37; ** Average value for the period 1974–78.
Source: Tirumalai (1940); Guhan (1983); Palakurichi village records (2003–04; 2004–05; 2005–06; 2018–19).

of two crops of rice in Palakurichi village was, however, for a very short period of time in the whole span of a century of rice cultivation. The study by Guhan in 1983 mentions some cultivators growing two crops of rice. Discussions with village residents during the most recent household survey showed that, by the late 1980s, most cultivators grew only one crop of rice. Double cropping continued for two decades during the 1970s and 1980s. Thereafter, with the fall in water availability in the Cauvery irrigation system and problems of flooding and drought, most cultivators shifted back to a single crop of long-duration *samba* rice. Thus, except for a short period during the 1970s and 1980s, the village was single-cropped.

The third important feature of land use is a marginal increase in the area under millets and pulses in the early 2000s, noted in the study of 2004–05. This was largely because of the practice of growing a crop of black gram after the rice harvest. Black gram requires only residual moisture, and consecutive droughts in the region in the early 2000s prompted cultivators to grow short-duration crops with lower requirement of water. Black gram was introduced as a crop to be sown after the harvest of rice. This gave the farmers additional income without having to incur high levels of expenditure.

Rice cultivation and yields, costs, and incomes from rice cultivation are further discussed in chapter 11.

The Condition of Dalits in Palakurichi

The agrarian structure of Palakurichi (and the region) was highly polarised between a small number of land-owning caste Hindu cultivators who controlled the land, and a large number and proportion of landless agricultural labourers the majority of whom were Dalits. The prosperity emanating from rice cultivation was accumulated by landlords who exercised control over land and over the agricultural workers. Oppressive and exploitative agrarian relations were characteristic of the agricultural production system in Palakurichi village (see chapter 4).

Dalits constituted a significant share of the households in Palakurichi village. The first study of the village in 1917 reports that Dalit households constituted 51 per cent of the total population. This ratio was 50 per cent in 1938 and 49 per cent in 1983. Thereafter, the share increased to 57 per cent in 2004 and further to 61 per cent in 2019 (Table 2.12). Although Dalits constituted the largest social group in the village, the socio-economic conditions in which they lived were the worst among all households in the village. Historically, they faced different forms of social and economic discrimination, with Naidu landlord households in the village being their foremost oppressors.

Table 2.12 *Dalit households as a proportion of all households, Palakurichi village, 1918–2019*
in per cent

Year	Share
1918	51
1938	50
1983	49
2004	57
2019	61

Source: Survey data, 2019; Surjit (2008); Guhan (1983); Tirumalai (1940); Rajalu (1918).

Social Discrimination Against Dalits

Many scholarly studies on agrarian relations in Thanjavur region have described the *pannaiyal* system of cultivation that dominated rice cultivation in the region in different forms during the pre-colonial, colonial, and post-Independence period. Dalits in Palakurichi village, too, suffered from this oppressive regime.

The study by Rajalu (1918) showed that Dalits were landless and the different forms of oppression to which they were subjected. Dalit households lived outside the main village and untouchability was practised against people of the Scheduled Castes. Being *pannaiyals*, they were treated like slaves; Menon (1983) describes the *pannaiyal* system that existed during the colonial period as agrestic servitude. Most Dalit families lived in thatched huts away from and outside of the main village and near the paddy fields. Dalit houses did not have access to sources of water for domestic purposes. In 1918, Dalits were not permitted to walk through streets in the village that were occupied by Naidu households.

Most Dalit households worked as agricultural labourers in paddy fields owned by Naidu households. Dalit households were largely landless households and they did not have access to land, even through tenancy. The only source of employment for Dalit households was agricultural work in the village. Bondage was exploitative and oppressive. In earlier periods, Dalit workers were tied to the land and were transferred along with transfers of ownership of land.

The situation remained almost the same at the time of the study by Tirumalai in 1938. Wages were largely paid in kind and

> a pannayal, when he binds himself to a landowner gets Rs 75 for his marriage. The landlord also builds a hut for him. This is the nucleus of the perpetual debt of

> the pannaiyal who becomes a territorial serf. He can be transferred with the land and the landlord can get him back even if he runs away. (Tirumalai 1940, p. 141)

Guhan (1983, p. 102) notes that during his study of Palakurichi, old *pannaiyals* recalled that "it was normal for landlords to flog their pannaiyals, physically tie them to ploughs, and make them drink cow dung soaked in water as a punishment." This was the oppressive nature of discrimination that Dalits had to face from landlords during that period. So historically, Dalits in the village faced forms of discrimination worse than any other social group. They faced social discrimination in the form of untouchability and servitude to landlords, and in the process of agricultural production.

Mobilisation of Dalits Against Oppression

In the 1960s, as a result of agricultural development programmes and improvements in irrigation infrastructure, cultivators began to grow improved short-duration varieties, and many parts of the delta were brought under double cropping (Surjit 2008). This increased the demand for labour in cultivation and enhanced employment opportunities in rice cultivation, which, in turn, opened new opportunities for agricultural workers. Along with these developments, there were conscious efforts to mobilise agricultural workers, including Dalit workers in the region, under the leadership of the Communist Party. Workers were mobilised to fight for higher wages, against the inhuman treatment of Dalits, for improvements in living standards, and against other forms of discrimination (Sivaraman 1973).

The Keelavenmani massacre of 1968 when Dalit agricultural labourers and their children were burnt to death inside a hut in Keelavenmani village of Nagapattinam district was an important turning point in the agrarian movement in the region and in the State (Sivaraman 1973; Gough 1989; Menon 1983). This brought into the forefront the oppressive nature of agrarian relations that denied human beings their freedom and entitlements. It also caused the administration to give serious attention to discrimination against agricultural workers, particularly Dalit agricultural workers in the delta region. The Ganapathia Pillai Commission appointed to enquire into issues related to agrarian unrest in the region, clearly brought out the social and economic discrimination faced by Dalit agricultural labourers in the Thanjavur region (GoTN 1969). In Palakurichi, Dalits in the village organised themselves under the leadership of the Communist Party and took active part in protests against all forms of oppression. Their organisation and participation in building up a resistance against discrimination resulted in the election of a Dalit representative in the local body election. He became vice president of the Palakurichi Gram Panchayat in 1972. Dalit workers gained new confidence and opportunities to voice their concerns, and new access to public programmes. This was a slow process, but marked a turning point in the history of Palakurichi village in terms of the freedom of its people from an oppressive and discriminatory social and economic order. Representation in local governments and in higher levels of district administration and the legislature improved the access of Dalits to housing programmes, the public distribution system, credit support from cooperative banks, and other programmes. All of these contributed significantly to bringing about change in the continuous discrimination faced by Dalits in the region and in Palakurichi.

Another major change was the slow disappearance of the practice of severe forms of untouchability against Dalits. Studies in the village in 1983, 2004 and 2019 also note the slow but gradual improvement in the social and economic conditions of the Dalits in the village. The starting point of transformation was their mobilisation under the leadership of the Communist Party in the region and in the village. Guhan (1983) notes that, in his conversations with Dalit workers, "We have no fear so long as the red flag flies" was a statement that was frequently repeated (p. 103). These changes were also facilitated by the social and economic changes among other households in the village. By the late 1980s, the second generation of Naidu households, who gained new levels of education in cities such as Chennai and Coimbatore, moved out of the village to jobs in urban areas. Meanwhile, returns from rice cultivation were slowly declining because of low levels of productivity, the decline in availability of irrigation water from the Cauvery, natural calamities such as floods and drought that caused damage to crops, and issues arising from the demand for fair wages and the regulation of work hours. As a result of these factors, landed households began to lease out land to other households in the village. In this process, Dalit households gained some access to operational holdings of land through tenurial arrangements.

Changes in Living Conditions of Dalits in Palakurichi

As mentioned previously, the living conditions of Dalit households at the time of the early surveys was appalling. Historically, the only source of livelihood for Dalit households in the village was their earnings from selling their labour power. Although there have been some changes in the occupational pattern among Dalits in the village, manual work still remains the major source of livelihood. In a period of declining employment opportunities in the village, the Mahatma Gandhi National Rural Employment Guarantee Act

(MGNREGA) has provided some relief to workers in the period after 2005. Some Dalit households have gained employment in non-agricultural sector because they are now better educated than before, and are able to make use of opportunities provided by government programmes.

At Guhan's study of the village in 1983, only two Dalit households (out of total 186 Dalit households) in the village had a terraced or tiled house to live in. The remaining 184 households lived in thatched houses. No Dalit household had a private toilet for its use. In 2019, housing conditions had improved. Out of 249 Dalit households, 105 houses were terraced or tiled and the remaining houses were thatched or made of mixed material. Also, most households had access to electricity. Nearly 50 per cent of Dalit households had private toilets built in their houses. This was largely because of the public-supported housing programme called Indira Awaas Yojana (IAY) started in 1985, and the Pradhan Mantri Awaas Yojana-Gramin (PMAY-G) started in 2015. These were schemes to construct houses for below-poverty-line (BPL) households in rural areas. In 2019, there was thus a marginal improvement in the living conditions of Dalit households. A detailed analysis of the living conditions and asset position of the households in Palakurichi village is in chapter 15.

Summary and Conclusions

Palakurichi village, located at the tail end of the Cauvery delta, has been studied six times since 1916. These studies sketch out the socio-economic changes in the village over the last one century.

When Palakurichi was first studied in 1916, it was dependent on a single crop of rice. The distribution of land ownership in Palakurichi was highly unequal, with Naidu households owning almost all the land in the village. Though Dalit households constituted the majority of households in the village, they were subjected to extreme forms of oppression and discrimination based on caste. Most Dalits were agricultural labourers and were bonded to landlord households through the *pannaiyal* system that prevailed during the pre-colonial period in the region and continued in various forms and ways even after Independence.

The second study of the village during the early 1930s indicated improvements in agricultural production conditions with the construction of the Mettur dam in 1934 and consequent improvements in irrigation and flood control.

The study of the village by Margaret Haswell in the 1960s indicates the early gains of green revolution technologies, particularly gains such as double cropping and improvements in yield levels. Though there were signs of progress in agricultural production, socio-economic conditions remained extremely unequal and biased against the Dalits in the village. An important feature of the socio-economic conditions of the Dalit households in this period was their mobilisation under the leadership of the Communist Party against different forms of oppression, social and economic. After the Keelavenmani atrocity of 1968, the movement against such atrocities became stronger.

Guhan's study in the early 1980s recorded increased yield levels, higher cropping intensity, and higher incomes than before from rice cultivation. However, the benefits of this prosperity were usurped by the Naidu landlords who still had control over the land in the village.

In the 1990s, new water-sharing arrangements between riparian States, a decline in the irrigation water available in the region, and natural calamities adversely affected agricultural production and profitability from rice cultivation. A new generation of landowners began to turn to new forms of non-agricultural employment and did not want to continue with cultivation as a main profession. In the 2000s, introduction of mechanisation in most agricultural operations, including harvesting, affected the employment opportunities provided by rice cultivation in the village. Declining prospects from rice cultivation and lack of employment opportunities prompted agricultural worker households to seek non-agricultural employment opportunities in nearby towns and to other cities and States.

As we shall see in the chapters that follow, the survey of 2019 adds a new chapter of change in the history of this village. The old forms of landlordism have changed, and the old forms of bondage and unfreedom have been changed forever by economic change and political struggle. Nevertheless, as discussed in chapter 4, "the personnel of the rich" has remained static in many ways. The landlord households in the village and those with the most land are still from the same families that have dominated the village across the last century, although their incomes are now substantially from non-agricultural sources. Middle castes have gained more land than in the past. Some Dalit families have acquired land through purchase.

After decades of struggle, the conditions of life of Dalit families have changed in myriad ways. Despite these changes, inequality in the distribution of economic resources and incomes affects Dalit households the most, and the legacy of cumulative deprivation continues to affect the lives of the households of the Scheduled Castes.

The economy of this village has been severely affected by the declining supply of water availability for surface irrigation. Palakurichi is once again a single-cropped village. The occupational pattern has shifted to the non-agricultural sector. The economic challenges facing Palakurichi at the present moment are formidable.

Appendix

Land for Tillers' Freedom (LAFTI)

C.A. Sethu

Land for Tillers' Freedom (LAFTI) is a non-government organisation founded by Gandhian activists Krishnammal Jagannathan and S. Jagannathan in the aftermath of the Keelavenmani atrocity. Influenced by Vinoba Bhave's Bhoodan movement, they sought to convince landlords to donate land for distribution to landless Scheduled Caste households. LAFTI led a programme in the mid-2000s in the Nagapattinam–Thiruvarur region, in which land was purchased from landowners and then sold to Dalit households. Krishnammal Jagannathan told us that LAFTI's mission is "to liberate Dalit women and their families from their misery and their servile bondage to the landlords in the Tanjore area, the rice bowl of Tamil Nadu."

LAFTI identified pieces of land to be purchased and persuaded landowners to sell at a negotiated price (not very different from the market price). LAFTI was able to persuade large landowners to sell small pieces of their land because many landowners became less interested in farming in the 2000s as the returns from agriculture declined, and many families migrated to urban areas.

To assist landless Scheduled Caste households with funds to purchase land, LAFTI facilitated access to government schemes. One-half of the cost of land purchase was subsidised by the Tamil Nadu Adi Dravidar Housing and Development Corporation Limited (TAHDCO), an entity created in 1974 to help housing and construction needs of Scheduled Caste families. For the balance, LAFTI arranged loans from the National Scheduled Caste Finance and Development Corporation (NSFDC). Women from landless Scheduled Caste households were asked to register their names with LAFTI for a nominal fee. Land acquired from landlords was sold to women beneficiaries. LAFTI approached the Government of Tamil Nadu to exempt these transactions from stamp duty.

Krishnammal Jagannathan first visited Palakurichi village in 2006. One woman from each landless Scheduled Caste household was asked to register with LAFTI. The same year, LAFTI negotiated with landowners in the village and purchased land at the rate of Rs 33,000 per acre. When the land was sold, Rs 16,500 per acre was given as a subsidy from TAHDCO and Rs 16,500 was advanced as a short term loan from NSFDC to each beneficiary, to be repaid with interest in three years. LAFTI allocated land to the registered beneficiaries on a first come, first served basis.

Our interviews brought out some concerns among the beneficiaries about the programme. Paperwork in respect of legalisation was sometimes incomplete. In some cases, beneficiaries received one acre in non-contiguous fragments. Some beneficiaries exchanged land amongst themselves (creating further legal complications). There were also concerns about the quality of land: some plots were flood-prone because they were close to canals and marshy terrain. Not everyone was able to repay their loans on time, and had to pay interest to the bank at a penalty rate.

Nevertheless, LAFTI has played an important role in reducing landlessness among Scheduled Caste households in the region. It assisted nearly 4,000 women in the Thiruvarur–Nagapattinam region in acquiring one acre of agricultural land each (LAFTI 2019).[8]

[8] Land for Tillers' Freedom LAFTI (2019), Annexure II, *Women Empowerment: From Bondage to Rural Entrepreneurship*, available at the office of Land for Tillers' Freedom, Kuthur, Kilvelur, Nagapattinam District, Tamil Nadu.

Appendix Table 2.1 *Number and share of households, by caste, Palakurichi village, 2004 and 2019* in number and per cent

Caste	2004		2019	
	Number of households	Share (in per cent)	Number of households	Share (in per cent)
Paraiyar	135	31.6	102	26.2
Pallar	112	26.2	124	31.8
Padayachi	67	15.7	77	19.7
Pillai	20	4.7	7	1.8
Naidu	18	4.2	11	2.8
Konar	15	3.5	3	0.8
Thevar	13	3.0	2	0.5
Vellalar	11	2.6	17	4.4
Kammalar	7	1.6	7	1.8
Chettiyar	5	1.2	6	1.5
Vanniyar	5	1.2	3	0.8
Asari	4	0.9	2	0.5
Vadukar	3	0.7	0	0.0
Yadhava	3	0.7	10	2.6
Brahman	2	0.5	1	0.3
Agamudayan	2	0.5	3	0.8
Pandaram	2	0.5	1	0.3
Kallar	1	0.2	0	0.0
Kownder	1	0.2	0	0.0
Muthaliyar	1	0.2	1	0.3
Porkollar	0	0.0	1	0.3
Vannar	0	0.0	1	0.3
Reddyar	0	0.0	1	0.3
Gurukul Iyer	0	0.0	1	0.3
Unspecified Dalit	0	0.0	8	2.1
Unspecified	0	0.0	1	0.3
Total	427	100	390	100

Source: Survey data, 2004 and 2019.

Appendix Figure 2.1 *Location of Palakurichi village in Tamil Nadu*

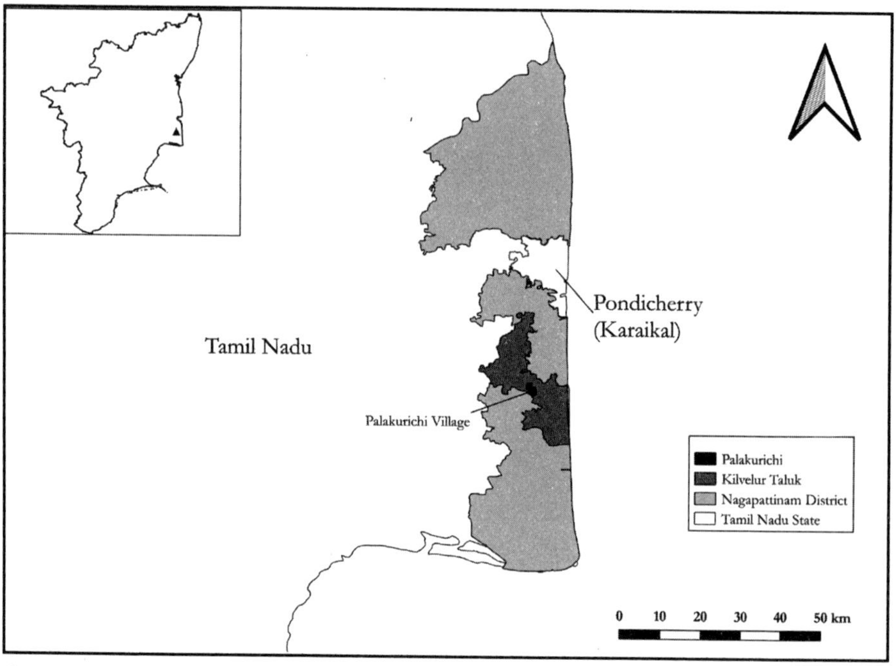

Source: Prepared by C. A. Sethu.

3

Venmani, 2019

C. A. Sethu

HIGHLIGHTS

Venmani village, Nagapattinam district, is located in the lower Cauvery delta. It is 7 kilometres from Kilvelur town and 20 kilometres from Nagapattinam, the district headquarters. The village has seven hamlets, of which Keelavenmani is the largest. The Keelavenmani hamlet is the site of the atrocity that took place on December 25, 1968, when landlords burnt alive 44 men, women and children from Dalit agricultural worker families because Dalit workers in the village refused to disband the union of agricultural workers.

At the Foundation for Agrarian Studies (FAS) survey of 2019, there were 415 households resident in the village. Almost a quarter of the households in the village were female-headed households. The bulk of the population of the village was in the age group 25–60, that is, of working age. Scheduled Castes (mainly Pallars and Paraiyars) constituted a majority of the village (63 per cent of all households). The main land-owning castes were Naidu (historically the landlords of the region) and Pillai. Nineteen Scheduled Caste households have acquired land through the work of Land for Tillers' Freedom (LAFTI), an organisation established in the aftermath of the atrocity by two Gandhian social workers.

There was a single season of cultivation in the village, with rice being the main crop, and green gram and black gram cultivated as subsidiary crops. All cultivation in Venmani was dependent on the Cauvery water, which comes to the village in accordance with the Mettur dam schedule. Salinity of ground water limited the use of borewells. In the reference year, Cyclone Gaja made landfall in the village and caused severe damage to crops and buildings.

Introduction

The village of Venmani is notable for encompassing the hamlet of Keelavenmani, which is the site of an atrocity that took place on December 25, 1968 when 44 people – including women and children – were burnt alive by local landlords as part of an attack in response to the unionisation of Scheduled Caste agricultural workers. Agrarian relations in Venmani, as in other parts of Thanjavur district, were characterised historically by a high concentration of land ownership in the hands of a few Brahman and upper caste landlords on the one hand, and a mass of impoverished landless Scheduled Caste workers on the other.

This chapter gives a brief account of the salient features of the village including location, geography, and demographic structure. I provide a brief commentary on the social structure and condition of the Scheduled Caste population in the contemporary period. The data come from the detailed household-level socio-economic survey conducted by the FAS in the summer of 2019. Much has changed in Venmani since 1968, and the FAS survey has captured features of a village in a period of transition from an agriculture dominated economy to one that depends on incomes from other sectors for the livelihoods of its people.

Location and Geography

Venmani is located approximately 25 kilometres to the west of the Bay of Bengal in central Tamil Nadu. It is located in Nagapattinam district's Kilvelur taluk. Venmani is located 7 kilometres to the south of Kilvelur town, the headquarters of the taluk. Nagapattinam city, the district headquarters, is 20 kilometres away from Venmani while Chennai, the state capital, is located at a distance of 315 kilometres. The village has seven component hamlets.

The village is in the Eastern Coastal Plains agro-ecological region of the classification of the Indian Council for Agricultural Research and in the Cauvery Delta region (by the classification of the Tamil Nadu government). It is characterised by red loam and alluvium soils.

Basic Features of the Population

Select data from the Census of India for 1961 to 2011 for Venmani are presented in Table 3.1. The population in the village nearly doubled between 1961 and 2011. The growth of the share of the Scheduled Caste population in the village suggests that the non-Scheduled Caste population has migrated

Figure 3.1 *Location of Venmani village in Tamil Nadu*

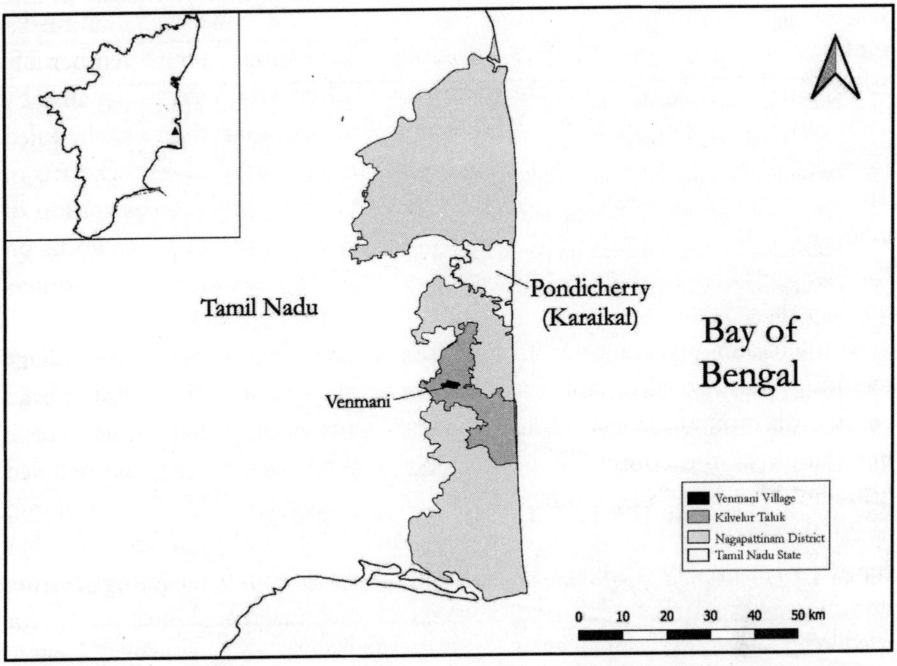

Source: Created by author.

from Venmani over the years. Other features of note include the decline in average household size, a sex ratio above 1,000, and a literacy rate that has stagnated since 1991.

The seven hamlets of Venmani are named Keelavenmani, Mela Venmani, Mayilangudi, Nanakudi, Kizh Kavalakudi, Mela Kavalakudi, and Sivaramapuram. A north–south road separates the village into unequal halves. The centre of the village is a junction on this road, with a large arch that heralds another path to the east. This path leads to the memorial of the Keelavenmani martyrs. The arch commemorates the 25th anniversary of the atrocity. The Panchayat office, the village administrative office, the building of the public distribution system shop, a primary agricultural cooperative society, a library, and a few small shops surround the archway, which also functions as a bus stop. Apart from this, the village houses a direct procurement centre of the Tamil Nadu Civil Supplies Corporation, which procures paddy cultivated in nearby areas. Venmani has two Panchayat Union primary schools, two anganwadis, and several temples. Hamlets other than Keelavenmani are located further away from this junction, at an increasing distance from this infrastructure. The people of Venmani rely on the nearby villages, chiefly Thevur, for secondary education, banking, markets, and other services.

Table 3.1 *Population characteristics, Venmani, Census of India, 1961 to 2011*

Sl. No.	Category	Year					
		1961	1971	1981	1991	2001	2011
1	Number of households	272	286	363	403	451	529
2	Population (in number)	1,146	1,302	1,506	1,575	1,740	2,005
3	Persons per household (2 divided by 1)	4.2	4.6	4.1	3.9	3.9	3.8
4	Scheduled Caste population (in number)	603	668	808	915	1,038	1,245
5	Scheduled Caste population (in per cent)	52.6	51.3	53.7	58.1	59.7	62.1
6	Change in share of Scheduled Caste population (in per cent)	–	-1.3	2.3	4.4	1.6	2.4
7	Male population (in number)	568	620	753	795	856	1,001
8	Female population (in number)	578	682	753	780	884	1,004
9	Sex ratio (females per 1,000 males)	1,018	1,100	1,000	981	1,033	1,003
10	Literacy rate (in per cent)	32.7	35.7	48.6	62.0	59.3	59.4

Source: Census of India (1961, 1971, 1981, 1991, 2001, 2011).

Table 3.2 *Distribution of population by hamlet, Venmani, 2019* in number and per cent

Hamlets	Households		Population		Scheduled Caste population in per cent
	Number	Per cent	Number	Per cent	
Keelavenmani	109	26	428	27	65
Mela Venmani	73	18	276	17	59
Mayilangudi	60	14	241	15	90
Naanakudi	51	12	171	11	65
Kizh Kavalakudi	81	20	333	21	65
Mela Kavalakudi	22	5	88	5	7
Sivaramapuram	19	5	77	5	72
All	415	100	1,614	100	64

Note: Population includes migrant workers.
Source: FAS survey data, 2018–19.

At the time of the FAS survey, the village had 415 households and a population of 1,614 persons. On average, there were 3.9 persons per household (Appendix Table 3.4). Keelavenmani is the largest of the seven hamlets, accounting for more than a quarter of the population. Almost two-thirds of the village population belonged to the Scheduled Castes. People of the Scheduled Castes were the largest population group in all but one hamlet as well (Table 3.2).

The Scheduled Castes predominate in the population (Table 3.3). Other

Table 3.3 *Distribution of population and households by social group, Venmani, 2019* in number and per cent

Caste	Population		Households	
	Number	Share	Number	Share
Scheduled Castes	1,041	65	263	63
Most Backward Classes	134	8	34	8
Backward Classes	411	25	109	26
Other caste Hindus	28	2	9	2
All	1,614	100	415	100

Note: Population data includes migrant workers.
Source: FAS survey data, 2018–19.

Table 3.4 *Distribution of population by gender and social group, Venmani, 2019* in number

Caste	Female	Male	All	Sex ratio (females per 1,000 males)
Scheduled Castes	549	492	1,041	1,116
Most Backward Classes	63	71	134	887
Backward Classes	210	201	411	1,045
Other caste Hindus	13	15	28	867
All	835	779	1614	1,072

Note: Population data include migrant workers.
Source: FAS survey data, 2018–19.

prominent castes are Naidu, Vellalar, and Nadar, all of which belong to the Backward Classes. There are also significant populations of Most Backward Classes, the most prominent of which are Ambalakarar and Padayachi. (Appendix Table 3.1)

A quarter of the households in Venmani are headed by women. This holds true when disaggregated by social group as well (Appendix Table 3.2.) The village has 835 women and 779 men, with a sex ratio of 1,072 females per 1,000 males. There are 59 girls and 41 boys under the age of six in the village. As seen in Table 3.1, the village has historically recorded a high sex ratio. Table 3.4 shows the sex composition of each social group in the village at the time of the survey. Though constituting only less than 10 per cent of the population, Most Backward Classes has an adverse sex ratio, as do the nine households that belong to Other caste Hindus.

In Venmani, more than half the population is older than 30 and children under the age of 19 comprise more than a quarter of the population. The majority of the population is aged between 25 and 60. This pattern holds when disaggregated by gender as well (Appendix Table 3.3.) The village therefore has a large share of persons of working age.

Hamlets

The revenue village of Venmani is coterminous with the Venmani Panchayat. The village is spread across seven distinct hamlets, each of which functions like a mini village. Most hamlets have separate settlements for the caste Hindus and others, though there are places in the margins where residences are not clearly demarcated by caste. The hamlets are also distinct in their caste composition. Access to amenities is another key feature that varies between the hamlets.

Keelavenmani

This is the largest hamlet in Venmani. Today, a memorial occupies the space of the hut where the atrocity of 1968 took place. Landlords committed this atrocity because the agricultural workers refused to give in to their demand that the workers disband their union. Today, red flags can be seen throughout

Figure 3.2 *Hamlets of Venmani revenue village*

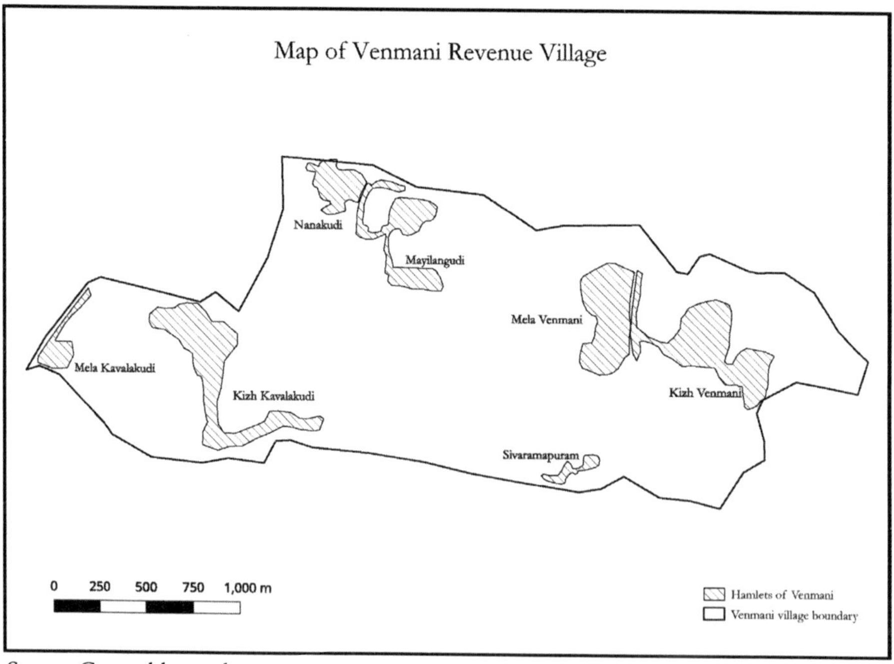

Source: Created by author.

the hamlet. More than half a century after the atrocity, most households are part of the communist movement.

The Scheduled Caste settlement is located near the rice fields, the Backward Class has large homesteads with big old buildings, while the Scheduled Caste settlement consists of newer and smaller houses densely packed and with little homestead land.

The hamlet had a population of 428 in 2018–19, more than a quarter of the population of Venmani. Almost two-thirds of this population are Scheduled Caste while Naidus form a little more than a fifth of the population. There are some households of Padayachi and Vellalar castes in the hamlet.

Keelavenmani has the best access to village amenities. The primary agricultural cooperative society for Venmani, the ration shop, the bus stop, Panchayat office, village administrative office, are all located in this hamlet. It has a Panchayat Union primary school as well.

Mela Venmani

This hamlet lies closest to Keelavenmani, on the other side of the main road that passes through the village. The hamlet is one of the smallest in the village, with 73 households and a population of 276. Scheduled Caste households form the majority in this hamlet as well. Nadar caste households constitute 13 per cent of the population.

The hamlet is settled on both sides of a road that makes a semi-circle to the main road. Each end of the road is settled by Backward Class and Scheduled Caste households, with some overlap in the middle.

Mayilangudi

The remaining hamlets are west of the main road in the village. Mayilangudi has the clearest separation between the Scheduled Caste and Caste Hindu settlements. They are separated by a paddy field, with the ownership of the path that leads to the Scheduled Caste settlement under dispute with the landlords.

The largest landlord households of Venmani live in this hamlet. They own more land than anyone else in the village, and live in old palatial structures. A paddy field away is the dense cluster of small, mostly semi-pucca, settlement of Scheduled Caste households. The hamlet has a population of 241, of them almost 90 per cent are Scheduled Caste. The second largest caste group is that of Naidus, who are 12 in number. The hamlet is not very large in area, but that is evidence of how dense the Scheduled Caste settlement is. There is an anganwadi in Mayilangudi.

Nanakudi

Nanakudi is to the west of Mayilangudi. The population of the village is 171 persons. The Scheduled Caste population in this village lives on the outer edges of its large ponds and along the canals, with no distinct separate settlement for Scheduled Caste and Backward Class households. The Scheduled Caste population constitutes almost two-thirds of the population of the hamlet. About 25 per cent of the households are Vellalar, Padayachi and Yadhava Castes. There is a small general shop and a small tea shop in the hamlet.

Kizh Kavalakudi

This hamlet is one of the farthest from the village centre. It is the second largest hamlet in the village, and consists of distinct Scheduled Caste and Backward Class areas, with the Scheduled Caste settlement located further from the main road than the others. The hamlet has a population of 333. Here too, nearly two-thirds of this population belonged to the Scheduled Castes. Households of the Vellalar caste constituted 14 per cent of the population. The population included households of the Yadhava, Nadar, and Padayachi castes.

The hamlet can be described as essentially a long and narrow space between a narrow road and a canal that is settled very densely. There are few pucca houses in this settlement. At the same time, it has some big old houses with large homesteads. The Backward Class settlement of the village has a primary school at its centre.

Mela Kavalakudi

From Kizh Kavalakudi, a road splits to the north-west, and Mela Kavalakudi is a few kilometres down this road. This is a small hamlet, with a population of 88 persons. It is the most remote hamlet in the village, with roads changing to mud paths near the hamlet. The hamlet is notable for dilapidated houses with large homesteads. Another notable feature of the hamlet is that it consists almost entirely of persons from the Ambalakarar caste; 74 out of the 88 persons belong to this caste. This is the only hamlet in which persons of the Scheduled Castes do not form a majority.

Sivaramapuram

This is a small densely populated hamlet at the south end of Venmani. The hamlet lies on both sides of the main road of the village, melding into the settlements of the neighbouring village. The population is 77, making it the smallest hamlet in the village. More than 70 per cent of the population belong to Scheduled Castes. Other castes in the hamlet are Vellalar and Padayachi.

In sum, Venmani village is atypical in that it consists of seven hamlets, each with its own distinct composition. The biggest hamlet is Keelavenmani, the site of the atrocity that took place 50 years before the survey. The village has a high sex ratio, low average household size, and the majority of the population are middle-aged. A quarter of the households are headed by women. Venmani historically was and still is a village with a majority Scheduled Caste population. There is some public infrastructure including a procurement centre for crops, an agricultural cooperative society, and two primary schools, among others. The hamlets differ in social composition and access to amenities.

Social Structure, Inequality in Land Ownership and Status of Scheduled Castes

Fifty years ago, Venmani, like Palakurichi, was an agricultural village, divided mainly between landlords and agricultural labourers. Today, 90 per cent of households receive incomes from secondary and tertiary activities. Agriculture in Venmani is limited to a single long crop of paddy per year, sometimes followed by a crop of black or green gram. Given the new situation with regard to the sharing of Cauvery river water, water availability is limited, often delayed, and fluctuating, all of which affect crop production. In 2018, Cyclone Gaja struck the village, causing much damage to crops and property. Frequent natural disasters add to the problems of agriculture in the village.

Landlessness remains high, with over one-half of resident households not reporting any ownership of crop land. The landless are almost entirely from the Scheduled Castes. At the same time, as documented in later chapters, there has been some acquisition of land by erstwhile landless Scheduled Caste households through the efforts of a Gandhian NGO, Land for Tillers' Freedom or LAFTI (see Appendix of chapter 2).

Findings from the FAS survey examined in this volume provide a detailed account of the patterns of employment, earnings, incomes, and assets among Scheduled Caste households. It is clear that there has been a diversification of employment and incomes and population of the Scheduled Castes are no longer restricted to living as agricultural workers. While there have also been improvements in living standards, social and economic inequalities persist.

Appendix

Appendix Table 3.1 *Distribution of population by caste, Venmani, 2019* in number

Social group	Caste	Population
Scheduled Castes		
	Pallar	602
	Paraiyar	364
	Kuravan	28
	Other Scheduled Castes	47
Most Backward Classes		
	Ambalakarar	101
	Padayachi	18
	Vanniyar	15
Backward Classes		
	Vellalar	142
	Naidu	108
	Nadar	62
	Pillai	36
	Yadhavar	26
	Kammalar	10
	Other Backward Classes	27
Other castes		
	Kamma Naidu	11
	Brahman	4
	Others	13
All		1,614

Note: All population data include migrant workers.
Source: FAS survey data, 2018–19.

Appendix Table 3.2 *Distribution of female-headed households by social group, Venmani, 2019* in number and per cent

Social group	Number	Per cent
Scheduled Castes	61	23
Most Backward Classes	9	26
Backward Classes	26	24
Other	2	22
All	98	24

Note: Population includes migrant workers.
Source: FAS survey data, 2018–19.

Appendix Table 3.3 *Distribution of population by age group and gender, Venmani, 2019* in number and per cent

Age group	Female	Male	All	Share	Cumulative share
Less than 6	59	41	100	6	6
6 to 14	98	87	185	11	17
15 to 19	80	81	161	10	27
20 to 24	82	76	158	10	37
25 to 29	78	67	145	9	46
30 to 39	128	119	247	15	61
40 to 49	131	107	238	15	76
50 to 59	87	101	188	12	88
60 to 69	51	61	112	7	95
70 or more	41	39	80	5	100
All	835	779	1,614	100	100

Source: FAS survey data, 2018–19.

Appendix Table 3.4 *Average household size by hamlet, Venmani, 2019* in number

Hamlet	Average household size
Keelavenmani	3.9
Mela Venmani	3.8
Mayilangudi	4.0
Naanakudi	3.4
Kizh Kaavalakudi	4.1
Mela Kaavalakudi	4.0
Sivaramapuram	4.1
All	3.9

Source: FAS survey data, 2018–19.

4

Classes

Arindam Das, Rakesh Mahato, Parvathi Menon, and V. K. Ramachandran

HIGHLIGHTS

This chapter attempts to classify households in the two villages into socio-economic classes. The socio-economic characteristics of the major agrarian classes have changed dramatically over the last half a century or so.

The Thanjavur region, a fertile region known for cultivation of rice for over a thousand years, was also known for a complex system of agrarian relations, with large landlords (*mirasdars*) at one end, and agricultural workers from Dalit and other oppressed castes – who toiled in conditions of extra-economic oppression – at the other. Today, the largest class in the villages is a class of wage labour, engaged in multiple agricultural and non-agricultural jobs. We demarcate this proletariat further by type of employment: those engaged in unskilled or semi-skilled tasks and others engaged in skilled tasks. At the other end of the spectrum, we identify a class of landlords cum big capitalist farmers. The number of landlords has declined over time, as has average size of land owned by a landlord family, while incomes have diversified to include a variety of business activities. In between lies the peasantry, a differentiated social group in transition. There has been a proletarianisation of the peasantry, with members of all peasant classes engaged in wage labour at a variety of agricultural and non-agricultural tasks. While the levels of inequality remain extremely high, with landlords and big capitalist farmers controlling a disproportionate share of land and other assets, old forms of landlordism have changed radically.

Introduction

The aim of this chapter is to classify the population of households in the two villages into socio-economic classes. The classification is based on empirical evidence from the household surveys of 2019. We begin with a brief historical overview of agrarian classes in the Thanjavur region.

Rural Classes in History

A notable feature of the Thanjavur delta, attested by a range of historical sources from at least the fifth-century CE, was its agricultural abundance. The relatively high levels of agricultural productivity and land revenue made it a coveted region of political control, and it passed through the hands of a series of ruling dynasties from an early period till 1799, when the colonial power assumed formal control over it (P. Menon 1986, pp. 6–8). High levels of surplus extraction sustained not only the requirements of the regime in control, but also of classes of superior-right holders in the land. By the eighteenth century, the rights and entitlements of the latter – essentially the class of landlords – had consolidated into a particular form of land control known as the *mirasi* system. Colonial intervention in the nineteenth century brought about changes in the *mirasi* system, and the forms of landlordism that emerged remained in place, in significant ways, until at least the 1950s.

The delta formed by the river Cauvery – 802 km in length, of which 357 km run through Tamil Nadu – is a distinct agrarian and geographical sub-region. It is terrain that allows the many distributaries of the main river to fan out into branches, and further into channels and sub-channels. The total length of the canals and sub-canals is about 25,000 km, and the canals once inundated a vast spread of alluvial soil (Guhan 1993).

In this deltaic triangle of fertility and plenty, the form of social and land control that evolved was characterised, on the one hand, by large landholdings with ownership and control exercised mainly by non-cultivating landlords, and, on the other, by poor tenants and a vast army of manual workers living in conditions of bondage, and oppressed additionally by untouchability and other features of the caste system.

Kathleen Gough notes that this was the situation as late as the 1950s (Gough 1989, p. 20). In 1950, at least half the cultivated land in Thanjavur was in large estates that each covered one or more villages and extended to several hundred to several thousand acres. In 1950, Thanjavur district had the highest concentration of land ownership in Tamil Nadu. The proportion of intensively cultivated irrigated paddy land in the gross cropped area of the district was high. Thanjavur was marked also by a high proportion of non-cultivating landlords among landowners, and a high proportion of poor peasants and agricultural labourers in the rural population as a whole (*ibid.*, p. 21).

Evolution of Superior Rights in Land

By the end of the eighteenth century, the search by British administrators for the "owner of the soil" in order to make land and revenue settlements in the Thanjavur delta led to their engagement with the class of *mirasdars*. The system of rights of the *mirasdars* to the land soon emerged as being far more complex than they first appeared to be.

What many administrators recognised and recorded but could not seem to fit into their Europe-centred notion of property rights was that, in south India, private and conjoint rights could exist together. *Mirasi* rights accommodated the property rights of *mirasdar*-landlords as well as landlord and upper-caste control over different aspects of village property and life, including control over village offices, over irrigation and crop-guarding, over artisanal services, and over the grant of plots of land tax-free for castes that provided village services. There were many non-*mirasi* villages as well, and here other forms of land rights were in existence. In Thanjavur, at the end of the eighteenth century, out of a total land-owning population of 62,048 persons, Brahmins accounted for 17,149 (27 per cent of the total). Those classed as *sudras* (or non-Brahman, including Hindus and Christians) totalled 43,442 (70 per cent); Muslim landholders made up the remaining 1,457 (3 per cent) (P. Menon 1986, pp. 224–5).

The Peasantry

With respect to property relations, the village presented an intricate combination of private and conjoint landholding rights. Private rights over the land were expressed in the individual's hereditary right to till a particular portion of land and also render the revenue assessed upon it. As mentioned earlier, there were various categories of superior-right holders who either cultivated the land with the help of agricultural labour, or leased out their land to peasant cultivators. These superior-right holders controlled the affairs of the village, and enforced the actual subordination of the other categories of village society, including the poor peasantry, village artisans and village servants.

The peasantry in the eighteenth century was not a homogenous stratum and property inequalities had already made inroads into the structure of peasant land holdings. Evidence from the period, qualitative and quantitative, testifies to the differentiation that had taken place and was intensifying within the peasantry (*ibid.*, pp. 164–9).

Agricultural Labour

The most oppressed sections of toilers in the village were agricultural workers and people of the Dalit and other oppressed castes. These social groups were essential for the maintenance of the system of agricultural production, and in terms of numbers, they formed the largest segment of village society. Farm servants and agricultural workers could also be employed by peasant cultivators when large numbers of hired hands were needed for transplanting, weeding and reaping (*ibid.*, pp. 185–8).

Dalit workers remained in conditions of abject subordination, very often in conditions of slavery. It appears that the landlords bought and sold Dalit workers like movable property (P. Menon 1986).

An official document of 1799 on Thanjavur tells us that there occurred a great decrease in the population of unfree labour in this province after the war with Hyder Ali in 1781. The report tells us, first, that "slave labour" was largely employed for cultivation previous to 1781. Secondly, a large proportion of the "slave" population was physically exterminated during the second Anglo-Mysore War (1780–84) and many went to other regions. Thirdly, the foregoing resulted in a new demand for labour by *mirasdars*, and lands were leased to tenant farmers who were paid in proportion to the fertility of the soil (Tanjore Commissioner's Report, 1799, para 35, cited in P. Menon 1986, pp. 187–8).

Changes in the Nineteenth Century

The nineteenth century saw the establishment of full-blown colonial rule in the Thanjavur delta.

The land settlements introduced by the British conferred direct private property in land by entering into settlements with *mirasi* property owners. The settlements delegitimised and eventually brought an end to a fairly widespread aspect of the *mirasi* right, namely that of joint proprietorship. Land settlements, while altering earlier forms of superior-right holdings in land, did not touch the oppressive institution of caste, by means of which an entire class of agricultural workers was tied down by harsh forms of bondage. The particular form of tied and socially excluded labour that existed in Thanjavur aided the extraction of surplus and, consequently, of land revenue by the colonial state. Although slaves were legally freed in 1843, landowners were allowed to hold workers in varying forms of debt-bondage (Gough 1989, p. 35).

Until 1803, the share of the produce paid as revenue was collected directly from *mirasdars*, with quantity varying annually in accordance with market price. From 1804 to 1807, a fixed money rate was established and the share of the crop commuted to a money rate. In 1807, the government rejected both the *ryotwari* (individual assessment) and the *zamindari* system (where landlord-intermediaries collected the revenue, as in Bengal) in favour of a village rent system in which a group of *mirasdars* paid a fixed amount of money calculated on the average of the commutation prices of several years (S. Menon 1983, p. 346). Landlords were made privately responsible for their tenants, village servants, and slaves and could evict them or raise rents. Thus, in the first 20 years of colonial rule, revenue policy was directed to establish fixed assessment or a fixed method of calculating the money assessment, although the village remained the unit of assessment.

It was after 1820 that the move towards establishing a *ryotwari* system gathered momentum. In this, the individual proprietor was to pay a fixed cash revenue to the government. With the Ryotwari Settlement of 1893, the government issued individual title deeds to shares of land of various sizes in villages. The steady rise in revenue extraction increased differentiation among landholders, consolidating those who could pay while simultaneously dispossessing smaller *mirasdars* who could not. All other customary rights of the *mirasdars*, such as rights over wasteland, were derecognised. Earlier corporate structures gave way to individual control and management (*ibid.*, chapters 5 and 6). This was a major change, given that, in 1805, around 62 per cent of Thanjavur's villages were held in joint proprietorship (Gough 1978, p. 31). Kathleen Gough summarised the broad impact of colonialism as follows: "The British gradually transformed land ownership into private property and established the legal basis for capitalist production relations among landlords, tenants, village servants and agricultural labourers." (*ibid.*, p. 35).

The transformation of superior-rightholders into full-fledged landowning landlords was not confined to the class of *mirasdars* in Thanjavur. Other strata of dominant right holders also acquired land rights. An example is that of *pattakdars*, who were revenue collectors and intermediaries between the *mirasdars* and the state in certain areas in pre-colonial times. In addition to revenue collection, *pattakdars* were also responsible for the distribution of advances for cultivation and for overseeing the maintenance of irrigation systems. This group attained further dominance in the nineteenth century, and, as revenue rates increased, played a role in the dispossession of small *mirasdars* by advancing money to them and sequestering land when they were unable to pay. In different ways, through the nineteenth century, sections of the non-Brahmin population, including families from the Mudaliar, Chettiar, and Kallar castes, made significant inroads into land control (S. Menon 1983, p. 284).

The decline in communal land control as a consequence of the investment of land ownership with the *mirasdar* had the effect of creating a new type of tenant, one who, unlike the *ulkudi* (resident tenants) and *parakudi* (non-resident tenants) of the eighteenth century, were tenants-at-will to the dominant landowner (*ibid.*, p 505). Other factors contributed to the impoverishment of tenants in this period. The poor peasantry lost customary rights to village produce, and many poor peasants lost land as a result of forced auctions or foreclosure of their debts, and joined the class of agricultural labourers. As noted in S. Menon (1983),

> Under colonialism, the condition of labourers changed. The relationship between the labourers and proprietors of land was essentially transformed. With the dispossession of the small peasantry, the agricultural labourers in Thanjavur increased substantially. (S. Menon 1983, p. 475; see also pp. 444–5)

A new form of tenancy thus grew as a result of the impoverishment of a section of *mirasdar*s and of the loss of rights that former peasants held.

A consequence of these changes was that agricultural workers lost their customary and inalienable (under the *mirasi* system) attachment to the village as a unit and that they came under the control of individual proprietors of land. Another aspect of the control landlords exercised over agricultural workers was through control over the house sites on which workers lived. Landlords used the threat of eviction to keep labourers from migrating out of the village and to exact extra-economic unpaid labour from them. (*ibid.*, p. 486) They also used the mechanism of the debt-bond. The landlord gave the labourer a sum of money for occasions such as a marriage, or for cultivation, or the purchase of livestock. Interest may or may not have been levied, but the worker was bonded to the landowner, and the loan bred debt bondage that could extend over generations (*ibid.*, p. 493).

Gough identified three types of agricultural labour in the Thanjavur delta in the early 1950s (Ramachandran 1990, pp. 11–12). Cultivation by *pannaiyal*s, or farm servants, most of whom belonged to the "untouchable" castes, was the dominant form. As in the nineteenth century, they were bonded by debt to the landlord and could not change employers or migrate until the debt was discharged, a repayment that rarely happened. They continued to have to do unpaid work in the village, including the upkeep of irrigation works and of animals. The second group consisted of farm servants who were of "non-untouchable" castes. By virtue of their caste status, there were differences between Dalit workers and non-Dalit workers with respect to the types of duties imposed on them and in the privileges to which they were entitled. The third type of labourer was the casual worker, but casual workers, as Gough noted, of the "most depressed variety" (Gough 1981, p. 55). They were technically free to leave their employer, and usually worked fewer hours than farm servants; they were vulnerable in the extreme, with no assurance of survival through periods of personal or natural crises. Over time, and with the development of capitalist relations in agriculture, and the growth of peasant unions, the numbers of farm servants declined and those of casual labourers increased.

Classifying Contemporary Village Populations

Our identification of classes in the contemporary countryside is based on the method discussed in Ramachandran (2011) and Study Group (2016). In particular, we use four criteria to identify socio-economic classes in the study villages: ownership of the means of production (mainly, land and machinery); labour (family labour on farms, labour hired in by cultivators, and labouring out by hired workers); occupation; and the level and sources of household income. We apply these criteria to the data from our survey of households in the two villages.

The rich definition of classes in the countryside that are discussed in Ramachandran (2011) and Study Group (2016) require detailed multi-year quantitative and qualitative information on households. Our database is limited in this regard: it comes from a survey of households taken at a point of time and covering the reference year 2018–19. A further specific feature of the database is that a natural disaster, Cyclone Gaja, affected crop production, livelihoods, and household incomes in a serious way, making 2018–19 a distinctly non-normal year. The specific class categories that we propose in this chapter and use in subsequent chapters are thus influenced – or constrained – by these aspects of the database and reference year.

One of the consequences of the classification being based on single-year data is that we give prominence to asset ownership as a criterion for dividing the peasantry into classes. This is because the value of land, buildings, and machinery is likely to be less changeable over a single year than the number of days of employment or the level and sources of household incomes.

We note three further features of the socio-economic environment of our study villages that affect the characteristics of classes in the villages. First, over the last two decades, agricultural production has suffered because of the sharp reduction of the volume of water in the Cauvery irrigation system and repeated cyclone damage.

Secondly, there has been a significant growth of higher secondary and tertiary education in the study villages (as in the rest of Tamil Nadu). This growth, which is associated with an increase in the share of non-agricultural sources of income in household incomes, has had a significant impact on class. Non-agricultural incomes here come from different forms of skilled and semi-skilled employment, remittances, and pensions.

Although most of the households in both villages are connected occupationally to farming and agriculture, either through cultivation or as wage workers, incomes from these activities do not predominate in household incomes. In Venmani, 181 out of 415 households held operational holdings of land. In Palakurichi, 184 out of 390 households held operational holdings of land. These households were directly involved in crop cultivation. However, only eight households in Venmani and 11 households in Palakurichi earned 50 per cent or more of their income from crop cultivation. Fewer than 25 per cent of households in the two villages gained 50 per cent or more of their aggregate incomes from crop cultivation, agricultural wages, and animal resources together.

Thirdly, class in rural Tamil Nadu is also profoundly affected by the wide dispersal of small towns in the State. Small towns demand a labour force in the service sector, and much of this labour force is drawn from villages surrounding the towns. These workers – mainly youth – are largely drawn from peasants and worker families, thus altering the incomes and occupational position of these families in village society.

In general, in India, our studies have shown that substantial changes have occurred in the characteristics of the historical categories of landlord, agricultural workers, and peasants. The description of characteristics of each of these classes today that follows shows the enormous change that has taken place in the Thanjavur delta over the last 50 years or so.

All relevant statistical material is available in Appendix Tables 4.1 to 4.9.

Landlords and Big Capitalist Farmers

In our understanding, landlords are

> the main pillar of the class power of the ruling classes and the state in the villages. Landlord households – now almost entirely capitalist landlords – own the most land and generally the best land in most Indian villages, and the members of landlord households do not participate in the major agricultural operations on the land. Their land is cultivated either by tenants, to whom land is leased out on fixed rent or share, or by means of the labour power of hired

> workers. Landlord families are, in general, historical participants in the system of land monopoly in the village. (Study Group 2016)

Landlordism in the lower Cauvery delta had special characteristics. Among them was the prevalence of land holdings and estates that were huge (particularly considering that these were *ryotwari* areas). Another specific characteristic was the extraction of the surplus by landlords from dependent, mainly landless, and in large part Dalit, workers. Despite the development of wage labour, pre-capitalist forms of dependence and exploitation persisted through the twentieth century.

There have been vast changes in these socio-economic characteristics.

First, in general, while modern landlords and big capitalist farmers own the largest holdings and the best land in each of the study villages, the extent of their land holdings is a fraction of the extent of the land holdings they held 50 years ago (and much less than their land holdings at the time of the early Slater surveys of 1916–17). Secondly, the part played by the exploitation of unfree labour and different forms of pre-wage labour in the extraction of surplus has declined.

At the same time, in both villages today, the families and individuals that own and operate the largest holdings and best land do not work at the main major manual operations on the land. They use their surpluses to invest in a wide range of activities outside direct crop production. They are almost all families of the Naidu caste, who historically monopolised the land and labour markets as landlords. The personnel of the richest families in the village remains the same, although on a different socio-economic basis, and although these families do not wield the same kind of pre-capitalist – or feudal – power as before.

In the literature on the socio-economic characteristics of different classes in the countryside, "a second, and newer, constituent part of the ruling class in rural India" has been identified – the big capitalist farmers.

> Big capitalist farmers also do not participate in the major manual operations on the land. The main difference between them and landlords is that the former did not traditionally belong to the class of landlords. Some of them came from rich peasant or middle peasant families that had a tradition of family labour, whose members, in fact, actually worked at major manual tasks even in the present or previous generation. Such families have been beneficiaries of post-Independence agricultural and rural policy and have been at the gaining end of the process of post-Independence differentiation in general. . . . Agriculture was or became the focal point of their activity, and the basis of their economic power. Thus, while the foundation of the class position of landlords was inherited

> property and status, the foundation of the class position of capitalist farmers is the development of the productive forces and accumulation, particularly in the post-green-revolution period. In general, capitalist farmers of this type belong to the "intermediate" or "cultivating" castes. . . . (Study Group 2016)

This category of big capitalist farmers has developed in the villages of the lower Cauvery delta, though perhaps less than in other parts of Tamil Nadu and India. In Palakurichi, two of the eight households in the richest group of farmers, both of the Padayachi caste, can be classified as relatively big capitalist farmers (the Padayachi caste is categorised as a Most Backward Class in Tamil Nadu). Neither family is traditionally landlord, both come from peasant families that benefited from post-green-revolution capitalist development in agriculture. In Venmani, all households in the richest group are descendants of traditional Naidu landlord families.

The incomes of these households no longer necessarily derive mainly from cultivation:

> Although the foundation or basis of the power of the class of landlords and big capitalist farmers is control over land, land is not the only resource controlled by it, nor is land its only or even its major source of wealth. Many landlords and big capitalist farmers are also involved in lucrative business activities, including, for example, moneylending, grain mills, dairying, trade and speculation in food grain and other agricultural, horticultural and silvicultural commodities, manufacturing, real estate, construction, cinema theatres, petrol pumps, lodging houses, transport, the sale and lease of agricultural machinery, proprietary educational institutions (educational entrepreneurship is a new and important source of income and social control for this class), receiving incomes from financial assets, and so on. (Study Group 2016)

Landlords in Palakurichi and Venmani

In 2019, eight households in Palakurichi have been classified as landlords and big capitalist farmers (Appendix Table 4.1).

In Palakurichi, six of the landlord and big capitalist farmer households were Naidu households and the other two households were Padayachi households that were not traditionally landlords but acquired land over time, and became relatively big landowners in the village (Appendix Table 4.2). In Guhan's (1983) classification, there were 28 Naidu, two Pillai, three Padayachi, and three other caste Hindu landlord households.

In Palakurichi, households in this category constituted 2 per cent of all households and owned 38 per cent of all land owned by households resident in the village. The extent of the average ownership holding of land held by a landlord was 26 acres. In 2018–19, six Naidu landlords and big capitalist farmers households owned 142 acres of land. Of the total value of the means of production held by households, 22 per cent, was owned by landlords and big capitalist farmer households. Of the total assets owned by landlord households, 93 per cent was immovable property such as land and buildings (Appendix Table 4.8).

In 1917, K. S. Rajalu, the student of Gilbert Slater who conducted the 1917 survey, observed that landlords owned most of the crop land in Palakurichi: "evidence from tradition shows that the whole village was for generations in the hands of landlords" (Rajalu 1918, p. 81). In 1983, Guhan identified 36 landlord households in Palakurichi, and showed that eight Naidu households owned 37 per cent of all land in the village. In 1983, of 920 acres of ownership holdings of land in Palakurichi, 529 acres were owned by 23 Naidu households resident in the village and 267 acres were owned by 52 non-resident Naidu households. Guhan further noted that

> in the span of 90 years (between 1896 and 1983) interesting changes have occurred in terms of land held by different caste groups. Pillai, Brahmin and the craftsman caste of Asari have lost land. Padayachi have emerged as landowners, but, given their numbers in the village, their collective share is very small. Other castes have also to an extent entered the landowning category. It is the Naidus who have tangibly improved their position. (Guhan 1983, p. 67)

The more recent study by Surjit (2008) recorded a decline in the number of landlord households resident in Palakurichi. This was because rich Naidu households migrated to nearby towns and cities.

In Venmani, there were three households in this class, all Naidu households and descendants of the traditional landlords of the village.

The remarkable change in the character of landlords over the last few decades is further illustrated by the description of landlords in Guhan's (1983) study (Box 1), and that of a landlord in Palakurichi (Box 2) and Venmani (Box 3) in the contemporary period.

The quantitative and qualitative data clearly show a decline in the numerical strength of the class of landlords and capitalist farmers, as well as their control over village administrative, economic and political institutions. While there was a fall in the average size of landholding of a landlord family, most landlords resident in the villages had diversified sources of income including from real estate and other business activities.

Box 1: Landlords of Palakurichi in S. Guhan's Study

Between 1950 and 1977, the President of Palakurichi panchayat was a Naidu landlord and 50 per cent of panchayat members were Naidu. The person Guhan called "KA," who was the head of the household with the second-largest land holding (the household owned 57 acres) was panchayat President from 1950 to 1965, and VRR, the biggest landlord in the village (who owned 72 acres), was panchayat President from 1965 to 1977.

The Agricultural Services Cooperative Society in Palakurichi was controlled by Naidu landlord households from Palakurichi and neighbouring villages. The office of village munsiff was also traditionally shared between two or three Naidu landlord families. Naidu landlord families also controlled key informal arrangements in the village, such as the control of community incomes and the appointment of common village watchmen (these activities were managed by the Grama Seva Sangham [Village Service Society], consisting entirely of landed Naidus). Contracts from the Public Work and Highways departments were signs of status and sources of income for Naidu families: two or three landlord families had won contracts for a bridge over the Vellayar river, road work in and around the village, the construction of government offices, and other panchayat union and panchayat construction contracts.

In 1917, K. S. Rajalu observed that the Naidus were "emphatically not a trading class." There were no Naidu rice traders in the village, but Naidu families owned textile and toddy shops and a rice mill. One Naidu landlord family was a professional money lender and an owner of a toddy shop, thus establishing a link, through his own activity, between informal moneylending and the liquor business.

Naidu landlords invested very little of their surplus income in land, houses, or other assets in the village. They invested mainly in real estate in Chennai, financial assets, and their children's education (pp. 98–102).

Box 2: A Landlord Household in Palakurichi, 2019

RKR is a big landlord of Palakurichi village. He belongs to the Naidu caste. He owns 55 acres of agricultural land in the village. He cultivated rice on the entire land holding. In addition to daily-rated workers, he employs a long-term worker for farm work. He supervises the whole cultivation process. He owns half an acre of homestead land. He has one pond, used to cultivate fish. He is a rice merchant and does business in fodder. His business activities contribute significant incomes to the household.

He owned a start-up software firm in Chennai, but the company collapsed after the implementation of goods and service tax (GST) and he now lives in the village and looks after the land and other family businesses.

Box 3: A Landlord Household in Venmani, 2019

RGN is a big landlord, of the Naidu caste, who lives with his family in Mayilangudi hamlet, Venmani village. He owns 33 acres of agricultural land in Venmani and land in three other villages, the extent of which he did not disclose. He cultivated rice on all 33 acres. He also owned 8 acres of orchards with teak, coconut, bamboo, banana and mango trees. This household had a homestead spread over 0.6 acres of land. The household owned a 0.7-acre pond. The landlord employed a long-term worker who oversaw the agricultural activity of the household. The total land owned by the household was divided into parcels and registered to different members of the family. The household owned electric pumps, diesel pumps, a tractor with a cage wheel, seed drill, and rotavator and other implements, machinery that was bought in recent years. The household also owned a petrol pump and ran a real estate business.

The Peasantry

Peasant households are households whose members work on all or some of the major manual operations on the land. The peasantry is not homogenous, but is differentiated into socio-economic classes. We initially used three broad criteria, that is, **ownership of the means of production and other assets**; the **labour ratio**, defined as the ratio between the sum of number of days of family labour and the number of days of labouring out of members of the household in agricultural and non-agricultural work (in the numerator) and the number of days of labour hired in by the household (in the denominator); and **household income**. Our classification was based on data from the 2018–19 crop season, an agricultural year in which crop incomes were severely curtailed by Cyclone Gaja.

After examining the data for patterns of association across the three criteria, the final classification of the peasantry was based on the value of assets owned by a household. The labour ratio was distinct for the three asset-based classes, ranging from 10 among poor peasants to 0.5 among rich peasants. Even in a year when the absolute value of crop income and the share of crop income in total income was low, on account of a natural disaster, cultivation continues to be the central feature of the annual labour calendar of a peasant household.

The final criteria for the Palakurichi and Venmani data are given in Table 4.1 below.

Poor peasants comprised the majority of peasants in both villages (33 out of 42 peasant households in Palakurichi and 19 out of 30 peasant households

Table 4.1 *Classification of the peasantry based on value of assets owned by a household in Palakurichi and Venmani*

	Value of household assets (in Rs lakhs)	
	Palakurichi	Venmani
Rich peasant	above 25	above 40
Middle peasant	10–25	10–40
Poor peasant	below 10	below 10

in Venmani). On average, a poor peasant household owned an acre of land and operated 1.6 acres (Appendix Tables 4.4 and 4.5). Only two per cent of all households in Palakurichi and Venmani belonged to the class of rich peasants. In both villages, a rich peasant household typically owned nine acres of agricultural land.

In both study villages, households classified as part of the Backward Classes were the largest constituent of rich and middle peasant households, while the majority of poor peasant households were Dalit. In Palakurichi, five out of eight rich peasant households belonged to the Padayachi caste (which is classified as part of the Most Backward Classes in the State list). Among middle peasant households, half belonged to the Backward Classes. Dalit poor peasant households constituted 85 per cent of all poor peasant households in Palakurichi (Appendix Tables 4.2 and 4.3). This was mainly because 118 Dalit households received one acre of land each in the scheme implemented through Land for Tillers' Freedom (LAFTI) (see Appendix of chapter 2).

In Venmani, there were Scheduled Caste (SC) households in all categories of the peasantry, although Dalit peasant households were concentrated among the poor peasantry. Conversely, Backward Class peasant households continued to constitute a greater proportion than Dalits of the middle and upper sections of the peasantry (Appendix Table 4.3).

The peasantry is a social group in transition (its socio-economic characteristics in the twentieth century require fresh and detailed examination).

Certain important changes have occurred among households of different classes of the peasantry. First, there has been a diversification of skills and occupations within peasant households. With the spread of different kinds of tertiary education – technical, vocational, and in other sectors – more and more youth from peasant households are drawn away from primary-sector employment to employment in the secondary and service sectors in towns in the vicinity of the village and beyond. Youth from peasant households who have completed different levels of tertiary education often remain unemployed rather than work at traditional manual farming tasks.

Secondly, a phenomenon among the peasantry as a whole in India – and this region is no exception – is its proletarianisation. Proletarianisation in this case is not restricted to the phenomenon of land-loss and of erstwhile peasants becoming landless workers. An important aspect of proletarianisation is that members of farming families spend more and more – and sometimes the major part – of their work time as wage workers on the land of others and at non-agricultural wage work. In other words, if we are to measure the total number of days spent at wage labour in the village, and the total wage earnings of all workers in the village, a large proportion of those aggregate days and earnings would be worked and earned by workers from *peasant* families.

Thirdly, labouring out for wages at agricultural and non-agricultural tasks now covers increasing sections of the peasantry, and involves all poor peasants and almost all middle-level peasants.

Box 4: A Poor Peasant Household in Palakurichi

Ravichandran and Kumudam are Scheduled Caste poor peasants from Palakurichi. Although the household has an operational holding of land of 3.5 acres, its main earnings came from casual wage employment.

Ten years ago, the household was an agricultural labour household. It then came to own one acre of land, which Kumudam received as part of the scheme implemented through Land for Tillers' Freedoms (LAFTI).

The family, which does not own any major means of production for cultivation, cultivated paddy on the entire operational holding in the summer season, using family and hired daily labour. The household incurred losses from crop production. The household had taken two loans of Rs 40,000 each from the Primary Agricultural Cooperative Society and the Bank of India for cultivation, using their land and gold ornaments as collateral.

The household depends financially on a single Naidu landlord household. The head of the household took loans from the landlord household, and as a result the head of the household and his wife have to go to work for the landlord whenever he calls them. During the reference year, both of them worked for 50 days for the landlord. Ravichandran was paid Rs 400 per day and a dhoti and Kumudam was paid Rs 200 per day as wage by the landlord. In addition to this, the head of the household and his wife labour out at various crop operations for 64 days a year in others' fields. Apart from this, Ravichandran and Kumudam received employment for 54 days under the Mahatma Gandhi Rural Employment Guarantee Scheme (MGNREGS) scheme during the reference period.

Mahesh, the son of Ravichandran and Kumudam received a Bachelor of Engineering degree in Mechanical Engineering from the Anna University in Chennai, and is currently working as a trainee.

These features of the peasantry are illustrated by the case of a poor peasant household from Palakurichi (Box 4).

Tenancy remains an important feature of crop cultivation in the region. In Palakurichi, in 2018–19, land leased in for cultivation accounted for one-third of all land operated by resident households. The Palakurichi village studies, from the first one (Rajalu 1918) to the MIDS (Madras Institute of Development Studies) study of the early 1980s (Guhan 1983) observed that tenancy was not widely prevalent in the village. The situation has changed in the last two decades. In 2003–04, 43 per cent of all operational holdings were on land leased in by tenant farmers (Surjit 2008). In 2018–19, although the proportion had declined, it was still high, 34 per cent.

In terms of population, 28 per cent of cultivator households in Palakurichi were tenants in 2018–19, and the majority of them were from Naidu families. The major tenant households in Palakurichi were from among the landlords and rich peasants, a phenomenon often loosely described as "reverse tenancy." More than one half of the total extent of land leased in was leased in by landlords and rich peasants. Three landlord households together had leased in 85 acres and a single rich peasant household had leased in 31 acres of crop land. Scheduled Caste households were not the major section of tenants: 19 per cent of all land leased in was held by Scheduled Caste households, and 18 per cent of Scheduled Caste cultivator households, largely poor peasants, leased in land. As noted elsewhere, about a third of Scheduled Caste households in Palakurichi had gained access to one acre of crop land each by means of the programme of land purchase and sale conducted by the organisation LAFTI.

The major lessors of the village were also Naidus, largely non-resident households. Landlord households resident in the village thus leased land from other Naidu landlord households no longer resident in the village, typically on a fixed-rent contract. Temple lands were also leased by residents. Historically, only caste Hindus were permitted to lease temple land. At present, Scheduled Caste households have some access to temple land: five out of 13 households leasing in temple land were Scheduled Caste households.

Turning to Venmani, in the survey year, 30 per cent of cultivator households participated in tenancy contracts but only 17 per cent of all operational holdings were leased in. Unlike Palakurichi, in Venmani, poor peasant households accounted for a big share of (45 per cent) of tenant households, amongst whom Scheduled Caste households were a significant section. No landlord household of Venmani had leased in land for cultivation. The main lessors in Venmani are the temple trusts.

Wage Workers

A large section of households derives the major share of their earnings from wage work. Workers belonging to the class of wage workers participated in a wide range of tasks, agricultural and non-agricultural.

We have given data separately for two sections among wage workers, unskilled and semi-skilled workers, and skilled workers. Unskilled and semi-skilled work included agricultural labour, work on Mahatma Gandhi National Rural Employment Guarantee Scheme projects, semi-skilled or unskilled construction work, and brick-kiln work. Workers at these tasks were paid daily wages and piece-rated wages. Skilled workers included plumbers, masons, welders, painters, cooks, rice-mill workers, drivers, electricians, salespersons, carpenters, and factory workers. They were paid a daily-rated wage, a piece-rated wage, or a monthly wage. They remained casual workers, not regular salaried employees.

The first big change among workers in this class is, of course, that workers are more proletarian than before, that the freedom of workers to sell their labour power to their employers is not constrained by forms of dependence and unfreedom on the all-pervasive scale of the past.

Secondly, in different parts of India, it is no longer possible to separate a distinct class of agricultural workers – that is, those who spend most of their labour time and earn most of their annual earnings from agricultural work alone – from rural workers in general. The rural workforce today works at agricultural and non-agricultural tasks in a village and in its environs, and, as migrant workers, in cities and villages far removed from their places of original residence. This is true of the two survey villages as well. It is neither easy nor analytically useful to identify and separate a class of agricultural workers from non-agricultural workers – they together constitute a single class of rural workers.

A further feature of the class of rural workers in the survey villages is that a significant section of the class consists of semi-skilled and skilled workers, a reflection of the relative advance of secondary and tertiary education among rural worker families in the lower Cauvery delta in particular and Tamil Nadu in general.

In Palakurichi, 36 per cent of surveyed households in the village were wage worker households, 24 per cent were wage workers with the major part of their earnings coming from unskilled and semi-skilled work and 12 per cent were wage workers with the major part of their earnings coming from skilled and formal-sector wage work. In Venmani, 39 per cent of households in the village were wage worker households – the major share of earnings of 28 per cent came from unskilled, semi-skilled manual work and of 11 per cent from skilled and formal-sector wagework.

Wage worker households come from all castes. Of 139 wage worker households in Palakurichi, about 60 per cent were from Dalit households. The other wage workers came from the Padayachi and other castes.

About 75 per cent of wage worker households in Venmani were from the Scheduled Castes. Of all Scheduled Caste households in the village, 46 per cent were wage workers. There were wage worker households among households of the Pillai and Padayachi castes; in Venmani, there were even Naidu households, traditionally landowners in the region, among those engaged mainly in different types of wage work, including manual wage work (Appendix Tables 4.2 and 4.3).

Landlessness is high among wage worker households. Eighty-one per cent of wage worker households in Palakurichi and 78 per cent in Venmani owned no agricultural land. In Palakurichi, only 3 per cent of wage worker households had small operational holdings of land; the proportion was 13 per cent in Venmani. In Palakurichi, Dalit wage worker households with operational holdings of land are likely to have received that land through the mechanism established by LAFTI.

In terms of asset ownership, wage worker households owned very few assets. Both in Palakurichi and Venmani, 8 per cent of total assets in the village were owned by wage workers with major income from unskilled, semi-skilled manual work. The corresponding figures for wage workers with major income from skilled and formal-sector wage work were 7 per cent in Palakurichi and 3 per cent in Venmani. These households rarely owned any productive assets. The share of value of means of production owned by this class was just 5 per cent of the total value of means of production in Venmani.

Changes in Labour Relations

At the "Slater Survey" of 1917, which was conducted by K. S. Rajalu, there were about 120 farm servants (*padiyal* or *pannaiyal*) in Palakurichi. Most were bonded workers, forced to work in the homes of the landlords who employed them. The wage for a farm servant was one "Madras measure" (1.3 kg) of paddy, the retail price of which was two annas. Farm servants were also given 0.25 acres of cultivable land. The prevailing wage rate for daily agricultural workers was twice that of wages paid to the farm servant (Rajalu 1918, p. 80).

S. Tirumalai, who studied the village in 1937, showed that there was a decline in the number of farm servants in the village. Thirumalai's study counted 95 farm servant families in the village. In order to attach the workers to landlord households, workers were given Rs 75 for wedding expenses, a hut and a parcel of land (one-fourth of an acre) for cultivation. On an average, a farm servant household earned about 17 quintals (60 *kalam*) of grain as payment in kind and Rs 8 as payment in cash for the entire year. Tirumalai recorded only eight landless agricultural workers who were not farm servants or other kinds of attached workers.

In Guhan's (1983) study, about 85 per cent of the workforce in Palakurichi was engaged in agriculture and 68 per cent of the total workforce were agricultural labourers. The proportion of agricultural labourers in the agricultural workforce had increased sharply from previous studies. This proportion was recorded as being 44 per cent in 1917 and 61 per cent in 1937 (Guhan 1983, pp. 20–21).

Employer–labour arrangements had changed; one factor in this change was the enactment of the Tanjore Tenants and Pannaiyal Protection Act in 1952.

Guhan (1983) describes three categories of agricultural labourers in the village: *pannaiyal*, permanent labour, and casual labourers (Appendix Table 4.10). Pannaiyals were old bonded labourers who continued to work with individual families of landlords for years. They received wages in cash and kind, but these were paid for the number of days actually worked. The wage for a *pannaiyal* was lower than the prevailing wage rate for other workers. Apart from this, they also received clothes at the Pongal festival and small loans, of Rs 1,000 to 2,000, at a nominal interest. "Permanent labourers" in Guhan's description were men and women, usually working as couples, who were informally attached to a single landlord household, and who were required first to meet the landlord's work requirements before seeking work elsewhere. They were paid the prevailing daily wage rate. Casual labourers were called when employers needed workers to supplement the labour of farm servants and permanent workers. They received cash wages for all tasks other than harvest and post-harvest tasks.

By the time of Surjit's study in 2008, the *pannaiyal* system had disappeared and work was done by agricultural workers who depended on casual work for their livelihood (Surjit 2008, p. 120). In his study, 64 per cent of all workers were agricultural wage workers. Apart from this, 8 per cent of workers were engaged in manual work in petty shops and hotels in Nagapattinam and casual work in private offices. However, the data also indicated a fall in the proportion of agricultural workers in the working population, a fall caused mainly by the migration of workers from the village to nearby districts and to Chennai and Kerala in search of work (*ibid.*, p. 141–2).

Our survey in 2019 recorded no old-style farm servants or bonded workers in the village. The majority of workers were wage workers, hired on daily-rated or piece-rated contracts. There were workers who each worked regularly for a

Box 5: A Wage Worker Household in Palakurichi

Chandran and Amritham are heads of a Dalit wage worker household in Palakurichi. Chandran owns one acre of agricultural land, which his mother gained through the scheme implemented by LAFTI ten years ago. For the last two years, however, the household has not had an operational holding of land, since they mortgaged their ownership holding in order to meet the wedding expenses of their daughter.

The household has five members. Three of them worked as wage workers at agricultural and non-agricultural tasks, on daily and monthly contracts. Together, the members of the household did wage work for more than 650 days in the agricultural year.

Chandran's mother, now 60, worked for 340 days in the reference year as a domestic worker in a Naidu household and Chandran and Amritham were employed for 100 days in the reference year by the head of the same Naidu household. They have traditionally responded to this household whenever they are asked to work. Chandran received Rs 400 a day and Amritham Rs 200 a day for agricultural work.

MGNREGS work was the major source of employment for Amritham. She worked for 94 days under the scheme during our reference year. Chandran also worked as a plumber for 15 days. It was a piece-rated job, and he earned an average of Rs 600 a day.

The number of days of wage work gained per worker in the year (150 days in the reference year) by the workers in this household is one of the highest among households in the village.

single owner. Such workers were also paid a daily wage for the specific number of days worked, similar to that paid to casual workers, and not a fixed monthly or annual wage. The case study above is of one such wage worker household in Palakurichi (Box 5).

Other Non-agricultural Classes

Other classes in the villages have been identified on the basis of the main source of income of each household. These households had diversified sources of income, and most operated land.

Self-employed in Business Activity

In Palakurichi, 5 per cent of households in the village gained the major part of their income from business activities. The corresponding figure for Venmani was 7 per cent. These households received income from entrepreneurial activities or petty businesses within and around their village of residence. Most of these activities were not capital-intensive. They included activities such as selling vegetables, coconut, milk, or fish, running small general goods shops and tea shops, making and selling rope, and running an autorickshaw. A few households owned businesses that required higher levels of investment, including owners of a brick-kiln, an auto-mechanic shop, a pharmacy, a grocery shop, a restaurant, and earth-moving equipment. A few households in this category supplemented their incomes by means of crop cultivation (and, among the owners of very small businesses, by means of manual work as well).

Salaried Persons

The major share of the earnings of these households comes from the salaries of people employed in the government or private sectors.

Guhan (1983) showed that 27 per cent of the workers employed in the non-agricultural sector were salaried employees. They included village officers and postal workers and persons employed in schools, creches, dispensaries, health sub-centres, veterinary sub-centres, and the village cooperative society.

In the present study, 6 per cent of households in Palakurichi and 7 per cent of households in Venmani earned the major part of their incomes from salaried employment. Government employees included drivers and bus conductors in the State Transport Corporation, clerks in cooperative societies and banks, assistants at the veterinary hospital, headmasters and teachers at government schools, an electrician in the Tamil Nadu State Electricity Board, a sub-inspector of police, a postmaster, and so on. Private-sector employees included managers at hotels and restaurants in the nearby pilgrimage town of Velankanni, laboratory technicians and teachers at private schools, nurses at private hospitals, bus conductors, data entry operators in private companies, cashiers, office assistants, and accountants in private companies, and assistants at private finance companies. Some of these households also had subsidiary incomes from crop cultivation, animal husbandry, and other wage work.

Persons Living on Pensions, Small Rents, and Remittances

These households derive most of their incomes from small rents or remittances from family members and pensions under old-age pension schemes. Most of these households are made up of older people whose children have migrated to other places for work. Some households in this category leased out their land and derived small incomes from rent. Many worked as casual workers at non-agricultural tasks. There were a few households in this category that cultivated land. In Palakurichi, 9 per cent of households in the village belonged to this category. The proportion was 15 per cent in Venmani.

Concluding Remarks

As noted earlier, there has been a sea-change in agrarian relations in the region and in the two villages studied over the last half a century. The socioeconomic characteristics of the three major agrarian sections, namely landlords, peasants and workers, have changed dramatically.

At the top of the class hierarchy are the landlords cum big capitalist farmers, with the former emerging from traditional Naidu landlord families. Landlords as a class do not wield the social, economic and political power that they earlier did. The average size of land owned by a landlord family has declined, while incomes have diversified to a variety of business activities. However, landlords continue to own a disproportionately large share of land and assets holdings of all village residents. The number of landlords has dwindled, and may decline further given the pull of urban jobs for educated youth and the push from low and variable returns to crop production.

The peasantry – in particular, poor peasants, who formed the biggest component of peasant households – is a class in transition. As elsewhere in India, there was a large-scale proletarianisation of the peasantry. Members of all peasant classes engaged in wage labour at a variety of agricultural and non-agricultural tasks.

At the other end of the class hierarchy is the class of wage workers, workers no longer identifiable as pure agricultural workers. While the majority of wage workers were engaged in unskilled and semi-skilled manual work, a significant proportion of workers were engaged in skilled and formal-sector jobs. Both sections of wage workers were predominantly landless, free to sell their labour power to any employer. The large majority of wage workers belonged to the Scheduled Castes. While old forms of landlordism have disappeared, inequality in ownership of means of production remained stubbornly high, as did deprivation among workers.

Appendix

Appendix Table 4.1 *Distribution of households, by socio-economic class, Palakurichi, Venmani, 2018–19* in number and per cent

Socio-economic class	Palakurichi		Venmani	
	Number	Per cent	Number	Per cent
Landlords and big capitalist farmers	8	2	3	1
Rich peasants	8	2	10	2
Middle peasants	26	7	38	9
Poor peasants	130	33	78	19
Wage workers with major income from unskilled, semi-skilled manual work	92	24	117	28
Wage workers with major income from skilled and formal-sector wage work	47	12	45	11
Self-employed in business activity	19	5	31	7
Salaried persons	23	6	29	7
Persons living on pensions, small rents, and remittances	37	9	64	15
All households	390	100	415	100

Source: FAS–PARI survey data, 2019.

Appendix Table 4.2 *Distribution of households, by social group and socio-economic class, Palakurichi, 2018–19* in per cent

Socio-economic class	As a percentage of row						As a percentage of column					
	SC	MBC	BC	Other	Unspecified	All	SC	MBC	BC	Other	Unspecified	All
Landlords and big capitalist farmers	0	25	63	12	0	100	0	3	8	12	0	2
Rich peasants	12	63	25	0	0	100	1	6	3	0	0	2
Middle peasants	46	27	27	0	0	100	5	9	11	0	0	7
Poor peasants	85	5	9	1	0	100	47	9	19	13	0	33
Wage workers with major income from unskilled, semi-skilled manual work	67	25	7	1	0	100	26	28	9	13	0	24
Wage workers with major income from skilled and formal-sector wage work	47	32	17	2	2	100	9	19	12	13	100	12
Self-employed in business activity	11	32	47	10	0	100	1	7	14	25	0	5
Salaried persons	44	26	26	4	0	100	4	7	9	12	0	6
Persons living on pensions, small rents, and remittances	43	27	27	3	0	100	7	12	15	12	0	9
All households	61	21	16	2	0	100	100	100	100	100	100	100

Note: SC – Scheduled Caste, MBC – Most Backward Class, BC – Backward Class.
Source: FAS–PARI survey data, 2019.

Appendix Table 4.3 *Distribution of households, by social group and socio-economic class, Venmani, 2018–19* in per cent

Socio-economic class	As a percentage of row						As a percentage of column					
	SC	MBC	BC	Other	Unspecified	All	SC	MBC	BC	Other	Unspecified	All
Landlords and big capitalist farmers	0	0	33	67	0	100	0	0	1	29	0	1
Rich peasants	40	10	40	10	0	100	1	3	4	14	0	2
Middle peasants	34	16	50	0	0	100	5	18	17	0	0	9
Poor peasants	57	10	33	0	0	100	17	23	24	0	0	19
Wage workers with major income from unskilled, semi-skilled manual work	74	8	18	0	0	100	33	26	19	0	0	28
Wage workers with major income from skilled and formal-sector wage work	76	9	13	0	2	100	13	12	5	0	50	11
Self-employed in business activity	62	3	29	3	3	100	7	3	8	14	50	8
Salaried persons	73	3	24	0	0	100	8	3	7	0	0	7
Persons living on pensions, small rents, and remittances	64	6	25	5	0	100	16	12	15	43	0	15
All households	64	8	26	2	0	100	100	100	100	100	100	100

Note: SC – Scheduled Caste, MBC – Most Backward Class, BC – Backward Class.
Source: FAS–PARI survey data, 2019.

Appendix Table 4.4 *Distribution of ownership and operational holding, by socio-economic class, Palakurichi, 2018–19* in per cent and acrre

Socio-economic class	Percentage of total households	Percentage of all ownership holdings	Average ownership holdings	Percentage of all operational holdings	Average operational holdings
Landlords and big capitalist farmers	2	38	25.9	39	35.9
Rich peasants	2	13	8.7	16	14.8
Middle peasants	7	11	2.3	11	3.1
Poor peasants	33	25	1.1	28	1.6
Wage workers with major income from unskilled, semi-skilled manual work	24	4	0.2	0	0
Wage workers with major income from skilled and formal-sector wage work	12	2	0.3	0	0.1
Self-employed in business activity	5	1	0.4	2	0.9
Salaried persons	6	2	0.5	3	1
Persons living on pensions, small rents, and remittances	9	3	0.5	1	0.1
All households	100	100	1.4	100	1.9

Source: FAS–PARI survey data, 2019.

Appendix Table 4.5 *Distribution of ownership and operational holding, by socio-economic class, Venmani, 2018–19* in per cent and acre

Socio-economic class	Percentage of total households	Percentage of all ownership holdings	Average ownership holdings	Percentage of all operational holdings	Average operational holdings
Landlords and big capitalist farmers	1	18	27	19	30.3
Rich peasants	2	20	8.9	18	8.7
Middle peasants	9	27	3.1	26	3.3
Poor peasants	19	17	1	25	1.6
Wage workers with major income from unskilled, semi-skilled manual work	28	5	0.2	1	0.1
Wage workers with major income from skilled and formal-sector wage work	11	1	0.1	1	0.1
Self-employed in business activity	7	1	0.2	1	0.2
Salaried persons	7	4	0.6	4	0.8
Persons living on pensions, small rents, and remittances	15	6	0.4	5	0.4
All households	100	100	1.1	100	1.2

Source: FAS–PARI survey data, 2019.

Appendix Table 4.6 *Distribution of asset holdings, by socio-economic class, Palakurichi, 2018–19* in per cent and rupees

Socio-economic class	Percentage of total households	Share in total assets	Average asset holdings
Landlords and big capitalist farmers	2	22	83,91,382
Rich peasants	2	14	55,61,930
Middle peasants	7	13	15,46,223
Poor peasants	33	18	4,19,531
Wage workers with major income from unskilled, semi-skilled manual work	24	8	2,54,205
Wage workers with major income from skilled and formal-sector wage work	12	7	4,93,754
Self-employed in business activity	5	6	10,63,570
Salaried persons	6	7	9,46,960
Persons living on pensions, small rents, and remittances	9	5	4,43,539
All households	100	100	7,98,358

Source: FAS–PARI survey data, 2019.

Appendix Table 4.7 *Distribution of asset holdings, by socio-economic class, Venmani, 2018–19* in per cent and rupees

Socio-economic class	Percentage of total households	Share in total assets	Average asset holdings
Landlords and big capitalist farmers	1	24	3,04,95,567
Rich peasants	2	16	60,09,870
Middle peasants	9	19	18,80,028
Poor peasants	19	9	4,51,423
Wage workers with major income from unskilled, semi-skilled manual work	28	8	2,68,300
Wage workers with major income from skilled and formal-sector wage work	11	3	2,80,897
Self-employed in business activity	7	4	4,60,248
Salaried persons	7	7	9,69,321
Persons living on pensions, small rents, and remittances	15	9	5,09,964
All households	100	100	9,09,120

Source: FAS–PARI survey data, 2019.

Appendix Table 4.8 *Share of asset value to the total household asset value, by socio-economic class and asset category, Palakurichi, 2018–19* in per cent

Socio-economic class	Land and buildings	Trees	Animal	Means of production	Means of transport	Other assets
Landlords and big capitalist farmers	93	0	0	4	2	1
Rich peasants	90	0	1	6	2	2
Middle peasants	91	0	1	1	4	3
Poor peasants	88	0	2	1	4	5
Wage workers with major income from unskilled, semi-skilled manual work	89	0	2	0	3	5
Wage workers with major income from skilled and formal-sector wage work	86	0	2	0	6	7
Self-employed in business activity	72	0	1	8	3	16
Salaried persons	91	0	1	0	4	4
Persons living on pensions, small rents, and remittances	91	0	1	0	3	5
All households	89	0	1	2	3	4

Source: FAS–PARI survey data, 2019.

Appendix Table 4.9 *Number of days of employment, Palakurichi village, 1982–83* in days

Operations	Pannaiyals		Permanent labour		Casual labour		All categories (weighted average)	
	Male	Female	Male	Female	Male	Female	Male	Female
Pre-harvest cultivation	195	92	100	50	85	43	109	58
Harvest	30	29	33	30	27	15	32	28
Re-threshing	11	10	17	15	10	3	15	12
Total	236	131	150	95	122	61	156	98

Source: Guhan (1983, p. 80).

II

Irrigation and Water Availability

5

Irrigation

V. Surjit

HIGHLIGHTS

The Thanjavur region of Tamil Nadu, comprising the present-day districts of Thanjavur, Tiruvarur, and Nagapattinam, was known as the "rice bowl" of south India on account of its prosperous (in an earlier time) rice production system. The oldest remaining irrigation structure in the region, the Grand Anicut, was constructed during the Chola period (around the second century CE). The most significant twentieth-century addition to the irrigation system was the Mettur dam, constructed in 1934.

This chapter documents the decline in the annual flow of irrigation water through the Grand Anicut from the 1950s to the present. The annual flow of water in recent years has been one-third the level of 1951, and water flow in the last decade (2010–2019) reached a historic nadir. The last few decades have also witnessed, with increasing frequency, natural disasters such as floods and droughts.

The deficiency in water availability has affected agricultural productivity and profitability adversely. An analysis of the costs and returns from the production of rice for cultivators in the three districts showed that, in most years and at current yields and prices, cultivators were unable to break even. In Nagapattinam district, cultivators recouped the costs of production in only two of the past 20 years. Cultivators at the tail end of the Cauvery delta have experienced a shift from agricultural prosperity to distress.

Introduction

This chapter discusses aspects of the evolution of the agrarian economy of Thanjavur with a focus on the development of irrigation. In this chapter, "Thanjavur" refers to the undivided Thanjavur district, which comprised the present districts of Thanjavur, Thiruvarur, and Nagapattinam.

The Thanjavur region has historically been known as the "rice bowl" of south India for its prosperous rice production system. The importance of this region in terms of its contribution to rice production in the country has been widely noted in the literature (Gough 1981; Schendel 1991; Swenson 1973; Menon 1983). According to Ramiah (1937), during the early decades of the twentieth century, the proportion of net sown area under rice cultivation in Thanjavur (70 to 80 per cent) was the highest among all districts of the Madras Presidency.

The region falls within the Cauvery delta and had assured irrigation from the Cauvery river. The irrigation system in the Cauvery delta is one of the oldest water control facilities in India and dates back to the Chola period during the second century A.D. (Bouton 1985). Alluvial soils of the delta are very good for wet rice cultivation.

Since the 1940s, Thanjavur has benefited from many government programmes aimed at augmenting rice production. These include the Grow More Food campaign (1942), the Intensive Agricultural Area Programme (IAAP) (1960–61), and the High Yielding Variety Programme (HYVP) (1966–67) (Rukmani 1994). Thanjavur was one among the seven districts selected for implementation of Intensive Agricultural District Programme (IADP) in 1962. The major criteria used for selection of districts for the IADP programme were "a well-organized and operating Community Development Programme; successfully functioning credit supply and marketing co-operatives; assured rainfall and irrigation facilities; and a readily available local agrarian leadership receptive to change" (Brown 1971).

The second section of the chapter provides a historical overview of irrigation development in the region, the third section analyses changes in irrigation water availability in the contemporary period, the fourth section examines the implications of water availability for agricultural productivity and profitability in the region, and the fifth section is a concluding section.

Irrigation Development in the Thanjavur Region

The Grand Anicut (an anicut is a masonry barrage), constructed during the rule of the Chola kings between the second and the third centuries CE, was the first structure constructed across the Cauvery river for utilising water for purposes of irrigation (Figure 5.1). The Grand Anicut prevented the flow of water from the Cauvery river into the Coleroon and diverted it for irrigation to the delta. This remained as the only irrigation structure on the Cauvery until 1836. In 1836, during British rule, two new irrigation structures – the Upper Anicut, located 28 kilometers upstream from the Grand Anicut, and the Lower Anicut, located 80 kilometers downstream from the Grand Anicut – were constructed. The Upper Anicut regulated the division of water between the Cauvery and Coleroon rivers. In normal years, the water was discharged into the Cauvery, which was then used to irrigate the command area of the Grand Anicut. At times of floods, the water was diverted into the Coleroon to prevent damage to the crops sown in the delta region. The Lower Anicut helped in exercising better control over irrigation water, particularly at times of water scarcity and floods, and brought more cultivated area under irrigation. In 1886, regulators were constructed at the Cauvery and Vennar branches of the main river at the Grand Anicut. This helped to improve the distribution of irrigation water between the two rivers that irrigated the delta and protected the area from floods (Frankel 1971).

The most significant improvement in the Cauvery irrigation system came with the construction of the Mettur dam and the Grand Anicut Canal in 1934.[1] The Cauvery-Mettur Project (CMP) aimed to overcome "uncertainty and unsteadiness" in the supply of irrigation water and to prevent flood waters from damaging crops in the delta (AERC 1961).[2] Construction of the Grand Anicut Canal brought nearly 300,000 acres of land in the western and southern part of Thanjavur under irrigation (Bouton 1985, p. 72) and came to be known as the "new delta" region. Area irrigated by Cauvery River prior to construction of the CMP was called the "old delta" region.

Gough (1981) writes that during the early 1800s, about 70 per cent of the net area cultivated in Thanjavur was irrigated. With the development of irrigation facilities, particularly the construction of the Grand Anicut Canal, by the 1950s, about 85 per cent of the region was brought under irrigation. Prior to construction of the Grand Anicut Canal, rainfed cultivation of rice was practised in the south-western parts of the delta. With the expansion of irrigation as a result of the construction of the Grand Anicut Canal, cultivation in some parts of the new delta shifted to wet rice cultivation. However,

[1] The work for Mettur dam was started in 1925 and the construction was completed in 1934.

[2] The major objectives of the Cauvery-Mettur project were "to provide an improved, controlled and steady supply of water to the land now irrigated in the delta and the second is to extend irrigation to an additional area of 3,01,000 acres" (AERC 1961, p. 8). For a more detailed account of various aspects of Cauvery-Mettur Project, see Barber (1940).

Figure 5.1 *Development of irrigation infrastructure and agriculture development in Cauvery delta*

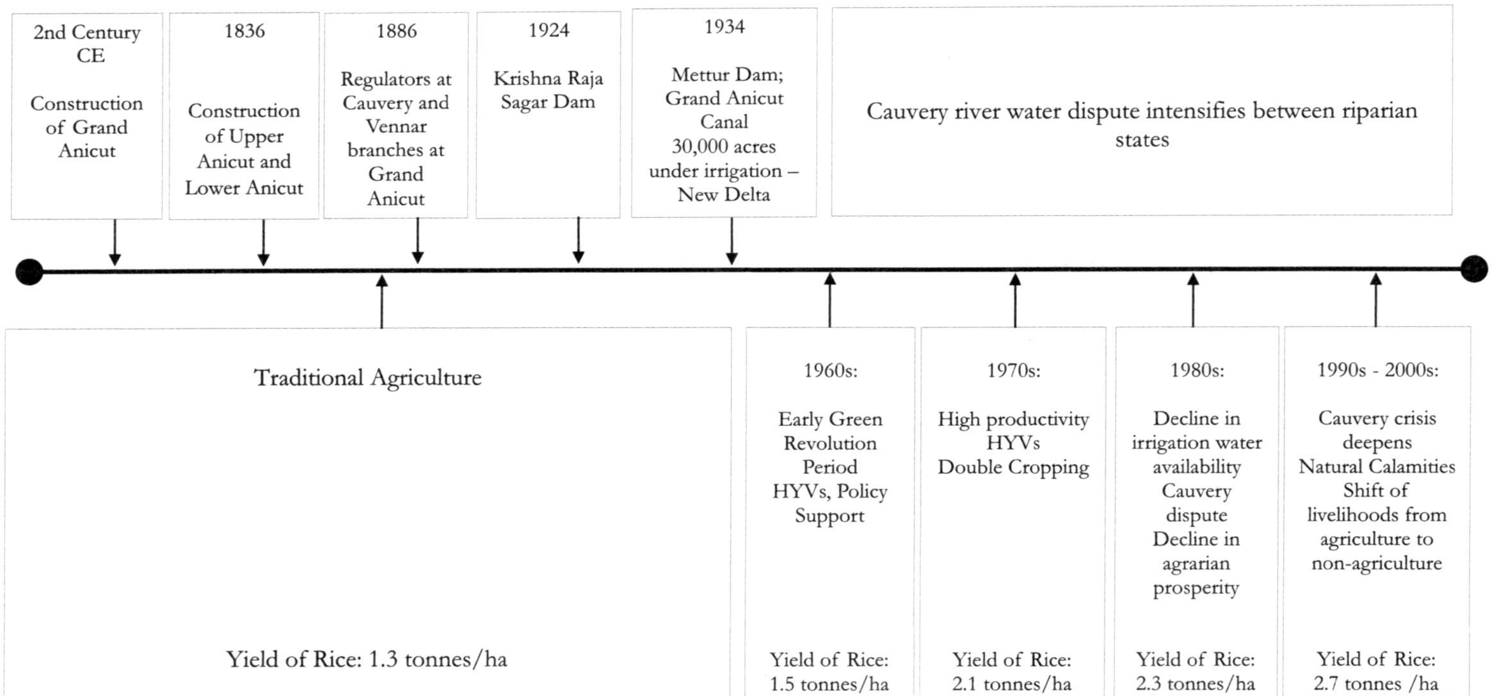

because of the limited availability of water, rainfed cultivation remained the predominant form of rice cultivation in the new delta (Bouton 1985).

No major irrigation structure has been constructed across the Cauvery in the Thanjavur region following the construction of the Mettur dam. With the introduction of agricultural development programmes like IADP in the early 1960s, intensive techniques of rice cultivation were adopted. Intensification of cultivation after the introduction of short duration high-yielding varieties increased the requirements of irrigation in the region. In order to meet the increased water requirement, cultivators in the old delta region began to use groundwater, extracted using tube wells driven by electric or diesel pumps, to supplement canal irrigation.

In the last decades of the twentieth century, scarcity and wide fluctuations in the availability of irrigation water from the Cauvery irrigation system has become the most important constraint on rice cultivation in the region. The problem has become severe in the last one and a half decades and has severely affected the prospects of rice cultivation and the livelihoods of cultivators in the region. Scarcity of water has also been a cause of the major dispute over sharing of Cauvery river water between the riparian states.[3]

A figurative representation of the development of irrigation infrastructure and agriculture production scenario in Cauvery delta is given in Figure 5.1. At present, the entire Cauvery delta is irrigated by a network of rivers and canals that branch out from the Cauvery river at the Grand Anicut. Irrigation water from the Grand Anicut is carried to the delta through its main branches and canals (Cauvery, Vennar, and the Grand Anicut Canal), which further branch out into small canals and rivulets.

Contemporary Concerns Related to Irrigation

Decline in Irrigation Water Availability: 1950s to 2019–20

The outflow from the Grand Anicut through a network of small rivers and canals determines the levels of availability of irrigation water for cultivation in different parts of the region. Although several factors influence the delivery of irrigation water at the field level, the volume of outflow from the Grand Anicut is a broad indicator of the availability of irrigation water. For the last four decades, from the 1980s, the decline in irrigation water in the delta has significantly affected the prosperity of agricultural production in the region. A detailed analysis of availability of irrigation water over the last seven decades

[3] For a historical account of the Cauvery river water dispute, see Guhan (1993).

indicated by the total flow from the Grand Anicut is given in Figure 5.2 and Table 5.1.

The analysis clearly shows that the annual water availability from the Grand Anicut has declined dramatically over the past seven decades, with the flow now reduced to one-third the level of 1951. The highest recorded flow of irrigation water was 359 tmcft in 1954–55, and the lowest recorded outflow was 9 tmcft in 2016–17. The second lowest recorded outflow from the Grand Anicut was in 2003–04, the reference year for my previous study on Palakurichi village. The average yield of rice recorded for Palakurichi village during 2003–04 was 1.24 tonnes per hectare, whereas, the State-level average yield was 3.5 tonnes per hectare. The decade-wise average flow of irrigation water shows that the flow has declined by almost half from 301 tmcft during the 1950s to 141 tmcft during the 1980s. This period also coincides with the years of the Cauvery river water dispute between Tamil Nadu and Karnataka. Thereafter, though there was marginal improvement in the 1990s, the outflow from the Grand Anicut fell to a historic low of 103 tmcft from 2010 to 2019 (Table 5.1). The trend in water availability for irrigation, plotted in Figure 5.2, points to a steady decline in water availability, a situation that is likely to worsen in the future. This will have serious implications for rice production systems, affecting profitability and impacting the lives and livelihoods of a significant share of the rural population of the delta.

Table 5.1 *Mean and median annual flow of irrigation water from the Grand Anicut during different periods from 1950–51 to 2019–20* in tmcft

Period	Mean	Median
1950s	301	327
1960s	252	243
1970s	251	259
1980s	141	125
1990s	178	177
2000–09	118	122
2010–19	103	116

Source: For data from 1950–51 to 1979–80: Records of the Superintending Engineer, Public Works Department, Thanjavur Circle, cited in TNAU (1985). For data from 1980–81 to 2006–07 and up to 2019: Records of the Office of Executive Engineer, Public Works Department, Cauvery Division.

Figure 5.2 *Total annual flow of irrigation water from the Grand Anicut 1950–51 to 2019–20 in tmcft*

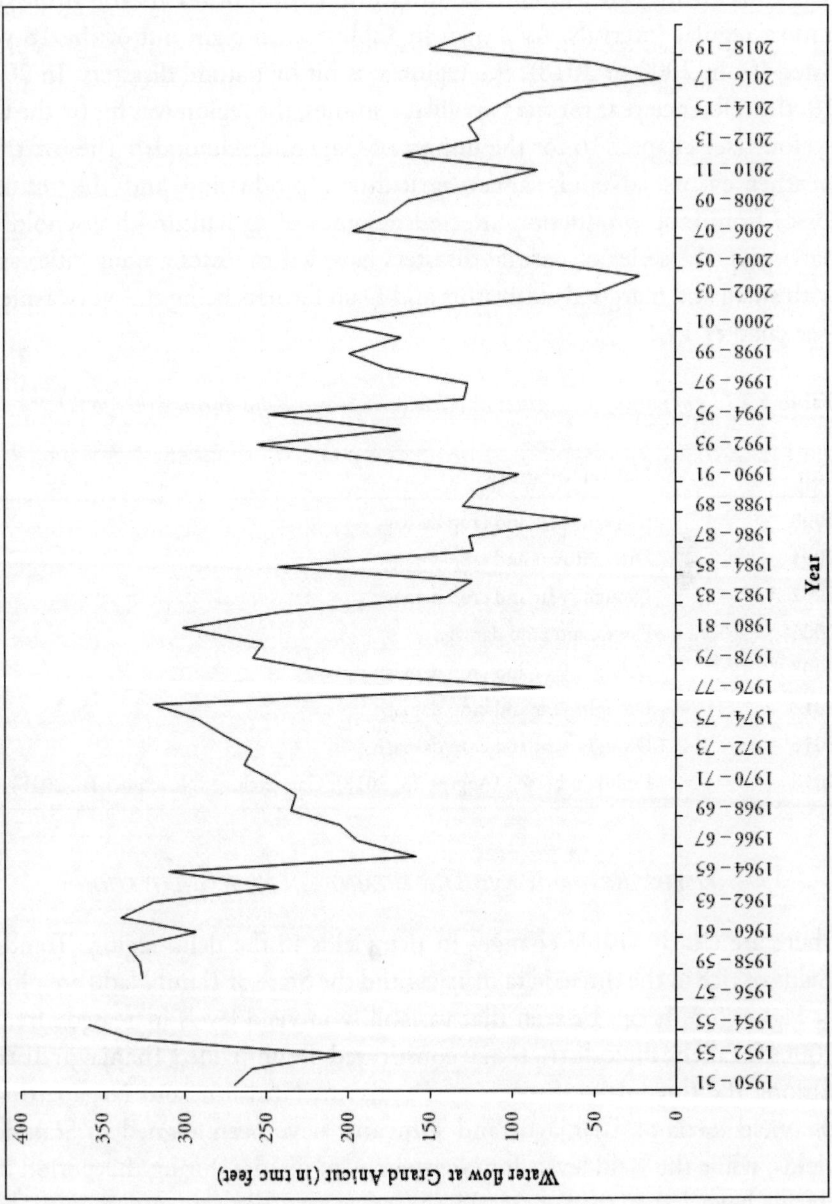

Natural Calamities and Disasters in the Region

In addition to the problem of declining water availability for irrigation, the region has witnessed natural calamities in the form of floods and drought at almost regular intervals. As shown in Table 5.2, in eight out of the 18 years listed (from 2000 to 2018), the region was hit by natural disasters. In 2018–19, the reference year for the two village studies, the region was hit by the Gaja cyclone (see chapter 16 for the impact of Gaja on livelihoods). These extreme weather events adversely affect agricultural production and the resultant losses from crop production affected incomes of agricultural households. In particular, the series of natural disasters have led to losses among cultivators, with small and marginal cultivators and Dalit farmers being the worst sufferers (see chapter 11).

Table 5.2 *List of natural calamities in the lower Cauvery delta during 2000 to 2018*

Year	Natural calamity
2000	Drought year and crop damage
2001	Drought year and crop damage
2002	Drought year and crop damage
2005	Floods and crop damage
2008	Drought year and crop damage
2012	Drought year and crop damage
2016	Drought year and crop damage
2018	Kollidam breach (August 23, 2018); Gaja cyclone (November 16, 2018)

Yields, Returns, and Uncertainty in Rice Cultivation

There are clearly visible changes in rice yields in the delta region. Trends in yields of rice in the three delta districts and the State of Tamil Nadu are plotted in Figure 5.3. It can be seen that variability in yield levels increased after the 2000s for all the three districts that constituted the undivided Thanjavur district. Among the three delta districts of Thanjavur, Tiruvarur, and Nagapattinam, the yield levels of Thanjavur and Tiruvarur have been aligned to State-level yields, while the yield levels for Nagapattinam district during this period have always been lower than yields in the other two districts and showed more variability as well. Nagapattinam, a coastal district and located towards the tail end of the delta, has been more prone than others to the impact of natural calamities, and this is reflected in lower and more variable yields.

The decline in availability of irrigation water from the Grand Anicut and the high incidence of natural calamities have been two major constraints on rice cultivation and have severely affected the prosperity of rice production systems in the Cauvery delta. The region once known for its prosperity based on rice cultivation has been struggling to support livelihoods based on rice cultivation.

In order to understand the levels and trends in productivity and profitability of rice cultivation in the delta, I analysed the cost of production for rice, minimum yield required to meet at least the cost of production of cultivators to sustain cultivation and the actual yield realised in the three delta districts for a period of two decades from 1998–99 to 2017–18. Based on the average cost of cultivation of rice at the State level, farm harvest prices received by the cultivators and the average yields of rice in the three delta districts, I estimated the minimum yield required to generate revenue that covered the cost of production or what is termed break-even yield. The break-even yields were calculated for each year for the three districts for the period from 1998–99 to 2017–18. The results of this exercise are presented in Table 5.3.

The cost of cultivation of rice per hectare for the State of Tamil Nadu during the period from 1998–99 to 2017–18 is given in column 1 of Table 5.3. The break-even yields for rice cultivation for each year were calculated based on the average farm harvest prices realised by cultivators in the districts of Thanjavur, Tiruvarur, and Nagapattinam (given in columns 2, 3, 4, and 5) respectively. The break-even yield represents the minimum yield that a farmer should realise from his field to meet the "paid-out costs" (Cost A2) of rice

Figure 5.3 *Yields of rice in Thanjavur, Tiruvarur, Nagapattinam districts, and Tamil Nadu, 1997–98 to 2018–19* in tonnes/ha

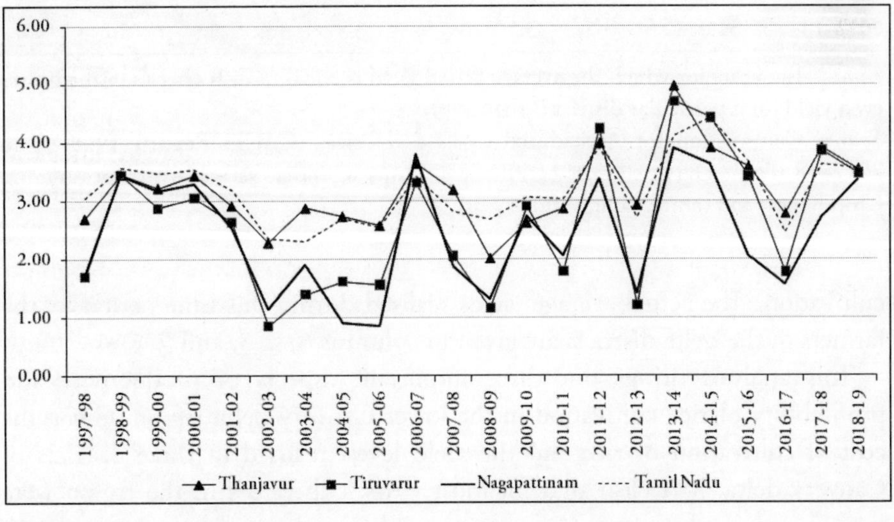

Table 5.3 *Productivity and Profitability of rice production in three districts of Cauvery delta region, 1998–99 to 2017–18*

Year	Cost A2	Break-even yields (tonnes per hectare)				Actual yields* (tonnes per hectare)			
	1	2	3	4	5	6	7	8	9
	(Tamil Nadu) Rs/hectare	Thanjavur	Tiruvarur	Nagapattinam	Tamil Nadu	**Thanjavur**	**Tiruvarur**	**Nagapattinam**	**Tamil Nadu**
1998–99	15,758	3.2	3.3	3.3	3.3	**3.5**	**3.5**	**3.5**	**3.6**
1999–00	17,509	3.5	3.5	3.6	3.5	**3.2**	2.9	3.2	**3.5**
2000–01	17,833	3.4	3.4	3.4	3.5	**3.4**	3.1	3.3	**3.5**
2001–02	18,432	3.9	3.9	3.9	3.7	2.9	2.6	2.5	3.2
2002–03	19,236	3.8	3.8	3.7	3.7	2.3	0.9	1.2	2.4
2003–04	19,287	3.7	3.6	3.6	3.6	2.9	1.4	1.9	2.3
2004-05	19,338	4.0	3.9	3.9	3.9	2.7	1.6	0.9	2.7
2005–06	19,924	3.8	4.3	4.4	4.0	2.6	1.6	0.9	2.5
2006–07	21,401	4.2	4.1	4.4	4.3	3.6	3.3	3.8	3.4
2007–08	23,373	3.5	3.4	3.6	3.3	3.2	2.1	1.9	2.8
2008–09	24,792	2.9	2.6	2.8	2.9	2.0	1.2	1.3	2.7
2009–10	29,001	2.8	3.2	3.2	3.1	2.6	2.9	2.7	**3.1**
2010–11	31,775	2.7	2.7	2.7	3.2	**2.9**	1.8	2.1	3.0
2011–12	37,913	3.8	3.8	3.8	3.8	**4.0**	**4.2**	3.4	**3.9**
2012–13	43,027	4.0	4.0	3.4	3.3	2.9	1.2	1.4	2.7
2013–14	44,879	3.1	3.1	3.1	3.2	**5.0**	**4.7**	**3.9**	**4.1**
2014–15	46,404	3.0	3.0	3.0	3.2	**3.9**	**4.4**	3.6	**4.4**
2015–16	47,532	3.4	3.7	3.7	3.6	**3.6**	3.4	2.1	**3.7**
2016–17	47,276	3.3	3.3	3.3	3.3	2.8	1.8	1.6	2.5
2017–18	51,048	3.5	3.5	3.5	3.5	**3.9**	**3.9**	2.7	**3.6**

Note: * The years for which the average actual yield is equal to or higher than the break-even yield for a particular district is shaded grey.

Source: Commission for Agricultural Costs and Prices (CACP) Reports 1998–99 to 2017–18, Farm Harvest Prices of Principal Crops in India, various years. Season and Crop Report for Tamil Nadu, various years.

cultivation. The actual average yields realised during this time period by the farmers in the delta districts are given in columns 6, 7, 8, and 9.

This analysis brings out three important aspects of productivity and profitability of rice cultivation in the lower Cauvery delta region. Given the cost of cultivation of rice and the yield levels realised in three districts of Cauvery delta, it is clear that, in most years, cultivators in the region were unable to meet the cost of cultivation and suffered losses. In Thanjavur district, in the last 20 years (1998–99 to 2017–18), cultivators were able to meet the cost of cultivation expenses only for nine years. In Tiruvarur district, the yield estimates show that cultivators were able to meet the cost of cultivation for only five years. The most worrisome performance of rice cultivation was in Nagapattinam district, where cultivators were able to recoup the cost of cultivation in only two of the last 20 years. This indicates the level of distress faced by cultivators in the region, particularly those cultivators who belonged to the tail end of the lower Cauvery delta.

Concluding Remarks

The Cauvery irrigation system has its origins in the second century CE. It supported a prosperous rice production system in the delta region, which accounted for a significant share of net sown area and supported a dense population that was unaffected by many of the food shortages that struck other parts of India. The abundant water resources earned the region the name "land of floods" and the early irrigation structures built and developed during the British period were largely to regulate the flow and control floods. The upper and lower anicuts built in the nineteenth century and the Mettur dam constructed in the early part of twentieth century improved the irrigation infrastructure in the delta and contributed further to agrarian prosperity.

In this context, green revolution strategies helped in increasing cropping intensity in the 1970s. After the 1980s, however, there was a decline in irrigation water availability that slowly affected the agrarian prosperity of the region. Data in this chapter show that the volume of water available for irrigation in the present decade is considerably less compared to the 1960s. The mean annual flow of irrigation water from the Grand Anicut in 2010s is only 41 per cent of the volume that was available in the 1960s. An exercise to study changes in productivity and profitability for two decades, from 1997–98 to 2017–18 showed that cultivators were unable to meet even the paid-out costs of cultivation in most years. The region once known as the "rice bowl" of south India for it prosperous rice production system, has now deteriorated to a situation where a major section of cultivators are unable to recover the expenditure incurred on rice cultivation.

6

Aridification

Charu Chandra Devshali and T. Jayaraman

HIGHLIGHTS

Is a process of aridification taking place in the lower Cauvery delta? This chapter examines one aspect of aridification, that is, soil moisture.

A sharp decline in the volume of water available to the Cauvery irrigation system in Tamil Nadu, combined with potential changes in water availability on account of climate change, raise serious concerns about crop yields and crop production in the lower Cauvery delta. This chapter explores the changes in soil moisture by estimating a moisture index based on rainfall and evapotranspiration for the three delta districts of Thanjavur, Nagapattinam, and Tiruvarur, using a consistent dataset for a period of 58 years, 1957–2015.

The main finding of the analysis is that there is a statistically significant declining trend in the moisture index in all the three districts. By this measure, there has been a rise in aridity in these districts over a relatively long period.

We argue that climate change, specifically a rise in annual mean temperatures, may be an important factor in changes in the moisture index (by affecting evapotranspiration), and we recommend further examination of the factors affecting the moisture index.

Introduction

In chapter 5, V. Surjit documents the steady decline in availability of irrigation water in the Cauvery irrigation system, the Grand Anicut. He also documents a rise in variability of rice yields and rice production in the three districts of erstwhile Thanjavur region, with the yields in Nagapattinam district being lower than those in the other two districts (see also Surjit 2011). These tendencies pose a major challenge to the livelihoods of almost 0.3 million cultivators and one million agricultural labourers residing in 1,843 villages of the region. The decline in water availability is likely to have long-run effects on cropping patterns with a fall in area sown to paddy and an increase in cultivable land that is left fallow, and a consequent threat of increased perennial weed infestation and soil degradation. In this chapter, we further explore the process of aridification of the Cauvery delta.

In recent years, there has been growing research on changes in the climatic features of Indian districts. Precipitation and evapotranspiration are two very important factors that have a direct effect on the hydrological cycle of a region, and thus the availability of moisture for crops and other vegetation. For improved monitoring of crop production and planning for climate adaptation, it is important to use indicators that involve both these parameters and their spatio-temporal variations. During the last few decades, studies have proposed a number of drought and moisture indices based on different parameters, including precipitation, evapotranspiration, soil moisture, runoff, and vegetation status (Mishra and Singh 2010).

One such study by Raju *et al.* (2013) reclassified many districts across India in terms of the specific climatic zone to which they belonged, based on a moisture index. The moisture index was based on two parameters: rainfall and potential evapotranspiration. The study found that 124 districts required to be reclassified into dryer categories, with many shifting towards semi-arid and arid categories from dry sub-humid and semi-arid categories, respectively. The three districts of Nagapattinam, Tiruvarur, and Thanjavur were reclassified by this study from the category of dry sub-humid to semi-arid. This is a major finding and needs further investigation.

Since the moisture index used in this reclassification is based on rainfall and evapotranspiration, it is important to investigate whether the observed shift of the three districts to the semi-arid category was driven mainly by a decline in rainfall or a decline in evapotranspiration, or both. Secondly, the data on rainfall used by Raju *et al.* (2013) were only for a 30-year period, and based on the simple mean value of rainfall for each district from 1975 to 2005. The reclassification of climatic zones was thus based on a comparison with an earlier classification, without ensuring consistency between the two periods by using a common dataset over a longer period.

Here, we re-examine the issue of aridification of the districts of the lower Cauvery delta using a consistent dataset for a longer time period. This re-examination shows that not all three districts need to be reclassified as semi-arid: Nagapattinam and Tiruvarur remain in the dry sub-humid category, while Thanjavur does shift to the semi-arid category. However, the analysis points to progressive aridification in all three districts due to a long-term decline in the moisture index. We show that this progressive aridification is due to both an increase in evapotranspiration and a decrease in rainfall. Taking note of the literature on evapotranspiration and anthropogenic global warming, our results suggest that this decrease is due to global warming of anthropogenic origin.

Data and Methodology

The moisture index of Raju *et al.* (2013) is based on annual rainfall data for the period 1971–2005 from 6,000 rain gauge stations spread across the country, which were used to develop a 0.5 x 0.5 degree grid map of rainfall for India. The potential evapotranspiration (PE) for the same time period was taken from published data of the India Meterological Department (IMD), which are collected from 144 locations and then used to develop a similar grid map of PE. The study then used the 30-year average annual precipitation and PE data for each district to compute the moisture index (MI) based on a formula originally developed by Thornthwaite and Mather (1955) and simplified by Venkataraman and Krishnan (1992) to the following form:

$$MI = \left[\frac{(P - PE)}{(PE)}\right] X\ 100$$

where MI is the moisture index, P the average annual rainfall and PE the average annual potential evapotranspiration.

In this chapter, we recalculate the MI using this same general method. However, we use data made available by the International Crops Research Institute for the Semi-Arid Tropics (ICRISAT) for a longer time period of 58 years to study precipitation, PE, and trends in the moisture index for the three districts of the lower Cauvery delta. The dataset on the ICRISAT website is based on TerraClimate (Abatzoglou *et al.* 2018), which is a climate and climatic water balance dataset for global terrestrial surfaces.[1] The TerraClimate data have a spatial resolution of about 4 km (or 1/24th

[1] http://data.icrisat.org/

Table 6.1 *Classification of climatic zones based on the moisture index (MI)*

Value of MI	Climatic zone
< –66.7	Arid
–66.6 to –33.3	Semi-arid
–33.3 to 0	Dry sub-humid
0 to 20	Moist sub-humid
20.1 to 99.9	Humid
100 or more	Per-humid

Source: Raju *et al.* (2013), following Venkataraman and Krishnan (1988).

of a degree) and monthly temporal resolution. TerraClimate uses climatically aided interpolation, combining high-spatial resolution climatological normals from the WorldClim dataset with coarser spatial resolution, but time-varying data from CRU Ts4.0 and the Japanese 55-year Reanalysis (JRA55). Mean statistics are used by ICRISAT to aggregate the pixel-level data to the district level for India.

Results and Discussions

We have computed the moisture index for three time periods: (i) for the total period for which data are available, 1957–2015; (ii) for the time period of the Raju *et al.* (2013) study, 1971–2004; and (iii) for the last 30 years of the available data, 1985–2015. The results are shown in Table 6.2.

Among the three districts, the lowest values of the MI in all the time periods was for Thanjavur district, putting the district clearly in the category of a

Table 6.2 *Moisture index values and climate zone for Cauvery delta districts for three time periods during 1957–2015*

District	1957–2015	1971–2004	1985–2015
Nagapattinam	–21.15 (dry sub-humid)	–24.18 (dry sub-humid)	–26.32 (dry sub-humid)
Thanjavur	–37.89 (semi-arid)	–40.45 (semi-arid)	–41.11 (semi-arid)
Tiruvarur	–26.27 (dry sub-humid)	–29.46 (dry sub-humid)	–32.66 (dry sub-humid)

Source: Authors' estimates based on ICRISAT data.

semi-arid climate zone in all the three time periods. The values of the MI for Nagapattinam and Tiruvarur indicate that these districts belong to the dry sub-humid category for all the three periods, although Tiruvarur is on the threshold of the semi-arid category in the most recent period (1985–2015).

To identify trends in the MI, we also calculated 30-year moving averages for the entire period 1957–2015 (Figure 6.1), since the inter-annual variability of the MI points to the need to smoothen the data before doing any trend analysis. A Mann-Kendall trend test showed a statistically significant decreasing trend for all three districts, clearly denoting progressive aridification (see Appendix). There were also differences across the three districts in terms of classification. Nagapattinam remained in the dry sub-humid category and Thanjavur in the semi-arid category throughout the period under consideration (Figures 6.1 and 6.2). However, Tiruvarur, based on the calculated MI, shifted from the dry sub-humid to the semi-arid category for the 30-year moving average starting from 1974, went back to the dry sub-humid category for the 30-year moving average starting from 1981, and continued to remain in the dry sub-humid category till 2015 as seen in Figure 6.3.

Figure 6.1 *Thirty-year moving average of the moisture index for Nagapattinam district*

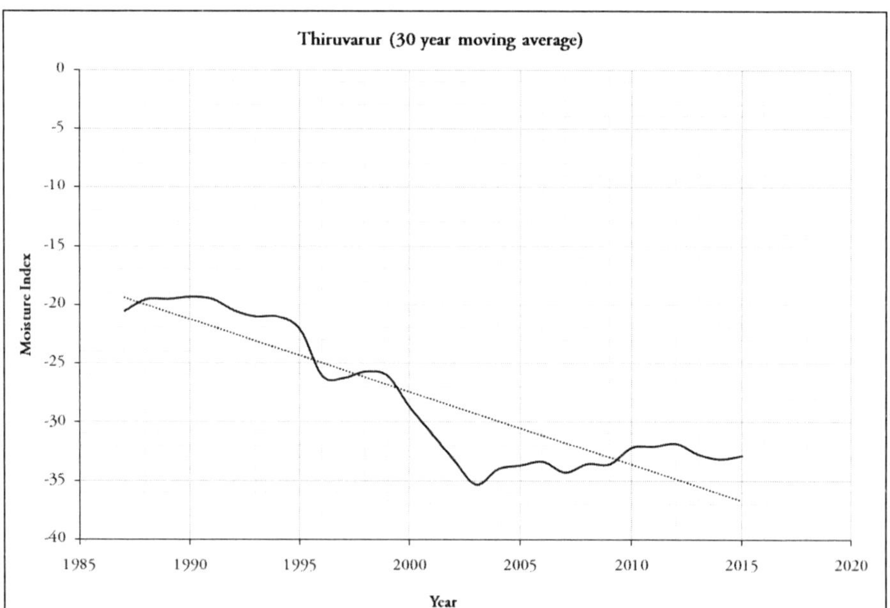

Note: Each data point is the moving average for the preceding 30-year period, with the x-axis label denoting the last year of this period. Hence, the graph begins from 1987 and ends at 2015. The dotted line indicates the trend for the entire period.
Source: Authors' calculation based on ICRISAT data.

Figure 6.2 *Thirty-year moving average of the moisture index for Thanjavur district*

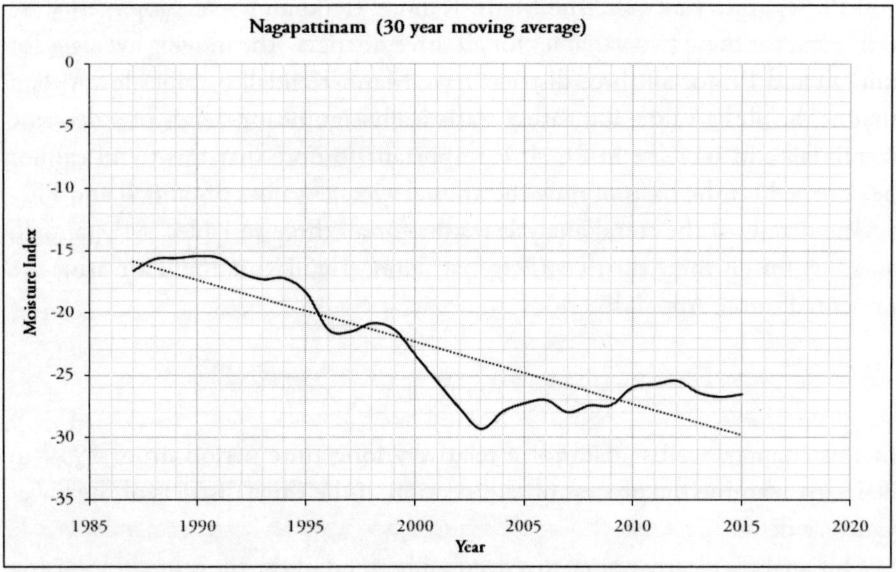

Note: Each data point is the moving average for the preceding 30-year period, with the x-axis label denoting the last year of this period. Hence, the graph begins from 1987 and ends at 2015. The dotted line indicates the trend for the entire period.
Source: Authors' calculation based on ICRISAT data.

Figure 6.3 *Thirty-year moving average of the moisture index for Tiruvarur district*

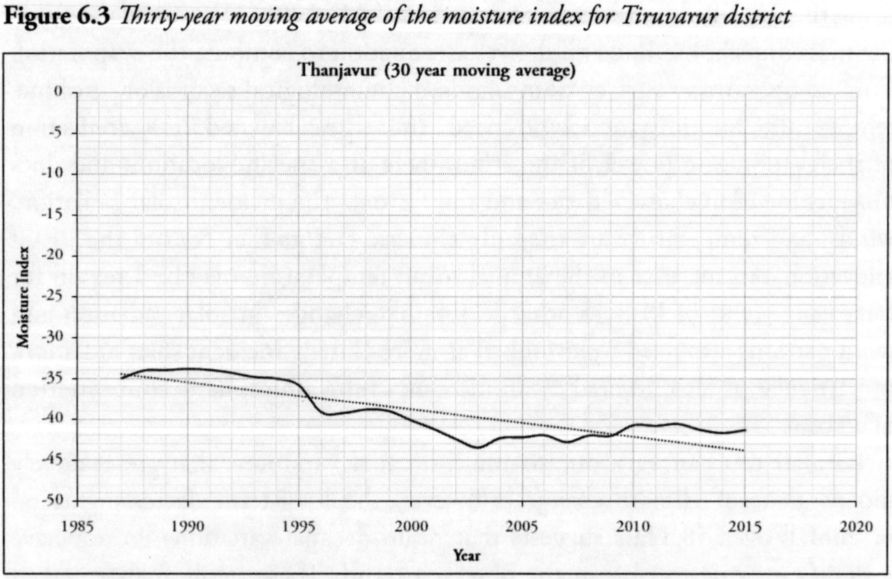

Note: Each data point is the moving average for the preceding 30-year period, with the x-axis label denoting the last year of this period. Hence, the graph begins from 1987 and ends at 2015. The dotted line indicates the trend for the entire period.
Source: Authors' calculation based on ICRISAT data.

Third, we examined trends in the 30-year moving averages of annual rainfall and PE separately as well. The Mann-Kendall trend and Sen's Slope test were estimated for these two variables for all three districts. The moving averages for rainfall and PE for all three districts have Mann-Kendall p-values lower than that of the alpha value, indicating statistically significant trends of a decrease in rainfall and increase in PE. It is important to note that this trend cannot be detected on the basis of only the annual average values of rainfall and PE.

The details of the trend analysis results for all three variables (MI, rainfall, and PE) for all three districts (Nagapattinam, Thanjavur, and Tiruvarur) are presented in the Appendix.

Conclusion

In this chapter, we use data for a relatively long time period, from 1957 to 2015, to examine the process of aridification of the three districts of the lower Cauvery delta.

Our analysis clearly points to a decreasing trend of the moisture index using 30-year moving averages, indicative of a rise in aridity in the three districts. The trend decline in the value of the MI can be linked to increasing PE and a decreasing rainfall trend in all three districts. The only factors that affect PE are climatic parameters, and the PE can be directly calculated from these variables using the FAO Penman-Monteith equation (FAO 1998). The calculation uses the mass transfer method and derives an equation to compute the evaporation from an open water surface from standard climatological records of sunshine, temperature, humidity, and wind speed. Thus, the calculated PE is a reflection of the evaporating power of the atmosphere at a specific location, and does not include crop characteristics and soil factors. The incident solar radiation, winds, and temperature are the only climatic factors that control the PE of a location. An increase in the annual mean temperature may be a reason for increasing trend of PE, yet other factors like changes in solar radiation and wind patterns also need to be looked at more closely. Incident solar radiation, in particular, is also lowered by an increase in the atmospheric concentration of aerosols.

Rainfall too can vary due to multi-decadal variations that are relatively independent of climate change. However, the long-term decreasing trend in rainfall over 58 years suggests that multi-decadal variations do not have a significant role to play in the observed trend. These trend analyses taken together suggest that it is climate change that is driving the overall declining trend in the moisture index. A more definitive conclusion however requires a deeper study that is beyond the scope of this analysis.

These results, together with the overall decline in moisture availability through irrigation, highlight the twin pressures on crop production in the lower Cauvery delta. Higher PE increases the irrigation demands of crops as the available moisture is removed at a faster rate. At the same time, crop production faces declining rainfall as well as declining availability of water from irrigation.

Although using modelled climate data has the advantage of higher resolution both temporally and spatially, there are also some limitations and uncertainties associated with such data. Long-term trends in data are inherited from parent datasets which may themselves have some inherent assumptions. The water balance models are also very simple and do not account for heterogeneity in vegetation types or their physiological response to changing environmental conditions.

Investigation and understanding of aridification, as in the Cauvery delta, is complex for several reasons (see Box 6 on the part played by cyclones). There are multiple climatic and biophysical drivers of aridification which are also mediated by socio-economic factors. An increase in fallow cultivable land in the districts of the lower Cauvery delta may also be an indicator of lower availability of irrigation water, especially in areas that are dependent on canal water for irrigation. This becomes especially important when resilient agricultural practices for productive areas like the lower Cauvery delta are developed keeping in mind the Sustainable Development Goal (SDG) 2 of doubling agricultural productivity and the incomes of small-scale food producers.

Box 6: Cyclone Events in the Cauvery Delta

Isaac M.

Aridification is quite consistent with the occurrence of cyclonic storms of varying intensity. Cyclone Gaja occurred in the year of the FAS field survey. The impact of Cyclone Gaja on crop production and trees, on amenities and incomes, is discussed separately in chapter 16 of this volume. A brief overview of cyclones in the Cauvery delta, drawing on the analysis in Manah (2022), is given below.

The bi-modal distribution of tropical cyclones and severe cyclonic storms in the Bay of Bengal basin is in contrast to the pattern in other tropical basins. Along the eastern coast of India, the coastal districts of West Bengal, Odisha, Andhra Pradesh, and Tamil Nadu are highly prone to tropical cyclones, placing them in the high and very high category of vulnerability. The analysis here, using satellite era data (Manah 2022), indicates a statistically significant decreasing trend in annual (monsoon and post-monsoon) occurrences of cyclonic disturbances in the Bay of Bengal basin, when we consider all scales of cyclonic disturbances.

The basin in which the lower Cauvery delta is located has recorded the deadliest storm surges. Tropical cyclones in the Bay of Bengal become comparatively disastrous due to a shallow continental shelf, a unique combination of high tide, funnel coastal configuration, and low flat coastal terrain, that, in association with high population density, leads to high mortality figures (Murty, Flather, and Henry 1986). However, the picture is somewhat different when assessments are carried out at the district level. In comparison to the lower Cauvery delta, the coastal districts of States such as Andhra Pradesh (Nellore, East Godavari, Krishna), Puducherry (Union Territory, Yanam district), West Bengal (South and North 24 Parganas, Medinipur, Kolkata), and Odisha (Balasore, Bhadrak, Kendrapara, Jagatsinghpur) are more prone to cyclone hazards (Mohapatra *et al.* 2012).

The findings of my analysis (Manah 2022) using historical time-series data (1891–2020) (IMD 2011) point to contrasting results as compared to that using only satellite era data (1961–2020). There is a decreasing trend in annual and monsoon season cyclonic disturbances, tropical cyclones, and severe cyclonic storms in the Bay of Bengal basin. However, there is an increasing trend for all three categories in this basin for the post-monsoon season. The same long-term dataset for the Arabian Sea also shows an increasing trend in annual and post-monsoon cyclonic disturbances.

A trend analysis for the lower Cauvery delta alone does not show any statistically significant trend. However, the distribution of tropical cyclones shows a bimodal distribution as noted for the entire basin. Tropical cyclones in these basins are an important feature of the northeast monsoon season, delivering the precipitation on which rain-fed agriculture systems largely rely for overcoming the moisture deficit in a semi-arid climate. On the other hand, the seasonal occurrence of tropical cyclones coinciding with crucial stages of agriculture production, as in the case of rice (peak sowing and harvesting season), makes agriculture vulnerable to tropical cyclones in the region under study.

References

IMD (2011), "Cyclone eAtlas: Tracks of cyclones and depressions over North Indian Ocean," from 1891 onwards, electronic version 2.0/2011, Cyclone Warning & Research Centre, IMD, Chennai, India, http://14.139.191.203/AboutEAtlas.aspx

Manah, I. (2022), "Tropical Cyclones in the North Indian Ocean Affecting the Lower Cauvery Delta," MSSRF, Chennai (unpublished manuscript).

Mohapatra, M., Mandal, G. S., Bandyopadhyay, B. K., Tyagi, A., and Mohanty, U. C. (2012),

"Classification of Cyclone Hazard Prone Districts of India," *Natural Hazards*, vol. 63, no. 3, pp. 1601–20, https://doi.org/10.1007/s11069-011-9891-8.

Murty, T. S., Flather, R. A., and Henry, R. F. (1986), "The Storm Surge Problem in the Bay of Bengal," *Progress in Oceanography*, vol. 16, no. 4, pp. 195–233, https://doi.org/10.1016/0079-6611(86)90039-X.

Appendix

The Mann-Kendall statistical test for trend analysis is used to assess whether a trend in either direction is statistically significant. The Mann-Kendall test does not assess the magnitude of change. If the p value in a Mann-Kendall trend analysis is lower than that of the significance, that is, alpha value (0.05), then it signifies that there is a definite trend in the series. Negative tau value indicates a decreasing trend and positive indicates an increasing trend.

The following table shows the results for the Mann-Kendall test done for 30-year moving averages of potential evapotranspiration (PE), rainfall, and moisture index for the three districts.

Appendix Table 6.1 *Mann-Kendall tests for trend analysis of 30-year moving averages of rainfall, potential evapotranspiration, and moisture*

Districts		Rainfall (30-year moving average)	PET (30-year moving average)	Moisture index (30-year moving average)
Nagapattinam	Kendall's tau	–0.562	0.956	–0.586
	p-value	<0.0001	<0.0001	<0.0001
	alpha	0.05	0.05	0.05
Thanjavur	Kendall's tau	–0.517	0.951	–0.562
	p-value	<0.0001	<0.0001	<0.0001
	alpha	0.05	0.05	0.05
Thiruvarur	Kendall's tau	–0.581	0.966	-0.601
	p-value	<0.0001	<0.0001	<0.0001
	alpha	0.05	0.05	0.05

Source: Authors' analysis from TerraClimate data.

III

Resources

7

Landholdings

M. Thangaraj

HIGHLIGHTS

This chapter examines landholdings in the two villages. More specifically, it examines the ownership of landholdings by size-class of holdings, by social groups, and by gender. It also examines land under tenancy, fragmentation of landholdings, and the extent of common land. The chapter draws upon data on landholdings from the Survey and Settlement of 1896 up to land records of 2019–20. It uses data from official land records, earlier village studies, and the FAS surveys of Venmani and Palakurichi conducted in 2018–19.

The first major change is a decline in the number of large landholdings (20 hectares and more) and a rise in the number of marginal (one hectare and below) landholdings. In 1896, 45 per cent of total holdings in Palakurichi village were marginal holdings; the proportion was 78 per cent in 2019.

Alongside changes in the size of landholdings, there have been changes in the caste composition of landowners. Naidus owned 71 per cent of land in Palakurichi in 1896, and 30 per cent in 2019. At the same time, land remains concentrated in the hands of a few upper caste landowners: 9 households accounted for 34 per cent of total land owned in Palakurichi in 2019.

A remarkable change is that Scheduled Caste households in 2019 had ownership rights to land, and together owned about 33 per cent of agricultural land in the two villages (although the average landholding of a Scheduled Caste household was 0.5 to 0.6 hectare). The share of ownership holdings of land owned by Scheduled Caste households was less than the share of Scheduled Caste households in the population, and the average ownership holding owned by a Scheduled Caste household was well below the average extent of an ownership holding of land. Nevertheless, the very fact that Scheduled Caste households together owned about one-third of all ownership holdings represents a change in land distribution.

Access to land for Scheduled Caste households did not come through land reform in these two villages, but through a purchase-cum-subsidy effort led by a Gandhian social work organisation that was established in the aftermath of the Keelavenmani atrocity.

Introduction

Historically, the lower Cauvery delta was known for huge disparities in the distribution of land: for centuries, the entire peoples of the depressed classes were denied access to land. They remained landless until redistributive and protective legislative measures were introduced in India after Independence. Land was concentrated in the hands of the economically powerful castes of East Thanjavur (now divided into Thiruvarur and Nagapattinanam districts) and there were tensions between landlords and hired landless agricultural workers since the early twentieth century. Attempts made by the colonial government to provide access to barren and other uncultivable wasteland to the landless does not seem to have made any impact in the area. Another unique feature of the region is that it has attracted social scientists, many of whom have conducted research on the vibrant movement by landless agricultural workers against the landlords' social oppression and economic exploitation. Many social scientists have also attempted to study the nature and distribution of landholdings and agrarian relations at the village level.

Early studies of the village economy of Tamil Nadu were undertaken by the University of Madras under the guidance of Professor Gilbert Slater, of the Department of Indian Economics. These village-level studies are known as studies of "Slater villages." Palakurichi village was one among them and was first studied in 1917 under Slater's guidance by K. Soundara Rajalu, Christian College, Madras, a native of Palakurichi village. A memorial to him was constructed in 1996 in Palakurichi village. Palakurichi village was resurveyed by S. Tirumalai, University of Madras in 1937 under the guidance of Professor P. J. Thomas. Further S. Guhan from Madras Institute of Development Studies, resurveyed Palakurichi in 1983. V. Surjit studied cultivators in Palakurichi in 2002–03. Palakurichi and Venmani villages were surveyed by the Foundation for Agrarian Studies (FAS) in 2019.

Objectives and Hypotheses

The objective of this chapter is to examine the structure and characteristics of landholdings in the two villages, namely Palakurichi and Venmani, located in Nagappattinam district. Specifically, I examine the ownership of landholdings by size-class of holdings, by social groups, and by gender. I also examine land under tenancy, fragmentation of landholdings, and the extent of common land. The following specific hypotheses are examined.

(1) The extent of land covered by marginal holdings (up to 2.5 acres/ 1 hectare) has continuously been increasing over a century.
(2) The ownership of land remains concentrated among the traditionally economically dominant community. In the recent past, however, Scheduled Caste households have been able to acquire land.
(3) The access of women to the ownership of land has increased in recent years.
(4) The area under tenancy is more prevalent on land owned by institutions than on land owned by individuals.
(5) People of the Scheduled Castes do not have access to land under tenancy because of social restrictions.
(6) Over the years, the average number of parcels per holding has decreased and the average area per parcel has increased.
(7) The area under *poramboke* land (common or public land) kept for common purposes for the villagers has declined over the years.

Data

These hypotheses are examined with data from official sources, including personal interviews with officials. Official data were collected from the following village land records: Survey and Settlement Records, Resurvey and Settlement Records, Updating Registry Scheme (UDR) Survey Records, *chitta*, and Record of Tenancy Rights (RTR), 1969. Data were also collected from prior studies of the two villages. Primary data collected by the Foundation of Agrarian Studies (FAS) from a census survey conducted in May–June 2019 are also used. The present author visited the villages of Palakurichi and Venmani in January 2020.

An examination of data on population shows that people of the Scheduled Castes constitute the largest population group in all five studies of Palakurichi, that is, those conducted in 1917, 1937, 1983, 2004, and 2019 (see chapter 2 in this volume).[1] Scheduled Castes also comprise the majority in the village of Venmani.

Structure of Landholdings

This section begins by setting out the record on landholdings for over a century.

[1] Guhan used the term "Harijan" for Scheduled Castes. Data on population by sub-castes among the Scheduled Castes was given by Tirumalai (1940) and Guhan (1983).

Landholdings in 1896

The first source of data on landholdings is the Survey and Settlement Record of 1896. In 1896, of the total 91 *patta* holdings, 41 (45.1 per cent) were in the size-class of less than 2.5 acres, that is, marginal holdings, and these together accounted for 54.49 acres or 6.2 per cent of the total *patta* land. At the other extreme, there were 10 *pattas* (11 per cent of all holdings) in the size-class of 25 acres and above. The extent of land owned was 552.97 acres or 59.2 per cent of total land. The data clearly indicate that the distribution of landholdings was very unequal (see Table 7.1). The data further indicate that the top three holdings, of more than 80 acres each, accounted for 318.82 acres or an average holding size of 106 acres. Guhan (1983) estimated the Gini coefficient to be 0.69 in 1896.

Landholdings in 1917

In K. S. Rajalu's study, the area of the Palakurichi village was recorded to be 1,238 acres, of which 952 acres was wet land, 92 acres was dry land, and 194 acres was *poramboke* land. In 1917, there were 132 landowners, of whom 127

Table 7.1 *Distribution of land ownership, by size-class of holdings, Palakurichi, 1896* in acres and per cent

Size-class	*Pattas*	Extent	Cumulative per cent of *pattas*	Cumulative per cent of land held
0.01–0.99	13	3.7	14.3	0.4
1.00–2.49	28	50.8	45.1	5.8
2.50–4.99	16	55.9	62.6	11.8
5.00–7.49	6	37.0	69.2	15.8
7.50–10.99	8	70.8	79.0	23.4
10.00–14.99	3	36.2	81.3	27.3
15.00–19.99	5	83.2	86.8	36.2
20.00–24.99	2	42.7	89.0	40.8
25.00–29.99	3	79.5	92.3	49.3
30.00–34.99	1	30.6	93.4	52.6
35.00–39.99	1	37.8	94.5	56.6
40.00–44.99	2	86.2	97.7	65.8
80.00 +	3	318.8	100.0	100.0
Total	91	933.3		

Source: Guhan (1983), p. 68.

landowners cultivated the land. Of the remaining five landowners, one was a "guru" (or spiritual teacher), one a temple priest, and three were widows. Three-fourths of the land was cultivated by landowners, 19 cultivators were pure tenants without ownership of land and 10 persons with small holdings also rented land. Rajalu notes:

> Rent is invariably paid in kind, the rate varying according to fertility, facility of irrigation and convenience. The rent per acre for the best land is about 360 measures of paddy, worth about Rs. 40; the average rent for all land rented in the village is equal to about Rs. 30. The owner pays the kist [land tax]. The total kist for the whole village is Rs. 4903-11-0*
>
> *This works out at an average of Rs. 4-11-0 per acre of all cultivated lands, wet and dry, the fertile wet land paying a little more than Rs. 6 per acre. (Rajalu 1918, p. 78)

Landholdings in 1924

Tirumalai (1940) reported that a Resettlement Survey was introduced by the government in 1924 in Palakurichi village. There was an increase of 4.09 acres from Cholavidyapuram due to resettlement of the village in 1924 and as a result, the total area of the village went up to 1,242 acres. Using data on land tax paid, Tirumalai (1940) reported that there were 170 holdings with a cultivated area of 1,049 acres in 1924. Tirumalai further reported that 105.9 acres of land were sublet and cultivated by tenants.

Landholdings in 1937

By 1937, the number of landholders had gone up to 215 *pattadar*s (Tirumalai 1940). Out of 215 *pattadar*s in the village, 90 *pattadar*s were non-residents and six had gone to the Straits Settlements. There were only 119 resident *pattadar*s, including seven local temple deities. Of all resident *pattadar*s, 22 were non-cultivating *pattadar*s. There were 10 pure tenants and eight agricultural workers (excluding *pannaiyal*s) who neither rented nor owned land.

The data further show that nearly 89 per cent of the holdings were below 10 acres (Table 7. 2). The average size of holding was 4.88 acres.

Landholdings in 1979

The Updating Registry Scheme (UDR) Survey Records of Palakurichi from the UDR Scheme, 1979, provides information on land ownership in terms of

Table 7.2 *Distribution of ownership of landholdings, by size-class, Palakurichi, 1937* in acres and per cent

Size of holdings	Number of holdings		Area cultivated	
	Number	Per cent	Area	Per cent
< 1.00	72	33.5	27.2	2.6
1.00–10.00	119	55.4	392.8	37.4
10.00–25.00	18	8.4	251.6	24.0
25.00–50.00	3	1.4	88.6	8.4
50.00–100.00	2	0.9	159.7	15.2
100.00–250.00	1	0.5	129.7	12.4
Total	215	100.0	1,049.6	100.0

Source: Tirumalai (1940), p. 124.

assessment paid.[2] The UDR of Palakurichi village indicates that the number of holdings had gone up to 299 in 1979. The total land area reported was 1,052.84 acres.

Landholdings in 1983

The distribution of land owned by individuals by size-class of landholdings is available for 1983 (Table 7.3). In Palakurichi village, the size of one-third (33.7 per cent) of ownership holdings was less than one acre each; together they constituted 2.1 per cent of the total extent of ownership holdings. About 74 per cent of the households owned less than five acres each, together owning 18.3 per cent of the total extent of all ownership holdings. The data further show that four holdings with 50 acres and more accounted for as much as 256.77 acres (or 27.9 per cent of total land owned). Thus, the data clearly indicate the unequal distribution of landholdings in 1983 in Palakurichi village. Guhan's study also shows that the Gini coefficient of land ownership rose from 0.69 in 1896 to 0.71 in 1983.

Landholdings in 1984/1987

As per official records, the number of landholdings in Palakurichi in 1984 was 294 and the extent of land owned was 430.14 hectares (or 1,062.45 acres) (Table 7.4). This is higher than the figures reported by the Guhan survey

[2] UDR (equivalent to the third survey and settlement) was carried out between 1979 and 1989 in Tamil Nadu.

Table 7.3 *Distribution of ownership of landholdings by size-class, Palakurichi, 1983* in acres and per cent

Size-class	Number of holdings	Extent in acres	Cumulative holdings in per cent	Cumulative extent in per cent
0.01–0.99	49	19.7	33.7	2.1
1.00–2.49	35	61.7	57.8	8.8
2.50–4.99	23	87.2	73.7	18.3
5.00–7.49	8	46.4	79.2	23.3
7.50–9.99	8	73.2	84.7	31.3
10.00–14.99	7	84.6	89.5	40.5
15.00–19.99	3	51.0	91.6	46.0
20.00–24.99	3	65.7	93.7	53.1
25.00–29.99	1	25.0	94.4	55.8
30.00–39.99	2	68.7	95.8	63.3
40.00–49.99	2	80.6	97.2	72.1
50.00–59.99	2	108.8	98.6	83.9
70.00–79.99	2	148.0	100.0	100.0
Total	145	920.6		

Source: Guhan (1983), p. 63.

(1983) (Table 7.3).[3] In the official record, out of 281 individual and joint holdings, 173 (61.6 per cent) holdings were in the marginal size-class. The average size of a holding (individual and joint) was 1.37 ha. Apart from individual and joint holdings, 11 temples and one *chatram* (charitable trust) also owned land in Palakurichi.

In Venmani village, 86.6 per cent of the holdings were marginal-sized holdings. The average size of individual and joint holdings was only 0.56 ha. It is significant to note that the average size of holding was 2.45 times higher in Palakurichi than in Venmani village.

The data presented in Table 7.5 indicate that the average size of landholding owned by individuals was smaller than the average size of institutional holdings. Of the total area of Palakurichi, of 502.72 ha, 75.4 ha (15 per cent) were under the control of the government and available for use to people in the village (UDR Survey Records 1984). A charitable trust (*chathram*) controlled 12.58 hectares of land. In Venmani, around 84 ha (18.6 per cent of land) was government-owned land and 46.3 ha (10. 9 per cent of land) was held by nine temples.

[3] Discrepancy between survey data and official records can occur for many reasons (for example, a person owning land in Palakurichi may not be resident in the village).

Table 7.4 *Number of holdings and extent of land ownership by size-class, Palakurichi 1984 and Venmani 1987* in number and hectares (ha)

Size-class	Palakurichi (1984)			Venmani (1987)		
	Number of holdings	Area of land	Remarks	Number of holdings	Area of land	Remarks
I. Individual and joint holdings						
Marginal	173	49.2	–	497	148.6	
Small	43	62.5	–	44	63.8	
Semi-medium	38	109.2	–	24	62.4	
Medium	26	154.8	–	9	45.7	
Large	1	10.2	–	–	–	–
All	281	385.9	–	574	320.4	
II. Institutional holdings (except *poramboke* and *natham* lands)						
Marginal	7	1.9	6 temples and 1 cooperative society land	5	2.7	Temple lands
Small	2	3.3	Temple lands	3	4.1	Temple and Veerasaiva Thirugnana-sambandha Matam
Semi-medium	1	3.6	Temple lands	1	4	Temple lands
Medium	2	13	Temple lands	–	–	–
Large	1	12.5	*Chathram* lands	1	36.6	Temple lands
Total	13	34.3	–	10	47.4	
All	294	430.1	–	584	367.8	

Notes: (1) Size-classes are as follows: marginal = up to 1 hectare, small = 1 to 2 hectares, semi-medium = 2 to 4 hectares, medium = 4 to 10 hectares, large = greater than 10 hectares. (2) *Poramboke* refers to public land; *natham* refers to land earmarked for housing; *chathram* is a charitable trust.

Source: A-Register documents of Palakurichi, 1984 and of Venmani, 1987.

Landholdings in 2019/2020

The most recent data from the A-Register of the two villages was compiled and the distribution of landholding by size-class of land owned in Palakurichi and Venmani is shown in Table 7.6.

In Palakurichi, a little less than three-fourths (72.1 per cent) of total holdings were in the marginal size-class and accounted for 111.03 hectares or 26.4 per cent of the extent of all holdings. 1n 2019, around 10 per cent of total land (41 ha) was under the control of institutions. The total number of

Table 7.5 *Number of holdings and extent of land ownership by type of holding, Palakurichi 1984 and Venmani 1987* in number and hectares

Nature of holdings	Palakurichi (1984)			Venmani (1987)		
	Number of holdings	Total area	Average area per holding	Number of holdings	Total area	Average area per holding
I. Individual and joint holdings						
Individual holdings	189	359.9	1.9	418	264.2	0.6
Joint holdings/*pattas*	92	25.7	0.3	156	56.1	0.4
Total individual and Joint holdings	281	385.6	1.4	574	320.4	0.6
II. Institutional holdings						
Government lands	–	75.4	–	–	84.2	–
Chathram	1	12.5	12.5			
Agricultural cooperative society	1	0.1	0.1			
Veerasaiva Thirugnana sambandha Matam	–	–	–	1	1.1	1.1
Temple	11	21.7	2	9	46.3	5.1
Total institutional holdings	13	109.8	8.4	10	131.6	13.2
Total landholdings/area	294	495.4	1.7	584	452	0.8

Notes: (1) Joint holdings in Venmani include a joint title of an individual and a temple. Total government land includes *poramboke* and *natham* lands. The data for this land were not included in Table 7.4. (2) *Poramboke* refers to commons/public land; *natham* to land earmarked for housing; *chathram* to a charitable trust; *matam* is a religious institution. (3) There is a slight discrepancy between the reported area and the area obtained from the A-Register of Venmani due to a few missing pages in the copy of the A-register document.
Source: A-Register documents of Palakurichi, 1984 and of Venmani, 1987.

holdings has risen from 294 in 1984 (Table 7.5) to 501 in 2019 (Table 7.6).

In Venmani too, the total number of holdings rose from 584 in 1987 (Table 7.5) to 678 in 2019 (Table 7.6). Institutional holdings accounted for 13 per cent of total holdings in Venmani. In addition to temples and religious trusts, a tiny extent of land (0.41 hectare in total) was owned by the Communist Party of India (Marxist) and the local Agricultural Cooperative Society and Civil Society Corporation in Venmani.

Landholdings in the FAS Survey, 2019

In the two recent village surveys, primary data were collected from all resident households (390 in Palakurichi village and 415 in Venmani). There were 181

Table 7.6 *Number of landholdings and extent of land owned by size-class, Palakurichi 2019 and Venmani 2020* in number and hectares

Size-class	Palakurichi 2019			Venmani 2020		
	Number of holdings	Area of land	Remarks	Number of holdings	Area of land	Remarks
I. Individual holdings						
Marginal	361	111.0		592	174.2	–
Small	77	111.9	–	52	73.7	–
Semi-medium	38	103.4	–	17	47.5	–
Medium	8	43.4	–	5	26.2	–
Large	1	10.0	–	–	–	–
Total	485	379.7	–	666	321.6	–
II. Institutional holdings						
Marginal	8	2.7		7	3.1	Temple, civil supply corporation, cooperative society and CPI(M) lands
Small	2	3.0	Temple lands	3	4.1	Temple and Veerasaiva Thirugnanasambandha Matam lands
Semi-medium	3	10.4		1	3.5	Temple lands
Medium	2	11.4	Temple lands	–	–	–
Large	1	13.3	*Chathram* lands	1	36.6	Temple lands
Total	16	40.9	–	12	47.3	–
	501	420.6		678	368.9	

Note: Total institutional holdings for Venmani exclude *poramboke* and *natham* lands. *Poramboke* refers to commons/public land; *natham* to land earmarked for housing.
Source: Compiled from A-Registers of Palakurichi, 2019 and of Venmani, 2020.

landowning households in Venmani and 212 in Palakurichi. The remaining households did not own land (Table 7.8).

Among the landowning households, the highest number were those with marginal holdings (one hectare and less) in Venmani (78 per cent) and Palakurichi (83 per cent). At the other end of the distribution, a few households held more than 10 hectares each. The data clearly exhibit that there is an unequal distribution of land in both Venmani and Palakurichi. Landlessness is a major problem; 56 per cent of households in Venmani were landless and the proportion was 46 per cent in Palakurichi village.

Table 7.7 *Number of landholdings and extent of land owned by type of holding, Palakurichi 2019 and Venmani 2020* in number and hectares

Nature of holdings	Palakurichi 2019			Venmani 2020		
	Total no. of *pattas*	Total area	Average area per holding	Total no. of *pattas*	Total area	Average area per holding
I. Individual holdings and joint holdings						
Individual *pattas*	313	266.8	0.9	512	252.8	0.5
Joint *pattas*	172	112.9	0.7	154	68.9	0.5
Total individual and joint holdings	485	379.7	0.8	666	321.6	0.5
II. Institutional holdings						
Primary health centre	1	0.9	0.9			
Civil supply corporation	1	0.1	0.1			
Total government lands	–	81.8	–	–	73.4	–
Cooperative	1	0.1	0.1			
Chathram	1	13.3	13.3			
Temple	10	19.6	2.0	8	45.8	5.7
Acute Infrastructure Private Ltd	2	6.8	3.4			
Veerasaiva Thirugnanasambandha Matam		–	–	1	1.1	1.1
Communist Party of India (Marxist)	–		–	1	0.2	0.2
Agricultural cooperative society	–		–	1	0.1	0.1
Civil supply corporation		–	–	1	0.1	0.1
Total institutional holdings	16	122.7	–	12	120.7	–
Total landholdings	501	502.5	–	678	442.3	0.7

Notes: (1) Total government lands include *poramboke* lands and *natham* lands. This land was not included in Table 7.6. *Poramboke* refers to commons/public land; *natham* refers to land earmarked for housing. (2) *Chitta* for Venmani was extracted from the *Amma e-Service of Land Records*, "Tamil Nilam," Government of Tamil Nadu. A photocopy of the *chitta* register, 2018 obtained from the office of VAO of Venmani was kept as a reference and the information on each *patta* number was retrieved by entering the *patta* numbers one by one. Despite our efforts of entering *patta* numbers, details for some *patta*s have not been obtained and there is a difference in the area of the holdings. Further, the A-Register of Venmani village for the year 2020 could not be availed. The figures for *poramboke* lands were taken from the abstract of the A-Register of 2018.
Source: Chitta extracts of Venmani, 2020, and *chitta* and A-Register in Palakurichi, 2019.

Table 7.8 *Number of households and area owned by size-class of land ownership, Venmani and Palakurichi, 2019* in number and hectares

Size-class	Venmani		Palakurichi	
	Number	Area	Number	Area
Landless households	234	–	178	–
Up to –1.00	141	64.3	176	82.6
1.01–2.00	22	28.4	20	25.3
2.01–4.00	10	26.3	6	16.0
4.01–10.00	6	31.5	7	40.7
10.01–20.00	2	26.1	2	34.4
More than 20 hectares	–	–	1	22.3
Landholding households	181	176.6	212	221.2
Total	415	176.6	390	221.2

Source: Survey data.

Marginalization of Holdings

There is a long history of discussion on the size of economic holdings in India. Recognising that there is not enough agricultural land to provide every cultivating family with an economic holding, Kumarappa argued for the transfer of surplus population on land to non-agricultural pursuits, and for cooperative joint farming of holdings smaller than basic holdings (Kumarappa 1949). In a discussion on October 10, 1927 on the Small holders' Relief Bill, Dr Ambedkar, as a member of the Bombay Legislative Council agreed on the question of the disadvantages of scattered farms. He, however, argued that whether a farm is economic or uneconomic depends not on the size of the farm but also on the other factors of production, labour and capital (Ambedkar 1982). He also accepted the introduction of cooperative agriculture and urged owners of small holdings to join in cultivation without affecting private ownership.

Marginalization of landholdings resulting in holdings of an uneconomic size is a process that has been ongoing in India. Marginal holdings (below 1.0 ha) accounted for 50 per cent of all holdings in 1970–71, 54.5 per cent in 1976–77 and 56.5 per cent in 1980–81 (Kurien 1987). Marginalization, it is argued, may be more on account of rising poverty than on account of division of property through inheritance (Bandyopadhyay 1986). Rao and Hanumappa (1999) suggest that the process is likely to get intensified in the coming years.

In Tamil Nadu, as per the latest Agricultural Census 2010–11, marginal and small operational holdings of land of less than 2 hectares each accounted for 92 per cent of all holdings and 61 per cent of the total operated area (GoI 2015).

Our first hypothesis is that land under marginal holdings (up to 2.5 acres or 1 ha) has been continuously increasing over a century.

In 1896, 45 per cent of total holdings in Palakurichi village were in the category of marginal holdings. In 1983, 57.9 per cent of holdings were marginal holdings; this went up to 61 per cent in 1984. In 2019, the proportion was 74 per cent according to official sources and 78 per cent according to the field survey.

In Venmani, we have data for a shorter period. The earliest data (for 1987) indicate that 85 per cent of all holdings were marginal holdings. The proportion was 88 per cent in 2020. In short, there has been a big increase in the number and proportion of holdings of marginal size over time, more dramatically visible in the data for Palakurichi village, which are available over a 100-year period.

Deshpande (2003) has observed that the share of landholdings belonging to Scheduled Castes is declining at a sharper rate than the general trend. In the study villages, most of the holdings owned by people of the Scheduled Castes landowners come under the category of marginal holdings: 95 per cent of the holdings in Palakurichi village and 88 per cent of the holdings in Venmani village (See Appendix Tables 7.3 and 7.4).

Caste and Landholdings

While speaking on the Report of the Commissioner for Scheduled Castes and Tribes for 1953, Dr. Ambedkar (Ambedkar 1997, p. 912) remarked that "the government should provide land to the Scheduled Castes so that they might obtain independent means of livelihood, cease to be afraid of anybody, walk with their heads erect, and live fearlessly and courageously" (Ambedkar 1997, p. 912). In rural India, land tends to be concentrated in the hands of the upper castes. Underprivileged sections of people are denied access to land.

In Palakurichi village (Table 7.9) most of the land was under the control of the Naidus, the economically powerful caste in the village. The data further show that the entire land of the village was owned by caste Hindus and people of the Schedule Castes did not own any land in the village in 1896. Rajalu (1918) in his study reported that the Naidu caste was the most influential in Palakurichi, that they owned most of the land, and that their holdings were large. They were not a trading class but were agriculturists. They did not sell their land except to repay debts, but bought land wherever and whenever possible.

The dominance of Naidu households in Palakurichi continued in 1983. Of all holdings, 51.7 per cent belonged to Naidu households, and these holdings covered 86.5 of the total extent of ownership holdings (Table 7.10). Thus, the

Table 7.9 *Land ownership by caste, Palakurichi, 1896* in per cent

	Caste	Share in land ownership (resident and non-resident)
1	Naidu	70.8
2	Brahmins	5.1
3	Padayachis	0.8
4	Pillais	11.4
5	Asaris	3.9
	Total	100.0

Note: From Survey and Settlement Record, 1896; cited by Guhan (1983).
Source: Guhan (1983), p. 69.

Table 7.10 *Number of holdings and extent of land ownership of residents and non-residents by caste, Palakurichi 1983* in hectares

Caste/ Institution	Residents		Non-residents		Total (Individual ownership)	
	Holdings	Extent	Holdings	Extent	Holdings	Extent
Naidu	23	214.3	52	108.0	75	322.2
Pillais	7	10.6	11	5.0	18	15.6
Padaiyachis	11	9.9	14	5.5	25	15.4
Chettiyars	1	7.0	–	–	1	7.0
Konars	4	3.5	7	1.3	11	4.8
Muslims	1	0.4	1	2.4	2	2.7
Asari	2	0.4	4	1.4	6	1.8
Harijan	3	0.7	1	0.8	4	1.6
Christian	–	–	1	1.1	1	1.1
Nadar	–	–	1	0.1	1	0.1
Brahmin	–	–	1	0.1	1	0.1
Institutions	12	32.5	–	–	–	–
Temples	4	17.0	–	–	–	–
Total	68	296.3	93	125.8	145	372.6

Note: Small shrines own 9.87 acres.
Source: Guhan (1983), p. 64.

Table 7.11 *Share of landowning and landless households in total population by caste, Palakurichi, 1983,* in per cent

Caste	Share in population	Share of residents among those who own land in village	Share of landless households
Naidu	6.4	86.8	3.8
Pillai	7.6	4.3	54.2
Padayachi	17.7	4.0	50.0
Other castes	19.7	4.6	67.2
Harijans (SCs)	48.6	0.3	92.5
All	100.0	100.0	72.5

Source: Guhan (1983), p. 66.

data clearly indicate that there was an inequality in distribution of land owned by different castes in Palakurichi village. Taking the extent of all individual landholdings, the share of non-resident land owners was 33.8 per cent.

Among 12 institutional holdings, the largest landowner was a local *chatram* (rest house) owning 34 acres (Guhan 1983). It was endowed by a leading Naidu family nearly a hundred years ago to feed pilgrims to the annual festival in the neighbouring village of Ettukudi. The charitable institution continues to function.

Details regarding caste-wise land ownership and the proportion of landless households in 1983 are given in Table 7.11. The data clearly show that most of the land in Palakurichi village was owned by Naidu households. Naidus constituted 6.4 per cent of the population and owned 86.8 per cent of the land. The share of landless among Naidus was very low (3.8 per cent of households). Guhan has compared his survey data (1983) with data from the Survey and Settlement record, 1896 (Table 7.9); the data showed that the domination of Naidu households in land ownership had continued for nearly 90 years.

PARI survey data

In Palakurichi village, none of the Dalits (Scheduled Castes) owned any land in 1896. The study conducted in 1983 by Guhan found that only four Dalit households owned 3.89 acres of land in the village. The picture was different in 2019.

According to the PARI survey, Scheduled Castes households owned 32 per cent of the total extent of land owned by households resident in Venmani and 33.7 per cent of the total extent of land owned by households resident in Palakurichi. It is striking that the landless, particularly from among the Scheduled Castes, have acquired ownership of land in both villages. No household from among the Scheduled Castes owned any land in Venmani village in 1968, when 44 persons were burnt alive by oppressor landlords. The data from the PARI survey show that 95 Scheduled Caste households together owned 141 acres in Venmani and 150 Scheduled Caste households owned a total of 184 acres of land in Palakurichi in 2019.

The average area owned by a Scheduled Caste household remains small: 0.6 hectare in Venmani and 0.5 hectare in Palakurichi. Most Scheduled Caste landowners (95.3 per cent in Palakurichi and 88.4 per cent in Venmani) owned marginal landholdings.

In the mid-1940s, East Thanjavur was known for the mobilization of agricultural workers under the banner of the Communist Party (and the Party was known as "Pallan-Paraiyan Katchi," or Party of the Dalits). The initial struggle of the Party was to eliminate the barbarous forms of "punishment," such as whipping and forced eating of cow dung, that were meted out to Scheduled Caste workers. All agricultural workers belonging to the Scheduled Castes were landless (Saravanan 2017).

Not long after the Venmani atrocity of 1968, two Gandhians, Krishnammal

Table 7.12 *Extent of land ownership by caste, Venmani and Palakurichi village, 2019* in hectares and per cent

Caste	Venmani		Palakurichi	
	Area	Per cent	Area	Per cent
Scheduled Castes	57.1	32.1	74.6	33.7
Aagamudaiyar	8.4	4.7	3.2	1.5
Ambalakarar	13.1	7.4	–	–
Brahmin	4.0	2.3	0.0	0.0
Chettiyar	0.9	0.5	2.8	1.2
Kammalar	0.0	–	1.2	0.6
Nadar	12.2	6.9	–	–
Naidu	44.8	25.2	66.8	30.2
Padayatchi	2.0	1.1	60.6	27.4
Pillai	31.3	17.6	4.8	2.2
Thevar	0.3	0.2	0.0	0.0
Yadava	3.8	2.1	7.2	3.3
Total	177.9	100.0	221.2	100.0

Source: Survey data.

and Jagannathan, came to Venmani to address the problems of landless agricultural workers. Initially, they asked landlords to donate land; they realised subsequently that this approach was not going to succeed in East Thanjavur. They formed an association called Land for Tillers' Freedom (LAFTI) in 1980. Their method was to purchase the land with the help of bank credit, to distribute the land to the landless, to get the stamp duty and registration fee on land transfers waived, and, in addition, to get a subsidy from the government (Thangaraj 2003). There was also a view that "LAFTI was operating to defuse agrarian unrest and thereby working against fundamental social transformation in the countryside" (Rigby 1987, p. 319).

In Venmani, 55 acres of land were distributed to landless Scheduled Caste households by LAFTI (Fernando 2018). According to FAS survey data, 134 Scheduled Caste households in Palakurichi reported receiving one acre of land each with the help of LAFTI. This has significantly influenced the nature of land distribution in the village, particularly among Scheduled Caste households (see chapter 2). Nevertheless, the livelihoods of the Scheduled Castes remain vulnerable to poverty because of the small size of the holdings they own.

In conclusion, evidence shows that ownership of land remains concentrated among traditionally economically dominant communities. Naidus comprise 2.8 per cent of the population but control 30 per cent of the land in Palakurichi village. At the same time, Scheduled Castes have acquired some land in the recent past.

Women's Ownership of Land

Women constitute nearly half of the total population. Women have been denied equal rights to access to education and land including of ancestral property of land by inheritance. While both colonial and post-Independence governments in India have enacted laws that permit women to inherit landed property, tradition however dictates that male members of a family inherit the land. As a result, women own much less land than men in India today.

In Palakurichi, in 1984, 23 per cent of the land was owned by women in individual or joint holdings, mainly the former (Table 7.13). The average area of an ownership holding of land owned by a woman was 62 per cent of the average area of an ownership holding of land owned by a man.

Similarly, in Venmani village in 1987, 24 per cent of the land was owned by women in individual or joint holdings; 67.6 per cent of the land was owned by men in individual or joint holdings (and the rest was held by institutions). The average area of a landholding owned by a woman was 0.55 acres, and the average area of land owned by a man was 0.67 acres.

Table 7.13 *Ownership of landholdings by gender in Palakurichi, 1984, and Venmani, 1987* in hectares

Nature of holdings	Palakurichi, 1984			Venmani, 1987		
	Number of holdings	Total area	Average area per holding	Number of holdings	Total area	Average area per holding
Individual holdings						
I. Individual *pattas*						
Women	64	86.7	1.4	132	73.1	0.6
Men	125	273.2	2.2	286	191.2	0.7
Total	189	359.9	1.9	418	264.2	0.6
II. Joint *pattas*						
All women	8	1.8	0.2	13	5.3	0.4
All men	52	13.8	0.3	69	25.7	0.4
Mixed	32	10	0.3	74	25.1	0.3
Total	92	25.7	0.3	156	56.1	0.4
Grand total	281	385.6	1.4	574	320.4	0.6

Source: A-Registers of Palakurichi, 1984 and of Venmani, 1987.

Data from official records for the most recent period (Table 7.14) show a small increase in the extent of land owned by women. In Palakurichi, land held by women in joint *pattas* rose, taking the total share of land in women's names to 31 in 2019. In Venmani, there was a small increase in women's holdings in individual *pattas*, taking the total share of women to 25.6 per cent in 2020.

Comparing data from the PARI surveys with earlier village records, it appears that while the extent of land owned by women is low, there has been an improvement over time in both Palakurichi and Venmani villages (Appendix Tables 7.5 and 7.6)

In Palakurichi, there were 72 holdings by women in individual and joint *pattas* in 1984, covering a total extent of 88 hectares. In 2019, the corresponding number of holdings was 164, covering an extent of 118 hectares. In Venmani, the number of holdings by women rose from 145 in 1987 to 179 in 2020, with the extent of area owned increasing from 78 to 110 hectares.

In conclusion, women's access to land owned was relatively low but has improved a little over the years.[4] Land owned by women increased from 23 per

[4] This is in line with other studies such as by Agarwal, Anthwal, and Malvika (2021) in 30 villages across nine states that found that the percentage of landowning rural households which have at least one woman owning agricultural land has gone up from 21.4 per cent in 2009 to 29 per cent in 2014.

Table 7.14 *Ownership of land patta/holdings by gender in Palakurichi, 2019, and Venmani, 2020* in hectares

Nature of holdings	Palakurichi, 2019			Venmani, 2020		
	Number of holdings	Total area	Average area per holding	Number of holdings	Total area	Average area per holding
Individual holdings						
I. Individual *pattas*						
Women	116	80.0	0.7	170	77.5	0.5
Men	197	186.8	1.0	342	175.2	0.5
Total	313	266.8	0.9	512	252.8	0.5
II. Joint *pattas*						
All women	48	38.1	0.8	9	4.7	0.5
All men	46	15.0	0.3	68	26.8	0.4
Mixed	78	59.8	0.8	77	37.5	0.5
Total	172	112.9	0.7	154	68.9	0.5
Grand total	485	379.7	0.8	666	321.6	0.5

Source: A-Register of Venmani, 2019 and *chitta* excerpts of Venmani, 2020.

cent of the total extent of land in 1984 to 31 per cent in 2019 in Palakurichi. In Venmani, the change was less: the land owned by women was 24.5 per cent of the total extent of land in 1987 and 25.6 per cent in 2020.

Tenancy

To study the nature and the extent of land under tenancy in the selected two villages, data were collected from records of tenants maintained by the Village Administrative Officer (VAO). The record provides information on the names of landowners, the extent of land owned, the names of tenants, and the area under tenancy. Post-Independence legislation on tenancy include the Unlawful Eviction Act, 1955, Fixation of Fair Rent Act, 1956, and the Record of Tenancy Rights (RTR) Act, 1969. The last envisages a record of tenancy in the State, with a view to regulating the working of other Acts intended to protect tenants. This Act enables the government to maintain a list of actual tenants in villages.

Rajalu reported that there were 19 "pure tenants" (that is, farmers with no operational holding other than the land they lease) in 1917; Tirumalai (1940) reported that 106 acres of land were leased out in 1924. He also reports that there were 10 "pure tenants" in 1937 in Palakurichi. The official records today

Table 7.15 *Area under own cultivation and tenancy by temples in Palakurichi, 1984* in hectares

Temple name	Area under self-cultivation	Area under tenancy
Thannilapadi Rasagopala Perumal	3.6	0.0
Varadaraja Perumal	2.2	6.0
Parvatheeswara Swami	0.9	3.9
Ayyanar	0.3	0.0
Pillaiyar Koil	0.4	0.0
Mariamman	0.3	0.0
Pidariamman	0.1	0.0
Nellukkadai Mariyamman	0.0	0.7
Karpaganadaswami	3.3	0.0
Total	11.1	10.5

Source: Column 2: compiled from the A-Register, Palakurichi, 1984; column 3: Record of Tenancy Rights, Palakurichi, 1972.

show only temple-owned land to have been leased to tenants in Palakurichi village. Three temples in the villages now lease land to tenants. Out of 53.47 acres of land owned by the temples, nearly half has been leased out to tenants.

Information in Appendix Table 7.2 clearly indicates that land belonging to temples alone have been recorded in the RTR of Palakurichi. The total area of land leased out was 26.15 acres consisting of 34 plots leased out to 35 persons (some names have been repeated). It is significant to note that one individual (a Naidu) is the trustee of all temple lands under tenancy (other than the land of the Nellukadai Mariyamman temple, Nagappattinam). There were no Scheduled Caste tenants in Palakurichi village.

Surjit's study (2004) of Palakurichi showed that Scheduled Castes had access to operational holdings of land. This was mainly because of struggles conducted under the leadership of the Communist Party of India (Marxist). Dalits gained access to temple land mainly as sub-tenants of official tenants. Of the total area operated by Dalit households, 68 per cent was leased in. Surjit's study further shows that

> A notable feature of temple-land tenancies is that the tenants are predominantly from caste Hindu families. Of the fourteen temple tenants in 2004, only one was a Dalit cultivator. However, thirteen of the fourteen tenants sub-leased some of the temple land to other cultivators. Historically, only other castes were tenants of the temple land. (Surjit 2004, p. 179)

Details of tenancy could not be accessed by us from the Venmani Village

Administrative Office. However, in an informal discussion with an older person of the village, we learned that nearly 90 acres of land in Venmani village was under the control of Devapureeswarar temple, Thevur (an adjacent village), and that this land was leased out to some 60 or 70 tenants who were working on the land when the RTR Act came into force. All of these tenants belonged to the Scheduled Castes.

In conclusion, first, data available are consistent with the hypothesis that tenancy is more prevalent on land owned by temples (institutions) than on land owned by individuals. Data as published in 1972 based on the Tamil Nadu Agricultural Lands Record of Tenancy Rights Act, 1969 show only temple land to have been leased out in Palakurichi. Secondly, Scheduled Castes do not have access to land under tenancy.[5] This is evident from the data given in Appendix Table 7.2. No Scheduled Caste name is found among the tenants in Palakurichi village.

The tenancy legislation enacted from 1955 to 1969 did not benefit Dalits in Palakurichi village. The Government of Tamil Nadu has not legally banned tenancy. It has permitted leasing out land and created a record of tenancy in which name of the landowner, name of the tenant, and the area under tenancy have been recorded. The prevalent system of tenancy is an oppressive and exploitative system in which tenants pay rent (although regulated) to the landowner that is higher than the land tax paid by the landowner to the government as land revenue/tax.

Fragmentation of Holdings

One of the characteristics of landholdings in India is that land held by a single household is unlikely to be in one compact block but in many parcels scattered in several places all over the village. Subdivision and fragmentation of holdings are major causes for low productivity in agriculture. As the *Report of the Committee on Doubling Farmers' Incomes* (Volume I) notes, fragmented and scattered holdings do not allow the efficient utilization of farm resources and technology adoption by farmers (GoI 2017, p. 12). Many States have enacted laws to consolidate landholdings; the government of Tamil Nadu, however, has not done so.

There is evidence of a reduction in the number of fragments and an increase in the average area per parcel between 1961–62 and 1981–82. This was on

[5] This is observed also by Nancharaiah (1988) in his study of Kanchakoduru village in Krishna district, Andhra Pradesh. He showed that Scheduled Caste households could not get any benefit from the tenancy laws. The Scheduled Castes have low access to tenancy and the landowners (Brahmins) hesitated to lease out their lands to Scheduled Castes on grounds of untouchability.

account of many factors, including government intervention, the acquisition of land by the owners of contiguous plots, and the exchange of land between landowners (Thangaraj 1995, p. 183).

In this section, I draw on village records to examine the number of parcels in landholdings, and the average area per parcel in the two villages.

The problems arising out of fragmented landholdings were reported in the first study of Palakurichi. K.S. Rajalu wrote:

> The [longest] distance of any plot of land from the home of the cultivator in the village is one mile (1.6 km). The intermixture of the holdings is a considerable inconvenience. One man reaps earlier than those who hold adjoining plots; he cannot graze his animals on the stubble till his neighbours have reaped. The conditions of water supply also may compel a man to grow the same crop as his neighbours, when he would prefer to grow another. In consequence, the villagers have adopted a system of mutual exchange of lands called *parivarthanai* (mutual exchange), by which plots of equal value are exchanged in such a way as to give the various owners as many contiguous plots as possible . . . . *Parivarthanai* is a difficult process, because in order that the two proprietors may agree to exchange, it is necessary to have equality in value, taking into consideration area, fertility, distance from the village, irrigation facilities, and other conveniences. The rich proprietor will frequently refuse to exchange in such a way as to convenience a small neighbour: and the small proprietor is very much at the mercy of a rich man who holds adjoining land. (Rajalu 1918, pp. 79–80)

commenting on the inconvenience of fragmentation (inter-mixture) of holdings, and pointing out that mutual exchange was a difficult process.

Twenty years later, Tirumalai in his study of Palakurichi village in 1937, reported that there was no mutual exchange of land (Tirumalai 1940.) His study has detailed information on the number of plots per holding for different size-classes (Appendix Table 7.7). The total number of landholdings reported in his study were 215. The number of plots was 976, or 4.54 parcels per holding, with an average plot size of 0.43 acres (Table 7.16).

Guhan too did not come across any case of mutual exchange of land. His data on the number of parcels and the average size of a parcel (Table 7.16) show that there was not much change in both parameters between 1937 and 1983. However, as the number of holdings was smaller, the number of parcels per holding was higher.

Data are available on the distribution of holdings and plots by gender (Appendix Tables 7.6 and 7.8).

Recent data from village land records show that in Palakurichi, the number

Table 7.16 *Number of parcels per holding and average size of parcels, Palakurichi, 1937 and 1983* in number and hectares

Year	Total extent of holdings	Number of holdings	Average size per parcel	Number of parcels	Average number of parcels per holding
1937	424.8	215	0.4	976	4.54
1983	426.1	161	0.4	987	6.13

Source: Guhan (1983), p. 75.

of parcels in individual landholdings has increased from 1,094 in 1984 to 1,123 in 2019. The average area per parcel has declined slightly from 0.35 hectares in 1984 to 0.34 hectares in 2019 (Appendix Table 7.10). There were no obvious gender differences in terms of the number of parcels per holding or the average size of a parcel in 2019.

In Venmani, land records for 1987 and 2020 show that there was a small decline in the total number of parcels, and number of parcels per holding, but no change in the average size of a parcel (Appendix Table 7.11). Again, there were no clear differences as between land owned by men and women in this respect.

To conclude, in Palakurichi, there has been a decline in the number of parcels per holding and a rise in the area of a parcel. In Venmani, there has not been much change in respect of parcelisation between 1987 and 2020.

Common Land in the Villages

In every village, certain lands are earmarked for the use of village people, land reserved for future housing, grazing for livestock, threshing floors, tanks, ponds, and so on. There are other types of common land that are preserved for public purposes. Some of this land has been encroached upon by people because of the scarcity of cultivable land and the mounting pressure of population on the land. *Poramboke* or common land is assessed for revenue purpose in the land records and the assessed lands [and, in specific circumstances, can be assigned to persons in the village].

In 1917, 194.36 acres of *poramboke* land were reported in Palakurichi village (Rajalu 1918). This included tanks, ponds, village site, roads, and common pasture. Rajalu also noted that there were 19 threshing floors in 1917 and two tanks, each about 12-feet deep and covering 2.5 acres. There were many small ponds in Palakurichi village. The different uses of *poramboke* land can be visualized from data for 1924 in Appendix Table 7.12.

Table 7.17 *Classification of communal poramboke lands, Venmani, 2018* area in hectares

Classification	Area in hectares	Per cent of total commons land area
Canal	2.49	3.39
Threshing floor	1.71	2.33
Pond	3.19	4.35
Crematory	0.19	0.26
Temple	0.33	0.45
Village *natham*	17.57	23.94
L.F. Road	1.81	2.47
Pichaikalaiyar river	4.91	6.69
Therkodiyar river	11.90	16.22
Pathway	1.40	1.91
Pool	0.23	0.31
River bank	0.65	0.89
Total	73.38	100.00

Source: A-Register enclosures abstract, Venmani, 2019.

There was no change in total *poramboke* land reported in 1937, and, not surprisingly, only a negligible proportion of this land was used for cultivation (Appendix Table 7.13).

The next data point, for 2019, shows the current uses of communal *poramboke* land in Palakurichi (Appendix Table 7.14). By village records, the total extent of *poramboke* had not changed much (188.12 acres). The highest share of this was under canals (21.74 hectares), followed by the Velliyar river (14.34 hectares). It is significant to note that land has been earmarked for dwelling purposes, the *natham*, covering 12.83 hectares, and the *cheri-natham*, covering 0.29 hectares. To our surprise, then, the area under *poramboke* land has not declined over the years in Palakurichi village.

Some Conclusions and Recommendations

As some observers suggest, structural change has occurred in rural Tamil Nadu; more specifically, caste and land relationships have been reconfigured in rural Tamil Nadu (Kalaiyarasan and Vijayabaskar 2021, p. 150). We place our observations for these two villages.

My first set of conclusions pertain to access to land, both in terms of ownership and operational landholdings, for Scheduled Caste households.

The data clearly exhibit that the distribution of land in Venmani and

Palakurichi is unequal. Ownership of land remains concentrated among traditionally economically dominant castes. Naidus comprise 2.8 per cent of the population but control 30 per cent of the land in Palakurichi village. At the same time, Scheduled Castes have acquired some land in the recent past.

In 1983, only four Scheduled Caste households in Palakurchi owned agricultural land. In 2019, 150 Scheduled Caste households owned land. Households of the Scheduled Castes historically owned only a negligible share of the extent of all ownership holdings of land; that share rose to about 33 per cent in 2019. Landlessness has decreased among Scheduled Castes.

This acquisition of land by Scheduled Castes has not come about through land reform. The Government of Tamil Nadu enacted the Ceiling on Land Holdings Act in 1961. No land has been declared as surplus under the land ceiling laws in Palakurichi. The largest resident landlord today owns 68 acres of wetland and 4 acres of dry land. His holding is equivalent to 47.5 standard acres and is recorded as owned by himself, his wife, two sons, and a daughter. It is possible for a household with five members to own more than 100 acres of double crop land without attracting the ceiling (Guhan 1983, p. 70). During the late 1950s, trusts were created to escape from the Ceiling on Landholdings Act. Charitable trusts are institutions established for a specific purpose, such as for education, health, or religious purposes. Trusts are exempted from the provisions of the Land Ceiling Act. A study conducted by LAFTI shows that a landlord from Valivalam village (adjacent to the study area) has transferred 600 acres of land to different trusts to avoid ceiling legislation (Jagannathan 2003).

There is no evidence of redistribution of land in Palakurichi village through the Tamil Nadu Land Reforms (Fixation of Ceiling on Land) Act, 1961 and The Tamil Nadu Land Reforms (Reduction of Ceiling on Land) Act, 1970 to the landless and other poor, including Dalit households, in the village.

As discussed in Chapter 2, Scheduled Castes in Palakurichi and Venmani have received small plots of land through the efforts of LAFTI, a non-government organization.

With regard to tenancy, first, the data available are consistent with the hypothesis that tenancy is more prevalent on land owned by temples (institutions) than on land owned by individuals. Secondly, Scheduled Castes do not have access to land under tenancy.

To reduce the domination of the economically powerful social groups, I argue that the ceiling limit of the land should be reduced to 10 standard acres and that the ceiling surplus land thus identified be redistributed to the landless poor irrespective of their social status.

The second set of conclusions relate to marginalization and fragmentation of landholdings. There has been a big increase in the number and proportion of holdings of marginal size (that is, ownership holdings of less than one hectare in extent) over time, dramatically visible in the data for Palakurichi village for a hundred years.

With regard to the fragmentation of landholdings, in Palakurichi, there has been a decline in the number of parcels per holding and a rise in the area of a parcel. In Venmani, there has not been much change in respect of parcelisation between 1987 and 2020. In light of this observation, I argue that individual farming should not be allowed on holdings that are smaller than basic holdings. They should be, in the course of time, brought under cooperative joint farming.[6]

Above all, it is time to remember and consider Dr Ambedkar's views on land policy. Dr Ambedkar has submitted a memorandum on safeguards for the Scheduled Castes to the Constituent Assembly in 1946 on behalf of the Scheduled Caste Federation. One of the demands in this proposal was for "agriculture to be a State industry," that is, for land to be nationalized. The proposal suggested that "the State divide land acquired in to farms of standard size acre" that could be either "cultivated as a collective farm" or by tenants who would share the produce among themselves after paying charges levied on the farm. Further state-owned land could be leased out to "villagers without distinction of caste or creed and in such manner that there will be no landlord, no tenant and no landless labourer" (Ambedkar 1979, pp. 396–97).

The author thanks Madhura Swaminathan for her comments on an earlier version of the paper, and an anonymous referee for useful comments and suggestions. The author also wishes to thank C. A. Sethu for his painstaking efforts to collect the village land records and R. Ashwath for collecting village land records and processing the data, enabling the author to utilise them for this study.

[6] My suggestion is along the lines of those made in Kumarappa (1949).

Appendix

Appendix Table 7.1 *Number of households and population by caste, Venmani and Palakurichi,* 2019

Caste	Venmani			Palakurichi		
	Number of households	Population (including migrants)	Population (excluding migrants)	Number of households	Population (including migrants)	Population (excluding migrants)
Brahmin	2	4	4	1	3	3
Chettiyar	2	8	7	6	19	18
Scheduled Caste	263	1,041	954	235	877	810
Naidu	28	115	101	11	40	30
Other caste Hindu	77	303	271	35	138	131
Padayatchi	9	33	28	79	279	266
Pillai	33	109	103	21	88	75
Thevar	1	1	1	2	4	4
All	415	1,614	1,469	390	1,448	1,337

Note: Other caste Hindu includes two households that did not specify their caste in Venmani and one such household in Palakurichi.
Source: Survey data, 2019.

Appendix Table 7.2 *Tenurial status, temple trustees and tenants by caste, Palakurichi, 1972*

Name of the landowner	Trustee name	Trustee caste	Tenant name	Tenant caste	Area (in acres)	Dryland/ Wetland
Nellukkadai Mariamman, Nagapattinam	–	–	D. Viswanathan	Pillai	1.62	Wetland
Sri Varadaraja Perumal Temple	Santhanakrishna Naidu	Naidu	1. R. Kunji Padaiyachi	Padaiyachi	0.37	Wetland
			2. R. Kunji Padaiyachi	Padaiyachi	1.08	Wetland
			3. Perumal Konar	Konar	1.54	Wetland
			4. K. Rajagopal Konar	Konar	1.54	Wetland
			5. Venkatrama Naidu	Naidu	0.08	Wetland
			6. Venkatrama Naidu	Naidu	0.37	Wetland
			7. i.Pappammal w/o Govindasamy ii. Pakkirisamy	Pillai	0.28	Wetland
			8. G. Ramakrishna Naidu	Naidu	2.42	Wetland
			9. i. Pappammal w/o Govindasamy ii. Pakkirisamy	Pillai	1.91	Wetland
			10. Venkatrama Naidu	Naidu	0.06	Wetland
			11. i. Pappammal w/o Govindasamy ii. Pakkirisamy	Pillai	0.08	Wetland
			13. Perumal Konar	Konar	0.18	Wetland
			14. K. Rajagopal Konar	Konar	0.18	Wetland
			15. G. Ramakrishnan	Naidu	0.4	Wetland

Appendix Table 7.2 *(continued)*

	16. K. Arumuga Padaiyachi	Padaiyachi	0.1	Wetland
	17. K. Arumuga Padaiyachi	Padaiyachi	0.18	Wetland
	18. Venkatrama Naidu	Naidu	0.08	Wetland
	19. Venkatrama Naidu	Naidu	0.26	Wetland
	20. Venkatrama Naidu	Naidu	0.06	Wetland
	21. K. Arumuga Padaiyachi	Padaiyachi	0.89	Wetland
	22. K. Arumuga Padaiyachi	Padaiyachi	0.22	Wetland
	23. K. Singaravelu Padaiyachi	Padaiyachi	1.89	Wetland
	24. K. Arumuga Padaiyachi	Padaiyachi	0.58	Wetland
	Total		14.85	
Parvatheeswaraswami	1. Venkatachalam	Padaiyachi	0.15	Dryland
	2. Venkatrama Naidu	Naidu	1.22	Wetland
	3. R. Sourirajulu	Naidu	1.12	Wetland
	4. R. Sourirajulu	Naidu	0.7	Wetland
	5. Kaliyamoorthi	Chettiyar	3.84	Wetland
	6. R. Venkatachalam	Padaiyachi	0.58	Wetland
	7. R. Venkatachalam	Padaiyachi	1.2	Wetland
	8. R. Sourirajulu	Naidu	0.8	Wetland
	9. R. Venkatachalam	Padaiyachi	0.05	Wetland
	10. R. Venkatachalam	Padaiyachi	0.02	Wetland
	Total		9.68	
	Grand Total		26.05	

Source: Record of Tenancy Rights, Palakurichi, 1972.

Appendix Table 7.3 *Number of households and area of land ownership by size-class and by social group (excluding homestead), Venmani, 2019* area in hectares (ha)

Ownership of holdings by size-class / Social groups	Scheduled Caste		Backward Class		Most Backward Class		Other		All	
	Number of households	Area	Number of households	Area	Number of households	Area	Number of households	Area	Number of households	Area
Landless	168	–	40	–	18	–	3	–	231	–
(0.01–1) ha	84	31.9	49	27.1	10	3.6	1	0.4	144	63.1
(1.01–2) ha	7	8.6	10	12.5	5	7.1	–	–	22	28.3
(2.01–4) ha	2	4	7	18.8	1	4.3	–	–	10	27.1
(4.01–10) ha	2	12.5	3	14.2	–	–	1	4	6	30.8
(10.01–20) ha	–	–	–	–	–	–	2	28.7	2	28.7
Landholding households	95	57.1	69	72.6	16	15.1	4	33.2	184	177.9
All households	263	57.1	109	72.6	34	15.1	7	33.2	415	177.9

Source: Survey data, 2019.

Appendix Table 7.4 *Number of households and area of land ownership by size-class and by social groups (excluding homestead), Palakurichi, 2019*
area in hectares (ha)

Ownership of holdings by size-class / Social groups	Scheduled Caste		Backward Class		Most Backward Class		Other		All	
	Number of households	Area	Number of households	Area	Number of households	Area	Number of households	Area	Number of households	Area
Landless	85	0	36	0	51	0	5	0	178	0
(0.01–1) ha	143	63.7	16	8.6	15	9.1	2	1.2	176	82.6
(1.01–2) ha	6	6.9	6	8.2	8	10.2	–	–	20	25.3
(2.01–4) ha	–	–	3	8.7	3	7.3			6	16.0
(4.01–10) ha	1	4.0	2	9.9	3	17.8	1	8.9	7	40.7
(10.01–20) ha	–	–	1	18.2	1	16.2	–	–	2	34.4
More than 20 ha	–	–	1	22.3	–	–	–	–	1	22.3
Landholding households	150	74.6	29	75.9	30	60.6	3	10.1	212	221.2
All households	235	74.6	65	75.9	81	60.6	8	10.1	390	221.2

Source: Survey data, 2019.

Appendix Table 7.5 *Women's land ownership by size-class of landholding, Palakurichi, 1984 and 2019* in hectares

Size-class	Palakurichi 1984		Palakurichi 2019	
	Number of holdings	Area	Number of holdings	Area
Marginal	43	17.615	126	45.299
Small	16	22.685	26	37.395
Semi-medium	8	23.765	11	29.755
Medium	5	24.445	1	5.590
Total	72	88.510	164	118.039

Note: Includes individual and joint *patta* titles held by women, but excludes mixed joint *pattas* held by men and women.
Source: A-Register of Palakurichi, 1984 and 2019 (also see Table 7.13 in this chapter for 1984 and Table 7.14 for 2019).

Appendix Table 7.6 *Women's land ownership by size-class of landholdings, Venmani, 1987 and 2020* in hectares

Size-class	Venmani 1987		Venmani 2020	
	Number of holdings	Area	Number of holdings	Area
Marginal	121	41.740	162	82.198
Small	20	27.545	13	18.163
Semi-medium	4	9.055	4	10.36
Total	145	78.340	179	110.721

Note: Includes individual and joint women *patta* titles, but mixed joint *pattas* of men and women are not included.
Sources: A-Register of Venmani, 1987 and *chitta* excerpts of Venmani, 2020 (also Table 7.13 for 1987 and Table 7.14 for 2020).

Appendix Table 7.7 *Distribution of plots by size, Palakurichi, 1937* in acres

Size	Plots		Area of land	
	Number	Per cent	Area	Per cent
1–5 cents	47	4.82	12.04	1.14
5–10 cents	100	10.25	18.60	1.82
10–20 cents	156	15.98	20.77	2.00
20–30 cents	82	8.40	19.56	1.90
30–40 cents	51	5.23	16.84	1.62
40–50 cents	44	4.51	19.62	1.90
50 cents – 1 acre	164	16.80	94.15	8.95
1–2 acres	151	15–47	196.27	18.67
2–3 acres	83	8–50	198.88	18.95
3–4 acres	37	3.79	124.98	11.90
4–5 acres	26	2.66	114.38	10.86
5–6 acres	21	2.15	116.20	11.05
6–7 acres	11	1.13	70.57	6.76
7–8 acres	1	0.10	7.24	0.66
8–9 acres	–	–	–	–
9–10 acres	2	0.20	19.54	1.90
Total	976	100.00	1,049.64	100.00

Source: Tirumalai (1940), p. 123.

Appendix Table 7.8 *Distribution of plots by gender, Palakurichi, 1984 and 2019* in number and hectares

Nature of holdings	Palakurichi – 2019*			Palakurichi –1984**		
	Total number of parcels	Average number of parcels per holding	Average area per parcel	Total number of parcels	Average number of parcels per holding	Average area per parcel
I. Individual holdings						
Women	247	2.13	0.32	221	3.45	0.39
Men	574	2.91	0.33	761	6.09	0.36
Total	821	2.62	0.32	982	5.20	0.37
II. Joint holdings						
All Women	63	1.31	0.60	11	1.38	0.16
All Men	59	1.28	0.26	65	1.25	0.21
Mixed	180	2.31	0.33	35	1.09	0.29
Total	302	1.76	0.37	111	1.21	0.23
Total individual and joint holdings	1123	2.32	0.34	1093	3.89	0.35
Total institutional holdings	444	–	–	311	–	–
Total holdings	1,567	–	–	1,404	–	–

Note: Total number of holdings and the total area are given in Tables 7.13 and 7.4.
Source: *Compiled from the *chitta* record and A-Register of Palakurichi, 2019; **A-Register of Palakurichi village, 1984.

Appendix Table 7.9 *Distribution of plots by gender in Venmani, 1987 and 2020* area in hectares

Nature of holdings	Venmani – 2020			Venmani – 1987		
	Total number of parcels	Average number of parcels per holding	Average area per parcel	Total number of parcels	Average number of parcels per holding	Average area per parcel
I. Individual holdings						
Women	420	2.47	0.19	404	3.06	0.18
Men	936	2.74	0.19	965	3.37	0.20
Total	1356	2.65	0.19	1369	3.28	0.19
II. Joint holdings						
All women	19	2.11	0.25	29	2.23	0.18
All men	128	1.88	0.21	139	2.01	0.19
Mixed	172	2.23	0.22	163	2.20	0.15
Total	319	2.071	0.216	331	2.12	0.17
Total individual and joint holdings	1675	2.52	0.19	1700	2.96	0.19
Total institutional holdings	102	–	–	377	37.7	0.35
Total holdings	1777	2.62	0.25	2077	3.56	0.22

Source: *Chitta* extracts of Venmani, 2020.

Appendix Table 7.10 *Distribution of plots by size-class of land owned, Palakurichi, 1984 and 2019* in hectares

Size-class	Palakurichi 2019			Palakurichi 1984		
	Number of parcels	Average number of parcels	Average area per parcel	Number of parcels	Average number of parcels	Average area per parcel
Individuals/Joint holdings						
Marginal	571	1.58	0.19	272	1.56	0.18
Small	206	2.68	0.54	165	3.84	0.38
Semi-medium	227	5.97	0.46	286	7.53	0.38
Medium	105	13.13	0.41	354	13.62	0.44
Large	14	14.00	0.72	17	17.00	0.60
Total	1123	2.32	0.34	1094	3.89	0.35

Source: Compiled from the A-Register document of Palakurichi, 1984 and 2019.

Appendix Table 7.11 *Land ownership by size-class of land owned, Venmani, 1987 and 2020*
area in hectares

Size-class	Venmani 2020			Venmani 1987		
	Number of parcels	Average number of parcels	Average area per parcel	Number of parcels	Average number of parcels	Average area per parcel
Individual/Joint holdings						
Marginal	1125	1.90	0.16	966	1.94	0.15
Small	316	6.08	0.23	339	7.7	0.19
Semi-medium	180	10.59	0.26	248	10.33	0.25
Medium	54	10.80	0.49	147	16.33	0.31
Total	1675	2.52	0.19	1700	2.96	0.19

Source: Compiled from A-Register document of Venmani, 1987 and *chitta* extracts of Venmani, 2020.

Appendix Table 7.12 *Classification of communal poramboke land, Palakurichi, 1924* area in hectares

Type of *poramboke*	Area
River	24.82
Canal	21.17
Village site	11.55
Tank	4.84
Threshing floor	4.11
*Odai**	2.63
Footpath	2.34
Cart-track	1.12
Road	0.83
Road and canal	0.45
Burial ground	0.44
Street	0.41
Bunds	0.32
Temple	0.18
Total	75.21

Note: **Odai* stands for stream.
Source: Tirumalai (1940), p. 121.

Appendix Table 7.13 *Distribution of area under cultivation by type of land, Palakurichi, 1937* in hectares and per cent

Type of land	Total area	Area cultivated	Cultivated area as per cent of total area
Wet	395.22	382.4	97
Dry	29.56	7.08	23
Assessed waste	1.4	0.05	4
Poramboke	75.21	0.87	1.1
Inam	1.32	0.23	16
Total	502.7	390.62	

Source: Tirumalai (1940), p. 129.

Appendix Table 7.14 *Classification of communal poramboke lands, Palakurichi, 2019* area in hectares

Classification	Area	Per cent of total *poramboke* land area
Canal	21.74	28.55
*Natham**	12.83	16.85
River bank	0.33	0.43
Threshing floor	3.39	4.45
Pond	4.84	6.36
School	0.08	0.11
Cart road	0.39	0.51
Footpath	2.55	3.35
Pidaari temple	0.08	0.11
*Cheri-natham**	0.29	0.38
Cemetery	0.44	0.58
Canal bank	0.08	0.11
Road	0.83	1.09
Road and canal	0.46	0.60
Edaiyar river	2.57	3.37
P. Edaiyar river	7.92	10.40
Vellaiyar river	14.34	18.83
Streets	0.42	0.55
Stream	2.63	3.45
Wells	0.01	0.01
Total	76.16	100.00

Note: **Natham* and *cheri-natham* refer to lands earmarked for housing.
Source: Revenue Assessment Abstract, Office of VAO, Palakurichi.

8

Livestock

A. Suresh

HIGHLIGHTS

With the spread of mechanisation and decline in use of cattle as a source of draught power, the composition of livestock holdings has changed. Small ruminants – goats, in particular – have become the major component of livestock in the villages. Ownership of goats was widespread: 82 per cent of households in Palakurichi owned goats whereas only 25 per cent owned cattle.

Livestock were owned by households from all castes and classes. The proportion of livestock-owning households was higher among lower-income groups, but the average size of holding was higher among relatively better-off households. In Palakurichi, three-fourths of poor peasants owned livestock; the proportion was one-third among landlords and capitalist farmers. In standard livestock units, however, the size of holding among the latter was four times that among poor peasants.

While income from livestock constituted only 3 to 4 per cent of aggregate household income, among households affected by losses in crop production, incomes from livestock agriculture helped reverse the losses. Among all types of livestock, the returns-to-expenditure ratio was highest for goat farming. This can explain why goats were so widely owned especially among poorer households. Not surprisingly, incomes from livestock were distributed more equally than incomes from crop production

With investment in better infrastructure (including veterinary care, extension and markets), livestock can provide income enhancement and less exposure to risk for poorer households.

Introduction

The lives and livelihood of people in Indian villages are closely related to livestock. However, the progress of mechanisation along with widespread usage of fertilizers in agriculture has weakened the crop-livestock linkage. The economic utility of cattle is reduced to that of a source of milk. Though cross-bred cattle are superior in milk-production capabilities, they are not preferred due to their increased disease-proneness compared to local cattle. The lack of green fodder in villages further accentuated the situation, as the hitherto available grazing lands were gradually transferred to other uses. Gradually, small ruminants like sheep and goats have attained widespread adoption due to their relatively low investment requirement, low maintenance expenditure, and high net return relative to expenditure. This makes small ruminants a major component of the livestock-holding pattern of smallholders and weaker sections of society (Suresh *et al.* 2008). Small ruminants are better suited for the arid and semi-arid regions of India and their population is increasing in such regions. The demand for meat and eggs continues to be high, and consequently, farming of small ruminants (goat and sheep), poultry (layer and broiler), and piggery have emerged as major enterprises.

Research Questions

The chapter uses data from village studies of Palakurichi and Venmani as well as official statistics to examine current patterns of livestock ownership across classes and changes in the structure of the livestock population over a period of time. Tracing this change and its reflection on various classes in the villages provides insights into the role the livestock sector plays in the broader socio-economic context. We argue that the role of livestock has changed from a supplier of milk for home consumption and input to crop farming by providing draught power to that of an income-generating asset, and thereby to livelihood security. An important question examined here is whether this transition has occurred across all socio-economic classes.

Secondly, it has been shown that the distribution of livestock is more egalitarian than the distribution of land (Taneja and Birthal 2004; Ali 2007). Even landless households participate in livestock farming by undertaking small-scale livestock enterprises (Birthal, Joshi and Gulati 2005; Kumar, Staal and Singh 2011). We examine the extent of livestock holdings across socio-economic classes.

Thirdly, the composition of livestock holding varies across classes and over time. We explain the observed pattern of holdings as a response to ease of investment, relative returns over expenditure, and regularity of returns.

Fourthly, access to markets is an important determinant of incomes and returns from livestock, and so understanding market participation across socio-economic classes becomes important. Using detailed data on household incomes, our study tries to examine the role of income from livestock farming for households in different socio-economic groups.

Changes in the Livestock Economy of Palakurichi, 1918 to 1983

Data from surveys of Palakurichi during the period from 1918 to 1983 show a decline in the population of draught animals and an increase in the populations of milch animals, small ruminants (sheep and goat), and poultry (Table 8.1). The population of draught animals increased from 199 in 1918 to 327 in 1970. With the mechanisation of agriculture, the population declined sharply and reached 76 in 1983. This tendency has continued, as we shall see in the next section. Correspondingly, the number of ploughs has declined, notably wooden ploughs fell from 150 in 1970 to 43 in 1983.

Tirumalai (1940) provides a vivid account of livestock in Palakurichi.

Table 8.1 *Trend in livestock population, carts, and ploughs, Palakurichi, 1918–83* in number

Item	1918	1937	1970	1983
Draught animals	199	234	327	76
a. Cattle	191	222		
b. Buffalo	8	12		
Milk animals	175	211	160	269
a. Cattle	124	151		
b. Buffalo	51	60		
Calves	NA	131	173	206
Sheep and goat	427	259	282	498
Poultry	NA	NA	682	797
Horse	1	NA	NA	NA
Total livestock	802	835	1,624	1,846
Carts	29	52	24	30
Ploughs	91	128	182	86
• Wooden	91	NA	150	43
• Iron	0	NA	32	24
• Rotator	0	NA	NA	19

Note: NA – not available.

Sources: Slater, ed. (1918); Tirumalai (1940); and Guhan (1983).

The traditional cattle breeds were known as *Tanjore Mottai*. Farmers mainly purchased them from local markets or private owners through brokers. A pair of oxen was used for 8 acres which was 60–100 per cent higher than their normal working capacity. He-buffaloes were seldom used for work in drylands but were used in some wetlands. The price of a pair of bullocks ranged between Rs 40 to Rs 100 (Rs 75 on average); they worked for a period not less than five years, and were sold afterward for Rs 25. The price of a pair of he-buffaloes ranged between Rs 20 to Rs 50. Among the available oxen and he-buffaloes, 10 to 20 per cent were unfit for work and were kept for sentimental reasons. Some of the cultivating tenants purchased dregs at the cattle markets at extremely low prices and disposed of them once the cultivating season was over. This tendency of frequent purchase and sale of cattle was practiced as it was uneconomical to keep work animals during the off-season. The villagers spent little on feed (2 to 4 annas per head) and animals had to depend on grazing lands, *poramboke*, or wasteland for grazing. Only a few animals belonged to fine breeds, and the rest were non-descript indifferent bred, and carelessly reared. The main purpose of keeping cattle was to breed the future stock of draught cattle, and the leftover milk after the suckling of the calves was a by-product. The milk yield ranged between 2 to 5 pounds, and the price was about 4–5 annas per 2 pounds. The cattle were priced between Rs 25 to Rs 50 per head (average Rs 30). A buffalo in milch was also priced at a similar range (average Rs 25), despite having better milk yield, longer lactation period, higher price for its milk (compared to cattle), and comparable maintenance cost. One reason could be that he-calves of buffaloes were less wanted and fetched poor prices.

In 1961, all cultivators in the village possessed at least one cow and one buffalo for their domestic use. Haswell (1961, p. 31) notes that "the number of beasts per family in 1961 was 4.88 and cattle per head of population was 0.585, compared with 0.663 in 1936 and 0.439 in 1916." Cultivators were reported to be in extreme difficulty as they could not procure sufficient feed for the cattle.

The increase in the population of milch animals, sheep goats, and poultry by 1983 is directly related to the ability of these species to provide supplementary income to the peasants (Guhan 1983), who kept them either under ownership or under *varam* (sharing) basis. Under the latter category, richer households provided small ruminants and poultry to the *varam* holders under the agreement that they maintain them and share the output with the owner on a 50:50 basis. Guhan (1983) noted that most of the draught animals in Palakurichi were owned by large landlords. The distribution of milch animals was less skewed.

The prevalence of several livestock diseases and death due to them are noted by Slater, ed. (1918), Tirumalai (1940), Haswell (1961), and Guhan (1983), as the veterinary infrastructure in the village was not well developed.

Features of Livestock Ownership, 2019

The population of livestock in the two villages, as per the survey of 2019, is shown in Table 8.2. It is clear that the number of cattle in Palakurichi is less than that reported in the study of 1983. In terms of absolute figures, goats and chickens predominate among different types of livestock.

It is interesting that over half of all households in both the villages owned one or other type of livestock (55 per cent in Palakurichi and 54 per cent in Venmani) (Table 8.3). Among the socio-economic classes, the proportion of livestock-owning households (LHH) is highest among peasants; the proportion of LHH increases as we go from poor peasants to rich peasants. The

Table 8.2 *Population of livestock in Palakurichi and Venmani, 2019* in number

Livestock	Palakurichi	Venmani
Cows/bullocks	126	241
Goats	703	599
Poultry (chicken)	291	661

Source: FAS survey data.

Table 8.3 *Proportion of livestock-holding households across socio-economic classes, Palakurichi and Venmani, 2019* in number and per cent

Socio-economic class	Livestock-holding households (LHH)		Share of LHH in total households (%)	
	Palakurichi	Venmani	Palakurichi	Venmani
Landlords and big capitalist farmers	3	1	38	33
Rich peasants	6	9	75	90
Middle peasants	19	29	73	76
Poor peasants	73	58	56	74
Manual wage workers	79	71	57	44
Persons living on pensions, small rents, and remittances	12	22	32	34
Salaried persons	12	19	52	66
Self-employed in business activity	11	16	58	52
All	215	225	55	54

Source: FAS survey data.

proportion of livestock-holding households is the lowest among landlords and big capitalist farmers and those living on pensions, small rents and remittances.

However, there is a departure from the livestock-holding pattern observed historically in that, households from classes other than the peasantry also own livestock. About 70 per cent of rich peasants in Palakurichi and 90 per cent in Venmani owned livestock. At the same time, 52 per cent of salaried households in Palakurichi and 66 per cent in Venmani also owned livestock. Cultivators traditionally owned cattle for agricultural operations, but with the emergence of mechanisation, the ownership of draught animals has fallen substantially. Indeed, even households without any operational holdings possessed livestock (52 per cent in Palakurichi and 42 per cent in Venmani). They engaged in stall-feeding of livestock.

There are variations in livestock ownership across caste groups. Ownership of livestock is disproportionately lower among Dalit households as compared to non-Dalits. About 50 per cent of Dalit households in Palakurichi and Venmani owned livestock; the proportion was 60 to 66 per cent for households from the Backward Classses.

To sum up, while there is inequality in the ownership of livestock across caste and class, reflecting inequality in ownership of agricultural land, the distribution of livestock among livestock holding households is more equal than the distribution of operational holdings among them (based on estimates of the Gini coefficient).

Composition of Livestock

The major livestock owned are cows, bullocks, goats, and backyard poultry. In the two villages, cattle are no longer the most important type of livestock. Poultry birds are possessed mainly for eggs for home consumption. Other livestock such as pigeon, turkey, rabbit, and sheep are also owned, but to a small extent (16 pigeons, three turkeys, and two rabbits in Palakurichi; and three sheep and 10 pigeons in Venmani). There were no buffaloes in the villages.

The distribution of various livestock across socio-economic classes shows that the livestock population is concentrated among poor and middle peasants, and manual wage workers (Table 8.4). These three groups together accounted for 65 per cent of cattle, 70 per cent of goats, and 74 per cent of poultry birds in Palakurichi. The respective figures were 78 per cent, 75 per cent, and 62 per cent in Venmani. Thus, livestock is largely owned by the peasantry and manual wage workers together, even though ownership is spread across all socio-economic classes.

Although cattle have been given higher priority in the livestock sector in

Table 8.4 *Distribution of livestock species across socio-economic classes, Palakurichi and Venmani, 2019* in number

Socio-economic class	Palakurichi			Venmani		
	Cow/ Bullock	Goat	Chicken	Cow/ Bullock	Goat	Chicken
Landlords and big capitalist farmers	9	23	3	2		
Rich peasants	14	69	6	23	12	60
Middle peasants	28	35	42	70	106	100
Poor peasants	29	214	124	69	150	123
Manual wage workers	25	243	49	41	209	188
Persons living on pensions, small rents, and remittances	9	42	5	15	50	38
Salaried persons	4	45	60	16	44	69
Self-employed in business activity	8	32	2	5	28	83
All households	126	703	291	241	599	661

Source: FAS survey data.

Table 8.5 *Proportion of households owning livestock and mean size of livestock holdings, Palakurichi and Venmani, 2019* in per cent and number

Village	Livestock-holding households (no.)	Proportion of households owning			Mean size of holding (no.)		
		Cattle	Goat	Poultry	Cattle	Goat	Poultry
Palakurichi	215	25	82	21	2	4	7
Venmani	225	47	65	44	2	4	7

Source: FAS survey data.

India, of late other livestock, particularly small ruminants (goat and sheep), have gained attention. The goat turns out to be the most widely owned livestock – owned by 82 per cent of households in Palakurichi and 65 per cent of households in Venmani (Table 8.5). In both Palakurichi and Venmani, the proportion of households with goats was higher than the proportion of households with cattle, in all socio-economic classes (except for landlords and rich peasants). In Palakurichi, the proportion of goat-owning households was more than 90 per cent among manual wage workers and persons living on pensions and remittances; between 80 and 90 per cent among self-employed and poor peasants; and 60 and 80 per cent among salaried persons and rich peasants. It was 33 per cent among capitalist farmers.

At the same time, the average size of holding was higher among rich peasants and capitalist farmers (17–23 heads per household) than households in other classes (3–5 heads per household). While only a small proportion of households that were neither peasants nor wage workers owned goats, the average holding size of goats with them was generally higher. Venmani shows a similar pattern of ownership of animals.

Thus, the nature of livestock holding depends on position in the class structure.

Size of Livestock Holding

The mean holding size of cattle, goats, and poultry was two, four, and seven, respectively, in Palakurichi and Venmani. Using standard FAO methodology, I have converted holdings of livestock into standard livestock units (Table 8.6). Using standard units, the average size of livestock holdings is higher among landlords and rich peasants than others in Palakurichi. Landlords and rich peasants had holdings that were four times higher than those held by manual workers. In Venmani, livestock holdings were higher for rich and middle peasants than others. Rich and middle peasants had holdings that were two to three times larger than those of manual workers.

Though livestock is an income-earning asset, the relatively prosperous socio-economic classes are in a better position to invest in them. Income from livestock accrues after a significant time gap: three to five years for a cattle calf

Table 8.6 *Mean and median size of livestock holding, by socio-economic class, Palakurichi and Venmani, 2019* in standard livestock units

Socio-economic class	Palakurichi		Venmani	
	Mean	Median	Mean	Median
Landlords and big capitalist farmers	2.3	2.3	1.0	1.0
Rich peasants	2.3	1.7	1.5	1.4
Middle peasants	0.9	0.9	1.6	1.5
Poor peasants	0.5	0.4	0.9	0.8
Manual wage workers	0.5	0.3	0.6	0.5
Persons living on pensions, small rents, and remittances	0.7	0.5	0.6	0.4
Salaried persons	0.6	0.4	0.7	0.2
Self-employed in business activity	0.7	0.4	0.4	0.3
All	0.6	0.4	0.8	0.5

Source: FAS survey data.

to reach a milk-producing age, and for goats, it would be about one to one-and-a-half years for first calving. Farmers usually sell the male goats keeping the female as stocks for the next crop. Therefore, it would take one and half to two years to realise economic returns from the sale of goat kids. Another significant factor is the regularity of income: while in-milch cattle yield milk regularly, the income from goats is a one-time event (at the time of sale). There is also irregularity in the flow of incomes while households incur high initial expenditure to build up a stock of animals and have to spend regularly on maintenance expenditure. These two factors can affect the investment in livestock by households from poorer socio-economic classes.

Asset Value

We turn now to the share of livestock in agricultural assets. With a mean asset value of about Rs 16,300 in Palakurichi and Rs 20,170 in Venmani, livestock accounted for about 5 to 6 per cent of the value of total agricultural assets and 2 per cent of the value of all assets (Table 8.7). The value of livestock assets varied widely across households – from Rs 12,100 to Rs 82,750 in Palakurichi

Table 8.7 *Livestock assets as a ratio of agricultural assets and total assets, Palakurichi and Venmani, 2019* in rupees and per cent

Socio-economic class	Palakurichi			Venmani		
	Value of livestock (Rs)	Livestock/ agricultural assets (%)	Livestock/ all assets (%)	Livestock (Rs)	Livestock/ agricultural assets (%)	Livestock/ all assets (%)
Landlords and big capitalist farmers	82,733	1	1	29,000	1	0
Rich peasants	51,500	2	1	39,950	1	1
Middle peasants	22,634	4	1	39,781	4	2
Poor peasants	12,662	7	3	20,507	13	4
Manual wage workers (skilled+unskilled)	12,109	35	3	14,857	39	5
Persons living on pensions, rent, remittances	18,733	22	3	13,705	12	2
Salaried persons	15,058	13	2	17,779	11	2
Self-employed in business activity	21,036	20	2	7,038	12	2
All	16,303	5	2	20,170	6	2

Source: FAS survey data.

and from Rs 7,000 to Rs 40,000 in Venmani. The value of livestock assets was highest for capitalist and landlord farmers of Palakurichi, mainly because of the large holding of goats by some farmers. The value of livestock assets was next highest for rich peasants, followed by middle peasants, and lowest for manual wage workers and poor peasants, in both villages.

The share of livestock in total agricultural assets was the highest for manual wage workers, mainly because of the lack of other means of production. The share of livestock assets in total agricultural assets was lower as we moved from manual wage workers to poor peasants, middle peasants, rich peasants, and landlords in Palakurichi and Venmani. It was the highest for manual wage workers (35 per cent and 39 per cent in Palakurichi and Venmani, respectively) and the lowest for rich peasants and landlords (less than 1 per cent).

Given their overall asset poverty (see chapter 9), livestock was an important component of assets for manual wage workers and poor peasants.

Earnings from Livestock

The inability of the agricultural sector – that is of crop and livestock farming – to generate a decent income can be gauged from an analysis of level and sources of income (Tables 8.8 and 8.9).

The net income of livestock-holding households (LHH) was estimated by netting out the expenses from agricultural activities including crops and livestock. The mean income of an LHH was Rs 1.4 lakh and Rs 1.6 lakh in Palakurichi and Venmani, respectively (Table 8.8). The median values indicate that about 50 per cent of LHH had income less than Rs 1.06 lakhs in Palakurichi and Rs 1.03 lakhs in Venmani.

On a per-capita basis, the annual net income of a livestock-holding household was about Rs 40,000 in Palakurichi and Rs 44,000 in Venmani. Per

Table 8.8 *Mean and median household income of livestock-holding households by source of income, Palakurichi and Venmani, 2019* in rupees

Village		Crop	Livestock	Other sources	Total household income
Palakurichi	Mean	7,081	6,565	1,25,855	1,39,501
	Median	179	3,600	99,830	1,05,741
Venmani	Mean	294	6,079	1,52,038	1,58,412
	Median	0	4,350	99,000	1,03,117

Source: FAS survey data.

Table 8.9 *Mean per capita income by source of income, Palakurichi and Venmani* in rupees and per cent

Village		Crop	Livestock	Other sources	All
Palakurichi	Rs	1,988	2,278	36,046	40,312
	%	5	6	89	100
Venmani	Rs	92	1,960	42,187	44,240
	%	0	4	95	100

Source: FAS survey data.

capita income from crops was very low in the survey year due to severe damage from Cyclone Gaja. The mean annual per capita income from livestock was Rs 2,278 in Palakurichi and Rs 1,960 in Venmani.

The mean annual income from livestock was about Rs 6,565 in Palakurichi, and Rs 6,079 in Venmani (Appendix Table 8.1) but there were sizeable variations across classes. In Palakurichi, capitalist farmers and big landlords received about Rs 40,000 a year from livestock. At the same time, the net income from livestock was Rs 4,000–5,000 for manual workers and poor peasants (that is, one-tenth). The differences in income from livestock across classes were smaller in Venmani.

In terms of composition of income, even among LHH, about 90 per cent of income in Palakurichi was from "other sources" while 5 per cent came from crops, and another 5 per cent from livestock. In Venmani, 96 per cent of income was from "other sources", while livestock contributed 4 per cent. Income from livestock accounted for 21 per cent of net income of rich peasants in Palakurichi (and 4 to 5 per cent for poor and middle peasants). In Venmani, livestock income was 7 per cent of total income for poor and middle peasants and 3 per cent for rich peasants (Appendix Table 8.1).

Livestock and Farm Income Variability

A significant feature of income generation in the two villages is that while crop production generated negative incomes for many households, livestock income was inevitably positive. For example, in Venmani, on average, a poor peasant household made losses of Rs 1,532 from crop production in the survey year and received positive net incomes of Rs 5,540 from livestock rearing. One can argue that it is the contribution from livestock that prevented many households from falling into the realm of negative incomes. Although crop failure has become very frequent in the region, livestock could withstand those

Table 8.10 *Coefficient of variation of net household income, by source of income, among LHH, Palakurichi and Venmani, 2019*

Village	Crop	Livestock	Non-farm	Household income
Palakurichi	1,983	193	85	128
Venmani	–3,926	135	122	121

Source: FAS survey data.

Table 8.11 *Adjusted agricultural income and share of livestock, for livestock-holding cultivators, Palakurichi and Venmani, 2019* in rupees and per cent

Socio-economic class	Palakurichi		Venmani	
	Total agricultural income (Rs)	Share of livestock in income (%)	Total agricultural income (Rs)	Share of livestock in income (%)
Landlords and big capitalist farmers	4,90,345	9	1,93,874	10
Rich peasants	31,378	100	11,009	100
Middle peasants	10,289	77	16,273	62
Poor peasants	7,053	70	5,540	100

Source: FAS survey data.

vulnerabilities and provide some income to households. In that sense, livestock contributes to reducing the variability of farm income.

Note also that the coefficient of variation (CV) for crop incomes was much higher than that for livestock (Table 8.10).

In 2018, the villages encountered a major cyclone, Gaja, resulting in severe crop loss and negative crop incomes (chapters 11 and 16). We recalculated all incomes by assuming negative crop incomes as zero incomes and then estimated adjusted agricultural income from the crop and livestock sectors (Table 8.11).

Adjusted farm income was low for all cultivator classes, except for landlords and big capitalist farmers. What is interesting, however, is that income from livestock turned out to be the largest contributor to farm income for all classes of peasants. The share of livestock in total income ranged from 62 to 100 per cent for the peasant classes in Venmani, and 70 to 100 per cent in Palakurichi.

Income from livestock was distributed more equitably across households than crop income. While the Gini coefficient for overall household income was 0.47 for Palakurichi and 0.51 for Venmani, the Gini coefficient for crop incomes was highest, followed by livestock and other sources in that order.

Table 8.12 *Gini coefficient by source of income, for livestock-holding households, Palakurichi and Venmani, 2019*

Village	Income from crop production	Income from animal resources	Income from other sources	Total income
Palakurichi	0.93	0.67	0.42	0.47
Venmani	0.88	0.59	0.52	0.51

Source: FAS survey data.

In both villages, income from goats was the biggest component of livestock income, to the extent of 55 per cent in Palakurichi and 48 per cent in Venmani (Appendix Table 8.2). Cattle contributed 39 per cent of livestock income in both villages. Goats generated higher income than cattle and poultry for households in most socio-economic classes.

An important finding from the economic analysis of livestock rearing is that it provides a good return over expenditure, which makes it a financially worthwhile enterprise (Figure 8.1). The share of expenses to gross income from livestock was 50 per cent in Palakurichi and 48 per cent in Venmani. This explains the economic viability of livestock in the villages and its role as a buffer for smoothening income fluctuations.

Looking at each type of livestock, the return over gross expenditure is highest

Figure 8.1 *Income and expenditure from livestock, Palakurichi and Venmani, 2019* in rupees

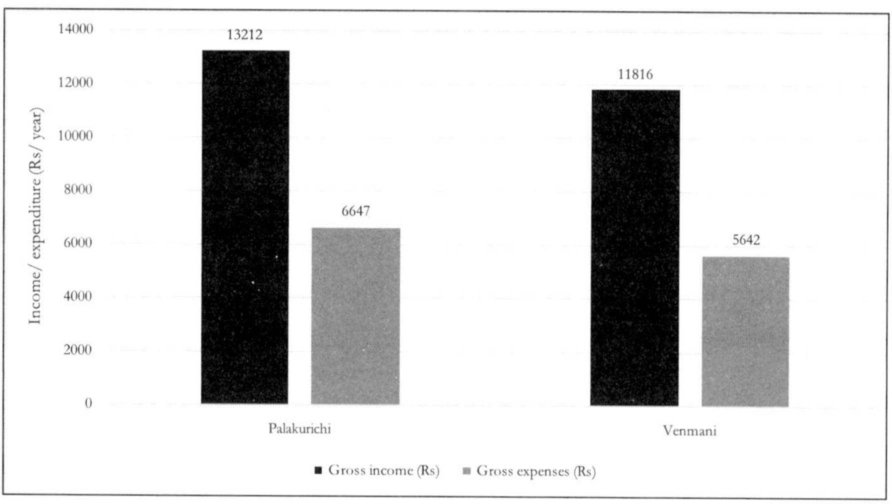

Source: FAS survey data.

for goats in both villages. The net income as a share of gross expenditure for goats was to the tune of about 200–300 per cent and that for poultry was to the tune of 100–220 per cent in both the villages as compared to a lower ratio for cattle (31 per cent in Palakurichi and 47 per cent Venmani). Expenditure on goat farming is relatively low, and return per rupee spent is relatively high, making goat farming a relatively good economic proposition.

Constraints to Higher Income

In the case of milk, 73 per cent of milk produced in Palakurichi (about 40,000 litres annually) is marketed whereas it was about 45 per cent in Venmani, with an annual production of 34,000 litres.[1] There is no organised milk collection, and the major milk marketing channel is direct sale to nearby households and shops. Price realised for milk varied across the villages and across classes. Farmers in Venmani, in general, realised a lower price compared to farmers of Palakurichi. The farmers of higher socio-economic classes realised better prices.

Notwithstanding quality differences in milk, one major reason for differences in price realisation is the relative underdevelopment of milk marketing facilities in the villages. Organised milk marketing through milk cooperatives helps to realise prices based on milk quality. The experience of dairy development in India points to the need to develop marketing facilities and supply inputs like feed, fodder, and veterinary facilities to raise production and returns.

Egg production is almost completely used for own consumption.

Turning to goats, the major determinant of the price of goats is their body weight and sex. Male goats with higher body weight fetch a better price. On average, the farmers sold four goats a year and realised a gross income ranging between Rs 10,500 to Rs 11,000. The average price of a goat was Rs 2,700 in Palakurichi and Rs 2,600 in Venmani. In Palakurichi, the price received by landlords and big capitalist farmers and rich peasants was higher than that realised by other socio-economic classes. Such clear differences were not observed in Venmani, and the overall price realised was in general lower for most of the socio-economic classes as compared to Palakurichi. The need to develop better marketing facilities is reflected in the case of the marketing of goats as well (Appendix Table 8.4).

[1] The low yield could be partly due to weather conditions, as milk yield is lower in high-temperature conditions.

Table 8.13 *Production and sale of milk, egg, and cow dung, Palakurichi and Venmani, 2019*

Village	Production			Sale/Production		
	Milk (litres)	Cow dung (trolley)	Egg (pieces)	Milk (%)	Cow dung (%)	Egg (%)
Palakurichi	40,458	153	3,811	73	2	5
Venmani	34,003	226	7,411	45	7	44

Source: FAS survey data.

Table 8.14 *Participation in milk markets, marketed surplus, and price of milk, across socio-economic classes, Palakurichi and Venmani, 2019* in per cent and rupees

Socio-economic class	Share of milk selling households in producing households (%)		Extent of sale/production (%)		Average milk price (Rs/litre)	
	Palakurichi	Venmani	Palakurichi	Venmani	Palakurichi	Venmani
Landlords and big capitalist farmers	100	0	96	0	25.0	24.0
Rich peasants	25	33	55	44	26.3	25.5
Middle peasants	88	29	67	44	25.9	23.9
Poor peasants	90	39	77	48	25.2	24.6
Manual wage workers (skilled+unskilled)	100	44	75	41	25.9	23.4
Persons living on pensions, small rents, and remittances	67	25	67	86	25.0	23.6
Salaried persons	100	20	88	5	30.0	26.2
Self-employed in business activity	100	50	82	56	30.7	24.5
Overall	85	34	73	45	26.1	24.4

Source: FAS survey data.

Fisheries Development

Even though the villages belong to the coastal district of Nagapattinam, the fisheries sector is not well developed. Gradually, inland fish culture is coming up in the village, utilising ponds and other water bodies. There were a few farmers who raised fish, by using fingerlings procured from the offices of the Fisheries Department of the Government of Tamil Nadu. Fish feed is procured from private shops. On maturity, the fish are sold on the basis of forward contracts. The contractors undertake the operations of harvest and sale. Using existing water bodies, expansion of fisheries can generate additional income.

Concluding Remarks

Livestock is an important component of the farming system in Palakurichi and Venmani today. It is undertaken as a supplementary income-generating activity and provides a buffer against fluctuations in crop income. The major types of livestock owned by households are cattle, goats, and poultry chicken.

The mean livestock-holding size is small and can be managed using household labour supply. The cattle and goat enterprises are carried out in an extensive farming system, making use of fodder available from public lands, pastures, and harvested crop fields. Occasionally a cut-and-carry system of fodder is also practiced. Backyard poultry is undertaken to meet household nutritional requirements. Fisheries has not developed into a major economic sector in the villages. However, the spread of aquaculture in nearby villages in the Nagapattinam is getting reflected in the villages too.

Milk sales were 73 and 45 per cent of production in Palakurichi and Venmani, respectively. Cow dung was used for crop farming and eggs were used for household consumption. Price realised for milk and goats varied among different socio-economic classes. The prices realised depend on the institutional mechanism available for marketing and the bargaining power of the households. Compared to a poor peasant, the prices received for goats were higher by 25 per cent for rich peasant households and 57 per cent for landlord households.

The infrastructure for livestock is underdeveloped – particularly, veterinary care and milk-marketing facilities. We argue that the relative underdevelopment of the villages in terms of marketing facilities, particularly concerning milk and live goats, has adversely affected the income generated. With adequate institutional arrangements for marketing and delivery of livestock services and feed, livestock has the potential to emerge as a major source of income for poor households in this region.

Appendix

Appendix Table 8.1 *Mean net annual income by source and socio-economic class, for livestock-holding households, Palakurichi and Venmani, 2019* in rupees

Class	Palakurichi				Venmani			
	Crop	Livestock	Other source	Total	Crop	Livestock	Other source	Total
Landlords and big capitalist farmers	447953	42392	392112	882457	175444	18430	750000	943874
Rich peasants	-38370	31378	157223	150230	-7354	11009	313087	316742
Middle peasants	2341	7948	143583	153872	6223	10050	120726	136999
Poor peasants	2099	4954	107434	114487	-1532	5540	79513	83521
Manual wage workers (skilled+ unskilled)	-71	4042	117352	121323	44	5488	105473	111005
Persons living on pensions, small rents, and remittances	2720	8388	94227	105336	-2788	4351	157792	159355
Salaried persons	14281	10240	206233	230754	-4465	5471	420373	421379
Self-employed in business activity	1159	3679	135634	140472	528	3014	223807	227349
All	7081	6565	125855	139501	294	6079	152038	158412

Source: FAS survey data.

Appendix Table 8.2 *Share of income of various livestock species, by socio-economic class, Palakurichi and Venmani, 2019* in per cent

Socio-economic class	Palakurichi				Venmani			
	Cattle	Goat	Chicken	Total	Cow/ Bullock	Goat	Chicken	Total
Landlords and big capitalist farmers	27	71	2	100	100	0	0	100
Rich peasants	35	63	2	100	76	2	21	100
Middle peasants	83	10	7	100	47	43	9	100
Poor peasants	36	53	11	100	43	47	10	100
Manual wage worker (skilled+unskilled)	18	78	4	100	28	60	12	100
Persons living on pensions, small rents, and remittances	61	38	1	100	23	65	12	100
Salaried persons	40	50	10	100	32	51	18	100
Self-employed in business activity	54	45	1	100	−1	68	33	100
All	39	55	6	100	39	48	13	100

Source: FAS survey data.

Appendix Table 8.3 *Expenditure pattern in livestock farming for livestock-holding households, Palakurichi and Venmani, 2019* in rupees and per cent

	Species	Palakurichi	Venmani
Net income from livestock	Cattle	2,589	2,386
	Goat	3,582	2,926
	Chicken	394	767
Net income from livestock as a share of gross expenditure	Cattle	31	47
	Goat	208	298
	Chicken	102	220

Source: FAS survey data.

Appendix Table 8.4 *Average sale of goats during the year, by socio-economic class, Palakurichi and Venmani, 2019* in number and rupees

Socio-economic class	Palakurichi		Venmani	
	Average goats sold (no.)	Average price per unit (Rs)	Average goats sold (no.)	Average price per unit (Rs)
Landlords and big capitalist farmers	23	4,200	–	–
Rich peasants	17	3,361	4	2,250
Middle peasants	3	2,792	6	2,739
Poor peasants	4	2,680	4	2,432
Manual wage workers	3	2,645	4	2,694
Persons living on pensions, small rents, and remittances	4	2,750	4	2,826
Salaried persons	5	2,931	4	2,598
Self-employed in business activity	4	2,476	4	2,429
Overall	4	2,706	4	2,597

Source: FAS survey data.

9

Assets

Nelson Mandela S.

HIGHLIGHTS

The distribution of assets among households is marked by high levels of inequality with a mass of asset-poor households at one end of the spectrum and a few rich households at the other end. In Venmani, the bottom 40 per cent of households owned 5 per cent of total assets while the top 10 per cent of households owned almost 60 per cent of all assets. Actual levels of inequality are likely to be substantially higher than the levels shown up by survey data, since the survey data did not cover a full inventory of the assets of the rich, and did not cover financial assets and holdings of gold and jewellery at all.

Land remained the largest single category of physical assets owned by households. Land and other means of production were concentrated in the hands of landlords and big capitalist farmers. Livestock was concentrated in the hands of rich and middle peasants. Wage workers, who constituted 39 per cent of all households in Venmani, owned 12 per cent of all assets. The household of an average wage worker possessed assets worth Rs 2.6 lakhs; the average asset holding among landlords and capitalist farmers was Rs 83.9 lakhs, a ratio of 1:32. Decomposition of the Gini coefficient across classes (using the Yitzhaki method) showed that between-class inequality contributed two-thirds or more of total inequality (within-class inequality contributed the rest).

Scheduled Caste households comprised the majority of the population but owned assets disproportionately less than their share in population. In Palakurichi, Scheduled Caste households constituted 60 per cent of households and owned 32 per cent of all assets. A similar situation prevailed among Most Backward Class households. The bulk of assets were owned by Backward Class and Other caste households.

Introduction

The ownership and control of land and other means of production form the basis of class power in Venmani and Palakurichi. This chapter analyses the level and composition of asset ownership in the study villages based on the PARI survey data collected in 2019. The chapter further investigates the distribution of asset ownership across categories of socio-economic class and caste. The Gini coefficient is used as a measure of inequality. Overall inequality is further decomposed into within-group and between-group inequality using the method developed by Yitzhaki (1994).

PARI survey data provide a rich source of information on various types of asset ownership in the study villages. The data offers information on household-wise ownership of agricultural land (both extent and value) in addition to the type of agricultural land and source of irrigation. It provides data on the ownership of non-agricultural land and buildings, means of production, means of transport, and other assets like domestic durable goods, stocks of grain, etc. Since it is difficult to gather reliable information on financial assets and jewellery, they were excluded from the survey.

Unequal Distribution of Asset Ownership in the Study Villages

In the survey year, an average household owned assets worth Rs 9.10 lakhs in Venmani and Rs 8 lakhs in Palakurichi. The mean value of total assets owned by households is higher than the median value in both the study villages indicating inequality in asset ownership (Table 9.1).

One household in Venmani had no assets of value while the topmost household in terms of assets ownership owned assets worth Rs 3.59 crores. In Palakurichi, the worst-off household possessed assets worth Rs 12,225, and the richest household owned assets valued at Rs 2.06 crores (Table 9.1).

Inequality in asset ownership is a striking feature of the study villages. In order to understand the concentration of asset ownership in the study villages,

Table 9.1 *Mean and median values of total assets owned by households in Palakurichi and Venmani, 2019* in rupees (at current prices)

Village	Number of households	Mean value of assets	Median value of assets	Min value	Max value
Venmani	415	9,10,687	3,17,360	0	3,58,79,520
Palakurichi	390	8,01,145	3,40,304	12,225	2,05,73,550

Source: PARI survey data.

Table 9.2 *Share of total assets by asset decile, Venmani and Palakurichi, 2019* in per cent

Deciles	Venmani	Palakurichi
D1	0.4	0.6
D2	1.0	1.4
D3	1.6	2.3
D4	2.2	3.1
D5	3.0	3.8
D6	4.1	4.8
D7	5.5	6.3
D8	7.8	8.9
D9	14.8	14.9
D10	59.5	54.2
Total	100.0	100.0

Source: PARI survey data.

households were ranked according to their asset ownership and divided into ten equal subgroups. In Venmani, the bottom 40 per cent of households owned only about 5 per cent of the total assets while the top 10 per cent owned a whopping 60 per cent of total assets. In Palakurichi, the bottom 40 per cent of households owned about 7 per cent of total assets while the top 10 per cent owned 54 per cent of total assets. Table 9.2 brings out the stark inequalities in asset ownership in the study villages. In both the study villages, the top decile owned more than 50 per cent of assets. The top two deciles, that is top 20 per cent, owned more than 74 per cent of assets in Venmani; the same figure for Palakurichi is about 69 per cent. The middle deciles (5, 6, 7, and 8) together owned about 20 per cent of assets in Venmani. In Palakurichi, the middle deciles owned about 24 per cent of assets.

Composition of Assets by Socio-economic Class

Land accounted for a major part of assets in both villages. The share of land and buildings in the total value of assets for the class of landlords and big capitalist farmers in Venmani was 97 per cent, and the same figure for Palakurichi was 93 per cent. For rich peasants, the share of land and buildings in total asset value was 94 per cent in Venmani and 90 per cent in Palakurichi. For middle peasants in both the villages, about 90 per cent of the total asset value came from ownership of land and buildings (Appendix Tables 9.1 and 9.2).

Tables 9.3 and 9.4 show the ownership of various types of assets by socio-economic class in Venmani and Palakurichi, respectively. The class of landlords and big capitalist farmers owned about 26 per cent of land and buildings (in value) in Venmani and about 22 per cent in Palakurichi. In short, three households owned more than a quarter of the total land assets in Venmani.

In Venmani, landlords and big capitalist farmers owned about 17 per cent of the means of production, rich peasants owned about 28 per cent, middle peasants about 33 per cent and poor peasants owned only 1 per cent. In Palakurichi, the ownership of means of production was highly concentrated in the hands of landlords and big capitalist farmers, and rich peasants. These two classes together owned about 67 per cent of the means of production.

In Venmani, animal assets were concentrated in the hands of middle and poor peasants; together, they owned about 51 per cent of animal assets (Table 9.3). In Palakurichi, landlords and big capitalist farmers owned about 7 per cent, rich peasants about 9 per cent, middle peasants about 12 per cent, poor peasants about 26 per cent, wage workers with major income from unskilled and semi-skilled manual work about 15 per cent, and wage workers with major income from skilled and formal sector wage work about 12 per cent (Table 9.4).

Table 9.3 *Share of asset value to total value of assets for each socio-economic class, by asset category, Venmani, 2018–19* in per cent

Socio-economic class	Land and buildings	Trees	Animal	Means of production	Means of transport	Other assets	All assets
Landlords and big capitalist farmers	26	7	1	17	9	3	24
Rich peasants	17	27	8	28	7	4	16
Middle peasants	19	33	25	34	13	14	19
Poor peasants	9	10	26	1	11	17	9
Wage workers with major income from unskilled, semi-skilled manual work	8	7	16	1	11	15	8
Wage workers with major income from skilled and formal sector wage work	3	3	7	0	11	8	3
Self-employed in business activity	3	2	2	4	12	16	4
Salaried persons	7	5	7	10	13	10	7
Persons living on pensions, small rents, and remittances	8	7	7	5	12	14	9
All households	100	100	100	100	100	100	100

Source: PARI survey data.

Table 9.4 *Share of asset value to total asset value for each socio-economic class, by asset category, Palakurichi, 2018–19* in per cent

Socio-economic class	Land and buildings	Trees	Animal	Means of production	Means of transport	Other assets	All assets
Landlords and big capitalist farmers	23	30	7	34	13	4	22
Rich peasants	14	5	9	33	9	6	14
Middle peasants	13	16	12	5	15	9	13
Poor peasants	17	16	26	5	22	23	18
Wage workers with major income from unskilled, semi-skilled manual work	7	12	16	0	8	10	8
Wage workers with major income from skilled and formal sector wage work	7	7	12	0	14	12	7
Self-employed in business activity	5	6	7	21	7	25	6
Salaried persons	7	2	5	1	9	6	7
Persons living on pensions, small rents, and remittances	5	6	6	0	4	6	5
All households	100	100	100	100	100	100	100

Source: PARI survey data.

Rich and middle peasants owned about 60 per cent of trees in Venmani. Tree ownership was concentrated in the hands of landlords and big capitalist farmers in Palakurichi. They owned about 30 per cent. The middle and poor peasants owned about 16 per cent each in Palakurichi (Table 9.4).

Distribution of Assets by Class and Caste

Table 9.5 shows the distribution of assets by socio-economic class in Venmani. Index of Access for a class is the ratio between its share of assets and share of households. If the index for a class is above one, then the share of assets owned by that class is higher than its share of population. The class of landlord and big capitalist farmers in Venmani owned about 24 per cent of total assets with a household average of Rs 3.05 crore. The Index of Access for landlords and big capitalist farmers was 34.6, the highest among all socio-economic classes. The Index of Access for rich peasants was 6.6 and they owned about 16 per cent of total assets with a household average of Rs 60 lakhs. The middle peasants owned about 19 per cent of the assets with an average of Rs 18.8 lakhs per household with an Access Index of 2.1. The Index of Access for

Table 9.5 *Distribution of total assets and Index of Access by socio-economic class in Venmani, 2019* in rupees and per cent

Socio-economic class	Number of households	Share of households	Mean asset value	Share of assets	Index of Access
Landlords and big capitalist farmers	3	0.7	3,04,95,567	24.2	34.6
Rich peasants	10	2.4	60,09,870	15.9	6.6
Middle peasants	38	9.2	18,80,028	18.9	2.1
Poor peasants	78	18.8	4,59,760	9.5	0.5
Wage workers with major income from unskilled, semi-skilled manual work	117	28.2	2,68,300	8.3	0.3
Wage workers with major income from skilled and formal sector wage work	45	10.8	2,80,897	3.3	0.3
Self-employed in business activity	31	7.5	4,60,248	3.8	0.5
Salaried persons	29	7	9,69,321	7.4	1.1
Persons living on pensions, small rents, and remittances	64	15.4	5,09,964	8.6	0.6
All	415	100	9,10,687	100	1.0

Note: Index of Access is the ratio between share of assets and share of households.
Source: PARI survey data.

salaried persons was 1.1. *For all other classes, the Index of Access was less than one.*

Poor peasants owned 9.5 per cent of total assets with a household average of 4.6 lakhs, and for this class, the Index of Access is 0.5. The largest class in numerical terms, the class of wage workers with major income from unskilled and semi-skilled manual work in Venmani, owned only 8.3 per cent of total assets with a household average of Rs 2.7 lakhs (the least among all the classes). The Index of Access for this class was 0.3.

Similarly, Table 9.6 shows the concentration of assets in hands of the class of landlords and big capitalist farmers in Palakurichi. The Index of Access for the landlords and big capitalist farmers was 10.2. They owned 21.5 per cent of total assets with a household average ownership of Rs 83.9 lakhs. Rich peasants owned assets worth 55.6 lakhs per household, on average, and their Index of Access was 6.8.

The Index of Access for middle peasants was 1.9 in Palakurichi and they owned about 13 per cent of total assets (with a household average of Rs 15.5 lakhs). In contrast to Venmani, the largest class in Palakurichi is the class of poor peasants and they held 17.5 per cent of total assets (Rs 4.2 lakhs per

Table 9.6 *Distribution of total assets and Index of Access by socio-economic class in Palakurichi, 2019* in rupees and per cent

Socio-economic Class	Number of households	Share of households	Mean assets value	Share of assets	Index of Access
Landlords and big capitalist farmers	8	2.1	83,91,382	21.5	10.2
Rich peasants	8	2.1	55,61,930	14.2	6.8
Middle peasants	26	6.7	15,46,223	12.9	1.9
Poor peasants	130	33.3	4,20,569	17.5	0.5
Wage workers with major income from unskilled, semi-skilled manual work	92	23.6	2,64,640	7.8	0.3
Wage workers with major income from skilled and formal sector wage work	47	12.1	4,94,477	7.4	0.6
Self-employed in business activity	19	4.9	10,63,570	6.5	1.3
Salaried persons	23	5.9	9,46,960	7.0	1.2
Persons living on pensions, small rents, and remittances	37	9.5	4,42,404	5.2	0.5
All	390	100.0	8,01,145	100.0	1.0

Source: PARI survey data.

household). The Index of Access for poor peasants was 0.5. The class of wage workers with major income from unskilled and semi-skilled manual work owned only 7.8 per cent of total assets (household average of Rs 2.6 lakhs). The Index of Access for this class was 0.3. In both villages, the average value of assets per household was lowest among wage workers with major income from unskilled and semi-skilled manual work, among all socio-economic classes.

Let us turn to the caste-wise distribution of assets (Table 9.7). Scheduled Castes constituted 63.4 per cent of total households in Venmani and owned about 40 per cent of total assets, with a household average of 5.8 lakhs. The Index of Access for the Scheduled Castes was 0.6, that is, they owned disproportionately fewer assets than their share in population.

The Index of Access for Most Backward Classes was 0.7. The Most Backward Classes owned 6 per cent of total assets, with a household average asset ownership of Rs 6.7 lakhs. While the Index of Access for the Backward Classes was 1.2, they owned about 33 per cent of total assets (an average of Rs 11.4 lakhs per household). Other castes group had the highest Index of Access of 12.2. The average asset value per household among Other castes was Rs 1.1 crore.

Similar to Venmani, Scheduled Caste households in Palakurichi had

Table 9.7 *Distribution of total assets and Index of Access by social group in Venmani, 2019*
in rupees and per cent

Social group	Number of households	Share of households	Mean asset value	Share of total assets	Index of Access
Scheduled Castes	263	63.4	57,8761	40.3	0.6
Most Backward Classes	34	8.2	6,67,960	6.0	0.7
Backward Classes	109	26.3	11,36,047	32.8	1.2
Other	7	1.7	1,12,08,703	20.8	12.2
Unspecified	2	0.5	3,60,075	0.2	0.4
Total	415	100.0	9,10,687	100.0	1.0

Source: PARI survey data.

Table 9.8 *Distribution of total assets and Index of Access by social group in Palakurichi, 2019*
in rupees and per cent

Social group	Number of households	Share of households	Mean hsset halue	Share of assets	Index of Access
Scheduled Castes	235	60.3	4,25,256	32.0	0.5
Most Backward Classes	81	20.8	12,08,613	31.3	1.5
Backward Classes	65	16.7	15,19,531	31.6	1.9
Other	8	2.1	19,37,337	5.0	2.4
Unspecified	1	0.3	3,45,450	0.1	0.3
All	390	100.0	8,01,145	100.0	1.0

Source: PARI survey data.

the lowest Index of Access of 0.5. The average value of asset ownership per Scheduled Caste household was Rs 4.2 lakhs (Table 9.8). The Index of Access for the Most Backward Classes and the Backward Classes were 1.5 and 1.9, respectively. On average, a Most Backward Class household owned assets worth Rs 12.1 lakhs and a Backward Class household owned assets worth Rs. 15.2 lakhs. The Index of Access for the Other caste households in Palakurichi was 2.4, with a household average asset ownership of Rs 19.4 lakhs. In both Venmani and Palakurichi, the Access Index was lowest (and less than one) for Scheduled Caste households.

Distribution of Landholdings by Socio-economic Class and Caste

Land is concentrated in the hands of landlords and big capitalist farmers. Table 9.9 shows that the landlords and big capitalist farmers owned about 17 per cent of the agricultural land in Venmani, with an average extent of 28.5 acres per household. In other words, three households in Venmani owned about 17 per cent of all agricultural land. Index of Access, defined as the ratio of "share in total extent" to the "share of households'," for the landlords and big capitalist farmers, was 24.3.

Rich peasants owned about 20 per cent of the land with an average extent of 10 acres per household. The Index of Access for rich peasants was 8.3. Middle peasants and poor peasants owned about 26 and 17 per cent of the agricultural land, and their respective household average ownership was 3.4 acres and 1.1 acres. In Venmani, 80 per cent of the agricultural land was owned by various classes of the peasantry and the class of landlords and big capitalist farmers.

In Palakurichi, the landlords and big capitalist farmers owned about 36 per cent of all agricultural land, with a household average extent of 26.8 acres (Table 9.10). The Index of Access for this class was 17.1, indicating a concentration of land in the hands of landlords and big capitalist farmers. The Index of Access for rich and middle peasants was 5.9 and 1.6, respectively. The average landholding size for a rich peasant household was 9.2 acres, and for a middle peasant household it was 2.5 acres. Poor peasants owned about 25 per

Table 9.9 *Distribution of total landholdings and Index of Access by socio-economic class in Venmani, 2019* in acres and per cent

Socio-economic class	Number of households	Share of households	Mean extent	Share in total extent	Index of Access
Landlords and big capitalist farmers	3	0.7	28.5	17.0	24.3
Rich peasants	10	2.4	10.0	19.8	8.3
Middle peasants	38	9.2	3.4	26.1	2.8
Poor peasants	78	18.8	1.1	16.7	0.9
Wage workers with major income from unskilled, semi-skilled manual work	117	28.2	0.3	6.4	0.2
Wage workers with major income from skilled and formal sector wage work	45	10.8	0.2	1.9	0.2
Self-employed in business activity	31	7.5	0.3	1.8	0.2
Salaried persons	29	7.0	0.7	4.1	0.6
Persons living on pensions, small rents, and remittances	64	15.4	0.5	6.2	0.4
Total	415	100.0	1.2	100.0	1.0

Source: PARI survey data.

Table 9.10 *Distribution of total landholdings and Index of Access by socio-economic class in Palakurichi, 2019* in acres and per cent

Socio-economic class	Number of households	Share of households	Mean extent	Share in total extent	Index of Access
Landlords and big capitalist farmers	8	2.1	26.8	35.9	17.1
Rich peasants	8	2.1	9.2	12.3	5.9
Middle peasants	26	6.7	2.5	10.9	1.6
Poor peasants	130	33.3	1.2	25.2	0.8
Wage workers with major income from unskilled, semi-skilled manual work	92	23.6	0.3	4.8	0.2
Wage workers with major income from skilled and formalsector wage work	47	12.1	0.3	2.7	0.2
Self-employed in business activity	19	4.9	0.5	1.5	0.3
Salaried persons	23	5.9	0.7	2.8	0.5
Persons living on pensions, small rents, and remittances	37	9.5	0.6	3.9	0.4
Total	390	100.0	1.5	100.0	1.0

Source: PARI survey data.

cent of all agricultural land, with an average extent of 1.2 acres per household. The Index of Access for poor peasants was 0.8. In Palakurichi, 84 per cent of the agricultural land was owned by various classes of the peasantry and the class of landlords and big capitalist farmers.

In Venmani, Scheduled Castes had the lowest Index of Access to land (0.5), with an average extent of mere 0.7 acres per household. The Access Index for all other caste groups was more than 1, and highest for Other caste households (10.2), who owned 12.4 acres on average (Table 9.11).

In Palakurichi, the Index of Access for Scheduled Caste households is 0.6 with an average size of 0.9 acres per household. The Access Index (and average extent of landholding) was similar for Backward Class and Other caste households in Palakurichi (Table 9.12).

Class power and caste privilege determines not only control over the extent of land in a village but also control over good-quality land. The quality of land owned is better reflected in the value of land than in extent.[1]

[1] Only those households that have reported separate values for land are included, even those with zero value of land. We have 349 households in Venmani and 377 households in Palakurichi.

Table 9.11 *Distribution of total landholdings and Index of Access by social group in Venmani, 2019* in acres and per cent

Social group	Number of households	Share of households	Mean extent	Share in total extent	Index of Access
Scheduled Castes	263	63.4	0.7	34.4	0.5
Most Backward Classes	34	8.2	1.2	8.4	1.0
Backward Classes	109	26.3	1.8	39.8	1.5
Other	7	1.7	12.4	17.3	10.2
Unspecified	2	0.5	0.1	0.1	0.2
Total	415	100.0	1.2	100.0	1.0

Source: PARI survey data.

Table 9.12 *Distribution of total landholdings and Index of Access by social group in Palakurichi, 2019* in acres and in per cent

Social group	Number of households	Share of households	Mean extent	Share in total extent	Index of Access
Scheduled Castes	235	60.3	0.9	34.4	0.6
Most Backward Classes	81	20.8	2.0	27.4	1.3
Backward Classes	65	16.7	3.1	33.5	2.0
Other	8	2.1	3.5	4.7	2.2
Unspecified	1	0.3	0.0	0.0	0.0
Total	390	100.0	1.5	100.0	1.0

Source: PARI survey data.

In Venmani, the class of landlords and big capitalist farmers own land that commands 31.9 per cent of the total land value with a mean land value of Rs. 1.84 crores per household. They controlled 17 per cent of land in terms of extent. By contrast, poor peasants accounted for 9.7 per cent of value of land but 16.7 per cent of extent (Table 9.13).

In Venmani, 38.5 per cent of total land value is held by Backward Class households, and 31 per cent by Scheduled Caste households, but the mean value of land per household is very low among Scheduled Castes (Rs 2.49 lakhs) as compared to Other caste households (56 lakhs per household) (Table 9.14).

Turning to Palakurichi village, landlords and big capitalist farmers held 30.5 per cent of total land value, with a mean land value of Rs. 65.3 lakhs per household. Poor peasants, the largest socio-economic class, held 18.4 per cent of total land in terms of value with a mean holding of Rs. 2.46 lakhs (Table 9.15). The Index of Access for landlords and big capitalist farmers was 14.5,

Table 9.13 *Distribution of total value of land owned and Index of Access by socio-economic class in Venmani, 2019* in rupees and per cent

Socio-economic class	Number of households	Share of households	Share in total land value	Mean land owned in value	Index of Access
Landlords and big capitalist farmers	3	0.9	31.9	1,84,46,000	35.4
Rich peasants	10	2.9	20.1	34,94,543	6.9
Middle peasants	38	10.9	21.9	9,99,823	2.0
Poor peasants	75	21.5	9.7	2,23,655	0.5
Wage workers with major income from unskilled, semi-skilled manual work	85	24.4	4.8	97,413	0.2
Wage workers with major income from skilled and formal sector wage work	34	9.7	1.5	79,131	0.2
Self-employed in business activity	26	7.4	2.3	1,50,944	0.3
Salaried persons	23	6.6	3.3	2,46,559	0.5
Persons living on pensions, small rents, and remittances	55	15.8	4.6	1,45,469	0.3
Total	349	100.0	100.0	4,97,471	1.0

Source: PARI survey data.

Table 9.14 *Distribution of total value of land owned and Index of Access by social group in Venmani, 2019* in rupees and per cent

Social group	Number of households	Share of households	Share in total land value	Mean land owned in value	Index of Access
Scheduled Castes	217	62.2	31.1	2,49,172	0.5
Most Backward Classes	28	8.0	7.7	4,79,293	1.0
Backward Classes	96	27.5	38.5	6,96,429	1.4
Other	7	2.0	22.6	56,06,400	11.3
Unspecified	1	0.3	0.0	25,000	0.0
Total	349	100.0	100.0	4,97,471	1.0

Source: PARI survey data.

Table 9.15 *Distribution of total value of land owned and Index of Access by socio-economic class in Palakurichi, 2019* in rupees and per cent

Socio-economic class	Number of households	Share of households	Share in total land value	Mean land owned in value	Index of Access
Landlords and big capitalist farmers	8	2.1	30.5	65,32,275	14.5
Rich peasants	8	2.1	14.2	30,41,488	6.8
Middle peasants	26	6.9	12.6	8,28,846	1.8
Poor peasants	128	34.0	18.4	2,46,112	0.5
Wage workers with major income from unskilled, semi-skilled manual work	86	22.8	7.0	1,40,040	0.3
Wage workers with major income from skilled and formal sector wage work	44	11.7	4.6	1,78,525	0.4
Self-employed in business activity	19	5.0	2.7	2,44,179	0.5
Salaried persons	22	5.8	5.1	3,97,223	0.9
Persons living on pensions, small rents, and remittances	36	9.5	4.8	2,29,164	0.5
Total	377	100.0	100.0	4,54,030	1.0

Source: PARI survey data.

Table 9.16 *Distribution of total value of land owned and Index of Access by social group in Palakurichi, 2019* in rupees and per cent

Social group	Number of households	Share of households	Share in total land value	Mean land owned in value	Index of Access
Scheduled Castes	229	60.7	32.3	2,41,421	0.5
Most Backward Classes	78	20.7	29.4	6,44,228	1.4
Backward Classes	61	16.2	33.3	9,33,536	2.1
Other	8	2.1	4.9	10,48,538	2.3
Unspecified	1	0.3	0.2	3,00,000	0.7
Total	377	100.0	100.0	4,54,030	1.0

Source: PARI survey data.

6.8 for rich peasants and 1.8 for middle peasants. The Index of Access was less than one for all other classes.

In Palakurichi, households belonging to the Scheduled Castes, the Most Backward Classes and the Backward Classes each owned about a third of the total land value, but the average value of land per household varied widely. The mean value of land was Rs 2.41 lakhs for a Scheduled Caste household, Rs. 6.4 lakhs for a Most Backward Class household and Rs 9.3 lakhs for a Backward Class household. The Access Index was greater than one for all caste groups other than Scheduled Castes (Table 9.16).

Decomposition of Inequality in Asset Ownership

This section analyses the inequality in asset ownership in the study villages using the Gini coefficient, a widely used measure of inequality. The Gini coefficient takes a value between zero and one. If every household owned an equal amount of assets in the village, the Gini coefficient would be equal to zero. And, if one household owned everything and the rest of the households owned nothing, then the Gini coefficient would be equal to one. Overall inequality is further decomposed into between-group and within-group inequality using the method suggested by Yitzhaki (1994). The groups for our analysis are socio-economic classes and social (caste) groups.

Table 9.17 presents the results of Gini decomposition of asset ownership by class in Venmani and Palakurichi. The Gini coefficient of asset ownership in Venmani was 0.703, and in Palakurichi it was 0.646. These are high levels of inequality. Further, the inequality between classes was the major contributor to overall inequality in both the study villages. The contribution of between-class inequality to the overall asset inequality was 74.5 per cent in Venmani and 64.6 per cent in Palakurichi. Whereas, the contribution of within-class Gini to total Gini was 25.5 per cent in Venmani and 35.4 per cent in Palakurichi.

We repeat the Gini decomposition exercise by caste group (Table 9.18). In Venmani, within-caste inequality contributed 81.3 per cent to overall inequality, and between-caste inequality contributed 18.7 per cent. Similarly, in Palakurichi the share of within-caste inequality to overall asset inequality was about 87.7 per cent, whereas that of between-caste inequality was 12.3 per cent.

Unlike the case of inequality by class, overall inequality is primarily explained by inequality within caste groups. This is because members of a caste group occupy different class positions. For example, in Venmani, four of the Scheduled Caste households were rich peasants, while a majority of Scheduled Caste households were manual workers. Similarly, in Palakurichi, a majority of the Scheduled Caste households were poor peasants and manual workers,

Table 9.17 *Gini decomposition of asset ownership by socio-economic class in the study villages, 2019* in number and per cent

Socio-economic class	Venmani		Palakurichi	
	Coefficient	Share	Coefficient	Share
Overall Gini	0.703	100.0	0.646	100.0
Within-group	0.179	25.5	0.228	35.4
Between-group	0.524	74.5	0.417	64.6

Source: PARI survey data.

Table 9.18 *Gini decomposition of asset ownership by social group in the study villages, 2019* in number and per cent

Caste	Venmani		Palakurichi	
	Coefficient	Share	Coefficient	Share
Overall Gini	0.703	100.0	0.646	100.0
Within-group	0.572	81.3	0.567	87.7
Between-group	0.131	18.7	0.08	12.3

Source: PARI survey data.

while one household was a rich peasant. Therefore within-caste inequality is a significant component of the overall inequality in both the villages.

Both Venmani and Palakurichi have very high inequality in ownership of agricultural land (area), with Gini coefficients of 0.772 and 0.728, respectively. The Gini coefficient for the value of land ownership in Venmani was 0.804, and in Palakurichi, 0.729. In Venmani, inequality in the extent of land owned is lower than inequality in the value of land owned. In Palakurichi, the inequality levels are similar for the extent of land owned and the value of land owned.

Conclusions

The villages of Venmani and Palakurichi are characterised by a high level of inequality in asset ownership. In both villages, the bottom 40 per cent of households owned about 5 to 7 per cent of all assets. An important finding from our analysis is that the high level of inequality is primarily driven by the inequality between socio-economic classes. While there are sharp differences across caste groups, the Gini decomposition results suggest that caste groups were not homogenous in terms of asset ownership. In both villages, Scheduled Castes comprise more than 60 per cent of the population but their share in asset ownership is disproportionately low.

A major part of land and other means of production are owned by the various classes of the peasantry, and landlords and big capitalist farmers. There is no observable trend of agricultural means of production getting concentrated in the hands of non-cultivating households in both the study villages.

The basis of class power and a primary source of accumulation in rural areas is the ownership and control of land. A disproportionate share of land is concentrated in the hands of rich peasants and landlords and big capitalist farmers. A highly unequal distribution of asset ownership is essentially a consequence of the highly unequal distribution of land and other means of production.

The value of asset ownership per household across caste categories reflect the traditional caste hierarchies. Scheduled Caste households had the lowest per household ownership of assets, while the Other castes had the highest ownership of assets per household.

It is important to acknowledge the progress made in addressing caste-based inequalities through various social welfare measures and policies over the century. At the same time, the persistence of caste-based inequalities in the twenty-first century and the poor socio-economic status of Dalits remain a key challenge to achieving social justice in Tamil Nadu.

Appendix

Appendix Table 9.1 *Share of asset value to total household asset value, for socio-economic class by asset category, Palakurichi, 2018–19* in per cent

Socio-economic class	Land and buildings	Trees	Animals	Means of production	Means of transport	Other assets
Landlords and big capitalist farmers	93	0	0	4	2	1
Rich peasants	90	0	1	6	2	2
Middle peasants	91	0	1	1	4	3
Poor peasants	88	0	2	1	4	5
Wage workers with major income from unskilled, semi-skilled manual work	89	0	2	0	3	5
Wage workers with major income from skilled and formal sector wage work	86	0	2	0	6	7
Self-employed in business activity	72	0	1	8	3	16
Salaried persons	91	0	1	0	4	4
Persons living on pensions, small rents, and remittances	91	0	1	0	3	5
All households	89	0	1	2	3	4

Appendix Table 9.2 *Share of asset value to total household asset value, for socio-economic class by asset category, Venmani, 2018–19* in per cent

Socio-economic class	Land and buildings	Trees	Animals	Means of production	Means of transport	Other assets
Landlords and big capitalist farmers	97	0	0	1	1	1
Rich peasants	94	1	1	3	1	1
Middle peasants	90	1	2	3	2	3
Poor peasants	85	0	3	0	4	7
Wage workers with major income from unskilled, semi-skilled manual work	86	0	2	0	4	7
Wage workers with major income from skilled and formal sector wage work	78	0	3	0	10	9
Self-employed in business activity	71	0	1	2	10	16
Salaried persons	86	0	1	2	5	5
Persons living on pensions, small rents, and remittances	88	0	1	1	4	6
All households	90	0	1	2	3	4

Appendix Table 9.3 *Share of asset value to the total village asset value, for asset category by socio-economic class, Palakurichi, 2018–19* in per cent

Socio-economic class	Land and buildings	Trees	Animals	Means of production	Means of transport	Other assets	All assets
Landlords and big capitalist farmers	23	30	7	34	13	4	22
Rich peasants	14	5	9	33	9	6	14
Middle peasants	13	16	12	5	15	9	13
Poor peasants	17	16	26	5	22	23	18
Wage workers with major income from unskilled, semi-skilled manual work	7	12	16	0	8	10	8
Wage workers with major income from skilled and formal sector wage work	7	7	12	0	14	12	7
Self-employed in business activity	5	6	7	21	7	25	6
Salaried persons	7	2	5	1	9	6	7
Persons living on pensions, small rents, and remittances	5	6	6	0	4	6	5
All households	100	100	100	100	100	100	100

Appendix Table 9.4 *Share of asset value to the total village asset value, for asset category by socio-economic class, Venmani, 2018–19* in per cent

Socio-economic class	Land and buildings	Trees	Animals	Means of production	Means of transport	Other assets	All assets
Landlords and big capitalist farmers	26	7	1	17	9	3	24
Rich peasants	17	27	8	28	7	4	16
Middle peasants	19	33	25	34	13	14	19
Poor peasants	9	10	26	1	11	17	9
Wage workers with major income from unskilled, semi-skilled manual work	8	7	16	1	11	15	8
Wage workers with major income from skilled and formal sector wage work	3	3	7	0	11	8	3
Self-employed in business activity	3	2	2	4	12	16	4
Salaried persons	7	5	7	10	13	10	7
Persons living on pensions, small rents, and remittances	8	7	7	5	12	14	9
All households	100	100	100	100	100	100	100

Appendix Table 9.5 *Average value of assets, by socio-economic class and asset category, Palakurichi, 2018–19* in '000 rupees

Socio-economic class	Land and buildings	Trees	Animals	Means of production	Means of transport	Other assets	All assets
Landlords and big capitalist farmers	7,800	39	83	326	157	59	8,391
Rich peasants	4,997	5	52	324	109	90	5,562
Middle peasants	1,408	6	25	19	57	46	1,546
Poor peasants	369	2	14	6	17	23	420
Wage workers with major income from unskilled, semi-skilled manual work	225	2	12	0	9	14	254
Wage workers with major income from skilled and formal sector wage work	422	2	15	1	29	32	494
Self-employed in business activity	760	3	26	177	35	171	1,064
Salaried persons	861	3	15	8	40	35	947
Persons living on pensions, small rents, and remittances	404	3	19	1	12	21	444
All households	709	4	18	40	25	33	798

Appendix Table 9.6 *Average value of assets, by socio-economic class and asset category, Venmani, 2018–19* in '000 rupees

Socio-economic class	Land and buildings	Trees	Animals	Means of production	Means of transport	Other assets	All assets
Landlords and big capitalist farmers	29,613	52	29	315	357	166	30,496
Rich peasants	5,625	51	40	203	83	63	6,010
Middle peasants	1,694	17	40	63	39	52	1,880
Poor peasants	385	3	21	2	17	32	451
Wage workers with major income from unskilled, semi-skilled manual work	231	2	15	2	11	19	268
Wage workers with major income from skilled and formal sector wage work	219	2	19	1	27	26	281
Self-employed in business activity	327	2	8	51	45	75	460
Salaried persons	833	3	18	70	52	50	969
Persons living on pensions, small rents, and remittances	447	2	14	16	21	31	510
All households	818	5	21	40	27	36	909

10

Credit and Indebtedness

Madhura Swaminathan and Ritam Dutta

HIGHLIGHTS

In rural Tamil Nadu today, the formal credit sector accounts for more than 75 per cent of total household borrowing, which is much higher than the all-India share of formal credit in rural debt. At the same time, there has been a significant increase in the role of the private sector in formal credit. This chapter provides evidence on the growth and importance of new private sector lenders other than commercial banks, mainly small finance banks, NBFCs (non-bank financial companies), and NBFC–MFIs (microfinance institutions). While these new lenders are easily accessible at the village level and provide small-size, collateral-free loans, credit from these agencies comes at a very high cost. Officially, the interest rates they charge are of the order of 23–24 per cent a year (as compared to Kisan Credit at 4 per cent from commercial banks and interest-free loans from cooperative societies). Realised rates of interest are even higher on account of the method of repayment.

Access to lenders varies systematically across castes and classes. Credit from public sector banks and cooperatives dominates the credit portfolio of landlords and capitalist farmers, and, to a smaller extent, of rich and middle peasants, and salaried households. All other classes are highly dependent on the new private "microfinance" lenders in addition to traditional informal sector lenders. Among unskilled wage workers in the village of Venmani, for example, 59 per cent of the principal borrowed was from private formal sector lenders and another 24 per cent from informal sector lenders.

A significant part of borrowing by the poor (wage workers and poor peasants) was for construction and improvement of houses (often to supplement government housing subsidy), and for meeting other consumption needs. As housing does not generate direct returns, housing loans are usually long-term and are advanced at relatively low interest rates. In rural Tamil Nadu, the poor bear a heavy interest burden on loans taken to secure basic housing facilities.

Introduction

The rural credit market in the two study villages of Tamil Nadu, Palakurichi and Venmani, has undergone an important structural shift. There has been a formalisation of rural credit with formal or regulated sources of credit forming the dominant component of aggregate credit of rural households (75 per cent of total borrowings in the two study villages). A closer look into the data, however, shows that there are two distinct segments of formal credit: older public sector scheduled commercial banks and cooperatives, and newer private financial agencies, notably small finance banks, non-bank financial companies (NBFCs), and NBFC–MFIs (microfinance institutions). The institutions in the latter group are qualitatively different from commercial banks and cooperatives in respect of the types of loan offered, the size of loans, duration, collateral secured, rates of interest, and forms of repayment.

The growth of the newer private sector financial agencies is linked to policy changes. From 2011 onwards, the Reserve Bank of India (RBI) introduced new regulations for microfinance institutions, and also created new institutions such as small finance banks (SFBs). The stated objective of this exercise was to provide credit to poorer sections of the population.

In this chapter, we empirically establish three features of rural credit markets as reflected in the field data. First, private sector formal credit has grown exponentially, and private formal lenders account for a substantive part of total formal credit. Secondly, while the new private sector institutions offer a range of services and loans, the bulk of credit is in the form of microfinance loans issued without any collateral security. The terms and conditions of microfinance loans are onerous, with extremely high rates of interest and tight repayment schedules. Thirdly, private formal credit is more important in the loan portfolio of the poor than that of the rich. This emerges from our analysis of access to credit disaggregated by caste and class. These features of the rural credit market have serious implications for the rural poor, as we argue in the concluding section.

Policy Background

The problem of rural debt and indebtedness of the peasantry acting as a constraint to income generation and to the alleviation of poverty has been recognised widely in the development literature. It was recognition of this problem and the need to provide credit for a variety of reasons – be it for smoothing of consumption, or as investment in education and housing, or for productive activities – to rural households, and the poor in particular, that was a major driver of credit policy after Independence.

Specifically, banking policy was directed towards "social and development banking" from 1969 onwards, starting with the nationalisation of major banks. This resulted in an unprecedented growth of rural banking: of bank branches, of credit, and of deposits. These policies of social and development banking were reversed in 1991 with the introduction of financial liberalisation. The effects of the consequent withdrawal of banks from rural lending became evident a decade later, and there were new efforts towards expansion of credit to rural areas in the mid-2000s. While the flow of agricultural credit rose from 2004 onwards, credit did not actually reach small and marginal farmers (Ramakumar 2019). In 2005, the policy of financial inclusion brought renewed focus on rural banking with measures such as opening of basic savings accounts and credit flow to poorer sections.

Since 2011, there have been important changes in rural credit institutions with the emergence of new formal sector financial institutions. Following the recommendations of the Malegam Committee, in 2011, the RBI created a regulatory structure for a new institution, namely the NBFC-MFI. An NBFC-MFI does not take deposits but is permitted to lend relatively small loans to relatively low-income rural households. Further, in 2016, the RBI permitted the creation of a new type of private sector bank, the small finance bank or SFB. Existing financial institutions like NBFCs, MFIs, and local area banks (LABs), along with residents/professionals with 10 years of experience in banking and finance, were eligible to apply for setting up of SFBs. The main objective of these new banks was to

> undertake basic banking activities of acceptance of deposits and lending to unserved and underserved sections including small business units, small and marginal farmers, micro and small industries and unorganised sector entities. (RBI 2014)

Equitas, headquartered in Chennai, emerged as the first SFB; it began operations in September 2016. Fincare, headquartered in Bangalore, started in 2017.[1]

Database

Detailed evidence from household surveys in two villages of Nagapattinam district, Venmani and Palakurichi, conducted in May–June 2019, provides an opportunity to study the nature of rural credit at a disaggregated level and to

[1] These policies to bring in unregulated or inadequately regulated private finance companies under the rubric of RBI regulation are in line with tendencies in global finance (Swaminathan 2023).

examine actual loans available to poorer households: households of manual workers and poor peasants, and of those belonging to Scheduled Castes and other oppressed castes. This chapter is based mainly on cross-section data from the two study villages, but we briefly examine changes in patterns of borrowing from the early 2000s to the present in Palakurichi village.

The data on indebtedness include information on all outstanding loans, including the principal borrowed, the purpose and source of borrowing, collateral offered, rate of interest, and extent of repayment. While the households were questioned carefully, it is likely that there is an underestimation of borrowing in our survey. Households do not accurately report interest payments, and hence this has been calculated based on additional information from lenders where available. Also, the regularity of repayment differs widely across type of loan, ranging from every week or fortnight for microfinance loans to once a year for crop loans. For this reason, on some loans (gold loan, for instance) interest is paid regularly, while on others (crop loan) it is paid at the end of the term, and in some cases the principal and interest are repaid in instalments. For this reason, the analysis in this chapter is based on information given on principal borrowed, and thus, the term credit or debt refers to the amount/principal borrowed and not to total outstanding debt.

Of the 415 resident households of Venmani, 360 households had some amount of outstanding debt. The total number of loans recorded in the survey was 1,061 and the average amount borrowed was Rs 51,000. In Palakurichi, of 390 resident households, there were 1,020 outstanding loans borrowed by 336 households, with an average loan size of Rs 50,000. On average, we found 3 loans per household, each of around Rs 51,000. In both villages, the principal borrowed per household averaged around Rs 1,50,000. A substantial section of the population in both villages, over 85 per cent of the population, had an active loan at the time of the PARI survey.

The New Lenders and Their Role in the Rural Credit Market

Lenders in the credit market in rural India are typically classified into two groups: formal and informal. In Tamil Nadu, as shown in Table 10.1, there has been a big spurt in the share of formal credit agencies in total debt outstanding of rural households over the last two decades. In 2019, 73 per cent of debt outstanding of rural households was from formal sources of credit (the corresponding proportion at the all-India level was 66 per cent), up from 47 per cent in 2002.

In the two study villages, too, the formal sector predominated. Of total principal borrowed (credit) by households resident in the two villages, the

Table 10.1 *Share of debt outstanding of rural households, by source, Tamil Nadu and India, 2002, 2012, and 2019* in per cent

Credit Agency	2002		2012		2019	
	Tamil Nadu	India	Tamil Nadu	India	Tamil Nadu	India
Formal	46.7	57.1	61.5	53.6	72.9	66.1
Informal	53.3	42.9	38.5	46.4	27.1	33.8
All	100.0	100.0	100.0	100.0	100.0	100.0

Note: Self-help group (SHG)–bank-linked credit and SHG–NBFC credit are included under "formal" sources of credit.
Source: NSSO, various rounds.

major share was from formal sector lenders: 72.5 per cent in Venmani, 81.2 per cent in Palakurichi, and 76.7 per cent for both villages combined.

There are, however, two distinct segments within the formal sector of credit demarcated by the criterion of ownership, that is, as between public and private ownership. The public sector comprises scheduled commercial banks and credit cooperatives.[2] The private sector has four types of lenders: private scheduled commercial banks, small finance banks, NBFCs, and NBFC–MFIs. Below, we elaborate on these institutions operating in the two villages. (Although private scheduled banks are normally classified with public sector scheduled banks, in the specific context of these two villages, as we demonstrate, their pattern of lending is closer to that of the other private sector agencies.) The lenders operating in the two villages are mapped in Figure 10.1.

There were 19 private sector regulated lenders with active loans, as compared to 12 public sector credit agencies. This is not surprising as there has been a tremendous growth of small finance banks, MFIs and NBFCs in Tamil Nadu. Tamil Nadu is among the top States in the country on various parameters of MFIs – in terms of loan portfolio outstanding (second, after West Bengal), active loan accounts (topmost), and number of MFIs (fifth)[3] – and has the highest number of branches of small finance banks in the country.[4]

Segmentation of the Formal Sector: The Role of Collateral

The justification for the subdivision of formal sector creditors proposed in this chapter comes from the distinctiveness of loans given by the two sub-sectors.

[2] While cooperatives are membership-based organisations, they are controlled by the State government.
[3] *Quarterly Financial Report*, April–June 2019, Sa-Dhan.
[4] Source: *Branch Banking Statistics*, RBI, 2019.

Figure 10.1 *Types of lenders, segmented by ownership and regulation*

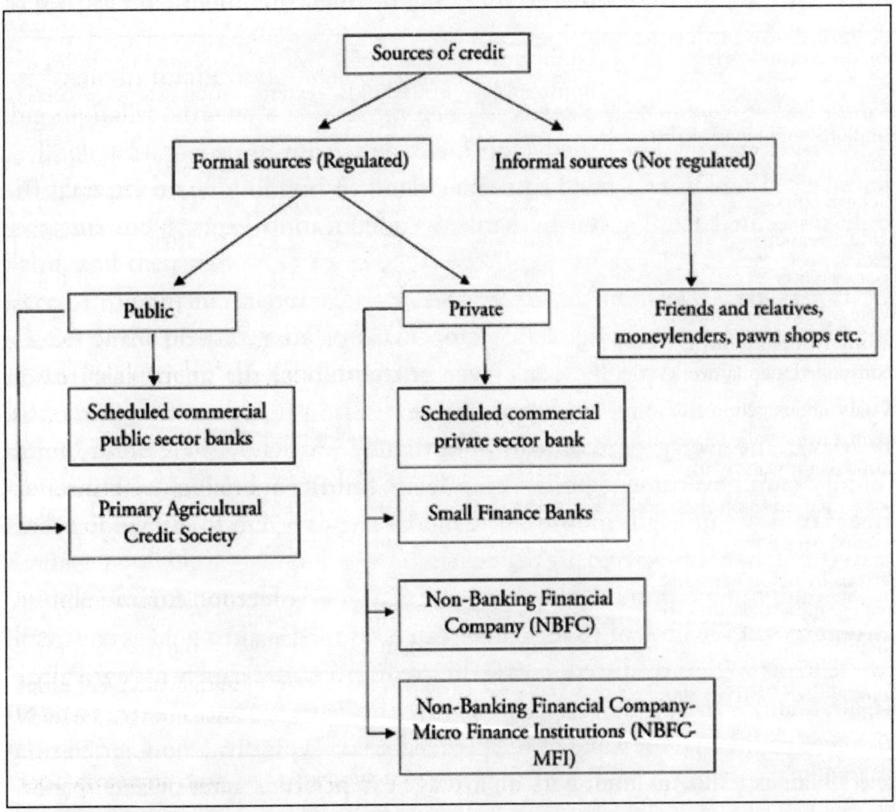

Note: The specific agencies functioning in the two villages are:

Scheduled commercial public sector banks: Bank of India, Canara Bank, Bank of Baroda, Central Bank of India, Corporation Bank, Indian Bank, Indian Overseas Bank, Punjab National Bank, State Bank of India, Vijaya Bank.

Scheduled commercial private sector banks: Axis Bank, HDFC Bank, RBL Bank, IDFC First Bank.

Small finance banks: Equitas Small Finance Bank, Suryoday Small Finance Bank, Fincare Small Finance Bank.

Non-bank financial companies (NBFCs): Five Star Business Finance Limited, Fullerton India, Hero Fincorp, L&T Financial Services, Mahindra Finance, Manappuram Finance Limited, Muthoot Finance, Muthoot Fincorp, Shriram Transport Finance Company Limited, TVS Finance.

Non-bank financial companies–microfinance institutions (NBFC–MFIs): Asirvad Microfinance Limited, Credit Access Grameen Limited, Impact Microfinance, Madura Microfinance Limited, SMILE Microfinance Limited, Samasta Microfinance.

Primary Agricultural Credit Societies (PACS): Kilvenmani Primary Agricultural Credit Society and Palakurichi Primary Agricultural Credit Society.

Specifically, there is a clear association between type of lender and type of loan, with the private formal sector being distinguished by the prevalence of collateral-free microfinance loans.

Public Sector Commercial Banks and Cooperatives

These agencies mainly issued crop loans and loans against gold and silver jewellery. There were a few loans where land or building was collateral. The only unsecured loans given by banks were education loans. Here are some examples.

(i) *Primary Agricultural Credit Societies or PACS* were active in both villages; members of PACS are eligible for crop loans or Kisan Credit Card (KCC) loans. These were typically loans given at the start of the kharif crop season (July onwards), to be repaid before the next season (usually after 10 months, in May). The average size of loan in our study was Rs 57,345. According to Tamil Nadu government policy, crop loans from cooperatives were interest-free if paid within eight months. The modal rate of interest (and median) was zero (the range was zero to 14 per cent).

Secondly, agricultural gold loans – a category of crop loans which are structured on the lines of KCC loans – can be availed against gold as collateral. These loans were introduced to ease the credit needs of farmers for agriculture (Nair, Shankaranarayana, and Ram 2015). The loan amount is meant to be 80 per cent of the market value of the pledged gold. Typically, a non-agricultural gold loan is given to members of PACS at 8 per cent interest and to non-members at 11.7 per cent interest per annum.

(ii) *Public sector commercial banks.* Crop loans from scheduled commercial banks were of two types – KCC loan and agriculture gold loan. In the case of KCC loans, the scale of finance for paddy was Rs 20,000 per acre in 2018–19. The interest rate was 9 per cent per annum with a subvention or subsidy of 5 per cent a year, so that the borrower paid 4 per cent if the loan was repaid within 12 months. If the loan was overdue beyond 12 months, a penal interest of 2 per cent kicked in, making the interest rate 11 per cent per annum. In the case of the second type of loan, namely agriculture gold loans, ideally, the scale of finance, or crop cultivated or gross area operated should have been the criterion for the disbursement of loans, but the gold value was used instead for loan disbursal (*ibid.*). The principal issued was, for example, fixed at Rs 2,050 per gram by Bank of India.[5] Again, the rate of interest was 4 per cent if repaid in 12 months; if overdue, it went up to 11 per cent. This was for gold

[5] This is decided by the headquarters of each bank.

loans of less than Rs 3 lakhs; for loans above Rs 3 lakhs, the interest rate was 11.45 per cent.[6]

The average size of a crop loan was Rs 1.7 lakhs in Venmani and Rs 2.3 lakhs in Palakurichi, confirming that it was larger landowners who took crop loans. The average "gold" loan was Rs 90,493, given at a modal rate of interest of 10 per cent per annum (the median was 9.6), and the range was 5.8 to 18. There were six active loans given by branches of Bank of India and Canara Bank for various non-income-generating activities that were reported to be at an interest rate of 18 per cent per annum.

Private Formal Lenders

There were four types of financial institutions in this group, with many types of credit in their loan portfolio. Our fieldwork however revealed that collateral-free microfinance loans were the most important category of credit issued to rural households. A distinctive feature of microfinance loans is that they are usually given to a woman member of a women's group. This is not, however, the earlier type of bank-linked self-help group, as the group does not engage in any independent activity (be it savings or micro-enterprise). The group is only for the purpose of enforcement of repayment.[7]

(i) *Private commercial banks*. The average size of collateral-free loans from private commercial banks was Rs 42,900 and the average rate of interest was 15 per cent. The highest rate of interest reported was 28 per cent on an unsecured group loan from IDFC First Bank.[8]

(ii) *Small finance banks or SFBs*. The bulk of loans given by SFBs were loans without collateral (82 per cent of credit). The rest were loans against land, house, and gold as security. Fincare, an SFB, gave loans to women in groups (comprised of three to 40 members) for "income-generating activities." The time period for paying the loans is 24 months in equated monthly instalments. For example, a loan of Rs 30,000 was paid in equated instalments of Rs 1,640 per month for a period of two years. There is a compulsory insurance component and a processing fee. Employees of Fincare collect these loans from the women individually. If the loanee is not able to pay the instalment, the other group members have to share the amount and pay it on her behalf, and the onus of making sure that happens falls on the group leader.

[6] There was one loan of Rs 70,000 at 14 per cent annual rate of interest, an agricultural gold loan issued by a public commercial bank. The loan was taken for a duration of 36 months and was unpaid on the date of the survey.

[7] This was admitted to us in interviews with local agents of SFBs and MFIs.

[8] This was a JLG loan of Rs 30,000 at a rate of interest of 27 per cent with an additional 1 per cent as processing fee.

(iii) *NBFC–MFIs*. All loans issued by NBFC–MFIs were unsecured microfinance loans, averaging Rs 30,000. The schedule of repayment varied with each loan – weekly, fortnightly or monthly. For example, Madura Microfinance, a non-deposit-taking microfinance institution, gave credit to groups of women using the "self-help group" model. The tenure of loans was between 24 and 30 months, and repayment was in equated monthly instalments. The base principal amount was Rs 33,000 and the highest was Rs 65,000 – based on credit history. The reported rate of interest was 20.6 per cent per annum with an additional 1 per cent as processing fee.

(iv) *NBFCs*. Over 75 per cent of the principal borrowed from NBFCs was in the form of unsecured microfinance loans. There were some loans taken with gold, land, and houses as collateral. Fullerton India Credit Company Limited, an NBFC, gave credit to members of women's groups at an annual interest of 23–25 per cent, with an additional rate of up to 3 per cent of the loan amount charged as processing fee. The tenure was between 18 and 24 months, and the loan size ranged from Rs 22,000 to Rs 45,000. For example, a loan borrowed from Fullerton India under the Solidarity Group Loan scheme of Rs 45,000 was to be repaid in 24 equated monthly instalments of Rs 2,620.

NBFCs such as Muthoot Finance also offered gold loans, at interest rates as high as 22 per cent. A single household in Venmani, self- employed in business activity, reported three active loans against gold from Muthoot Finance, at a rate of 22 per cent per annum, taken for marriage expenses.

Structure of the Rural Credit Market

For this analysis, we pooled data from both villages, as the types of lenders and types of loans were almost identical in the two villages. The analysis here is based on information relating to 2,080 loans and principal borrowed of Rs 1,058.9 lakhs. (A cross-tabulation of all loans by type of lender and type of collateral is given in Appendix Table 10.1.)

Formal sources of credit accounted for 76.7 per cent of principal borrowed in the two villages. Disaggregating by type of ownership, 45.6 per cent of credit came from public formal lenders and 31.1 per cent from private formal lenders. The remaining 23.3 per cent was from informal (private) lenders. The share of public sector banks and cooperatives was higher in Palakurichi (52 per cent of principal borrowed) than in Venmani (39 per cent of principal borrowed). And, the share of private financial agencies – SFBs, NBFCs, and NBFC–MFIs – was higher in Venmani than in Palakurichi (see Appendix Table 10.4).

Secondly, using type of collateral security to demarcate loans, we find that, of the total borrowing of Rs 10.58 crores by households in the two villages,

5.1 crores was without collateral. In short, 48.2 per cent of credit borrowed in these two villages was by way of unsecured loans. These two aspects, namely, the sizeable role of private formal agencies and the extent of collateral-free loans, are closely related.

Of unsecured loans, 1.6 per cent came from public formal lenders (in the form of education loans), 56.1 per cent from private formal lenders, and 42.3 per cent from informal lenders.[9] Indeed, it is the *predominance of collateral-free loans at relatively high rates of interest that justifies the separation of public and private sectors within formal financial institutions.*

Gold loans were the second most important type of loan, accounting for Rs 2 crores (Rs 20 million) or almost 20 per cent of total credit taken by residents of the two villages. While all categories of lenders gave loans against gold as collateral, 90 per cent of the amount borrowed was from public sector lenders, that is, banks and PACS. For borrowers with gold, given the difference in rate of interest across the three categories of lenders, the first preference was clearly public sector lenders.

At the same time, it is important to note that gold loans – agricultural gold loans, in particular – have become an important component of public sector lending; they accounted for 41 per cent of loans from public scheduled banks and 28 per cent of loans from PACS. Loans secured by gold, with little or no risk to the lender, are of course only available to borrowers with gold assets. These loans are receiving a boost from the demand side as well as the supply side – the banks and cooperatives promote these to improve their priority sector lending targets with zero or minimal risk and a guarantee of timely repayment, while the borrowers (with gold in hand) prefer it due to timely and easy access to liquidity (Nair, Shankaranarayana, and Ram 2015). Gold loans by definition are not available to the poorest sections of the population.

Crop loans or direct loans for crop production were given only by public formal lenders. They amounted to Rs 1.06 crores or 10 per cent of total credit. Crop loans are loans with government subsidy or subvention on interest (often nil rate of interest). Crop loans accounted for less than 10 per cent of total credit from public sector banks and 68.7 per cent of loans from cooperatives. These are cheap working capital loans, available to households with land holdings and membership in the cooperative society.

In terms of collateral, the remaining credit was distributed as follows: 4.3 per cent against land as collateral, 7.3 per cent against houses, 1.1 per cent against other assets, 2.4 per cent against pay slips (for salaried employees), and 6.9 per cent was unspecified on account of missing information.

[9] Among informal sources of credit, loans without collateral were 87.2 per cent of total credit, but around 11.4 per cent of these loans were at nil rates of interest from friends and relatives.

Distinctive Terms and Conditions of Loans

The two segments of the formal credit sector are distinct in respect of collateral securities, and rate of interest charged and other conditions on loans. The rate of interest rises sharply as we move down from public sector formal lenders to private sector formal lenders to informal lenders (see Table 10.2).[10]

Crop loans (KCC) from PACS were provided at zero interest, and from public scheduled commercial banks at 4 per cent with interest subvention. Regular gold loans from PACS were charged 11 per cent interest.

In the private formal sector, unsecured microfinance loans were charged a minimum of 20 per cent, with additional charges such as for processing and insurance. The rate of interest on loans from SFBs and NBFC–MFIs was officially declared to be 23–24 per cent. However, the effective rate of interest on microfinance loans is even higher as the loan is repaid in instalments and a reducing principal implies a rise in interest charged over time (Swaminathan 2023). Gold loans from Equitas, a small finance bank, were charged interest rates between 11 and 23 per cent, and Muthoot Finance levied a rate of interest of 21 per cent. Lastly, enforcement of repayment was ensured through personal visits and pressure on women (and their groups).

The rates of interest were, of course, the highest for informal lenders: some private finance companies charged 24–30 per cent, just a little higher than private formal lenders, but moneylenders charged exorbitant rates of interest (up to 240 per cent).

To sum up, we argue that the structure of the rural credit market has evolved, and while regulated or formal lenders account for nearly four-fifths of total credit, there is clear segmentation within the formal sector. Our first proposition is that a substantial component of formal sector lending is now from the newly regulated/created financial institutions (NBFCs, SFBs, and NBFC–MFIs). Our second proposition is that public and private formal sector lenders are in different leagues in respect of the rate of interest charged. In Palakurichi village, for example, public lenders charged a maximum of 10 per cent per annum on crop loans, while private formal lenders reported a maximum rate of interest of 34–39 per cent. These data are evidence of the "burden" of borrowing from private lenders, and raise questions about lumping together all types of formal sector financial institutions in one category. Thirdly, as microfinance loans are largely given to women, this new pattern of lending has gender implications that need to be explored further.

[10] We have not calculated rates of interest on microfinance loans; rather, we have taken the rates of interest reported by the agencies on their website.

Table 10.2 *Rates of interest by type of lender and type of loan* in per cent per annum

Type	Name of lender	Type of loan	Reported rate of interest (in per cent)
Formal (Public sector)	Canara Bank	KCC loan (land as collateral)	4–9**
		Agricultural gold loan	4–9##
		Education loan	10–10.5***
	PACS	KCC loan	0
		Agricultural gold loan	0@
		Regular gold loan	11.25
		Joint Liability Group loan	12.5
Formal (Private sector)	IDFC First Bank	Joint Liability Group loan	24–28
	Equitas Small Finance Bank	Microfinance loans (without collateral/JLG model)	23–24@@
		Gold loan#	11–23
	Muthoot Finance (NBFC)	Gold loan#	21
		Micro loan#	20.12
	Samasta Microfinance (NBFC-MFI)	Joint Liability Group loan#	22.76
Informal	Moneylender	Without collateral	5–243.3*
	Abirami Finance	Without collateral	24–30
	Lok Finance	Without collateral	5–28

Notes: * Rate of interest charged by informal lenders has been calculated.

An additional 1–2 per cent processing fee is added.

** There is a subsidy component of 5 per cent, effective interest rate being 4 per cent. The subsidy is applicable if repaid within 12 months; if overdue, an additional 2 per cent is added.

There is a subsidy component of 5 per cent, effective interest rate being 4 per cent. The subsidy is applicable if paid within 12 months; if overdue, an additional 2 per cent is added. However, if the principal is above Rs 3 lakhs, the rate goes up to 11.45 per cent.

*** 10 per cent for girls and 10.5 per cent for boys.

@ The rate of interest is zero if repaid within 8 months; if overdue, the rate is 7 per cent.

@@ 23 per cent when the principal is greater than Rs 25,000, else 24 per cent (an additional 1 per cent as processing fee is charged on loans above Rs 25,000).

Source: FAS survey data, 2019.

Variations in Access to Credit by Socio-economic Class

Our third proposition is that the composition of the credit portfolio of households differs systematically across socio-economic classes and castes. To examine this further, we discuss each village separately, as the caste and class composition is unique to a village. Unless otherwise specified, data in this section are from the FAS–PARI 2019 surveys.

Source of Borrowing

There are clear-cut differences across socio-economic classes in terms of access to the formal public sector credit agencies vis-a-vis the new private sector formal agencies and informal lenders.

In Venmani, the entire debt of the landlord class was outstanding from public sector banks and cooperatives. Among rich and middle peasants, and salaried persons, public sector lenders accounted for 60 per cent of total credit. For all other classes, the share of the public sector, a source of cheap credit, was less than 50 per cent of total credit (Table 10.3).

At the other end of the socio-economic hierarchy, we have the class of wage

Table 10.3 *Principal borrowed, by socio-economic class and source, Venmani, 2019* in per cent

Socio-economic class	Number of borrowing households	Formal		Formal (combined)	Informal	All sources
		Public	Private			
Landlords and big capitalist farmers	1	100.0	0.0	100.0	0.0	100
Rich peasants	10	60.0	24.1	84.1	15.9	100
Middle peasants	38	60.8	24.2	85.0	15.0	100
Poor peasants	69	45.5	27.4	72.9	27.1	100
Wage workers with major income from skilled and formal sector wage work	40	16.5	35.2	51.7	48.3	100
Wage workers with major income from unskilled, semi-skilled manual work	99	16.8	59.1	75.9	24.1	100
Self-employed in business activity	26	12.3	31.4	43.7	56.3	100
Salaried persons	26	61.4	14.6	76.0	24.0	100
Persons living on pensions, small rents, and remittances	51	24.9	53.0	77.9	22.1	100
All classes	360	39.5	33.0	72.5	27.5	100

workers, skilled and unskilled, constituting 39 per cent of all households in Venmani and 36 per cent in Palakurichi. Wage labour households had restricted access to public sector formal agencies, and were dependent on private sector formal agencies and, of course, informal lenders. Among skilled wage workers in Venmani, for example, 48 per cent of credit was from informal lenders and 35 per cent from private formal lenders. Among unskilled workers, private agencies accounted for 59 per cent of credit and informal lenders for another 24 per cent.

The patterns of borrowing were similar in Palakurichi, where credit from public sector lenders accounted for 83 per cent or more of total borrowing for landlords and rich peasants (Table 10.4). Loans from public banks and cooperatives accounted for 24 per cent of total credit among skilled wage workers, and only 4 per cent among semi-skilled and unskilled wage workers. Informal sources of credit accounted for 40 per cent of credit among those dependent on pensions and remittances, and about 33 per cent among unskilled wage workers.

If credit from public and private formal institutions is aggregated, as is normally done, then it appears that formal credit has become the mainstay of rural credit. Making a sub-categorisation, as we have proposed, shows that the relatively new private lending institutions, comprising SFBs, NBFCs, and

Table 10.4 *Principal borrowed, by socio-economic class and source, Palakurichi, 2019* in per cent

Socio-economic class	Number of borrowing households	Formal		Formal (combined)	Informal	All sources
		Public	Private			
Landlords and big capitalist farmers	7	88.8	10.7	99.5	0.5	100
Rich peasants	8	82.9	8.3	91.2	8.8	100
Middle peasants	25	61.1	24.7	85.8	14.2	100
Poor peasants	123	44.8	32.4	77.2	22.8	100
Wage workers with major income from skilled and formal sector wage work	43	24.0	52.8	76.8	23.2	100
Wage workers with major income from unskilled, semi-skilled manual work	74	4.0	63.1	67.1	32.9	100
Self-employed in business activity	15	76.6	9.0	85.6	14.4	100
Salaried persons	19	64.9	20.0	84.9	15.1	100
Persons living on pensions, small rents, and remittances	22	32.9	26.3	59.1	40.9	100
All classes	336	52.2	29.0	81.2	18.8	100

MFIs, have come to occupy an important position in the debt portfolio of households from economically weaker sections of the population. For wage labour and poor peasant households, as well as those dependent on pensions and remittances, the informal sector also remained a critical source of credit.

Purpose of Borrowing

To better understand credit needs, we examine the reasons given for borrowing and classify them into three broad categories: loans taken for productive uses or income-generating activities, loans for house repair and construction, and loans to meet consumption needs. Production loans include loans taken for agricultural activities, business, rearing of animals, etc. Consumption loans comprise loans taken for marriage and other family events, daily expenses, repaying existing loans, medical bills, etc.

In Venmani, loans to meet consumption needs accounted for the largest share (46 per cent) of aggregate credit (principal borrowed), followed by loans for house construction or repair, accounting for around 32 per cent of principal borrowed (Appendix Table 10.7). Loans for productive uses accounted for less than 22 per cent of the total amount borrowed. The broad picture was similar in Palakurichi village, though loans for consumption were less important here (38 per cent of total principal borrowed) than in Venmani village, and loans for productive uses and house construction each accounted for around 30 per cent of total borrowings (Appendix Table 10.8).

In short, consumption loans dominated the credit portfolio of households in both villages, while credit for productive uses was around one-fifth of total credit. What is surprising and interesting to note is the extent of borrowing for house repair and construction. In terms of size of loan, on average, loans for house construction were the largest among the three purpose-wise categories of loans. In Venmani, the average loan taken by a household for housing was Rs 1.6 lakhs and in Palakurichi, it was more than Rs 2 lakhs.

The main purpose of borrowing was very different across classes. Borrowing for productive uses dominated the credit portfolio of landlords and rich peasants in both villages. In Venmani, for all other socio-economic classes (with a few exceptions), the main purpose of borrowing was to meet a variety of consumption needs (Appendix Table 10.2). Among wage workers with unskilled work, poor peasants, and persons living on pensions and remittances, around one-third of borrowing was for the purchase, repair, or construction of houses. Loans for production amounted to 42–50 per cent of total borrowing among rich peasants, middle peasants, and self-employed in business households, and 100 per cent among landlord and big capitalist farmer households.

In Palakurichi, loans for productive uses accounted for more than 80 per cent of the total amount borrowed among rich peasants and self-employed business households (and 62 per cent among landlords). For households in all other socio-economic classes, loans for consumption and house repair accounted for the bulk of total borrowings. Among poor and middle peasants, and workers with unskilled work, 35–40 per cent of the amount borrowed was for house improvement, and the proportion was 81 per cent among households with salaried persons (Appendix Table 10.3).

A major finding that emerges from these data is that over 50 per cent of borrowing was to meet consumption needs among wage labour households, reflecting the inadequacy of incomes to meet expenditure on basic needs (Appendix Tables 10.9 and 10.10). In Venmani, among skilled wage workers, 68.7 per cent of the principal borrowed was for consumption, and almost half of this was to repay previous loans. Among unskilled wage workers, 52.5 per cent of borrowing was for consumption purposes, of which loans for meeting day-to-day expenses and marriage expenses accounted for 30 per cent each (Appendix 10.9). In Palakurichi, 54 per cent of the debt of skilled wage workers was for consumption purposes, of which around 40 per cent was to meet their daily needs. Among unskilled wage workers, 75 per cent of the debt incurred was for consumption purposes, of which 45 per cent was for meeting daily expenses (Appendix 10.10).

A second notable observation is that around a third of total credit availed was for purposes of house repair and construction, reflecting widespread investment in housing funded by loans. In Venmani, 34 per cent of credit taken by unskilled and semi-skilled wage labour households was for house construction and repair. In Palakurichi, 39 per cent of credit taken by skilled wage labour households was for house improvement. The proportion was much less among unskilled wage labour households in Palakurichi.

The question thus arises as to how wage labour households meet their demand for credit for consumption needs and investment in housing.[11] To examine this question we identified the source of credit for each specific purpose of loan; we illustrate with evidence on housing loans (Appendix Tables 10.5 and 10.6).

House Improvement: Repair and Construction

In both villages, loans for housing were taken from a variety of lenders including scheduled commercial banks, small finance banks, credit cooperatives,

[11] Less than a quarter of all credit for consumption purposes was from public financial institutions. These were usually gold loans, and hence more accessible to better-off landed households. Informal sector credit remained important for consumption credit.

non-bank financial companies, friends and relatives, self-help groups, and moneylenders.

Taking all classes together, in Venmani, only 49 per cent of housing loans came from public credit institutions. For poorer households, unskilled and semi-skilled manual worker households, however, 61 per cent of housing loans were from private financial agencies and another 27 per cent from informal lenders (Appendix Table 10.5). This tendency was even more marked in Palakurichi (Appendix Table 10.6). Among semi-skilled and unskilled wage workers, the main source of credit for house improvement was private lenders, with zero credit from public lenders.

As Gopinath points out, government schemes have played an important role in improving housing, especially among the Scheduled Castes. At the same time, these housing schemes have not yet reached all Scheduled Caste households, and the funds allocated for new houses do not cover the full costs of construction (chapter 15).

Thus, for investment in housing, an important constituent of human development and a route to social and economic mobility, wage labour households and Dalit households needed finance but did not have access to low-interest credit from public sector banks. A wage worker household borrowing from "formal" private financial agencies could be charged an official interest rate of between 22 and 26 per cent on a collateral-free loan (with the effective rate of interest being even higher), probably unique among housing loans across the world. *This is a high price to pay for better housing, a basic human right.*

Loans for Crop Production: Case Study of Palakurichi

In his 2003–04 study of farming households in Palakurichi, Surjit (2008) examined credit for agriculture by size-class of operational holding of the borrower and source of credit. We examined the credit portfolio of households engaged in crop cultivation (landlord and peasant classes) 15 years later, in 2018–19 (all data are at constant prices). The main changes observed are as below.

First, loans for agriculture were predominantly from the formal sector in 2003 (92 per cent of total principal borrowed) and this has remained so in 2018–19 (with 98 per cent of borrowing for productive uses by cultivators coming from the formal sector). In 2018–19, however, public banks and cooperatives accounted for 81 per cent of credit, and private sector agencies had stepped in to provide 17 per cent of credit.

Secondly, in real terms, the average credit per hectare has fallen for all classes of cultivators except the very large (with 20 hectares or more). Thirdly, there

Table 10.5 *Amount of credit per hectare and share of formal sector in crop credit, Palakurichi village, 2003 and 2019* in rupees and per cent (at 2019 constant prices)

Size-class of operational holding	Number of borrowing households	2003		2019	
		Amount of loan	Share of formal sector	Amount of loan	Share of formal public sector
0–1 hectare	282	22,742	74.8	15,831	58.6
>1–2 hectares	31	22,500	50.3	15,913	81.1
>2–4 hectares	7	1,958	100.0	16,416	42.8
>4–10 hectares	11	12,280	100.0	11,259	67.2
>10–20 hectares	3	32,482	100.0	25,832	100.0
>20 hectares	2	26,469	100.0	36,855	100.0
All	336	22,102	92.4	18,642	80.6

Note: Inflator used is CPI-RL with base year as 1986–87. Also, the 2003 data are from a sample survey whereas the 2019 survey was a census.
Sources: Surjit (2008) and FAS–PARI survey data.

were notable differences across cultivators in terms of quantum of credit and source of credit. Marginal cultivators operating less than one hectare reported crop loans of Rs 15,831 in 2018–19, whereas very large cultivators received more than double this amount (Rs 36,855). Further, while all cultivators in the village had access to crop loans due to an active PACS, marginal cultivators received 58 per cent of their crop credit from public sector financial institutions as compared to 100 per cent among those with 10 hectares or more.

Lastly, total crop credit was less than the recommended scale of finance (Rs 20,000 per hectare at 2018–19 prices as per the State Level Bankers' Committee) for all cultivators other than those with more than 10 hectares. The credit needs of these large cultivators were met adequately and entirely by low-cost credit from public sector banks and cooperatives.

Caste and Access to Credit

The share of public formal sources in total credit was higher for households higher up in the caste hierarchy. For Scheduled Caste households, credit from public sector lenders accounted for one-third of total credit in both villages; the proportion was much higher for all other caste groups (Tables 10.6 and 10.7). Private formal agencies accounted for 40 per cent of total amount borrowed by Scheduled Caste households in both villages. On the other hand, among households belonging to "Other" castes (Brahmin, Kamma Naidu, and Pillai caste Hindu households), public sector agencies were the *only* source of credit in Venmani, and in Palakurichi, public sector agencies accounted for 74 per cent of the principal borrowed.

As documented in this chapter, the cost of credit from the private formal sector is much higher than from the formal public sector. Scheduled Caste households thus get access to credit on terms much less favourable than households belonging to Backward Classes and Other castes.

The loans taken by Scheduled Caste households were primarily to meet consumption needs, and to invest in house repair and construction, and not for productive activity (the share of production loans in total credit was less than 15 per cent among Scheduled Caste households, as given in Tables 10.8 and 10.9). So, loans taken at relatively high interest rates from private formal (as well as informal) lenders by Scheduled Caste households were for activities that were unlikely to give economic returns, placing a high burden of repayment on the borrowing households.

Table 10.6 *Principal borrowed, by social group and source, Venmani, 2019* in per cent

Source of loan	Number of borrowing households	Scheduled Castes	Most Backward Classes	Backward Classes	Other
Formal (public)	162	33.1	39.7	53.2	100.0
Formal (private)	234	39.1	25.4	20.5	0.0
Formal (combined)	396	72.2	65.2	73.7	100.0
Informal	197	27.8	34.8	26.3	0.0
All sources	593	100.0	100.0	100.0	100.0

Note: The number of households is different from the number of borrowing households as a household can have loans from more than one source.

Table 10.7 *Principal borrowed, by social group and source, Palakurichi, 2019* in per cent

Source of loan	Number of borrowing households	Scheduled Castes	Most Backward Classes	Backward Classes	Other
Formal (public)	166	34.6	65.1	59.1	73.9
Formal (private)	216	41.3	22.9	17.1	16.8
Formal (combined)	382	75.9	88	76.2	90.7
Informal	210	24.1	11.9	23.8	9.3
All sources	592	100	100	100	100

Note: The number of households is different from the number of borrowing households as a household can have loans from more than one source.

Table 10.8 *Principal borrowed, by social group and purpose, Venmani, 2019* in per cent

Social group	Production	Consumption	Purchase, construction or repair of house	Unspecified	All
Scheduled Castes	14.2	46.5	36.3	3	100
Most Backward Classes	35.6	34.1	29.2	1.2	100
Backward Classes	36.8	37	22.5	3.7	100
Other	37.9	62.1*	0	0	100
All	21.7	43.4	31.8	3.1	100

Note: * The share of consumption for Other social group is high by virtue of a single loan of 2 lakh rupees taken from a PSU by pledging gold.

Table 10.9 *Principal borrowed, by social group and purpose, Palakurichi, 2019* in per cent

Social group	Production	Consumption	Purchase, construction or repair of house	Unspecified	All
Scheduled Castes	14.5	51.3	33.8	0.4	100
Most Backward Classes	31	31	38.1	0	100
Backward Classes	53.1	26.6	20.2	0	100
Other	78.7	20	1.3	0	100
All	31.8	37.7	30.4	0.2	100

Concluding Remarks

For many years, one of the goals of credit policy in India has been to make available adequate credit at affordable cost to rural households, and, in particular, to the poor and marginalised sections of rural households. In the name of financial inclusion, policy measures initiated from 2011 have attempted to regulate and promote microfinance lending. Three types of new private lenders have come under the purview of the Reserve Bank of India (RBI), namely, SFBs, NBFCs, and NBFC–MFIs. Field data from two villages of Tamil Nadu surveyed in 2019 give us an opportunity to assess the on-the-ground effects of these policy changes.

Our major findings are as follows. First, in aggregate, formal sources of credit dominate the credit portfolio of rural households. Disaggregated analysis shows that the newly regulated private agencies play a substantive role in the borrowings of rural households. Secondary data from Tamil Nadu show the rapid growth of NBFC–MFIs and other private lenders.

Secondly, the new private lenders operate very differently from the earlier generation of scheduled commercial banks and cooperatives. They specialise in microfinance loans, that is, small-size, collateral-free loans, repaid in regular instalments, with the group as a form of security. In particular, lending is to women who are a part of a women's group (not a self-help group) and this has changed access to credit for women. Unlike the earlier bank-linked women's self-help group model, women in this women's group are not engaged in any joint activity, be it savings or micro-enterprise. Interest rates on such loans are very high, and more than three times the rates charged by commercial banks and cooperatives. Such "microfinance" loans accounted for one-half of the total principal borrowed in the two villages. The contemporary phase of expansion of formal credit in rural areas is thus not an expansion of direct subsidised credit for agriculture and marginalised sections of the population.

Thirdly, households of poorer sections – that is, wage workers and poor peasants, and a high proportion of Scheduled Caste households – had less access to banks and cooperatives and were more dependent on "microfinance" borrowing from private formal lenders than better-off households. The bulk of borrowing by the poor was for house construction or repair and to meet consumption needs. As these activities do not generate immediate returns, these households shouldered a heavy burden of repayment. Better-off households – of landlords and rich peasants – were able to benefit both from crop loans at an almost nil rate of interest, as well as from low-interest rate loans against gold as collateral, from banks and cooperatives.

The earlier division of the rural credit market was such that only better-off households had access to formal credit and the poor had to rely on informal sector lenders. Now, the poor rely on informal sector lenders as well as the new formal private lenders. In short, there remains a division in respect of access to credit along the axes of class and caste, with those at the bottom of the hierarchy being at the mercy of RBI-recognised, profit-making microfinance lenders. The access of women to microfinance is also likely to change gender equations within the family.

Appendix

Appendix Table 10.1 *Structure of rural credit market: principal borrowed by type of lender and collateral, Palakurichi and Venmani villages combined* in Rs lakhs and per cent

Collateral/Lender	Public scheduled commercial banks	PACS	Private scheduled commercial banks	Small finance banks	NBFCs	NBFCs–MFIs	Informal	All sources	Share of total principal
Crop(land)	28.5	83.3	0	0	0	0	0	111.8	
% of row total	25.5	74.5	0	0	0	0	0	100	10.6
Land(other)	26.5	4.3	0	4	9	0	1.6	45.4	
	58.4	9.5	0	8.8	19.8	0	3.5	100	4.3
Gold/silver	148.2	33.6	0	3	6.3	0	11.8	202.9	
	73.0	16.6	0	1.5	3.1	0	5.8	100	19.2
House	51	0	0	8.6	11.1	0	7	77.7	
	65.6	0	0	11.1	14.3	0	9	100	7.3
Employment	25.4	0	0	0	0	0	0	25.4	
	100	0	0	0	0	0	0	100	2.4
Other	1.2	0	0	0	0	0	10	11.2	
	10.7	0	0	0	0	0	89.3	100	1.1
No collateral	8.3	0	105.5	70.6	85.7	25.1	216	511.2	
	1.6	0	20.6	13.8	16.8	4.9	42.3	100	48.3
Unspecified	73.4	0	0	0	0	0	0	73.4	
	100	0	0	0	0	0	0	100	6.9
All types	362.5	121.2	105.5	86.2	112.1	25.1	246.3	1058.9	
	34.2	11.4	10	8.1	10.6	2.4	23.3	100	100

Appendix Table 10.2 *Share of principal borrowed, by socio-economic class and purpose, Venmani, 2019* in per cent

Socio-economic class	Production	Consumption	House repair or construction	Unspecified	All
Landlords and big capitalist farmers	100	0	0	0	100
Rich peasants	42.8	7.6	18.7	30.9	100
Middle peasants	51	31.7	17.1	0.1	100
Poor peasants	21.9	48.3	29.7	0.2	100
Wage workers with major income from skilled and formal sector wage work	1.3	68.7	25.2	4.9	100
Wage workers with major income from unskilled, semi-skilled manual work	9.7	52.5	34.2	3.5	100
Self-employed in business activity	39.7	32.5	24	3.8	100
Salaried persons	5.8	36.2	56.7	1.3	100
Persons living on pensions, small rents, and remittances	10.4	51.6	33.5	4.5	100
All classes	21.7	43.4	31.8	3.1	100

Note: There was one loan of Rs 4 lakhs taken by a rich peasant household (with operational holdings of 15 acres) from a scheduled commercial bank, where the reason was not mentioned.

Appendix Table 10.3 *Share of principal borrowed, by socio-economic class and purpose, Palakurichi, 2019* in per cent

Socio-economic class	Production	Consumption	Purchase, construction or repair of house	Unspecified	All
Landlords and big capitalist farmers	61.9	19.1	19	0	100
Rich peasants	82.3	17.7	0	0	100
Middle peasants	24.3	34.7	40.9	0	100
Poor peasants	18.8	45	35.7	0.6	100
Wage workers with major income from skilled and formal sector wage work	7.2	54.1	38.7	0	100
Wage workers with major income from unskilled, semi-skilled manual work	5.8	75.3	18.9	0	100
Self-employed in business activity	85.9	13.3	0.8	0	100
Salaried persons	9.6	9.4	81	0	100
Persons living on pensions, small rents, and remittances	21.6	71.1	7.3	0	100
All classes	31.8	37.7	30.4	0.2	100

Appendix Table 10.4 *Principal borrowed and share of total borrowed by specific source of borrowing, Venmani and Palakurichi, 2019* in rupees and per cent

Source of loan	Name of source	Venmani	Palakurichi
Formal (public)	Public sector banks	1,51,84,800 (27.9)	1,70,83,200 (33.1)
	Credit cooperatives	33,52,500 (6.2)	87,67,194 (17.0)
	Other formal sources	29,14,000 (5.4)	10,70,000 (2.1)
Formal (public)		2,14,51,300 (39.5)	2,69,20,394 (52.2)
Formal (private)	Private sector banks	46,45,000 (8.5)	59,03,000 (11.5)
	Small finance banks	52,46,000 (9.6)	33,75,000 (6.5)
	NBFC	62,80,000 (11.6)	49,29,000 (9.6)
	NBFC–MFI	17,74,000 (3.3)	7,39,000 (1.4)
Formal (private)		1,79,45,000 (33.0)	1,49,46,000 (29.0)
Formal (combined)		3,93,96,300 (72.5)	4,18,66,394 (81.2)
Informal	Friends and relatives	23,77,000 (4.4)	5,60,000 (1.1)
	Moneylenders	56,77,840 (10.4)	32,95,645 (6.4)
	Private finance company	25,04,000 (4.6)	24,45,035 (4.7)
	Self-help group	22,92,800 (4.2)	17,89,300 (3.5)
	Other informal sources	21,19,150 (3.9)	15,91,000 (3.1)
Informal		1,49,70,790 (27.5)	96,80,980 (18.8)
All sources		5,43,67,090 (100.0)	5,15,47,374 (100.0)

Note: Private finance company comprises non-government companies, pawn shops, and private finance companies. Other informal sources comprise employer, unspecified, and any informal source that does not fall into any of the other categories.

Appendix Table 10.5 *Principal borrowed for housing activities, by socio-economic class and source of borrowing, Venmani, 2019* in per cent

Socio-economic class	Formal		Formal (combined)	Informal	All sources
	Public	Private			
Rich peasants	0.0	85.5	85.5	14.5	100.0
Middle peasants	55.7	33.2	88.9	11.1	100.0
Poor peasants	62.8	14.2	77.0	23.0	100.0
Wage workers with major income from skilled and formal sector wage work	45.0	30.5	75.5	24.5	100.0
Wage workers with major income from unskilled, semi-skilled manual work	11.6	61.2	72.8	27.2	100.0
Self-employed in business activity	34.2	12.2	46.4	53.6	100.0
Salaried persons	79.0	5.6	84.6	15.4	100.0
Persons living on pensions, small rents, and remittances	15.7	64.2	79.9	20.1	100.0
All classes	49.1	28.9	78.0	22.0	100.0

Note: The share of private formal sources in borrowings of rich peasant households is high on account of a single loan of Rs 2 lakhs, which alone comprised 58 per cent of all borrowings by rich peasants for housing.

Appendix Table 10.6 *Principal borrowed for housing activities, by socio-economic class and source of borrowing, Palakurichi, 2019* in per cent

Socio-economic class	Formal		Formal (combined)	Informal	All sources
	Public	Private			
Landlords and big capitalist farmers	97.3	2.7	100.0	0.0	100.0
Middle peasants	65.0	19.0	84.0	16.0	100.0
Poor peasants	66.4	18.9	85.3	14.7	100.0
Wage workers with major income from skilled and formal sector wage work	38.8	45.1	83.9	16.1	100.0
Wage workers with major income from unskilled, semi-skilled manual work	0.0	73.2	73.2	26.8	100.0
Self-employed in business activity	0.0	100.0	100.0	0.0	100.0
Salaried persons	72.6	17.9	90.5	9.5	100.0
Persons living on pensions, small rents, and remittances	16.7	63.2	79.9	20.1	100.0
All classes	61.3	25.3	86.6	13.4	100.0

Appendix Table 10.7 *Proportion of loans and principal borrowed, and principal borrowed per household, by purpose of borrowing, Venmani, 2019* in per cent and rupees

Purpose	Share of loans	Share of principal borrowed	Principal borrowed per household per purpose
Production loans	22.1	21.7	74,192
Purchase, construction or repair of house	19.6	31.8	1,61,416
Consumption loans	58.2	46.5	62,621
All	100	100	1,51,020

Appendix Table 10.8 *Proportion of loans and principal borrowed, and principal borrowed per household, by purpose of borrowing, Palakurichi, 2019* in per cent and rupees

Purpose	Share of loans	Share of principal borrowed	Principal borrowed per household per purpose
Production loans	22.7	31.8	98,604
Purchase, construction or repair of house	15.4	30.3	2,00,866
Consumption loans	61.9	37.9	47,589
All	100	100	1,53,415

Appendix Table 10.9 *Share of principal borrowed by specific purpose of borrowing for wage workers with major income from skilled and formal sector wage work, and wage workers with major income from unskilled and semi-skilled manual work classes, Venmani, 2019* in per cent

Purpose of borrowing	Skilled workers	Unskilled and semi-skilled workers
For agricultural expenses	0.2	7.0
Animal resources	0.0	2.6
Purchase and maintenance of productive durable assets	1.1	0.2
Production loans	*1.3*	*9.7*
Purchase, construction or repair of house	*25.2*	*34.3*
For day-to-day expenses	8.1	16.2
Marriage and other ceremonies	9.2	15.9
Educational expenses	5.1	5.7
Medical expenses	6.5	5.4
To repay previous loan	32.8	6.8
Purchase and maintenance of domestic durable assets	6.2	2.3
Other	0.7	0.1
Consumption loans	*68.7*	*52.5*
Unspecified	4.9	3.5
All	100	100

Appendix Table 10.10 *Share of principal borrowed by specific purpose of borrowing for wage workers with major income from skilled and formal sector wage work, and wage workers with major income from unskilled and semi-skilled manual work classes, Palakurichi, 2019* in per cent

Purpose of borrowing	Skilled workers	Unskilled and semi-skilled workers
For agricultural expenses	2.4	1.9
Animal resources	1.2	2.4
Business and trade	3.6	0.9
Purchase and maintenance of productive durable assets	0.0	0.6
Production loans	*7.2*	*5.8*
Purchase, construction or repair of house	*38.7*	*18.9*
For day-to-day expenses	21.3	33.8
Marriage and other ceremonies	14.5	13.2
Educational expenses	2.0	3.1
Medical expenses	3.0	12.1
Purchase and maintenance of domestic durable assets	8.6	1.8
To repay previous loan	4.5	11.4
Consumption loans	*54.1*	*75.3*
All	100	100

IV

Earnings

11

Farm Business Incomes

V. Surjit and Arindam Das

HIGHLIGHTS

The cultivation of paddy, the main crop in villages of the lower Cauvery delta, was damaged severely by Cyclone Gaja in the reference year (2018–19). Fifty-five per cent of cultivating households in Palakurichi and 44 per cent of cultivating households in Venmani suffered crop losses (negative incomes) from cultivation in that year. On average, a cultivator in Palakurichi lost Rs 210 per hectare (ha) in 2018–19.

There were clear variations in net income obtained from crop farming by households with different farm sizes or operational holdings of land. In Palakurichi, the net income per hectare among large cultivators was ten times the net income gained by cultivators with marginal (less than 1 ha) and small (1–2 ha) landholdings, mainly because of the higher yields and higher product prices realised by large cultivators. The average farm harvest price of paddy received by marginal cultivators, for instance, was Rs 16.80 per kg, while the average price received by cultivators with more than 10 hectares was Rs 18.90 per kg. In Venmani too, farm business income per hectare rose with the size of operational holding.

In line with observations made by Surjit (2008) in 2003–04, there were systematic differences in crop incomes as between Scheduled Caste and non-Scheduled Caste cultivators. Farm business incomes from paddy cultivation among Scheduled Caste households was significantly different (at the 10 per cent level of significance) from farm business income received by non-Scheduled Caste households in both villages. These differences are related to differences in farm size (as the majority of Dalit cultivators operate marginal or small landholdings), and differential access to other resources in the cultivation process.

Introduction

This chapter draws on data from the two study villages to examine four sets of questions concerning yield and profitability from crop production in the lower Cauvery delta.

The chapter is organised into five sections. In the second section, we discuss agricultural production conditions in the two study villages. In the third and fourth sections, we first discuss income and profitability from crop production in aggregate, then for paddy cultivation, in Palakurichi and Venmani villages. The fifth section is the conclusion.

Palakurichi village has been studied at different points of time since 1918 and the second section of the chapter also discusses changes in the costs of cultivation and farm business incomes in Palakurichi during the last two decades between 2003–04 and 2018–19.

To estimate costs and incomes from cultivation, we used the method provided in FAS (2015). We define farm business income as net income from the operated farm. The net income is defined as the gross value of output minus paid-out costs (Cost A2). Gross value of output (GVO) is defined as sum of value of main product and by-product. For each crop, the GVO and cost are calculated separately and aggregated to estimate farm business income for the operational holding. "Operational holding" refers to the total area operated by the household in the reference agricultural year. To estimate cost, we considered Cost A2 as defined by the Commission for Agricultural Costs and Prices (CACP). The components of Cost A2 are listed in Appendix Table 11.1.

Agricultural Production Conditions in Palakurichi and Venmani Villages

Palakurichi and Venmani are both in the tail end of the Cauvery delta and belong to the Old-Delta Coastal Zone (Bouton 1985).[1] The agro-ecological and socio-economic conditions of the villages are very similar. Palakurichi is closer to the tail end of the Cauvery delta than Venmani. Although both villages are located in the same agro-ecological zone, there are certain differences in the production conditions in the two villages that contribute to differences in yields and the incomes realised by cultivators.

[1] The region is classified as part of the Eastern Coastal Plain, Hot Sub-Humid to Semi-Arid Eco-region with coastal alluvium derived soils in the Agro-Ecological Regions classified by the Indian Council of Agricultural Research (ICAR). It is classified as part of the Cauvery Delta Zone in the National Agricultural Research Project (NARP) classification.

Production Conditions in Palakurichi Village

Palakurichi village has been studied at various points of time for nearly a century from 1918, and the study of 2018–19 is the sixth and perhaps the most comprehensive study so far of agrarian relations and production conditions in the village. The Cauvery delta region has the distinction of being the oldest irrigation system in the country. A vast network of very old canals that have been renovated and expanded at different periods of time constitute the irrigation system that supports agricultural production in the Cauvery delta. The major irrigation structures that form the backbone of the system that sustains agricultural production in the delta have been laid out since the construction of the Grand Anicut by the Cholas during the second century CE. Following this, the construction of the upper and lower anicuts during the later part of nineteenth century, and the Mettur dam in 1938, built a robust and effective water control mechanism that fostered a prosperous agricultural production system. In the 1970s, this paddy production system supported the introduction of green revolution technologies, which involved the cultivation of short-duration high-yielding varieties. All these resulted in higher yield levels and greater cropping intensity in the Cauvery delta, changes that also occurred in tail-end villages such as Palakurichi.

Until the late 1970s, a single crop of long-duration paddy was grown in the village in the *samba* (or monsoon) season. When Guhan (1983) surveyed the village, cultivators grew two crops, thanks to improved irrigation-water availability and control and the new supply of short-duration varieties of paddy. However, with the decline in irrigation-water availability and uncertainties associated with the availability of irrigation water through canals at the tail end of the delta, cultivators went back to a single crop of long-duration paddy in the 1990s. The performance of this single crop of long-duration paddy depended on irrigation-water availability, and since the 1990s, there has been an increased incidence of intermittent floods and drought. In 2003–04, the reference year of the study by the first author (Surjit 2008), the village witnessed the severest drought recorded, with yield levels plummeting to 1.24 tonnes per hectare. A detailed analysis of the natural disasters in the region and how it has affected agricultural production and livelihoods is in chapter 16.

In a normal crop year, cultivators grow a single crop of long-duration paddy. Land preparation starts in June–July, with the arrival of Cauvery irrigation water through the canals leading to the villages. The crop may also receive some rainfall as part of the onset of south-west monsoon. Once land preparation is complete, and with the arrival of water through canals in the Cauvery irrigation system, direct sowing is practiced. The seedlings get established in a month's time by August–September. For direct-sown paddy, two rounds of weeding are practised; one month after sowing and another round after three months of sowing. With herbicides becoming more prevalent, only one weeding remains. The crop matures by January–February and is harvested from March. Currently, the majority of cultivators use combine harvesters. Some cultivators make use of the residual moisture in the fields and grow a crop of black gram or green gram immediately after harvesting the paddy. It is grown in two ways: some cultivators sow the seeds of black gram or green gram in the fields while there is a standing crop of paddy, and the crop gets established after the harvest of the paddy crop. The second practice (common in Palakurichi) is to sow the seeds in paddy fields after the harvest of the crop. This system is practiced in most paddy fields in the taluk. A second crop of black gram or green gram provides some additional income to cultivators and some fodder to the livestock population.

During the study period, 2018–19, cultivators in both the villages raised a *samba* crop after the arrival of the Cauvery irrigation water in July 2018. However, in August 2018, there was a breach in the upper anicut, and water from the anicut was drained away through the Kollidam river (instead of the normal course through the Grand Anicut and the Cauvery irrigation system emanating from there) to prevent damage from the excess flow of water through canals to the paddy fields. As a result, the standing crop was largely raised by direct sowing; the crop could have been well established 30–40 days after sowing, but water was insufficient. The impact was severe at the tail end of the delta, where there was little groundwater for irrigation. This resulted in excess weed growth in the field, which, in turn, suppressed a paddy crop that was already suffering from water scarcity. A substantial portion of the paddy crop was damaged, and the only option was to replant the damaged parts of fields. The problem was aggravated, as mentioned, by excess weed growth that would otherwise have been suppressed by standing water in the field. Since the crop season had already been advanced by a month, direct sowing of the damaged part of the field became unviable. The most practical solution was to bring seedlings from neighbouring villages or from their own nurseries (possible for few large cultivators in Palakurichi) and fill the gaps in the main field where the crop was damaged. This, however, was not without cost. The cultivators had to incur extra expenses for buying seedlings, transporting them and transplanting them in the field wherever there were patches of crop damage. The data show that, out of a net sown area of 299.4 hectares, 51.1 hectares of paddy crop (17 per cent) were replanted in this manner.

In addition to this, on November 16, 2018, Cyclone Gaja hit the village with continuous rain and heavy winds. This affected the standing crop of paddy at the panicle initiation stage. Although the crop was not completely destroyed, the cyclone affected yield levels severely. The combined impact of natural setbacks during the crop season lowered yields and crop incomes.

Production Conditions in Venmani Village

Venmani village is in the same agro-ecological zone as Palakurichi village. It is also entirely dependent on the Cauvery irrigation system for cultivation, and the cropping pattern is similar to Palakurichi village. Palakurichi is nearer the tail end of the Cauvery delta than Venmani. Venmani village is better endowed with irrigation facilities, and is relatively less prone to flooding than Palakurichi. In Venmani, farmers cultivate a single crop of paddy (*samba* crop) and few cultivators grow a second crop of green gram or black gram immediately after paddy. The cultivation practices of paddy in Venmani village are similar to Palakurichi, except for the fact that a higher proportion of farmers in Venmani raise nurseries and transplant seedlings, and a higher proportion harvest the crop with combine harvesters.

Paddy cultivation in Venmani village was also affected by Cyclone Gaja during November 2018. The details of the impact of the cyclone and associated damage are discussed in chapter 16. The intensity of impact on paddy cultivation varied, but the impact of water scarcity followed by the cyclone was similar to their impact in Palakurichi village.

Income from Crop Production and Farm Incomes in Palakurichi Village

Income from Crop Production

In 2018–19, *samba*-season paddy was the single most important crop cultivated in Palakurichi village. Paddy accounted for 97 per cent of the total gross cropped area of the village. A small proportion of cultivators raised a second crop of green gram or black gram after paddy (7.57 hectares as monocrop and 2.42 hectares as intercrop in 2018–19). Of all cultivators in the village, 87 per cent were small and marginal farmers, operating less than 2 hectares of agricultural land.

In the last decade, nearly 118 Dalit households received up to one acre of land in Palakurichi through the Land for Tillers' Freedom (LAFTI) programme. This has significantly influenced the nature of land distribution in the village, particularly among Dalit households.

During the reference year (July 2018–June 2019), despite the damage caused by the breach in the upper anicut in August 2018 and later from

Cyclone Gaja, the average yield reported for paddy in Palakurichi was 3.3 tonnes per hectare. This is the highest yield recorded in the six studies of Palakurichi village conducted since 1918.

Our data from Palakurichi show that 55 per cent of all cultivators suffered income losses from crop production. The main reason for low or negative incomes from crop production was the replanting of paddy crop during the early crop-growing period, which increased the cost of cultivation.

Even with a relatively good yield, cultivators incurred an average net loss of Rs 758 per hectare. The losses are on account of replanting the damaged paddy crop and the complete failure of the pulses crop in the second season. Of 185 cultivators in Palakurichi, 97 cultivators had negative farm business incomes, that is, suffered losses from crop production. Crop incomes varied across size-classes of cultivators. The data show that there was a positive relationship between farm size and level of crop incomes. First, the gross value of output per hectare on an operational holding varied from Rs 53,234 for marginal farmers to Rs 88,471 for the largest land operating household in Palakurichi (Table 11.1). This variation was on account of differences in yield from paddy and price received by the farmers.

On an average, the gross value of output and paid-out costs were Rs 57,081 and Rs 57,839 per hectare, respectively. The largest land-operating households (>20 hectares of land) gained an income of Rs 41,457 per hectare. On the other hand, substantial losses were incurred by marginal cultivators (that is, in the 0.1 to 1 hectare category). Among marginal cultivators, 59 per cent incurred losses from crop production.

Though the cost of cultivation (Cost A2) per hectare was lowest for households with 20 hectares or more, we did not find any systematic negative

Table 11.1 *Gross value of output, Cost A2, and farm business income, by size-class of operational holdings, Palakurichi village, 2018–19* in rupees per hectare

Size-class (in hectares)	Number of households	Gross value of output	Cost A2	Farm business income
0.1–1.0	131	53,234	57,393	-4,159
1.01–2.0	30	63,842	59,411	4,431
2.01–4.0	7	70,907	65,110	5,797
4.01–10.0	11	65,451	54,078	11,373
10.01–20.0	4	69,456	63,662	5,794
> 20.0	2	88,471	47,015	41,457
All	185	57,081	57,839	-758

Source: Survey data, 2019.

Table 11.2 *Farm business incomes and yields from crop production in Palakurichi, 2018–19* in tonnes per hectare and number

Item	Number of households	Average yield	Median yield
Negative farm business income	97	2.7	2.57
Positive farm business income	88	4.13	4.07
Negative income from paddy	91	2.46	2.32
Positive income from paddy	79	4.2	4.1

Source: Survey data, 2019.

relationship between farm size and cost of cultivation. Our data show that gross value of output rose as we move from small and marginal to middle and large size categories of cultivators in Palakurichi. The net income per hectare obtained by large cultivators was ten times the net income obtained by small and marginal cultivators. The average yield of paddy cultivation reported by the two biggest households was 4 tonnes and 6 tonnes per hectare, respectively, whereas the village-level yield reported was 3.3 tonnes per hectare. Thus, households in bigger farm size categories achieved higher yields and realised higher prices for their produce than households in smaller size-categories of land holdings.

Secondly, households with positive crop incomes had significant yield advantages over those making losses (Table 11.2). It is important to note here that for households with negative farm business incomes from crop production, the average yield of paddy was much lower (2.7 tonnes per hectare) than for those with positive farm business income (4.13 tonnes per hectare; see also the results of the t-test in Appendix Table 11.7).

A large number of small farmers obtained yields higher than the average yield in the village. However, there is a statistically significant difference in paddy yields obtained by small farmers (who operated 2 acres or less) and large farmers (who operated 2 hectares or more). The average yield of paddy was 3.7 tonnes per hectare for large farmers and 3.16 tonnes per hectare for small farmers. This difference in yield was statistically significant at the 5 per cent level of significance in Palakurichi. The yield advantage of the large farmer is a major reason for the higher gross values of output that they achieve and the higher farm business incomes they earn.

Analysis of crop incomes among various social groups of cultivators shows that Dalit cultivators suffered greater losses and earned lower farm incomes than non-Dalit cultivators (Table 11.3). We tested for differences in the average gross value of output, Cost A2 and net incomes per hectare across social groups (Appendix Table 11.5). The difference in gross value of output

Table 11.3 *Gross value of output, Cost A2, and farm business income of operational holdings, by social group, Palakurichi, 2018–19* in rupees per hectare

Social group	Number of households	GVO	Cost A2	Farm business income
Dalit	129	53,962	56,399	-2,437
Non-Dalit	56	64,266	61,155	3,111
All	185	57,081	57,839	-758

Source: Survey data, 2019.

and Cost A2 was statistically significant at a 10 per cent level of significance. The reason seems to be on account of low productivity due to crop damage and differences in the farm harvest prices of paddy received by different households (Appendix Table 11.6). A large number of Dalit cultivators replanted paddy to make up for poor crop-growth caused by poor irrigation.

All Dalit cultivators (bar one) are small and marginal farmers. Discussions with farmers suggest that the land distributed through LAFTI was less endowed than other land with respect to irrigation facilities, and this may have contributed to lower farm incomes among Dalit cultivators.

Farm Business Incomes from Paddy Cultivation in Palakurichi Village

The two varieties of paddy cultivated in the village were CR-1009 and BPT-5204. The gross values of output, Cost A2, and net incomes from paddy cultivation across various categories of cultivators are in Table 11.6. Contrary to the finding of negative returns from operational holdings, the income from paddy cultivation per household was low but positive. The average per hectare farm business income from paddy cultivation for all households was Rs 1,274 per hectare.

There are three important features of the data on costs and returns from paddy cultivation in Palakurichi. First, the gross value of output increased with the size-class of operational holding. Large cultivators gained higher gross values of output and hence higher farm business incomes per hectare than small and marginal cultivators. The average gross value of output for farmers cultivating operational holdings of more than 20 hectares was Rs 81,865. The gross value of output from paddy cultivation was Rs 51,092 per hectare for those cultivating operational holdings of less than 1 hectare. The higher gross value of output gained by large cultivators (i.e., farmers cultivating operational holdings >10 hectares) was because of advantages with respect to yields and output prices (Table 11.4). In 2018–19, average yields gained by cultivators operating 10–20 hectares and more than 20 hectares were 3.8 tonnes and 4.5

Table 11.4 *Yield and farm harvest price of paddy cultivation, by size-class, Palakurichi, 2018–19* in tonnes per hectare and rupees per kg

Size-class (in hectares)	Yield	Price
0.1–1.0	2.7	16.8
1.01–2.0	3.1	17.2
2.01–4.0	2.6	18.2
4.01–10.0	3.6	18.4
10.01–20.0	3.8	18.9
> 20.0	4.5	17.3
All	3.4	17.6

Source: Survey data, 2019.

tonnes per hectare, respectively. The figure for operational holdings of less than a hectare was 2.7 tonnes per hectare. Guhan's study of 1983 recorded an average yield of 3.16 tonnes per hectare; the average yield in 2018–19, 3.3 tonnes per hectare, was only marginally higher.

There was a significant variation in the farm harvest price across different classes of cultivators. On average, the price received by cultivators farming more than 20 hectares was Rs 17.3 per kg, the price received by cultivators farming 10–20 hectares was Rs 18.9 per kg, and the price received by cultivators farming less than 1 hectare was Rs 16.8 per kg. These differences corresponded to differences in the marketing agencies used by cultivators. In Palakurichi, there was a direct procurement centre (DPC) operated by the State government for the procurement of paddy. There were also private traders who bought directly from cultivators. About 43 per cent of the paddy marketed was sold to the DPC. The average price for paddy paid by the DPC was Rs 18 per kg and the price paid by private traders was Rs 17 per kg. Almost all large cultivators sold paddy to the DPC. They also aggregated paddy by purchasing from small and marginal cultivators during the harvesting season and later selling it to the DPC at higher prices. These purchases were mostly linked to credit market transactions between large landholders and small and marginal cultivators. Most small and marginal landholders, particularly Dalit cultivators, took credit from large landholders, and sold their produce to them at harvest time. This interlinkage between credit and the sale of produce is reflected in the lower average prices received by small and marginal holders and Dalit cultivators in the village (Table 11.5)

Secondly, costs of cultivation of paddy were not very different for small and marginal cultivators and large cultivators. A major component of the costs of cultivation is the cost of hiring labour power, and it is a feature of

Table 11.5 *Yield and farm harvest price of paddy cultivation, by social group, Palakurichi, 2018–19* in rupees per kg and tonnes per hectare

Social group	Yield	Price
Dalit	2.8	16.8
Non-Dalit	3.3	18.2
All	3.4	17.6

Source: Survey data, 2019.

cultivation today that hired labour is used extensively across all size-classes of operational holdings. Hired labour accounted for 70 per cent of the total labour use of farmers cultivating marginal holdings and 96 per cent of the total labour use of farmers cultivating operational holdings of 10–20 hectares. This has resulted in the share of hired labour in total cost being almost equal across different size-categories of operational holdings. Small and marginal cultivators incur higher costs than large farmers on the use of farm machines, seeds, irrigation, and credit. The higher cost of credit for small and marginal farmer is because of their dependence on private sources of credit for working capital requirements (see chapter 12).

Thirdly, there is a clear positive relationship between farm business incomes from paddy and size-class of operational holding. The average net incomes per hectare gained by farmers cultivating less than one hectare, 10–20 hectares, and more than 20 hectares were (–) Rs 4,391, Rs 24,925, and Rs 29,940.

Dalit cultivators gain lower gross values of output and lower farm business incomes per hectare from the cultivation of paddy than non-Dalit cultivators (Table 11.7). Although the average cost is lower for Dalit cultivators, the lower

Table 11.6 *Gross value of output, Cost A2, and farm business income of paddy, by size-class of operational holding, Palakurichi, 2018–19* in rupees per hectare

Size-class of operational holding (in hectares)	Number of households	GVO	Cost A2	Farm business income
0.1–1.0	131	51,092	55,484	-4,391
1.01–2.0	30	60,644	56,655	3,989
2.01–4.0	7	66,144	65,005	1,140
4.01–10.0	11	68,404	59,601	8,802
10.01–20.0	4	81,275	56,350	24,925
> 20.0	2	81,865	51,925	29,940
All	185	57,655	56,381	1,274

Source: Survey data, 2019.

Table 11.7 *Gross value of output, Cost A2, and farm business income of paddy, by social group, Palakurichi, 2018–19* in rupees per hectare

Social group	Number of households	Gross value of output	Cost A2	Farm business income
Dalits	129	53,783	55,531	-1,749
Non-Dalit	56	63,868	57,989	5,880
All	185	57,413	56,149	1,265

Source: Survey data, 2019.

gross value of output realised (because of low productivity and because Dalit cultivators receive, on average, lower product prices) results in lower farm business incomes for Dalit farmers. The difference between Dalit and non-Dalit cultivators in this regard is statistically significant at a one per cent level of significance (Appendix Table 11.6). In other words, the data show that non-Dalit farmers had significant yield and price advantages, and, consequently, gained higher gross values of output and net incomes than Dalit farmers (Appendix Table 11.6).

Input Use Pattern in Paddy Cultivation across Size-class and Caste Groups in Palakurichi

The largest share of total costs in paddy cultivation was taken by hired labour (35 per cent of Cost A2). This was followed by the cost of machine labour (20 per cent). Other major components of the cost of cultivation of paddy were irrigation, plant protection, rent for leased land, and interest on working capital. There are notable variations in the level and pattern of input use across cultivators of different size-classes.

Four features of the data on the costs of hired labour are worth noting.

First, there is no significant variation in the share of expenditure on hired labour cost across size-classes of cultivators in the village.

Secondly, though small and marginal farmers used relatively more family labour, the share of wages in total costs was still high. Two specific features of the reference season – the need to replant paddy and to spend on additional weeding – added to these costs.

Thirdly, tasks in paddy cultivation are performed by hired daily workers. Large farmers had the first choice of workers, since workers were willing to accept lower wages for agricultural work in exchange for other benefits, such as credit.

Fourthly, women's participation in the hired labour market was significant

– 72 per cent of the total hired labour used for paddy cultivation was female. The transplantation of paddy and weeding were carried out exclusively by women workers. Male workers were hired mainly for land preparation, including ploughing, applying fertilizer, and plant protection. Harvesting was done jointly by men and women workers, generally working in pairs. Manual harvesting is, however, being replaced by combine harvesters. An annual payment in kind for guarding the harvested crop was made by large cultivators to the traditional village guard (*thalayari*).

Appendix Table 11.11 shows item-wise costs of cultivation for cultivators by caste group in Palakurichi. The data show that non-Dalit households spent more per hectare than Dalit households on human labour, mainly because Dalit farmers put in more family labour on their operational holdings than others. Rich households also hired long-term workers for paddy cultivation. The data also show that Dalit farmers spent more per hectare than non-Dalit households for seed and for machine labour.

The cost incurred for machine labour was the second largest component of the costs of paddy cultivation in Palakurichi (Appendix Table 11.10). Other than sowing, transplanting, and weeding operations, most field operations were mechanised. While all farmers used machines, large farmers owned more machines than small farmers, and small and marginal farmers spent more on the use of machinery than large cultivators.

With respect to the costs of irrigation, farmers operating less than one hectare incurred a cost of Rs 3,605 per hectare, and farmers operating more than 20 hectares spent Rs 2,436 per hectare. These differences arose from differences in ownership of the means of production, particularly of diesel pumps and tractors. All households operating more than 10 hectares of land owned diesel pumps for irrigation in Palakurichi, whereas only 4 per cent of households operating less than one hectare owned pumps (Table 11.8). Only 16 per cent of Dalit cultivators owned diesel pumps, while 50 per cent of non-Dalit cultivators owned diesel pumps (Table 11.9). This inequality creates differences in access to irrigation water, and in farmers' capacities to save crops and sustain yields, particularly during situations of water shortages at critical stages of plant growth.

With regard to tractor ownership, all households with 20 hectares or more owned and used tractors for cultivation, and no small or marginal cultivator owned one. In 2018–19, no Dalit household owned a tractor. The number of tractors owned by residents of the village declined from 16 in 2003–04 to 13 in 2018–19. This was because of an increase in absentee landlordism; as mentioned earlier, rich farmers have leased their land out and left to live in urban areas.

Table 11.8 *Ownership of diesel pumpsets among cultivators, by size-class of operational holdings, Palakurichi, 2018–19*

Size-class (in hectares)	No of households	Number of households owning diesel pumps	Proportion of households owning diesel pumps
0.1–1.0	131	12	9
1.01–2.0	30	15	50
2.01–4.0	7	6	86
4.01–10.0	11	9	82
10.01–20.0	4	4	100
> 20.0	2	2	100

Source: Survey data, 2019.

Table 11.9 *Ownership of diesel pumpsets among cultivators, by social group, Palakurichi, 2018–19*

Social group	Number of households	Number of households owning diesel pumps	Proportion of households owning diesel pumps
Dalit	129	20	16
Non-Dalit	56	28	50

Source: Survey data, 2019.

The average share of expenditure on seeds in the total costs of paddy cultivation was 9 per cent. Seed costs per hectare were higher for small and marginal farmers than for large farmers. As discussed earlier, paddy cultivation during 2018–19 was affected by damage to standing crops immediately after sowing. While large farmers managed the damage by transplanting seedlings from their own nurseries, small and marginal farmers had to buy seedlings from neighbouring villages, thus raising the costs of cultivation on their farms.

Expenditure on fertilizer is the third largest component of the costs of paddy cultivation in Palakurichi village. The most important source of formal sector farm credit in the village is the Primary Agricultural Co-operative Society (PACS). A part of the credit sanctioned to a cultivator is provided in kind in the form of fertilizers and plant protection chemicals. Large cultivators meet most of their credit needs from the PACS, and per hectare fertilizer use by large cultivators is higher than per hectare fertilizer use by small and marginal cultivators.

In summary, there is a clear positive relationship between farm business incomes from paddy cultivation per hectare and the size-class of operational holdings. Large cultivators realise higher gross values of output and incur lower costs than small and marginal cultivators. Dalit cultivators realised lower levels of gross value of output because of lower yields and product prices.

Changes in Costs of Cultivation in Palakurichi, 2003–04 to 2018–19

The estimates of costs and returns from paddy cultivation in Guhan (1983) are based on selected case studies of farmers operating various sizes of land holding. The studies of the village in 2003 and 2018 used standard methodologies and costs concepts for measuring costs and returns, and are comparable. We consider below certain features of change in the structure of the costs of cultivation of paddy in Palakurichi village from 2003–04 to 2018–19. It is to be noted that 2003–04 was a drought year, the year of the lowest irrigation water flow from the Grand Anicut in seven decades. As a result of this, the yield of 1.23 tonnes per hectare of paddy recorded in 2003–04 was the lowest recorded yield after 1918.[2] Although yield levels were low and returns were negative in 2003–04, a comparative assessment of structure of cost of cultivation gives an idea of changes in production conditions. A detailed item-wise cost of cultivation for paddy in Palakurichi village in 2003–04 and 2018–19 (in constant 2018–19 prices) is in Table 11.10.

At constant (2018–19) prices, the average Cost A2 was Rs 52,528 per hectare in 2003–04 and Rs 57,593 per hectare in 2018–19. The composition of the costs of cultivation remained almost the same. The notable changes between the two time periods (2003–04 and 2018–19) were increases in expenditure on hired human labour, machine labour, plant protection chemicals, and seeds. The increase in machine labour cost was largely because of the increase in mechanisation of crop operations, particularly the use of combine harvesters in 2018–19. In 2018–19 (unlike in 2003–04), cultivators used weedicides, increasing the expenditure on plant-protection chemicals. There was also an increase in the share of cultivators buying seed from the market, resulting in an increase in seed costs. In addition to this, cultivators replanted a portion of their one-month-old crop due to damage in 2018–19. The rental value of leased-in land declined in 2018–19, which could be because of the improvement in access to land among Dalits.

[2] The yield reported during the first study of Palakurichi village was 1.13 tonnes per hectare (Rajalu 1918).

Table. 11.10 *Average cost of cultivation of paddy, by item of cost, Palakurichi, 2003–04 and 2018–19, 2018–19 prices (CPI–AL)* in rupees per hectare

Item of cost	2018–19		2003–04	
	Cost A2	Share in Cost A2	Cost A2	Share in Cost A2
Hired human labour	18,245	31	18,035	34
Machine labour	11,696	17	8,853	17
Fertilizer	7,437	14	8,458	16
Seed	5,861	9	3,699	7
Plant protection	3,656	7	722	1
Irrigation	3,453	5	3,591	7
Farmyard manure	404	1	1,008	1
Rental value of leased-in land	2,545	8	5,162	10
Depreciation and maintenance	226	1	533	1
Interest on working capital	1,302	2	2,239	4
Miscellaneous	2,748	4	193	0
Cost A2	57,593	100	52,528	100

Source: Survey data, 2019; survey data of Surjit, 2008.

Income from Crop Production and Farm Business Incomes in Venmani Village

We now turn to the economics of farming in Venmani village in 2018–19.

Income from Crop Production in Venmani Village

The general characteristics of agricultural production conditions in Venmani village are similar to Palakurichi village. However, there are differences in cropping intensity and irrigation endowments and, consequently, differences in levels of cost, returns, and incomes from cultivation.

In Venmani village, paddy (*samba*) accounted for 57 per cent of the gross cropped area, followed by green gram and black gram (43 per cent). Green gram/black gram is cultivated as a monocrop on 99.1 hectares of land, as an intercrop on 49.81 hectares. The average gross value of output, Cost A2, and farm business income per hectare by size-class of operational holding in Venmani village in 2018–19 are given in Table 11.11.

The returns from cultivation were very low. The average income per hectare of operational holding was Rs 3,078. Crop incomes were higher than in Palakurichi, mainly because of higher cropping intensity in Venmani (as

Table 11.11 *Average gross value of output, Cost A2, and farm business income on operational holding, by size-class of operational holdings, Venmani, 2018–19* in rupees per hectare

Size-class (in hectares)	Number of households	Gross value of output	Cost A2	Farm business income
0.1–1.0	133	64,579	61,163	3,416
1.01–2.0	33	57,818	58,237	-419
2.01–4.0	9	53,251	53,464	-213
4.01–10.0	4	69,774	55,768	14,006
10.01–20.0	2	63,200	38,793	24,406
All	181	62,840	59,762	3,078

Source: Survey data, 2019.

mentioned, cultivators grew a second crop of green/black gram following the long-standing paddy crop). In 2018–19, 44 per cent of cultivators incurred losses in crop production. Most of them were small and marginal farmers. Cyclone Gaja caused severe damage to the standing paddy crop in Venmani. Large farmers gained higher crop incomes per hectare than small and marginal farmers in the village. On an average, farmers cultivating 10–20 hectares obtained incomes that were ten times higher than incomes gained by marginal farmers. Cost A2 per hectare was negatively related to the size-class of operational holding, and farm business income was positively correlated with the size-class of operational holding. Net income per hectare of operational holding averaged Rs 24,406 for farmers cultivating 10–20 hectares, Rs 14,006 for farmers cultivating 4–10 hectares, and Rs 3,416 for farmers cultivating less than one hectare. Cultivators whose operational holdings were 1–2 hectares and 2–4 hectares incurred losses.

Dalit cultivators had lower levels of incomes from crop production than non-Dalit cultivators (Table 11.12), the difference in crop incomes being statistically significant at a 10 per cent level of significance.

An interesting feature of the data is that the average paddy yield for farmers with positive farm business incomes was 1.5 times higher than the average paddy yield for farmers with negative farm business incomes. A similar pattern was observed with respect to farm business incomes from paddy cultivation. The yield difference between farmers with positive business incomes and negative business incomes was statistically significant (Appendix Table 11.7)

The key finding of our study is that a large number of households with marginal holdings suffered losses. These were 57 households comprising 54 per cent of marginal cultivators and 44 per cent of all cultivators.

Small and marginal farmers suffered greater losses than large farmers in the

Table 11.12 *Gross value of output, Cost A2, and farm business income on operational holding, by social group, Venmani, 2018–19* in rupees per hectare

Social group	Number of households	Gross value of output	Cost A2	Farm business income
Dalit	99	60,930	60,650	280
Non-Dalit	82	65,145	58,690	6,456
All	181	62,840	59,762	3,078

Source: Survey data, 2019.

Table 11.13 *Number of households with negative and positive incomes from crop production and yield from paddy cultivation in Venmani, 2018–19* in tonnes per hectare and number

Item	Number of households	Average yield	Median yield
Negative farm business income	84	2.63	2.66
Positive farm business income	96	3.87	3.9
Negative income from paddy	78	2.41	2.47
Positive income from paddy	92	3.94	4.13

Source: Survey data 2019.

study villages. To illustrate, 46 per cent (59 households) of marginal cultivators, 53 per cent (18 households) of households cultivating 1–2 hectares, 40 per cent (four households) of households cultivating 2–4 hectares, and 50 per cent (three households) of households cultivating 4–10 hectares incurred losses from crop production. We found that yields of households with positive farm business income was significantly (at one per cent level of significance) higher than yields of households with negative farm business income (Appendix Table 11.7). The three major reasons for crop losses in the reference year were Cyclone Gaja, high input costs, and the low product prices realised by many farmers, particularly poor farmers (Tables 11.16 and 11.17).

Farm Business Incomes from Paddy Cultivation across Various Size-classes and Social Groups in Venmani Village

Average farm business income from paddy cultivation alone during 2018–19 was Rs 3,195 per hectare. Cultivators farming 10.01–20.0 hectares of land realised a farm business income of Rs 25,745 per hectare, and cultivators with less than one hectare realised an average income of Rs 3,194 per hectare. Overall, there was a positive relationship between the size of operational holding and farm business income per hectare. Small and marginal cultivators incurred higher costs per hectare than large cultivators, indicating a negative relationship between Cost A2 and the size of operational holdings. There was a positive relationship between farm size and gross value of output per hectare

We also found significant variations in the product prices received by farmers cultivating different size-classes of holdings. All farmers sold their produce at a price lower than the official minimum support price (MSP). Two factors contributed to price variation across size-classes of operational holdings. First, the moisture content (and, consequently, the quality) of paddy was affected by Cyclone Gaja. Secondly, the quantity of rough paddy procured by the direct procurement centre (DPC) in Venmani was low, causing variations in the product price realised by farmers. Although the DPC was situated within the village, only 32 per cent of the total marketed output was sold to it. Of the total quantity sold to DPC, 68 per cent was sold below MSP (Rs 17.50 per kg) in Venmani. A large share (52 per cent) of the marketed output was sold to private merchants and commission agents by farmers in Venmani.

As in Palakurichi, Dalit cultivators achieved lower gross values of output, incurred higher costs of cultivation, and realised lower farm business incomes per hectare than non-Dalit households (Table 11.15). Most importantly, the average farm business income from rice cultivation realised by non-Dalit cultivators was almost four times the farm business incomes per hectare realised by Dalit households. Most Dalit households operated small and marginal holdings. They achieved lower yields from cultivation than non-Dalit households, and received lower prices for the paddy they sold.

As mentioned, non-Dalit cultivators had a yield advantage and price advantage (Table 11.17) over Dalit cultivators. The average yield achieved by non-Dalit cultivators was 3.5 tonnes per hectare and average yield achieved by

Table 11.14 *Gross value of output, Cost A2, and farm business income from paddy cultivation, by size-class of operational holdings, Venmani, 2018–19* in rupees per hectare

Size-class (in hectares)	Number of households	GVO	Cost A2	Farm business income
0.1–1.0	133	56,054	52,860	3,194
1.01–2.0	33	50,482	49,771	711
2.01–4.0	9	39,254	40,904	–1,650
4.01–10.0	4	60,379	46,422	13,957
10.01–20.0	2	65,516	39,771	25,745
All	181	54,009	50,814	3,195

Source: Survey data, 2019.

Table 11.15 *Average gross value of output, Cost A2 and farm business income per hectare of paddy, by social group, Venmani, 2018–19* in rupees per hectare

Social group	Number of households	GVO	Cost A2	Farm business income
Dalit	99	53,613	52,385	1,229
Non-Dalit	82	54,440	49,103	5,336
All	181	54,009	50,814	3,195

Source: Survey data, 2019.

Table 11.16 *Productivity and farm harvest price of paddy in Venmani, by size-class, 2018–19* in rupees per kilogram and tonnes per hectare

Size-class (in hectares)	Yield	Average price
0.1–1	2.7	15.4
1.01–2	3.1	15.6
2.01–4	2.6	16.8
4.01–10	3.6	16.5
10.01–20	4.3	15.4
All	3.4	15.7

Source: Survey data, 2019.

Table 11.17 *Productivity and price of paddy received by cultivators in Venmani, by social group, 2018–19* in rupees per kilogram and tonnes per hectare

Social group	Average price	Yield
Dalit	15.4	3.3
Non-Dalit	16.0	3.5

Source: Survey data, 2019.

Dalit cultivators was 3.3 tonnes per hectare. Non-Dalit cultivators in Venmani earned farm business incomes from paddy cultivation that were four times higher than the incomes from paddy cultivation earned by Dalit cultivators.

Input Use Pattern in Paddy Cultivation among Size-classes and Social Groups of Cultivators in Venmani Village

On average, the paid-out cost for cultivating one hectare of paddy in Venmani village was Rs 50,814 (Appendix Table 11.12). The item-wise cost of cultivation shows that the expenditure on hired human labour, machine labour, seed, and fertilizer constituted 75 per cent of the total cost of cultivation (Appendix Table 11.10). The largest share of expenditure of cost was on human labour (37 per cent), followed by the costs of machinery (20 per cent), fertilizers (13 per cent), and seeds (7 per cent).

The data show clearly that large farmers incurred lower costs of cultivation per hectare than small and marginal farmers. The average paid-out costs of paddy cultivation were estimated to be Rs 39,771 per hectare for large farmers and Rs 52,860 per hectare for marginal farmers. Large cultivators had an advantage largely because of the means of production owned by them and greater access than others to low-interest credit.

Dalit cultivators incurred higher costs of cultivation than non-Dalit cultivators (Appendix Table 11.13). The average cost of cultivation A2 per hectare incurred by a Dalit cultivator in Venmani village was Rs 52,385; the corresponding figure for a non-Dalit cultivator was Rs 49,103. Inequalities in the ownership of the means of production put Dalit cultivators at a disadvantage.

Conclusions

Palakurichi and Venmani villages have similar production conditions and are dependent predominantly on a single crop of long-duration paddy, *samba*. In terms of agricultural production conditions, Venmani is slightly better endowed than Palakurichi with respect to irrigation facilities and soil fertility. This is reflected in the marginally higher yield levels and farm business incomes from paddy cultivation in Venmani.

The major conclusions that emerged from a detailed analysis of costs and returns from crop production among various size-classes and social groups of cultivators were the following.

First, paddy agriculture in the lower Cauvery delta is characterised by low yields, in fact, by yields that are low by the standards of the green revolution years of the 1970s. Yields are unstable, and were strongly affected in the reference year by damage to the Grand Anicut system early in the monsoon paddy season and then by Cyclone Gaja.

Secondly, our data are a clear refutation of any argument for the existence of an inverse relationship between size and returns per hectare in agriculture. Every important parameter of economic improvement – yield, price received, gross value of output, access to credit, and farm business income – was related positively to size of operational holding. Conversely, costs of cultivation per hectare were inversely related to size of operational holding.

Thirdly, in terms of yield, price obtained, and GVO, Scheduled Caste cultivators fare significantly worse than non-Scheduled Caste cultivators in

Palakurichi. The historical dominance of non-Dalit large cultivators over ownership and access to the means of production helps them realise higher farm business incomes.

Appendix

Appendix Table 11.1 *Items included in the cost of cultivation calculation*

Paid-out cost (or Cost A2)
Seed (farm saved and purchased)
Manure (home-produced and purchased)
Chemical fertilizer
Plant protection
Irrigation
Hired labour
Animal labour (own and hired)
Machine (owned and hired)
Rent paid for leased-in land
Marketing expenses
Land revenue
Crop insurance
Interest on working capital
Depreciation on own machinery

Source: FAS (2015) and CSO (2008).

Appendix Table 11.2 *Ownership of diesel pumpsets among cultivators, by size-class of operational holding, Venmani, 2018–19*

Size-class (in hectares)	Number of households	Number of households having pumps	Proportion of households owning diesel pumps
0–1	129	9	7
1.01–2	34	6	18
2.01–4	10	6	60
4.01–10	6	3	50
10.01–20	2	2	100

Appendix Table 11.3 *Ownership of diesel pumpsets among cultivators, by social group, Venmani, 2018–19*

Social group	Number of households	Number of households having pumps	Proportion of households owning diesel pumps
Backward Classes	62	14	23
Most Backward Classes	16	2	13
Other	4	3	75
Scheduled Castes	99	7	7

Appendix Table 11.4 *Test for difference in mean (t-test) of productivity of paddy per hectare, by farmer category, study villages, in 2018–19*

Village	Small farmer	Large farmer	T-value	P-value
Venmani	3.3	3.5	–0.33	0.74
Palakurichi	2.8	3.7	3.86	0*

Notes: *Statistically significant at one per cent level of confidence; small farmer: <=2 hectare of operational holding, large farmer: >2 hectares.

Appendix Table 11.5 *T-test for gross value of output, Cost A2, net income on operational holding, by social group, Palakurichi, 2018–19*

Type	Dalit	Non-Dalit	T-value	P-value
GVO	53,961	62,266	–1.8	0.07
Cost A2	56,399	61,155	–1.76	0.08
Net income	–2,437	3,111	–1.7	0.79

Appendix Table 11.6 *T-test for gross value of output, Cost A2, net income, productivity, and price received of paddy, by social group, Palakurichi, 2018–19*

Type	Dalit	Non-Dalit	T-value	P-value
Productivity (tonnes per hectare)	2.8	3.3	–1.98	0.05
Price (in kg)	16.8	18.2	–4.16	0
GVO in hectares	53,783	63,868	–2.64	0.01
Cost A2 in hectares	55,535	57,989	–0.94	0.35
Net income in hectares	–1,749	5,880	–1.97	0.05

Appendix Table 11.7 *Test for difference in mean (t-test) of productivity of paddy per hectare of households with negative and positive income from crop production on operational holdings, study villages, 2018–19*

Type	Venmani		Palakurichi	
	T-value	P-value	T-value	P-value
Negative farm business income VS Positive farm business income	-7.98	0	−10.67	0*
Negative income from paddy VS Positive income from paddy	-10.29	0	−11.98	0*

Appendix Table 11.8 *T-test for gross value of output, Cost A2, net income on operational holding, by social group, Venmani, 2018–19*

Type	Dalit	Non-Dalit	T-value	P-value
GVO	60,930	65,145	-1.5	0.14
Cost A2	60,650	58,960	0.67	0.51
Net income	280	6,456	-1.86	0.07

Appendix Table 11.9 *T-test for gross value of output, Cost A2, net income, productivity, and price received of paddy, by social group, Venmani, 2018–19*

Type	Dalit	Non-Dalit	T-value	P-value
Productivity (tonnes per hectare)	3.3	3.5	-0.08	0.93
Price (in kg)	15.4	16	-0.9	0.36
GVO in hectares	53,613	54,440	-0.27	0.78
Cost A2 in hectares	52,358	49,103	1.64	0.1
Net income in hectares	1,229	5,336	-1.41	0.16

Appendix Table 11.10 *Average cost of cultivation for paddy, by size-class of operational holdings, by item of cost, Palakurichi, 2018–19* in rupees per hectare

Item of cost	0.1–1.0	1.01–2.0	2.01–4.0	4.01–10.0	10.01–20.0	>20	All
Hired human labour	17,375	16,198	20,861	19,530	17,633	17,165	17,491
Machine labour	11,650	10,393	9,208	8,739	6,435	9,073	10,681
Seed	5,884	5,300	5,055	4,659	4,063	3,328	5,452
Plant protection	3,357	3,250	3,024	3,446	4,984	4,431	3,462
Farmyard manure	334	683	484	255	458	200	398
Fertilizer	7,336	7,071	6,851	5,999	8,643	9,205	7,279
Irrigation	3,605	2,816	3,555	2,686	2,029	2,436	3,250
Interest on working capital	1,417	1,468	1,580	1,367	1,194	1,222	1,409
Rental value of leased-in land	1,163	5,825	6,163	6,946	6,754	0	3,012
Depreciation and maintenance	482	1,040	5,725	3,327	2,073	1,810	1,177
Land revenue	18	17	97	9	36	9	21
Miscellaneous	2,860	2,593	2,403	2,818	2,047	3,046	2,749
Cost A2	55,483	56,655	65,004	59,602	56,350	51,925	56,381

Source: Survey data, 2019.

Appendix Table 11.11 *Average cost of cultivation for paddy, by social group, by item of cost, Palakurichi, 2018–19* in rupees per hectare

Item of cost	Dalit	Non-Dalit	All
Hired human labour	16,765	18,657	17,491
Machine labour	11,540	9,301	10,681
Seed	5,877	4,772	5,452
Plant protection	3,195	3,890	3,462
Farmyard manure	241	649	398
Fertilizer	7,439	7,023	7,279
Irrigation	3,400	3,011	3,250
Interest on working capital	1,453	1,337	1,409
Rental value of leased-in land	1,968	4,686	3,012
Depreciation and maintenance	647	2,028	1,177
Land revenue	15	31	21
Miscellaneous	2,991	2,360	2,749
Cost A2	55,531	57,744	56,381

Appendix Table 11.12 *Average cost of cultivation for paddy, by size-class, by item of cost, Venmani, 2018–19* in rupees per hectare

Item of cost	0.1–1.0	1.01–2.0	2.01–4.0	4.01–10.0	10.01–20.0	All
Hired human labour	20,260	17,517	12,158	16,565	13,040	18,792
Machine labour	10,547	9,973	8,072	8,257	10,894	10,154
Seed	3,419	3,274	3,203	3,034	2,657	3,341
Plant protection	2,996	2,895	2,541	1,714	2,445	2,877
Farmyard manure	1,629	1,097	880	2,923	0	1,484
Fertilizer	6,410	6,527	6,102	6,224	4,375	6,367
Irrigation	463	629	578	641	1,478	534
Interest on working capital	1,314	1,318	933	1,124	1,065	1,275
Rental value of leased-in land	2,887	3,774	3,111	127	0	2,923
Depreciation and maintenance	795	612	1,685	2,291	1,712	900
Miscellaneous	2,140	2,157	1,641	3,521	2,104	2,166
Cost A2	52,860	49,771	40,904	46,422	39,771	50,814

Source: Survey data, 2019.

Appendix Table 11.13 *Average cost of cultivation for paddy, by social group, by item of cost, Venmani, 2018–19* in rupees per hectare

Item of cost	Dalits	Non-Dalits	All
Hired human labour	19,785	17,709	18,792
Machine labour	10,111	10,202	10,154
Seed	3,440	3,234	3,341
Manure	1,039	1,969	1,484
Fertilizer	6,656	6,052	6,367
Plant protection	2,919	2,831	2,877
Irrigation	496	575	534
Rent	3,808	1,960	2,923
Depreciation	644	1,178	900
Land revenue	13	18	16
Interest on working capital	1,305	1,242	1,275
Miscellaneous	2,166	2,134	2,150
Cost A2	52,385	49,103	50,814

Source: Survey data, 2019.

12

Employment and Wages

B. Satheesha and Jayan Jose Thomas

HIGHLIGHTS

Macrostatistics and village-level data show a major structural shift in patterns of employment in rural Tamil Nadu from agricultural to non-agricultural employment, particularly among men. The diversification of employment out of agriculture, however, is lower for persons from the Scheduled Castes and Most Backward Classes than for workers from other castes. A lower proportion of Scheduled Caste and Most Backward Class workers than Backward Class workers had regular jobs. The majority of wage workers came from the Scheduled Castes.

Data on days of employment point to persistent underemployment. On average, a male worker obtained 140 to 150 days of employment a year, of which only one-seventh came from agriculture. A woman worker obtained only 80–90 days of employment a year, of which more than half was employment through the Mahatma Gandhi National Rural Employment Guarantee Scheme (MGNREGS). MGNREGS was an important source of employment in both villages, especially for women.

Wage rates of male casual workers in agriculture and for non-agricultural tasks were higher than the corresponding all-India wage rates. The gender gap in wage rates persisted, with the wage rate for women being one-half the wage rate for men, a difference greater than the corresponding all-India level.

Introduction

This chapter examines key features of the labour market, the nature of employment and wages, in Palakurichi and Venmani. It is based on detailed surveys carried out by a census of households in these villages in 2019 as part of the Project on Agrarian Relations in India (PARI) conducted by the Foundation for Agrarian Studies (FAS). The two villages are located in Nagapattinam district of Tamil Nadu, in the Thanjavur region of the Cauvery delta. A number of scholars have studied agrarian relations in the Thanjavur region, which is described as the "rice bowl" of south India (see Surjit 2008). The study by Surjit (2008), which is based on a survey of a sample of households in Palakurichi and Sathanur, allows us to understand the labour market changes in this region between 2004 and 2019.

The changes in India's labour market, especially during the years after the mid-2000s, have been well documented in the literature. Most of these are studies that used data from household surveys on employment carried out at the national level – mainly the National Sample Surveys (NSS) on employment and unemployment and the Periodic Labour Force Surveys (PLFS). According to the PLFS data for 2017–18, agriculture and allied activities accounted for 44 per cent of India's total workforce and nearly 60 per cent of the country's rural workforce (188 million out of a total estimated rural workforce of 316 million in 2017–18; see NSO 2019). At the same time, there has been a growing shift of the country's workforce away from agriculture and allied activities, markedly so from the mid-2000s onwards (Thomas 2020a).

The above-referred structural transformation has occurred during a period of rapid expansion of the working-age population and increasing enrolment of young persons in educational institutions. Studies have shown that the increase in non-agricultural employment opportunities has been far less than the growth of the *potential* workforce, which is based on the increase in the working-age population and the shift of the workforce away from agriculture (*ibid.*). The resultant crisis in employment has intensified after 2011–12. The shift of the workforce away from agriculture during the period from 2004–05 to 2011–12 was driven more by "pull" than by "push" factors, as this period was characterised by rising rural wages and a large increase in rural construction jobs. However, the period after 2012 witnessed a slowdown in employment diversification in India with a substantial decline in non-farm employment opportunities, particularly for women. Besides, the growth of agricultural incomes and wages also experienced a deceleration after 2012 (*ibid.*; Thomas and Satheesha 2021).

It will be important to see the extent to which the broad labour market transformations described above have occurred at the level of a village. Among Indian States, Tamil Nadu has had a relatively good record with respect to achieving economic growth as well as ensuring that the gains from growth reach the disadvantaged sections of society. Studies have attributed this success mainly to the interventions by the Dravidian political parties and the high level of social expenditures by the State government (Kalaiyarasan and Vijayabaskar 2021). Tamil Nadu has been a leading region in India with respect to agricultural and industrial growth. Also, the structural transformation of the workforce is more advanced compared to the rest of the country. In 2017–18, the proportion of the rural workforce engaged in agriculture and allied activities was 42.5 per cent in Tamil Nadu compared to the national average of 60 per cent. At the same time, the growth of employment opportunities in the State in recent years has not been too high, especially for educated workers.

Previous studies point out that the agrarian structure in the Thanjavur region, even in the initial decades after Independence (1947), had been characterised by a high degree of inequality, with upper caste Hindu landlords at the top of the hierarchy and tenants and agricultural labourers at the bottom (Surjit 2008). Political mobilisation, especially by the Communist parties, provided some degree of empowerment, with tenants receiving a higher share of the crop produce and workers receiving better wages. Given such a context, it is important to see how the various social groups have fared in the labour market of the study villages over time.

Village-level studies are important to address some of the limitations of national-level official statistics in capturing the complexity of India's rural labour markets. One issue much discussed in the literature is the underestimation of women's work by official labour force surveys in India (Swaminathan 2020; Usami, Patra and Kapoor 2018). Another important problem with official labour force surveys is with respect to the identification of rural labour households. NSS surveys relied on the "self-perception" of the respondents to identify rural labour, which could lead to an underestimation of wage employment. Households, especially small landholder households, that obtain a major share of their income from wage employment, could still perceive themselves as "self-employed" and are likely to be excluded from the category of labouring households (Dhar 2012; Rawal 2014).

The second section of this chapter discusses the major features of population and workforce in the study villages. The third section examines the structure of employment, while the fourth section analyses manual employment and wages in Palakurichi and Venmani. The fifth section concludes the chapter by summarising the major findings of the study.

Population and Workforce in the Study Villages

The census comprised 1,448 persons in Palakurichi and 1,614 persons in Venmani. Of the total population, persons who were in the labour force were 897 (524 men and 373 women) in Palakurichi and 943 (561 men and 382 women) in Venmani (see Table 12.1 for the distribution of the population by activity status in Palakurichi and Venmani in 2019).

The structure of the population with respect to activity status was broadly similar in Palakurichi and Venmani. The proportion of workers (persons who were employed) to population was 83–84 per cent (15 years and above) among men in both the villages. The corresponding proportion among women was much lower: only 55.5 per cent in Venmani and 63 per cent in Palakurichi (see Table 12.3).

It will be worthwhile to compare the workforce participation rates (WPR) as observed from the village-level studies conducted by the FAS with the WPRs estimated from the official employment surveys conducted at the national level (NSS or PLFS).[1] According to the PLFS for 2017–18, WPRs among men and women (15 years and above) in rural India were 72 per cent and 23.7 per cent, respectively. The corresponding WPRs in rural Tamil Nadu were the following: 71.6 per cent among men and 36.7 per cent among women (Table 12.3). It may be noted here that as a proportion of the total population, the population in the age group of 15 to 59 years was 66 per cent in Tamil Nadu and 60.3 per cent in India in 2011 (Thomas 2021).

At the same time, it is important to note that the WPRs observed from the PARI surveys in Palakurichi and Venmani were at least 12 percentage points higher, for both women and men, than the WPRs for rural Tamil Nadu according to the PLFS data. One possible reason for the higher level of WPR as per the PARI survey is the nature of the survey itself. The proportions (in total population) of students, persons who are too young, and persons who are very old in the census from the study villages are considerably lower than the corresponding proportions for India as a whole or for rural Tamil Nadu as estimated from the PLFS survey.[2] This can happen on account of the specific

[1] WPR for Palakurichi and Venmani are based on the main occupation of persons. WPR for Tamil Nadu and India are based on the usual principal and usual subsidiary status (UPSS) of workers.

[2] According to PLFS for 2017–18, for India as a whole, the proportions in total population of students, population in the age group of 0 to 4 years, and population aged 65 years and above were as follows: 26.7 per cent, 8.5 per cent, and 6 per cent, respectively. The combined share of these three population categories (which, by their nature, cannot contribute to the economy) was 41.2 per cent. At the same time, students, those who are too young to work, and those who are too old comprised 20.6 per cent, 4.7 per cent, and 1.3 per cent respectively in Palakurichi. The combined share of these three population-categories was 26.6 per cent and 28.9 per cent in Palakurichi and Venmani, respectively.

characteristics of the study villages or due to the differences (between PARI and PLFS) in the sampling methodologies, or both.

Previous studies have shown that, in India, official employment surveys underestimate the economic contribution of women. The definition of economic activity, according to the official statistical agencies, is rather narrow and it excludes various types of women's work, which are largely home-based (Swaminathan 2020; Usami, Patra and Kapoor 2018; Mazumdar and Neetha 2011). According to the time-use survey of 2019, the WPR of rural women aged 15 years above in Tamil Nadu was 53.6 per cent, which was strikingly higher than the corresponding WPR reported in the official employment (PLFS) surveys (Vijayamba 2022).

Other factors attributed to the low and falling rate of female workforce participation in India are: increased participation of women in education, the gradual withdrawal of women from agriculture, especially with mechanisation, the absence of sufficient employment opportunities for women, unsafe working environment, and lack of fall-back options for women within the workforce (Abraham, Basole and Kesar 2021; Azim Premji University 2021; Seema 2021; Thomas 2020b; Abraham 2013; Thomas 2012). Given the above context, it appears that the village-level survey conducted by FAS has managed to capture the scenario of women's work better.

MGNREGS was an important source of non-farm employment for females in Palakurichi and Venmani (this aspect will be discussed in detail in a later section). Pointing to the high level of participation of women in MGNREGS work in different parts of India, Swaminathan (2020) notes that women do enter the labour market if suitable employment opportunities are available for them.

Students accounted for 19–21 per cent of the male population and 23–25 per cent of the female population in Palakurichi and Venmani (see Table 12.1). It is remarkable that students as a proportion of the population are higher for women than for men in these villages. In comparison, as per PLFS data for 2017–18, students as a proportion of the population in India as a whole were 28.5 per cent among men and 24.6 per cent among women. About 19–22 per cent of women in the study villages reported their activity status as attending domestic work. At the same time, as per the PLFS data, 44.4 per cent of all women in India (rural and urban combined) were attending to domestic duties (and, therefore, they were not in the labour force).

As per this study, migrants are persons who belong to a household but whose sphere of activity (say, as a worker, as a student, and so on) for a major part of the year falls outside the village. Migrants comprised 8–10 per cent of the total population in the two study villages (Palakurichi and Venmani). At the

Table 12.1 *Distribution of population aged 15 and above by activity status, Palakurichi and Venmani, 2019* in number and per cent

	Palakurichi				Venmani			
	Male		Female		Male		Female	
	Number	%	Number	%	Number	%	Number	%
1. *Workers*	509	69.9	370	51.4	542	69.6	377	45.1
2. *Unemployed*	15	2.1	3	0.4	19	2.4	5	0.6
3. In labour force (1+2)	524	72.0	373	51.8	561	72.0	382	45.7
4. Not in labour force	204	28.0	347	48.2	219	28.1	454	54.4
4.1 Students	136	18.7	163	22.6	162	20.8	207	24.8
4.2 Attending domestic work	1	0.1	136	18.9	2	0.3	180	21.5
4.3 Elderly, not working	10	1.4	9	1.3	11	1.4	14	1.7
4.4 Children, not working	41	5.6	27	3.8	31	4.0	44	5.3
4.5 Other	16	2.2	12	1.7	13	1.5	8	1.0
All persons	728	100	720	100	779	100	835	100

Source: FAS survey data, 2019.

Table 12.2 *Indicators of the extent of migration from Palakurichi and Venmani*

	Palakurichi	Venmani
Number of households	390	415
Total population	1,448	1,614
Number of migrants	121	155
Number of households receiving remittances	92	115
Migrants as percentage of population	8.4	9.6
Remittance-receiving households as percentage of all households	23.6	27.6

Source: FAS survey data, 2019.

Table 12.3 *Workforce participation rates (WPR) for males and females in Palakurichi, Venmani (2019), and rural areas of Tamil Nadu and India (2017–18)* in per cent

	All ages		15 years and above		
	Male	Female	Male	Female	Person
Palakurichi	69.9	51.4	84.2	63.0	73.8
Venmani	69.5	45.1	83.1	55.5	69.1
Tamil Nadu	55.9	29.4	71.6	36.7	53.7
India	51.7	17.5	72.0	23.7	48.1

Source: FAS survey data, 2019 and PLFS, 2019.

same time, the proportion of households which received remittance incomes was 23.6 per cent in Palakurichi and 27.6 per cent in Venmani. These figures suggest that there are a number of persons who have permanently migrated out of the study villages but who nevertheless maintain close familial or social ties with the village (see Table 12.2).

Employment Structure

Agriculture and allied activities continue to be important sources of employment in Venmani and Palakurichi, with combined shares of close to 40 per cent among male workers and 50 per cent or more among female workers (Figure 12.1). At the same time, it is clear that there has been some degree of diversification of the employment structure towards non-farm activities. The study by Guhan (1983) in Palakurichi shows that the ratio of agricultural workforce to total workforce was 80 per cent in 1983. In 2004, according to a study conducted by Surjit (2008), the ratio declined only marginally, to 78 per cent (see Surjit 2008, p. 142).

It is notable that the proportions of workers in agriculture and allied activities in the study villages are broadly in line with the figures we obtain for rural Tamil Nadu from the PLFS survey. The proportion of workers engaged in agriculture and allied activities was 38 per cent among men and 51 per cent among women in rural Tamil Nadu, according to the PLFS survey for 2017–18. The corresponding figures for rural India were 55 per cent and 73 per cent, respectively.

The diversification of the employment structure has been slower among the socially disadvantaged groups than others. Agriculture employed 55 per cent or more of the total workforce in the case of Scheduled Castes in Palakurichi and Most Backward Classes in Venmani. The Backward Classes were more successful in diversifying their income sources to non-farm sectors. The diversification of income sources among the Most Backward Classes has been greater in Palakurichi than in Venmani (see Figures 12.1 and 12.2).

Workers who have regular jobs are proportionately less among the Scheduled Castes and Most Backward Classes than others. The proportion of workers with regular jobs was in the range of 25–26 per cent among Backward Classes in both study villages. The corresponding proportion was 6 per cent among Scheduled Caste workers in Palakurichi and 11 per cent among Most Backward Class workers in Venmani. It is possible that the survey does not adequately capture the levels of occupational mobility achieved by some of the socially privileged groups not resident in the village any longer. Surjit (2008) found that many persons belonging to the Naidu caste, who were traditional

Figure 12.1 *Proportion of workforce employed in agriculture, males and females, in Palakurichi, Venmani (2019), and rural areas of Tamil Nadu and India (2017–18)* in per cent

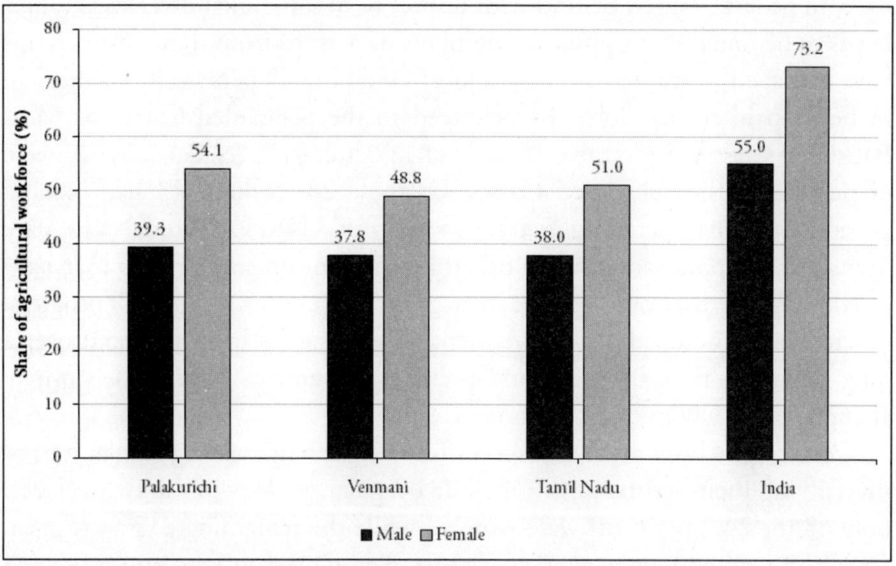

Source: FAS survey data, 2019 and PLFS, 2019.

Figure 12.2 *Proportion of workforce employed in agriculture by social group, Palakurichi and Venmani, 2019* in per cent

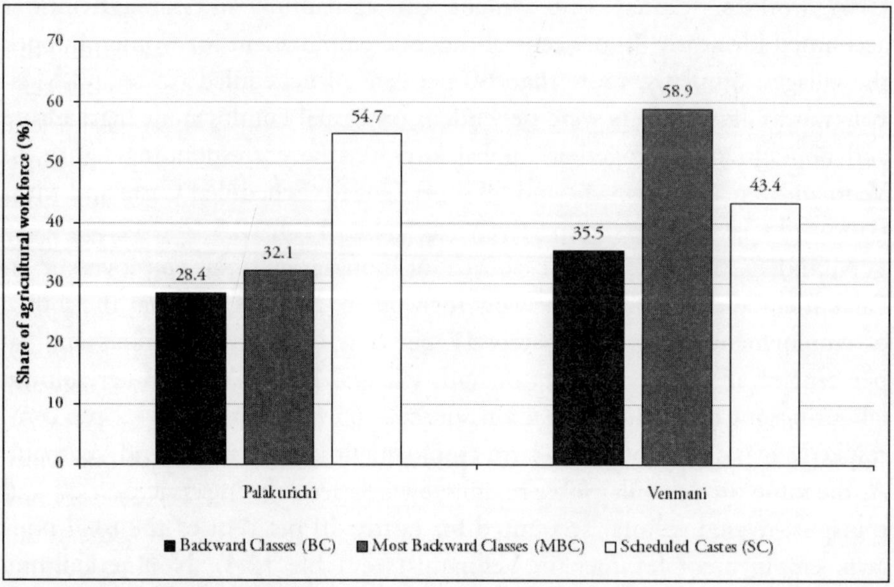

Source: FAS survey data, 2019.

landowners in this region, had permanently migrated out of the village and settled in cities.

While workers from the Scheduled Castes and Most Backward Classes have, in general, lagged behind with respect to occupational diversification, it needs to be noted that significant numbers of persons from these caste groups have managed to secure better-paid jobs. Of all the 30 persons in Palakurichi in better-paid regular jobs, 18 belonged to the Scheduled Castes or Most Backward Classes. In Venmani, of all 41 in better-paid regular jobs, 20 were of persons of the Scheduled Castes. Of these 20 workers, 13 had secured government jobs, including as teachers, staff of TNSTC (Tamil Nadu State Transport Corporation), and in other government offices. Groups that have faced historical disadvantage have managed to achieve some degree of progress. As chapter 14 notes, the empowerment and aspiration brought about over a long period of time by social and political movements have made positive changes, especially in case of Venmani.

Women have been much less successful than men in securing regular jobs or diversifying their occupations. Of all 281 regular workers in the two villages, only 68 (or 24.2 per cent) were women, while the remaining 213 were men. Of all 68 women regular workers, 52 were employed in low-paid jobs such as ICDS (Integrated Child Development Services) workers and teachers in private schools.

The major type of employment in Palakurichi and Venmani was casual employment, especially for women, Scheduled Caste, and Most Backward Class workers. Casual employment (in agriculture or non-agriculture) accounted for nearly 70 per cent of the total employment for women in both the villages. Similarly, more than 60 per cent of Scheduled Caste and Most Backward Class workers were dependent on casual employment (agriculture and non-agriculture together) in Palakurichi. The corresponding figures in Venmani were 60.9 per cent and 53.4 per cent for Scheduled Caste and Most Backward Class workers, respectively (see Tables 12.4, 12.5, and 12.6).

MGNREGS was a major source of non-agricultural employment in Palakurichi and Venmani, especially for women. MGNREGS was the source of employment for approximately 17 per cent of all male workers and 30 per cent of all female workers in both villages. For males, non-agricultural labouring out constitutes the main source – 65 per cent and 44.2 per cent, respectively – of the total non-farm employment in Palakurichi and Venmani. At the same time, regular jobs, mainly low-salaried jobs in services, sales, and transport-related sectors, accounted for nearly 40 per cent of the total non-farm employment for men in Venmani (see Table 12.4). Non-agricultural labouring out, including MGNREGS, was a particularly important source of

Table 12.4 *Distribution of workers by sector and nature of employment, Palakurichi and Venmani, 2019* in numbers and per cent

	Palakurichi				Venmani			
	Male		Female		Male		Female	
	Number	%	Number	%	Number	%	Number	%
1. Agriculture and allied	200	39.3	200	54.1	205	37.8	184	48.8
1.1 Self-employed	128	25.1	75	20.3	120	22.1	64	17.0
1.2 Casual labour	72	14.1	125	33.8	85	15.7	120	31.8
2. Non-agriculture	309	60.7	170	45.9	337	62.2	193	51.2
2.1 Regular wage/salaried persons	78	15.3	24	6.5	135	24.9	44	11.7
High salaried	22	4.3	8	2.2	33	6.1	8	2.1
Low salaried	56	11.0	16	4.3	102	18.8	36	9.5
2.2 Self-employed in non-agriculture	29	5.7	11	3.0	53	9.8	14	3.7
Business	5	1.0	0	0.0	7	1.3	3	0.8
Shop keepers	12	2.4	6	1.6	16	3.0	5	1.3
Other self-employed activity	12	2.4	5	1.4	30	5.5	6	1.6
2.3 Non-agricultural labouring out	202	39.7	135	36.5	149	27.5	135	35.8
Manufacturing-related	12	2.4	14	3.8	12	2.2	13	3.4
Building/metal, machinery-related trades*	66	13.0	3	0.8	49	9.0	0	0.0
Transport, service and sales workers	51	10.0	3	0.8	29	5.4	3	0.8
Construction	29	5.7	2	0.5	8	1.5	1	0.3
MGNREGS	38	7.5	111	30.0	41	7.6	117	31.0
Helpers (loading, cleaning, etc.)	6	1.2	2	0.5	10	1.8	1	0.3
All workers	509	100.0	370	100.0	542	100.0	377	100.0

Note: *Workers in building/metal, machinery-related trades include electricians, masons, plumbers, welders, carpenters, etc.
Source: FAS survey data, 2019.

Table 12.5 *Distribution of workers by social group and by sectors and nature of employment, Palakurichi, 2019* in numbers and per cent

	Backward Classes		Most Backward Classes		Scheduled Castes		All workers	
	Number	%	Number	%	Number	%	Number	%
1. Agriculture and allied	38	28.4	54	32.1	306	54.7	400	45.5
1.1 Self-employed	27	20.1	22	13.1	153	27.4	203	23.1
1.2 Casual labour	11	8.2	32	19.0	153	27.4	197	22.4
2. Non-agriculture	96	71.6	114	67.9	253	45.3	479	54.5
2.1 Regular wage/salaried persons	34	25.4	26	15.5	35	6.3	102	11.6
High salaried	12	9.0	11	6.5	7	1.3	30	3.4
Low salaried	22	16.4	15	8.9	28	5.0	72	8.2
2.2 Self-employed in non-agriculture	20	14.9	15	8.9	3	0.5	40	4.6
Business	2	1.5	2	1.2	1	0.2	6	0.7
Shop keepers	8	6.0	8	4.8	1	0.2	18	2.0
Other self-employed activity	10	7.5	5	3.0	1	0.2	16	1.8
2.3 Non-agricultural labouring out	42	31.3	73	43.5	215	38.5	337	38.3
Manufacturing-related	1	0.7	2	1.2	23	4.1	26	3.0
Building/metal, machinery-related trades*	7	5.2	21	12.5	39	7.0	69	7.8
Transport, service and sales workers	7	5.2	8	4.8	38	6.8	54	6.1
Construction	3	2.2	6	3.6	22	3.9	31	3.5
MGNREGS	24	17.9	35	20.8	86	15.4	149	17.0
Helpers (loading, cleaning, etc.)		0.0	1	0.6	7	1.3	8	0.9
All workers	134	100.0	168	100.0	559	100.0	879	100.0

Note: *Workers in building/metal, machinery-related trades include electricians, masons, plumbers, welders, carpenters, etc.
Source: FAS survey data, 2019.

Table 12.6 *Distribution of workers by social group and by sector and nature of employment, Venmani, 2019*, in numbers and as per cent

	Backward Classes		Most Backward Classes		Scheduled Castes		All workers	
	Number	%	Number	%	Number	%	Number	%
1. Agriculture and allied	82	35.5	43	58.9	260	43.4	389	42.3
1.1 Self-employed	62	26.8	24	32.9	94	15.7	184	20.0
1.2 Casual labour	20	8.7	19	26.0	166	27.7	205	22.3
2. Non-agriculture	149	64.5	30	41.1	339	56.6	530	57.7
2.1 Regular wage/salaried persons	60	26.0	8	11.0	107	17.9	179	19.5
High salaried	20	8.7	1	1.4	20	3.3	41	4.5
Low salaried	40	17.3	7	9.6	87	14.5	138	15.0
2.2 Self-employed in non-agriculture	25	10.8	2	2.7	33	5.5	67	7.3
Business	5	2.2		0.0	2	0.3	10	1.1
Shop keepers	7	3.0	2	2.7	9	1.5	21	2.3
Other self-employed activities	13	5.6		0.0	22	3.7	36	3.9
2.3 Non-agricultural labouring out	64	27.7	20	27.4	199	33.2	284	30.9
Manufacturing related	1	0.4		0.0	24	4.0	25	2.7
Building/metal, machinery-related trades*	12	5.2	2	2.7	35	5.8	49	5.3
Transport, service and sales workers	8	3.5	4	5.5	19	3.2	32	3.5
Construction	1	0.4		0.0	8	1.3	9	1.0
MGNREGS	41	17.7	13	17.8	104	17.4	158	17.2
Helpers (loading, cleaning, etc.)	1	0.4	1	1.4	9	1.5	11	1.2
All workers	231	100.0	73	100.0	599	100.0	919	100.0

Note: *Workers in building/metal, machinery-related trades include electricians, masons, plumbers, welders, carpenters, etc.
Source: FAS survey data, 2019.

Table 12.7 *Distribution of non-farm employment by location* in per cent

	Including MGNREGS		Excluding MGNREGS	
	Palakurichi	Venmani	Palakurichi	Venmani
Within village	48.5	43.2	26.1	19.4
Within district	28.3	25.7	40.3	36.3
Other districts	18.2	27.7	26.4	39.5
Outside State	2.1	1.7	3.0	2.4
Outside India	1.9	1.7	1.5	2.4

Source: FAS survey data, 2019.

employment for Scheduled Caste and Most Backward Class workers (Tables 12.5 and 12.6).

Nearby towns and cities within the district were the locations for 37 to 40 per cent of the total non-farm employment (without including MGNREGS) in Venmani and Palakurichi (Table 12.7). Tamil Nadu has a significant number of urban locations, including small towns and cities, which have high levels of connectivity, and they have played an important role in employment diversification towards the non-farm sector (Harriss and Jeyaranjan 2016).

Pluriactivity

Another important feature of the labour market in the study villages is the large share of "pluriactive" workers – workers who engage in multiple activities over a particular time period to secure their livelihoods. Various village studies show that multiple occupations of workers is a dominant feature of present-day Indian countryside (Yadu and Satheesha 2016). Based on their panel study of six villages in central Tamil Nadu, Lindberg *et al.* (2014) note that,

Table 12.8 *Average number of occupations per worker by primary occupation*

	Palakurichi	Venmani
Self-employed in agriculture	2.9	2.8
Casual labour in agriculture	2.8	2.8
Self-employed in non-agriculture	2.0	1.8
Regular salaried	1.3	1.2
Casual labour in non-agriculture	1.7	1.8
Total	2.2	2.1

Source: FAS survey data, 2019.

Table 12.9 *Number of workers reporting various secondary sources of occupation: by their primary occupation, Palakurichi*

Primary occupation	Workers with secondary occupation (in numbers)								All workers in primary occupation	Workers with secondary occupation as % of all workers in a primary occupation
	Cultivation	Animal husbandry	Agricultural labour	SE in non-agriculture	MGNREGS	Non-agricultural labour	Regular salaried	All		
Cultivation	0	9	76	10	63	13	4	175	196	89.3
Animal husbandry	1	0	0	0	1	1	0	3	7	42.9
Agricultural labour	18	4	0	1	138	23	0	185	197	93.9
Self-employed (SE) in non-agriculture	11	1	3	1	10	0	0	26	40	65.0
MGNREGS	4	20	30	3	0	3	0	60	149	40.3
Non-agricultural labour	17	2	15	1	32	10	0	77	188	41.0
Regular salaried	12	0	1	2	10	0	0	25	102	24.5
All	63	36	125	18	254	50	4	551	879	62.7

Source: FAS survey data, 2019.

Table 12.10 *Number of workers reporting various secondary sources of occupation: by their primary occupation, Venmani*

Primary occupation	Workers with secondary occupation (in numbers)								All workers in primary occupation	Workers with secondary occupation as % of all workers in a primary occupation
	Cultivation	Animal husbandry	Agricultural labour	SE in non-agriculture	MGNREGS	Non-agricultural labour	Regular salaried	All		
Cultivation	0	5	45	7	73	11	7	148	174	85.1
Animal husbandry	0	0	0	0	6	0	0	6	10	60.0
Agricultural labour	9	2	0	5	137	30	0	183	205	89.3
Self-employed (SE) in non-agriculture	4	3	4	5	13	5	0	34	67	51.0
MGNREGS	12	11	31	3	0	5	0	62	158	39.2
Non-agricultural labour	15	1	7	0	14	6	0	43	126	34.1
Regular salaried	15	0	2	1	8	1	0	27	179	15.1
All	55	22	89	21	252	58	7	503	919	54.7

Source: FAS survey data, 2019.

> about half of all households now live by working solely in agriculture (as workers and farmers), while the rest are "pluriactive": combining farm work with various forms of non-farm work and tiny businesses. (*Ibid*., pp.351)

According to Lindberg *et al.* (2014), the non-farm (often urban) linkage has become almost as important as farming for the livelihoods and social life of agrarian population in the villages.

Our study shows that an agricultural worker in the study villages took part on an average in three different activities during the year prior to the survey to earn her livelihood. At the same time, an average non-agricultural worker was engaged in two or fewer activities during the reference year 2018–19 (see Table 12.8). More than 85 per cent of all agricultural workers in Palakurichi and Venmani reported that they were pluriactive (see Tables 12.9 and 12.10). At the time of the survey, crop cultivation occurred only in one season in both the villages, and the number of employment days generated in agriculture was strikingly low during 2018–19 (see Table 12.12). Moreover, the decline in water availability from canals and Cyclone Gaja that occurred in the survey year adversely affected incomes from crop production in Palakurichi and Venmani (see chapter 11 in this volume). Therefore, workers were compelled to adopt more than one activity to secure their livelihoods.

The proportion of pluriactive workers was higher among females than males in both the villages. In 2018–19, in Palakurichi and Venmani, 70–78 per cent of all female workers were pluriactive, while the corresponding proportion for male workers was 53–61 per cent.

In both villages, the major source of secondary employment was MGNREGS, especially so for those reporting agricultural work as their primary occupation. In Palakurichi, there were 185 agricultural labourers who were pluriactive, and 138 of them reported MGNREGS as their secondary activity (Table 12.9). In Palakurichi and Venmani, MGNREGS accounted for 46 (254 out of 551) and 50 per cent (252 out of 503), respectively, of all reported secondary activities. Agricultural labour was the second biggest secondary activity followed by non-agricultural labouring out, which included employment as masons, construction workers, and other manual workers mostly outside the village (particularly for men).

Manual Employment and Wages

Households whose major source of income is wage work – including work that is unskilled, semi-skilled, skilled, or work that is part of the formal-sector – are classified as wage worker households (see chapter 4 in this volume). In

Palakurichi and Venmani, wage worker households comprised more than 35 per cent of all households (Figure 12.3). In both the villages, Scheduled Caste households were the largest constituent – accounting for more than 60 per cent – of all wage worker households (Table 12.11).

Table 12.12 clearly indicates the persistence of underemployment among workers belonging to manual worker households in Palakurichi and Venmani. The severity of underemployment was greater among female wage workers than among male wage workers. Male wage workers received an average of 144 and 147 employment days, respectively, in Palakurichi and Venmani

Figure 12.3 *Proportion of wage worker households (as % of all households)*

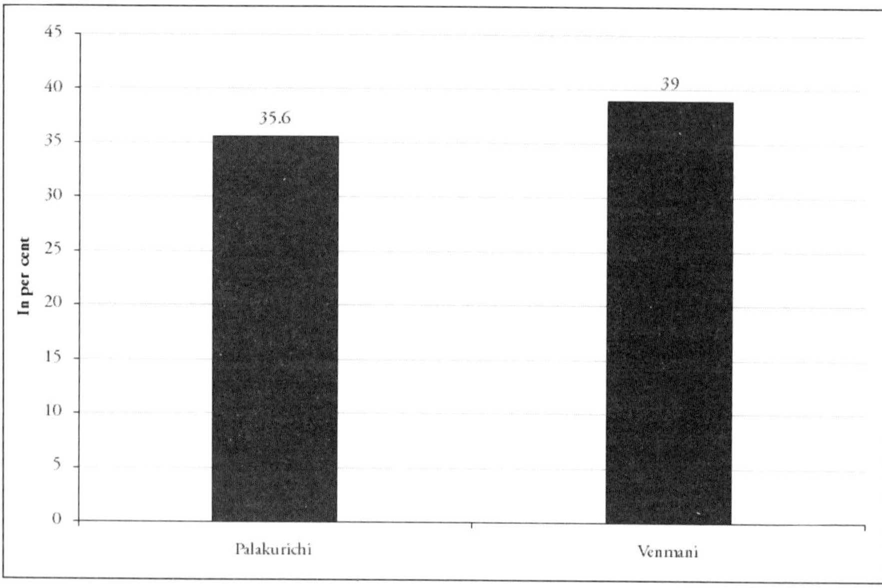

Source: FAS survey data, 2019.

Table 12.11 *Caste composition of wage worker households (as % of all households)*

	Palakurichi	Venmani
Scheduled Castes	60.3	63.4
Backward Classes	16.7	26.3
Most Backward Classes	20.8	8.2
Other	2.1	1.7
All	100	100

Source: FAS survey data, 2019.

during the reference year. On the other hand, female wage workers secured less than 100 working days. Compared to Venmani, underemployment is more severe among female wage workers in Palakurichi. The major source of wage employment for women was MGNREGS, which accounted for more than 50 per cent of the total days of employment. For males, non-agricultural wage employment accounted for nearly half of the total reported days of employment. In the study villages, for both male and female manual workers, the non-agricultural sector (including MGNREGS) provided a higher number of employment days than the agricultural sector.

Another important feature of the labour market in Palakurichi and Venmani was the relatively high level of wages of casual workers in both the agricultural and non-agricultural sectors. The average daily wage rate of a casual male worker in agriculture was Rs 496 in Palakurichi and Rs 450 in Venmani. The corresponding figure for females was Rs 220–223 in both the villages. At the same time, the daily wage in construction was Rs 605 for men and Rs 278 for women in Palakurichi. The wage rate for brick kiln male workers was strikingly lower than the wage rate for agricultural labour in both the villages (see Table 12.13).

In 2019, the officially approved minimum wage for a construction worker

Table 12.12 *Average days of employment for wage (skilled+unskilled) workers*

	Palakurichi		Venmani	
	Female	Male	Female	Male
Agriculture	23	16	23	17
MGNREGS	45	18	49	22
Non-agricultural casual labour	5	79	10	73
All work	79	144	92	147

Source: FAS survey data, 2019.

Table 12.13 *Average daily wages for wage workers by type of work*

	Palakurichi		Venmani	
	Female	Male	Female	Male
Agriculture	223	496	220	450
MGNREGS	174	176	147	149
Brick kiln workers	253	369	–	376
Construction workers	278	605	253	468

Source: FAS survey data, 2019.

was Rs 337 per day in Tamil Nadu (GoTN 2019). It needs to be noted that the wages per day received by male casual workers in agriculture and construction in the study villages were higher than the minimum wage level, but this was not true in the case of female casual workers.

PLFS data shows that the wage rates of male rural casual workers in agriculture and non-agriculture in Tamil Nadu were significantly higher than the respective national averages. In 2017–18, the nominal daily wage rate of male casual workers engaged in agriculture and related activities was Rs 308 in rural Tamil Nadu while the corresponding national average was Rs 229. Similarly, the wage rate for a male construction worker was Rs 400 in rural Tamil Nadu against Rs 289 at the national level. At the same time, female casual workers in rural Tamil Nadu received wages that were more or less similar to the corresponding national averages, especially so in the agriculture sector (See Figure 12.4).

Studies show that the growth of non-farm employment and the expansion of social welfare policies, in particular PDS and MGNREGS, resulted in labour shortages and a tightening of rural labour markets in Tamil Nadu, that pushed up real wages (Heyer 2013; Carswell and Neve 2014; Harris and Jeyaranjan 2016).

The wage gap between male and female wage workers is, however, high in the study villages. In both the villages, the daily wage earning of a female worker in agriculture was only 45–50 per cent of the wage rate of a male

Figure 12.4 *Average daily wages for rural casual labour in agriculture and construction, Tamil Nadu and India (2017–18)* in rupees

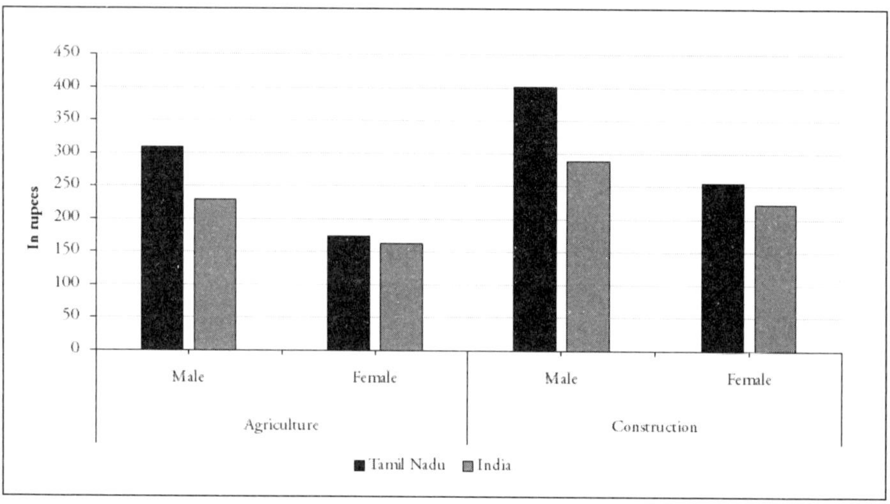

Source: PLFS, 2019.

Table 12.14 *Ratio of female to male wages for workers in agriculture and non-agricultural sectors*

	Palakurichi	Venmani
Agriculture	45.0	48.9
MGNREGS	98.9	98.7
Brick kiln workers	68.6	–
Construction workers	46.0	54.1

Source: FAS survey data, 2019.

worker in agriculture (see Table 12.14). NSS and PLFS data also show that the gap between the wages of female and male casual workers was relatively high in Tamil Nadu (Thomas and Satheesha 2019).

Summary of Major Findings

This chapter examined employment and wages in Palakurichi and Venmani, villages located in Nagapattinam district of Tamil Nadu.

First, the study villages were characterised by relatively high workforce participation rates (WPR), especially for females and especially in comparison with the WPR figures for rural Tamil Nadu and rural India as obtained from official labour force surveys. The reasons for the higher levels of WPR include a better reporting of women's work by the PARI village-level studies, availability of MGNREGS work, and possible differences in methodology (between PARI and official national-level surveys).

Secondly, agriculture and related activities employed close to 40 per cent of all male workers and 50 per cent or more of all female workers in Palakurichi and Venmani. The diversification of the employment structure has been slower among socially disadvantaged groups. The share of agricultural and casual employment in total employment was relatively high among Scheduled Caste and Most Backward Class workers. At the same time, persons from the Backward Classes have been more successful in securing regular jobs and in diversifying their income sources, in both villages. Chapter 14 notes that an important factor that has influenced the changing occupational structure in the study villages is the rapid expansion of education, especially higher education, over the last few decades. MGNREGS employment was a major source of non-farm employment for women as well as for persons from Scheduled Caste and Most Backward Class households. Nearby towns and cities within the district accounted for a large share of non-farm employment (excluding MGNREGS).

Thirdly, migrants comprised 8–10 per cent of the total population in the two study villages. It appears that the extent of permanent migration from the villages is much higher, given that approximately one-fourth of all households received remittance incomes.

Fourthly, the proportion of pluriactive workers in the workforce was high in Palakurichi and Venmani, indicating that incomes from agriculture were not sufficient to meet the livelihood needs of the workers' households. In these two study villages, the average days of employment for a wage worker in agriculture, for men as well as women, was less than 20 days during the reference year. The decline in water availability and the frequent occurrence of natural calamities have adversely affected incomes from cultivation, and necessitated the diversification of household income sources into non-farm sectors (see chapter 13 in this volume). This clearly points towards the deepening crisis in agriculture in the study villages and the low labour-absorptive capacity of that sector.

Finally, the wage rates of casual workers (both in agriculture and non-agriculture) in the two study villages were higher than the averages reported for rural Tamil Nadu and rural India.

13

Household Incomes

Tapas Singh Modak and Madhura Swaminathan

HIGHLIGHTS

Using FAS survey data for 2018–19, annual per capita income (excluding the value of subsidies paid in kind) was estimated to be around Rs 45,000 in Venmani and Palakurichi villages. The distribution of income was highly unequal, and 25 per cent of households in both villages received incomes below the two-dollars-a-day poverty line. One-half of all households earned incomes inadequate to buy a healthy diet (as defined by the FAO).

The large majority of households (over 90 per cent) reported some income from the agricultural sector, but in aggregate, the agricultural sector accounted for less than 20 per cent of household incomes. The bulk of incomes were generated in the secondary and tertiary sectors, and a large part of that income was generated in urban and semi-urban locations. This finding is consistent with our findings on the pattern of employment.

The size of income from non-agricultural sources and the extent of income diversification out of agriculture varied across socio-economic classes. Landlords were at the top of the income hierarchy and incomes from businesses such as rice mills accounted for a major share of household incomes. For wage workers and poor peasants who were at the bottom of the income distribution, incomes from non-agricultural labour played a vital role in annual earnings. On account of crop losses in the reference year, the share of income from farming was low for all sections of the peasantry.

There were statistically significant differences in the incomes of Scheduled Caste households and Backward Class households. Backward Class and Other caste households were concentrated in the upper-income quintiles, and Scheduled Caste households were concentrated in the lower-income quintiles of income distribution.

Introduction

In many parts of India, the village economy can no longer be characterised as mainly agricultural. Indeed, for a majority of households in rural India, income from agricultural activities is neither the main nor the sole source of income. This holds true for the two villages surveyed in southern Tamil Nadu, Palakurichi and Venmani.

According to the Situation Assessment Survey (SAS) of Agricultural Households, 2019, the share of agricultural households in rural India was 54 per cent.[1] It is a striking feature of the data that agricultural households received more income from wages and salaries than from crop production. In 2018–19, 40 per cent of the household income of an agricultural household, on average, was from wage earnings and salaries, and 37 per cent came from crop production (NSO 2021). In the case of rural Tamil Nadu, only 26 per cent of rural households were classified as agricultural households, and, on average, 55 per cent of their income came from wages and salaries.

Contemporary evidence from village surveys in different parts of the country collected by the Project on Agrarian Relations in India (PARI) shows substantial diversification of the incomes of rural households (Bakshi 2017; Modak and Swaminathan 2019; Bakshi and Modak 2021 – among others). We define incomes from the primary sector as incomes arising out of agriculture and allied activities, including incomes from crop cultivation, rental incomes from leasing out agricultural land, incomes from animal husbandry, fisheries, sericulture and other allied activities, and incomes from casual and long-term wage employment in agriculture.

The importance of the primary sector (used interchangeably with agricultural sector in this chapter) in total income generation, of course, varies across agro-economic regions (Appendix Tables 13.1 and 13.2). In the PARI studies, the share of income from the primary sector in the total income of village households ranged from 13 per cent in Venmani (Nagapattinam district, Tamil Nadu) to 81 per cent in Harevli (Bijnor district, Uttar Pradesh). At the same time, in terms of employment or work participation, a very large number of households participated in primary sector activity. To put it differently, while almost all households participate in primary sector work, the share of income from this sector varies. The share of income from the primary sector was generally high in irrigated villages in the PARI database. In villages with

[1] Agricultural households are defined as an "agricultural production unit" that produce field crops, horticultural crops, livestock, and the products of any of the other specified agricultural activities, with or without the possession and operation of any land, and which received a value of agricultural produce more than Rs 4,000 from agricultural activities during the last 365 days.

little or no irrigation, such as Zhapur in Kalaburagi district of Karnataka, the share of income from the primary sector was generally lower.

For the vast majority of households resident in Venmani and Palakurichi villages, non-agricultural incomes, or incomes from the secondary and tertiary sectors, now constitute the main source of aggregate household income. This is not surprising, particularly given the fact that the secondary and tertiary sectors constituted about 96 per cent of net state value added of Tamil Nadu in 2018–19 (NSO 2020). A large proportion of the workforce in rural Tamil Nadu (57 per cent in 2018–19) is employed in non-agricultural employment (including the manufacturing, construction, and service sectors) (NSO 2020).

Diversification in the sources of household income occurred across all socio-economic classes, but was most marked among manual worker households. Further, a substantial part of non-agricultural incomes accruing to households resident in the village was earned outside the village, reflecting close links between the village and the urban economy. These data on the sources of income at the household level are consistent with observations on the sectoral composition of employment (chapter 12 in this volume).

It is a striking fact that the diversification of incomes has not eliminated income-poverty. And there remain stark inequalities across castes, classes, and gender in respect of level of non-agricultural income.

Data and Method

Although household income is, for obvious reasons, a key indicator of living standards, it is not widely discussed in the Indian literature because of the absence of regular official statistics on household income. In the last few decades, data on household incomes have been collected by the Situation Assessment Surveys (SAS) of the National Statistical Office (NSO), but these pertain to only farming or agricultural households (and not all households) in the countryside.

The measurement of income in the rural economy is a complex process, as income flows are variable over the year, and most of the workers are engaged in the informal sector or in self-employment (Bakshi 2017). The Foundation for Agrarian Studies (FAS) has developed a detailed methodology for the calculation of incomes, beginning with the collection of disaggregated data on all sources of income (FAS 2015). Specifically, the questionnaire used in the FAS–PARI village surveys collects data separately for twelve sources of income from each household (Appendix). The estimates of income in the village surveys include all cash incomes and incomes in kind other than from borrowing and from the sale of assets (including cash transfers). All incomes are net of costs incurred by the households in the process of production or income generation.

Estimates of household income for the two villages of Tamil Nadu pertain to the agricultural year 2018–19, and are reported at current prices. An important caveat is that the reference year was not a "normal year" for crop production. As discussed in chapters 11 and 16 in this volume, there was a shortage of water in the early part of the kharif season, compounded by devastation from Cyclone Gaja in the latter part of the season. These events affected crop yields, costs of production, and incomes from cultivation for all households with operational holdings. In short, for cultivator households, the reference year was not a normal year; we have adjusted yields and incomes to assess crop incomes in a normal year. The incomes of wage worker households were, of course, less affected by these events, and therefore were more likely to reflect long-term incomes. We cannot gauge long-term changes in household incomes as no data on household incomes are available in any of the earlier studies of Palakurichi.

Annual Incomes, Poverty, and Inequality

Palakurichi and Venmani villages are in the same district and agro-ecological region, and, not surprisingly, the estimated annual income per household was similar in the two villages: Rs 1,53,000 (Rs 1.53 lakh) in Venmani and Rs 1,37,000 (Rs 1.37 lakh) in Palakurichi (Table 13.1).[2] In both villages, the median income was lower than the mean, indicating a disproportionate number of households with incomes lower than the mean. Annual household income ranged from –Rs 71,220 to Rs 17,49,208 in Venmani. In Palakurichi village, annual household income ranged from –Rs 2,67,708 to Rs 24,51,691.

Six households in Venmani and eight households in Palakurichi reported negative incomes in the reference year. This deficit in annual income was primarily on account of losses incurred in crop cultivation, mainly in rice cultivation. As many as 46 per cent of households in Venmani and 53 per cent of households in Palakurichi incurred losses in crop cultivation (chapter 11 in this volume), but after aggregating over all sources of income, the net household income was positive for most cultivator households.

At the other extreme, there were three households in Venmani with an annual income of over Rs 17 lakhs (Rs 17,00,000) in 2018–19. Of these, two were traditional Kamma Naidu landlord households and one was a household

[2] It is interesting that this is close to the average for Tamil Nadu for agricultural households, of Rs 1.43 lakh in 2018–19 (SAS).

Table 13.1 *Descriptive statistics of annual household and per capita incomes, Venmani and Palakurichi villages, 2018–19* in rupees

Statistics	Venmani		Palakurichi	
	Annual household income	Annual per capita income	Annual household income	Annual per capita income
Mean	1,52,794	45,328	1,36,849	45,515
Median	98,862	30,309	90,215	26,861
Minimum	–71,220	–24,426	–2,67,708	–1,33,854
Maximum	17,49,208	5,79,028	24,51,691	8,17,230
Households with negative income	6	–	8	–

with a salaried government employee. In Palakurichi, the highest income was reported by the landlord household that operated 73 acres of paddy land.

In both villages, our estimates of the incomes of the very rich households are serious underestimates. In Palakurichi, for example, the main landlord household had diversified into multiple business activities, such as business activities in the fisheries and coconut sectors, renting out commercial buildings, and running a real estate business and a private finance company. We were unable to get accurate estimates of incomes from these business activities.

Income inequality is sharp in both the study villages, with the richest ten per cent of households cornering about 35 per cent of total household incomes, and the poorest receiving a mere one per cent of all incomes.

To gauge income poverty, we used two benchmarks, two dollars a day at purchasing power (PPP) and four dollars a day at PPP. According to *The State of Food Security and Nutrition in the World 2020* (FAO, IFAD, UNICEF, WFP, and WHO 2020), 2.12 US dollars a day was needed for a nutrient-adequate diet and 4 US dollars a day for a healthy diet. At 2018–19 prices, the annual per capita income equivalent to two dollars a day is Rs 14,692, and the corresponding per capita income for four dollars a day is Rs 29,383.[3]

An important conclusion of our study is that a quarter of households in both villages had per capita incomes that amounted to less than two dollars a day, and more than 50 per cent of households were below the four-dollar-a-day poverty line; that is, around 50 per cent of households in both villages did not receive incomes that allowed them to buy a healthy diet.

[3] The calculation was made for South Asia separately in this report, and tallies with other studies of rural diets and expenditures (see Swaminathan 2020).

Composition of Income

In recent decades, on account of a decline in water availability as well as the frequent occurrence of natural calamities, rice production and productivity have suffered in both villages (see chapters 5, 11, and 16). The risks of agricultural production are one reason for the diversification of income sources. On average, the number of sources of income reported by a household was three.[4]

For residents of the villages, there was good connectivity to nearby urban centres, notably Nagapattinam, Thiruvarur, and Velankanni, as well as to more distant towns and cities.[5]

In both villages, although more than 90 per cent of households received some income from the primary sector, the share of the primary sector in total income was very low: 13 per cent in Venmani and 19 per cent in Palakurichi (Appendix Tables 13.3 and 13.4). Around 90 per cent of households reported at least one source of non-agricultural income, and secondary and tertiary sectors' incomes together accounted for 67 per cent of total incomes, on average. The rest came from transfers, particularly remittances.

Disaggregating further, in the primary sector, we distinguished between incomes from crop production, animal-rearing, agricultural labour, rent, and income from trees. The share of crop production was extremely low in the survey year (2 per cent in Venmani and 7 per cent in Palakurichi), explained by widespread losses in crop production caused by low rainfall followed by a cyclone. The share of income from agricultural labour was only 6 to 8 per cent of total incomes. In the survey year, the average income per household from crop production was lower than the average income per household from wage earnings in agriculture.

More than half of the households in both villages were engaged in animal-rearing, particularly goat-rearing. While the contribution of livestock incomes to total household incomes was only around 2 per cent, the share was significantly higher among households that actually had livestock holdings (for example, livestock contributed around 20 per cent of the income of rich peasants in Palakurichi; see chapter 8 in this volume). Further, as Suresh demonstrates, for peasant households that made crop losses, livestock was a significant and often the sole component of household agricultural income (see chapter 8).

Tenancy among resident households was low and, consequently, the share

[4] To measure income diversification, we have used a six-fold classification of sources of income.

[5] On Tamil Nadu's dispersed pattern of urbanisation and well-developed transport (particularly road transport) infrastructure, see Rukmani (1994).

of rental income from agricultural land was minimal. Income from trees was around 1.5 to 2 per cent of total incomes (Appendix Tables 13.3 and 13.4).

A majority of farm households incurred losses from crop production in the survey year. Since this was not a "normal" agricultural year, we re-calculated incomes from crop production to answer a hypothetical question: what would the incomes from crop production have been if farm households harvested at least the average yield of paddy in the survey year? In order to answer this question, we recalculated incomes using the average yield instead of the actual yield for 48 per cent of cultivators in Venmani and 57 per cent of cultivators in Palakurichi (that is, all households that reported yields lower than the village average).[6] As expected, crop incomes rose with this adjustment, and the increase was higher for poor and middle peasants than for landlords and big capitalist farmers (Appendix Table 13.5). Correspondingly, the share of income from crop production in total incomes rose. Among middle peasants, for example, in the survey year, crop income constituted 1–2 per cent of household income, but we estimated that in a "normal" year, this proportion would be 9 to 10 per cent (Appendix Table 13.6).[7] At the same time, as discussed in chapters 5 and 16 in this volume, the region of the lower Cauvery delta has been subject to frequent natural disasters including drought and floods and cyclones in the recent past. The survey year is thus not necessarily an outlier.

Incomes from non-agricultural activities were vital to all households. The most important components of this were wages from non-agricultural occupations, followed by salaries and returns from business and trade activities. About 90 per cent of households received some income from non-agricultural wage employment, and this component of income constituted 30 and 37 per cent of total income in Venmani and Palakurichi respectively.

There were numerous non-agricultural occupations among residents of the two villages. Workers commuted to nearby urban centres where they worked as drivers, workers loading and unloading goods, construction workers, carpenters, electricians, welders, and sales persons.[8] Some workers were short-duration migrants to cities including Chennai, Salem, and Coimbatore. The earnings from work on the Mahatma Gandhi National Rural Employment Guarantee Scheme (MGNREGS) was important for a large proportion of households (85 per cent of households in Venmani and 77 per cent in Palakurichi).

The share of income from salaried jobs in the public sector was 10–14

[6] The average yield of paddy was 3.4 tonnes/hectare in Venmani and 3.3 tonnes/hectare in Palakurichi in the survey year.

[7] This adjustment is not used in the rest of the chapter.

[8] In Mela Venmani hamlet in Venmani, rope-making was a cottage industry that employed a few, mainly Scheduled Caste, women.

per cent of aggregate household incomes. These were teachers in primary and secondary schools, clerks in government offices, police constables, transport workers, workers in the Integrated Child Development Services (ICDS) scheme of the government, and Accredited Social Health Activists (ASHA) in the two villages. Salaried employment in the private sector was scant. About 7 per cent of households received incomes from salaried jobs in private schools and colleges, finance companies, petrol pumps, hotels and eating-places, and other private enterprises.

Migration is an important phenomenon in these villages. About one-fourth of households received income from remittances, which accounted for as much as 14 per cent of aggregate income in Venmani and 8 per cent of aggregate income in Palakurichi. Members of households resident in the villages had migrated to many places, including Chennai, Coimbatore, Tiruchirappalli, Tiruppur, and Bengaluru. In addition, ten workers from Venmani and nine workers from Palakurichi had migrated to West Asian countries (Abu Dhabi, Dubai, Kuwait, Saudi Arabia, and Qatar), and Malaysia and Singapore, and worked as drivers, salesmen, electricians, and skilled workers in factories and oil fields.

There are some interesting contrasts here with other PARI villages (Appendix Tables 13.1 and 13.2). The share of the primary sector in total household incomes was high, above 60 per cent, in some of the villages located in irrigated, high-productivity, cereal-growing villages such as Ananthavaram in Guntur district, Andhra Pradesh (68 per cent), 25F Gulabewala in Sikar district, Rajasthan (70 per cent), and Hakamwala in Mansa district, Punjab (79 per cent). In most villages, however, the primary sector accounted for less than 60 per cent of total household incomes (18 out of 23 villages).[9] Of the 25 villages listed in Appendix Table 13.2, the two villages from Tamil Nadu reported the lowest share of income from the primary sector.

At the same time, and irrespective of the contribution of the primary sector to aggregate income, in every village in the PARI dataset with one exception, most households participated in some agricultural or allied activity. For example, in Panahar village in Bankura district, West Bengal, 97 per cent of households reported some income from agriculture, although the contribution of agriculture to total income was only 38 per cent. There are two implications of these findings. On the one hand, it is clear that returns to agricultural employment are on the whole low relative to employment in other sectors of the economy. On the other hand, almost every household resident in a

[9] The corresponding number is not available in published reports of SAS, as wages from agricultural and non-agricultural employment are not reported separately.

village had a stake in agriculture and engaged in agricultural activity some time during the year.

Variations in Household Income by Socio-economic Class

The picture changes when the data are disaggregated. There are systematic differences in the level and composition of income across castes and classes.

Venmani

Wage workers whose earnings were mainly from unskilled and semi-skilled manual work were at the bottom of the income hierarchy, followed closely by poor peasants (Table 13.2). These were also the two numerically most important classes in the village. Mean annual household income among unskilled wage workers was Rs 71,500, and among poor peasants, Rs 97,000. Wage worker households whose major income came from unskilled or semi-skilled manual work accounted for 28 per cent of all households, and only 13 per cent of all village income. Similarly, poor peasants accounted for 19 per cent of total households, but their share in the total income was only 12 per cent.

Table 13.2 *Number of households and mean annual household income, by socio-economic class, Venmani, 2018–19* in numbers and rupees

Socio-economic class	Number of households	Mean annual household income (in Rs)
Landlords and big capitalist farmers	3	14,56,678
Rich peasants	10	3,22,507
Middle peasants	38	1,68,934
Poor peasants	78	97,008
Wage workers with major income from unskilled, semi-skilled manual work	117	71,671
Wage workers with major income from skilled and formal-sector wage work	45	1,91,292
Self-employed in business activity	31	2,04,118
Salaried persons	28	3,38,882
Persons living on pensions, small rents, and remittances	65	1,38,743
All	415	1,52,794

Wage earnings accounted for 87 per cent of household income among unskilled wage workers (Appendix Table 13.7). This included earnings from agricultural wages (24 per cent of total income) and non-agricultural wages (63 per cent). Poor peasants were also largely dependent on incomes from wage labour. In the survey year, 54 per cent of household income of poor peasants came from agricultural and non-agricultural wages, with income from crop production accounting for only 7 per cent of their annual income. The share of income from "other" sources (including transfers and remittances) was 19 per cent, followed by 15 per cent from salaries and 5 per cent from petty businesses.

The mean incomes of middle peasants, wage workers with skilled employment, and those engaged in business and trade were around two to three times the mean incomes of unskilled wage workers (Table 13.3).[10]

Rich peasants and households with salaried persons constituted two distinctly better-off socio-economic classes. The mean income per household of these groups was four times the mean income per household of unskilled wage workers, and twice the village average. It is noteworthy that agricultural incomes constituted only one-fifth of the household incomes of rich peasant households. Self-employment in non-agricultural activity (owning brick kilns and petty businesses) was the most important source of income.

At the top of the class and income hierarchy were the three landlord and big capitalist farmer households, with an average annual income of around Rs 15 lakh. This estimate must be taken as a lower bound, as we believe incomes from non-farm sources have been underestimated for these households. The share of income from agriculture was reported to be 21 per cent of household incomes (this is an overstatement, since non-agricultural incomes were greatly underestimated). These households had investments in the rice trade, rice mills, and petrol pumps.

To illustrate, JK, a member of a traditional landlord household in Venmani, owned 30 acres of crop land and had mortgaged in another 10 acres. He and his brother cultivated rice on 40 acres. They ran a rice mill in the village, and procured paddy from cultivators in the village and nearby areas. In 2018–19, they received Rs 14 lakh as net earnings from the rice mill business, which accounted for about 81 per cent of their total household income. JK's son had migrated to Chennai, and worked as a salaried employee in a private establishment.

[10] Middle peasants are households with operational holdings, whose members work on their own farm, and with assets valued between Rs 10 lakh and Rs 40 lakh. Rich peasants are those with assets above Rs 40 lakh (see chapter 4).

Table 13.3 *Ratio of average income of a class to income of an unskilled wage worker, Venmani and Palakurichi, 2018–19*

Socio-economic class	Venmani	Palakurichi
Landlords and big capitalist farmers	20.3	11.5
Rich peasants	4.5	1.9
Middle peasants	2.4	2.1
Poor peasants	1.4	1.2
Wage workers with major income from unskilled, semi-skilled manual work	1.0	1.0
Wage workers with major income from skilled and formal-sector wage work	2.7	1.9
Self-employed in business activity	2.8	2.2
Salaried persons	4.7	3.7
Persons living on pensions, small rents, and remittances	1.9	1.1
All	2.1	1.7

Palakurichi

Variations in the level and composition of incomes of households in different socio-economic classes in Palakurichi are similar to those in Venmani (Tables 13.3, 13.4, and Appendix Table 13.8).

Wage workers whose major earnings were from unskilled and semi-skilled manual work were the poorest class in terms of average household income (Rs 78,475 in 2018–19). This class constituted 24 per cent of all households, and received only 14 per cent of total income. The major sources of income for the members of this class were non-agricultural wages (60 per cent of total income), agricultural wages (22 per cent of total income), and other sources such as remittances (12 per cent of total income). Poor peasants were a little better off than unskilled wage workers, reporting an annual income of Rs 95,077 in the survey year. Wage earnings accounted for 68 per cent of household incomes, on average, and crop production contributed only 3 per cent of total income.

The average incomes of middle peasants, skilled wage workers, and self-employed business households were twice the average incomes of unskilled workers. Skilled wage workers comprised 12 per cent of households and received 14 per cent of total village income. Earnings from non-agricultural wages was the largest component of the incomes of skilled wage worker households (84 per cent of total income).

Table 13.4 *Number of households and mean annual household income, by socio-economic class, Palakurichi, 2018–19* in number and rupees

Socio-economic class	Number of households	Mean annual household income (in Rs)
Landlords and big capitalist farmers	8	8,97,209
Rich peasants	8	1,50,515
Middle peasants	26	1,69,321
Poor peasants	130	95,077
Wage workers with major income from unskilled, semi-skilled manual work	92	78,475
Wage workers with major income from skilled and formal-sector wage work	47	1,57,337
Self-employed in business activity	19	1,78,316
Salaried persons	23	2,96,202
Persons living on pensions, small rents, and remittances	37	92,210
All	390	1,36,849

More than 50 per cent of peasant households in Palakuricihi made losses from agriculture in 2018–19. The mean household incomes were Rs 1.5 lakh, Rs 1.7 lakh, and Rs 95,000 for rich, middle, and poor peasants, respectively. In peasant families, the share of agriculture in total income ranged from 1 to 7 per cent. All peasant households had earnings from diverse sources. Rich peasant households ran small businesses such as grocery shops, tea shops, dairy farms, and fisheries. The share of these sources of income was 61 per cent of their total income. Middle peasant households depended on non-agricultural wages (46 per cent of total income), self-employment in non-agriculture (16 per cent of total income), and other sources including remittances (17 per cent of total income). Poor peasant households depended on wage earnings, agricultural wages (16 per cent of total income), and non-agricultural wages (52 per cent of total income).

Households dependent on salaried employment in Palakurichi had a mean income of Rs 3 lakh a year, with salaries accounting for 81 per cent of total income.

The class of landlords and big capitalist farmers were at the top of the income distribution, with an estimated average annual income of Rs 9 lakh. This is not high, and it is clear that the survey has underestimated the income of rich households. Income from self-employment in agriculture contributed about 56 per cent of total income, followed by 17 per cent from salaries, 16 per cent from self-employment in non-agriculture, and 8 per cent from other sources. Agriculture contributed a larger share of total income than in Venmani (Appendix Table 13.6).

There were significant variations of income within this class of landlords and big capitalist farmers, the range being from Rs –2.7 lakh to Rs +24.5 lakh. The household with negative incomes was one engaged exclusively in crop production, which suffered on account of crop losses during the survey year. Landlord households that had not diversified into business and trade were households in which the elders lived in the village and the younger generation had migrated to cities.

Female-headed Households

The share of female-headed households in both villages was significantly higher than the average reported at the national and state levels (17 per cent in Venmani and 24 per cent in Palakurichi, as compared to a national average of 11 per cent at the Census of 2011). The relatively large number of female-headed households in the two villages reflects the fact of widespread male-specific migration.

Female-headed households had significantly lower incomes than male-headed households (Table 13.5).[11] The former depended largely on remittances and pensions. There were few avenues of employment for women workers within the village other than in agriculture (some women in Venmani were employed in rope-making). Participation by women in MGNREGS was high

Table 13.5 *Number of female-headed and male-headed households, and average annual household incomes, Venmani and Palakurichi, 2018–19* in number and rupees

Type of household	Venmani		Palakurichi	
	Number of households	Annual household income	Number of households	Annual household income
Female-headed household	98	1,06,163	68	80,850
Male-headed household	317	1,67,210	322	1,48,675
All	415	1,52,794	390	1,36,849

[11] The t-test was significant for a difference in household incomes as between female-headed and male-headed households, but not statistically significant for per capita incomes, as female-headed households were usually smaller than male-headed households.

in both villages. Around two-thirds of female-headed households belonged to the Scheduled Castes.

Caste

For this discussion, we used a four-fold classification of households in terms of broad social groups: Scheduled Castes, Most Backward Classes, Backward Classes, and Other castes.[12]

Venmani

Venmani is a village in which people of the Scheduled Castes are a majority (belonging mainly to the Pallar and Parayar castes). Households from the Most Backward Classes constitute only 8 per cent of the village population. Ambalakarar is the largest caste group among the Most Backward Class households. The castes in the category of Backward Classes in Venmani village, which accounted for 25 per cent of the population, were the Naidu, Nadar, Vellalar, Pillai, Kammalar, and Yadhavar castes. All Other caste Hindus (Brahman, Kamma Naidu, and some others) comprised 2 per cent of the population.

In terms of average income, households from the Most Backward Classes were at the bottom rung of the ladder in Venmani village. The average annual household income in this group was Rs 90,084 (Table 13.6). Among Scheduled Caste households, numbering 263, the mean income was Rs 1,34,690. The

Table 13.6 *Mean annual household income, by social group, Venmani, 2018–19* in number and rupees

Social group	Number of households	Mean household income (in Rs)	Ratio of all social groups to Scheduled Castes
Scheduled Castes	263	1,34,690	1.0
Most Backward Classes	34	90,084	0.7
Backward Classes	109	1,86,696	1.4
Other caste Hindus	7	5,69,181	4.2
All	415	1,52,794	1.1

Note: Two households that did not report caste status are included in the "All" category but excluded from the caste-wise disaggregation.

[12] Others mainly comprised Other caste Hindu households.

highest mean income, as may be expected, was among Other Caste households (Rs 5.7 lakh).

A test of significance showed that mean incomes (using household income and per capita income variables) of Scheduled Caste and Most Backward Class households together (and separately) were significantly different from the mean incomes of Other caste households. Since the two large groups in the villages are Scheduled Caste households and Backward Class households, we also tested for differences in incomes between these two groups. As shown in Table 13.7, in both villages, and for both household and per capita income

Table 13.7 *A test for the null hypothesis of no significant difference in household income and per capita income of Scheduled Caste and Backward Class households, Venmani and Palakurichi*

Village	Variable	t value	P value
Venmani	Household income	2.2122	0.02862
	Per capita income	2.6101	0.01011
Palakurichi	Household income	2.2227	0.02959
	Per capita income	2.2153	0.03005

Figure 13.1 *Distribution of households by quintiles of per capita income, by social group, Venmani*

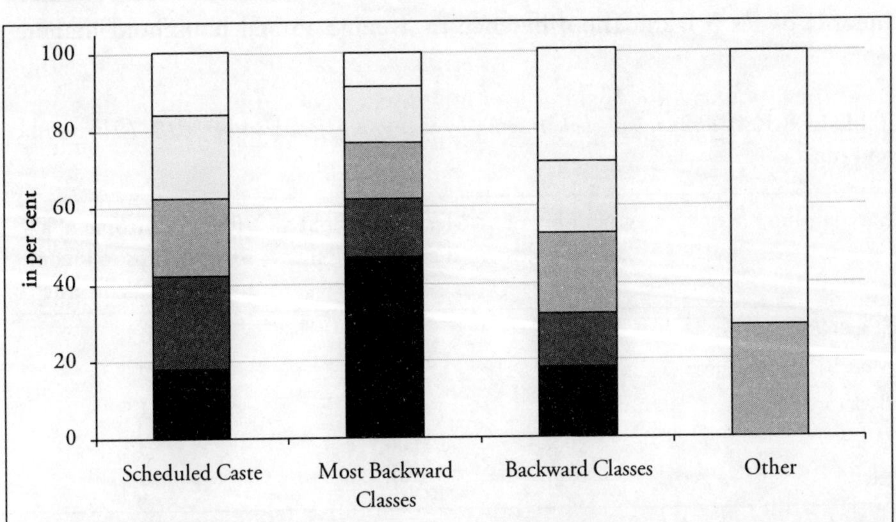

Note: Households are divided into five equal groups (quintiles), according to the value of per capita income. The quintile cut-off points are Rs 12,650, Rs 22,562, Rs 39,405, and Rs 62,733.

variables, there was a statistically significant difference in the mean incomes of Scheduled Caste households and Backward Class households.

Figure 13.1 shows variations in income levels across social groups based on quintiles of per capita income. If there were horizontal equality in the distribution of income, we would expect 20 per cent of each social group to belong to each quintile. In Venmani, more than 70 per cent of Other caste households were in the top per capita income quintile (shaded white). By contrast, about 16 per cent of Scheduled Caste households and 9 per cent of Most Backward Class households were in the top income quintile.

Palakurichi

Variations in income across social groups is not very different in Palakurichi. In this village, Scheduled Caste households constituted 60 per cent of the population, followed by Most Backward Class households (21 per cent), Backward Class households (17 per cent), and Other caste households (2 per cent). The lowest average annual household income was among Scheduled Caste households (Table 13.8). The mean annual per capita income among Scheduled Caste households was Rs 97,807, and the mean annual per capita income among Backward Class and Most Backward Class households was around Rs 1.9 lakhs.[13] Other caste households (Brahman, Chettiyar, Gurukul Iyer, Kamma Naidu, Pandaram, Saiva Vellalar) had an estimated per capita income of Rs 3 lakh. The difference in average annual household incomes

Table 13.8 *Mean annual household income, by caste group, Palakurichi, 2018–19* in number and rupees

Social group	Number of households	Mean household income (in Rs)	Ratio of income of all social groups to income of Scheduled Caste
Scheduled Castes	235	97,807	1.0
Most Backward Classes	81	1,91,448	2.0
Backward Classes	65	1,89,585	1.9
Other	8	3,00,774	3.1
All	390	1,36,849	1.4

Note: One household did not report caste status and is included in the "All" category but excluded from the caste-wise disaggregation.

<?> Most Backward Class households in Venmani (mainly fish workers) are poorer than Most Backward Class households in Palakurichi.

Figure 13.2 *Distribution of households by quintiles of per capita income, by social group, Palakurichi*

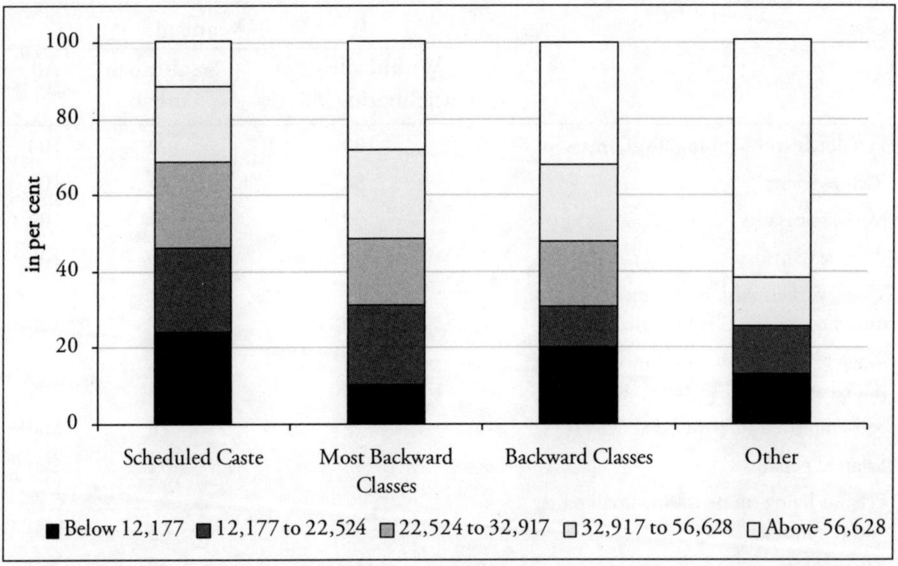

Note: Households are divided into five equal groups (quintiles), according to the value of per capita income. The quintile cut-off points are Rs 12,177, Rs 22,524, Rs 32,917, and Rs 56,628.

between Scheduled Caste households and Backward Class households was statistically significant (Table 13.7).

Figure 13.2 shows the distribution of households in each caste group across quintiles of per capita income. Households from Other castes, followed by Backward Class households, were over-represented in the top income quintile, whereas Scheduled Caste households were under-represented. In Palakurichi, Most Backward Class households were also over-represented in the top income quintile and under-represented in the lowest income quintile. In Palakurichi, Padayachi was the main caste in the Most Backward Class category, and some of these households belonged to better-off socio-economic classes.

Rural and Urban Incomes

Employment in urban locations was important for residents of the two villages. We attempted a two-way classification of household income: (i) income generated within the village or in neighbouring villages, and (ii) income generated in towns and cities. The first category comprised income from crop cultivation, animal resources, trees, agricultural wages, and some

Table 13.9 *Share of household income, by socio-economic class and location of income generation, Venmani* in per cent

Class	Venmani		
	Within village or neighboring villages	Semi-urban/ urban	All
Landlords and big capitalist farmers	100	0	100
Rich peasants	86	14	100
Middle peasants	59	41	100
Poor peasants	50	50	100
Wage workers with major income from unskilled, semi-skilled manual work	63	37	100
Wage workers with major income from skilled and formal-sector wage work	28	72	100
Self-employed in business activity	72	28	100
Salaried persons	48	52	100
Persons living on pensions, small rents, and remittances	37	63	100
All	55	45	100

Table 13.10 *Share of household income, by socio-economic class and location of income generation, Palakurichi* in per cent

Class	Palakurichi		
	Within village or neighboring villages	Semi-urban/ urban	All
Landlords and big capitalist farmers	86	14	100
Rich peasants	71	29	100
Middle peasants	52	48	100
Poor peasants	55	45	100
Wage workers with major income from unskilled, semi-skilled manual work	60	40	100
Wage workers with major income from skilled and formal-sector wage work	41	59	100
Self-employed in business activity	84	16	100
Salaried persons	46	54	100
Persons living on pensions, small rents, and remittances	48	52	100
All	58	42	100

non-agricultural wages (including MGNREGS), while the second comprised mainly non-agricultural wage earnings, salaries, and remittances.

Income generated in urban areas accounted for 45 per cent of total incomes in Venmani and 42 per cent in Palakurichi (Tables 13.9 and 13.10). The urban economy was thus a crucial direct contributor to the livelihoods of residents of the two villages.

Secondly, there were important variations in the urban–rural composition of income across socio-economic classes. Among households engaged in crop production, income within the village exceeded income generated outside the village for rich peasants and landlords. In Venmani, landlord and capitalist farmer households had diversified into businesses (petrol pumps, rice mills, paddy trading) that were located in the village or in nearby villages and towns. As Venmani is adjacent to a national highway, business opportunities were to be found in and around the village.

In Palakurichi, landlords and big capitalist farmer households were largely agriculturists (exceptions were one household that had a member with salaried employment and another with a business in a semi-urban area).

Among middle and poor peasants, the share of incomes earned from urban areas was greater than the share of incomes earned within the village. This reflects the crisis of crop production among the peasantry. Crop incomes were inadequate for poorer sections of the peasantry, and members of these households depended on non-agricultural earnings for their survival.

For households dependent on non-agricultural wage earnings, households dependent on remittances, and households dependent on salaries, incomes generated outside the village accounted for the major part of total household income (Table 13.9).

Among wage worker households, then, earnings came largely from urban locations, reflecting the lack of skilled employment opportunities within the village.

Remittances

As mentioned, remittances also played a big role in livelihoods inVenmani and Palakurichi (Table 13.11).

By definition, the contribution of remittances to household income was high for the class of households dependent on pensions, small rents, and remittances. Nevertheless, remittances were also important for middle and poor peasant households (constituting 8 to 17 per cent of their total income). Almost one-fourth of all households in both villages had at least one migrant who sent remittances.

Table 13.11 *Share of remittances in total income, Venmani and Palakurichi, 2018–19* in per cent

Class	Share of remittances in total income	
	Venmani	Palakurichi
Landlords and big capitalist farmers	–	1
Rich peasants	1	7
Middle peasants	10	8
Poor peasants	17	14
Wage workers with major income from unskilled, semi-skilled manual work	4	7
Wage workers with major income from skilled and formal-sector wage work	9	2
Self-employed in business activity	6	0
Salaried persons	3	2
Persons living on pensions, small rents, and remittances	59	49
All	14	9

Concluding Remarks

Diversification of incomes through participation in non-farm occupations is a prominent feature of the region, with incomes and earnings from non-agricultural labour, salaries, business and trade, and remittances constituting more than 80 per cent of aggregate income in both villages. While 90 per cent of households received incomes from activities in the primary sector, incomes directly from occupations in the primary sector contributed between 13 and 19 per cent of total household incomes in the two villages. The single most important source of income was earnings from non-agricultural wage employment, from MGNREGS within the village, and from wage employment in nearby urban centres. In addition, remittances from persons working in more distant towns and cities were also important as a supplementary source of income for poorer sections of the peasantry and for wage worker households. Salaried employment opportunities in government and in the private sector were limited. There was little factory-based employment in the neighbouring urban centres. Most wage workers from the village were employed as casual workers on daily wages.[14]

Crop incomes were low, in absolute terms and as a share of total incomes.

[14] These findings are consistent with the evidence on employment patterns examined by Thomas and Satheesha (chapter 12 in this volume) on a large, pluriactive workforce and on diversification of the employment structure.

The survey was conducted during a bad agricultural year, although data in chapters 6 and 16 in this volume suggest that natural disasters occur frequently in this region.

The incomes of a quarter of households in both villages were estimated to have been below the two-dollar-a-day poverty line, and of more than half the households below the four-dollar-a-day poverty line. These are measures based on the costs of a healthy diet, and the situation as reflected in our findings is deeply disturbing.

To understand income inequality, we disaggregated the data by socio-economic class. First, landlords and big capitalist farmers were at the top of the income ladder. Secondly, around 50 per cent of cultivator households incurred losses in crop production because of adverse agricultural conditions during the survey year. Thirdly, average incomes were the lowest among manual wage workers and poor peasants, and households of both these classes were heavily dependent on wage earnings. The employment available is relatively low-paid and insecure even when it is skilled or semi-skilled employment and in urban locations.The level and composition of incomes of the peasantry, especially poor peasants, point to the proletarianisation of the peasantry and support the view that the "peasantry is a class in transition" (chapter 4).

There were a large number of female-headed households in both villages, reflecting the fact of male-specific migration for employment. In this context, our finding of a statistically significant difference in the mean household incomes of female-headed households and male-headed households is a matter of pressing importance. The earnings gap is largely on account of the absence of employment opportunities for women in non-agricultural activities in and around the village, the large and persistent gender gap in agricultural wages (see chapter 12 in this volume), and the inadequacy of remittances.

Last but not least, caste remains a sure predictor of income. There were statistically significant differences in the incomes of Scheduled Caste and Backward Class households in both villages. Scheduled Caste households are concentrated in the class of wage workers: 60 per cent of wage worker households in Palakurichi and 75 per cent in Venmani were Scheduled Caste households.

Among Indian States, Tamil Nadu stands out in terms of structural transformation in respect of employment and output, and this is visible at the village level. The principal finding of this chapter is that access to non-agricultural employment and diversification of sources of income have not ended poverty among manual worker households, especially those from discriminated social groups.

Appendix

Incomes of households in the survey villages were estimated separately for the following sources. The survey used detailed modules on incomes from each of the following sources.

1. Crop production
2. Animal resources
3. Wage labour
   i) Agricultural labour (casual)
   ii) Agricultural labour (long-term)
   iii) Non-agricultural labour (casual)
   iv) Non-agricultural labour (monthly/long-term)
4. Salaried jobs
   i) Government salaried jobs
   ii) Other salaried jobs
5. Business and trade
6. Moneylending
7. Income from savings in financial institutions and equity
8. Pensions and scholarship
9. Remittances and gifts
10. Rental income
    i) Rental income from agricultural land
    ii) Rental income from machinery
    iii) Rental income from other assets
11. Artisanal work and work at traditional caste calling
12. Any other sources

The definition of "costs of cultivation" closely follows the definition of the "Cost A2" category used under the Comprehensive Scheme for Studying Cost of Cultivation/Production of Principal Crops (CCPC), of the Commission of Agricultural Cost and Prices (CACP), India. It includes the cost of all material inputs (purchased and home-produced), the cost of hired labour, rental payments, the imputed value of interest on working capital, and depreciation of owned fixed capital other than land. It excludes cost of family labour and rental value of owned land.

Data are collected at various levels of disaggregation, to assist in more accurate reporting and better recall from respondents. For example, crop incomes and costs of production are reported and calculated for each crop and crop-mix during the agricultural year. Livestock incomes are calculated for each type of livestock. Similarly, for wage labour income in agriculture, each worker was asked questions on the number of days of employment and on earnings (in cash, kind, or both) for each season, crop, and crop operation.

Appendix Tables

Appendix Table 13.1 *Sources of household income, PARI villages* in per cent

Village	District	State	Year of survey	Per cent of households reporting		
				Primary	Secondary and tertiary sectors	All other sources
Ananthavaram	Guntur	Andhra Pradesh	2005–06	88	52	32
Bukkacherla	Anantapur	Andhra Pradesh	2005–06	94	38	19
Kothapalle	Karimnagar	Telangana	2005–06	89	54	22
Harevli	Bijnor	Uttar Pradesh	2006	97	55	32
Mahatwar	Ballia	Uttar Pradesh	2006	96	83	74
Warwat Khanderao	Buldhana	Maharashtra	2007	95	62	17
Nimshirgaon	Kolhapur	Maharashtra	2007	97	65	17
25F Gulabewala	Sri Ganganagar	Rajasthan	2007	93	52	28
Rewasi	Sikar	Rajasthan	2010	100	68	58
Gharsondi	Gwalior	Madhya Pradesh	2008	97	71	48
Alabujanahalli	Mandya	Karnataka	2009	98	86	35
Siresandra	Kolar	Karnataka	2009	100	73	32
Zhapur	Kalaburagi	Karnataka	2009	84	73	47
Panahar	Bankura	West Bengal	2010	97	86	27
Amarsinghi	Maldah	West Bengal	2010	95	95	43
Kalmandasguri	Koch Bihar	West Bengal	2010	98	95	44
Tehang	Jalandhar	Punjab	2011	50	79	45
Hakamwala	Mansa	Punjab	2011	95	60	41
Katkuian	West Champaran	Bihar	2012	95	86	51
Nayanagar	Samastipur	Bihar	2012	77	79	57
Mainama	Dhalai	Tripura	2016	95	93	56
Khakchang	North	Tripura	2016	99	98	67
Muhuripur	South	Tripura	2016	98	96	71
Venmani	Nagapattinam	Tamil Nadu	2019	94	96	48
Palakurichi	Nagapattinam	Tamil Nadu	2019	91	96	48

Appendix Table 13.2 *Composition of household income, PARI villages* in per cent

Village	District	State	Year of survey	Share in total income (per cent)		
				Primary	Secondary and tertiary sectors	All other sources
Ananthavaram	Guntur	Andhra Pradesh	2005–06	68	20	12
Bukkacherla	Anantapur	Andhra Pradesh	2005–06	59	32	9
Kothapalle	Karimnagar	Telangana	2005–06	44	53	3
Harevli	Bijnor	Uttar Pradesh	2006	81	15	4
Mahatwar	Ballia	Uttar Pradesh	2006	24	61	15
Warwat Khanderao	Buldhana	Maharashtra	2007	60	37	3
Nimshirgaon	Kolhapur	Maharashtra	2007	47	47	6
25F Gulabewala	Sri Ganganagar	Rajasthan	2007	70	19	11
Rewasi	Sikar	Rajasthan	2010	35	38	27
Gharsondi	Gwalior	Madhya Pradesh	2008	54	44	2
Alabujanahalli	Mandya	Karnataka	2009	58	39	3
Siresandra	Kolar	Karnataka	2009	73	25	2
Zhapur	Kalaburagi	Karnataka	2009	47	49	4
Panahar	Bankura	West Bengal	2010	38	54	8
Amarsinghi	Maldah	West Bengal	2010	47	44	9
Kalmandasguri	Koch Bihar	West Bengal	2010	45	43	12
Tehang	Jalandhar	Punjab	2011	39	39	22
Hakamwala	Mansa	Punjab	2011	79	18	3
Katkuian	West Champaran	Bihar	2012	48	49	3
Nayanagar	Samastipur	Bihar	2012	36	55	9
Mainama	Dhalai	Tripura	2016	22	72	6
Khakchang	North	Tripura	2016	40	51	9
Muhuripur	South	Tripura	2016	21	62	17
Venmani	Nagapattinam	Tamil Nadu	2019	13	67	20
Palakurichi	Nagapattinam	Tamil Nadu	2019	19	67	14

Appendix Table 13.3 *Source and composition of household income, Venmani, 2018–19* in per cent

Income source	Per cent of households reporting	Share in total income (per cent)	Average income (Rs)
Crop production	44	2.1	7,294
Animal resources	54	2	5,567
Agricultural labour	59	6.4	16,632
Rental income from agricultural land	5	0.3	10,776
Income from trees	45	2	6,899
Primary sector	**94**	**12.8**	**20,818**
Non-agricultural casual labour earnings	90	29.6	50,405
Government salaries	7	14.2	3,00,034
Private salaries	6	4.8	1,16,677
Business and trade	17	18.2	1,62,288
Rental income	4	0.6	23,290
Secondary and tertiary sectors	**96**	**67.4**	**1,06,769**
Pension and scholarship	25	5.5	33,378
Transfer and other remittances	28	14.2	79,075
Any other sources	4	0.1	4,256
All other sources	**48**	**19.8**	**63,232**
All households	100	100	1,52,794

Appendix Table 13.4 *Source and composition of household income, Palakurichi, 2018–19*
in per cent

Income source	Per cent of households reporting	Share in total income (%)	Average income (Rs)
Crop production	47	6.5	18,823
Animal resources	53	2.8	7,031
Agricultural labour	62	7.9	17,390
Rental income from agricultural land	5	0.3	9,396
Income from trees	21	1.4	8,988
Primary sector	**91**	**18.9**	**28,311**
Non-agricultural casual labour earnings	89	37.8	58,028
Government salaries	5	10.1	2,82,473
Private salaries	6	5.1	1,14,293
Business and trade	16	12.5	1,07,338
Rental income	3	1.2	48,248
Secondary and tertiary sectors	**96**	**66.7**	**95,150**
Pension and scholarship	28	4.8	23,205
Transfer and other remittances	23	8.8	51,518
Any other sources	3	0.8	42,332
All other sources	**48**	**14.4**	**41,211**
All households	100	100	1,36,849

Appendix Table 13.5 *Mean income from crop production, by socio-economic class, Venmani, 2018–19* in rupees

Class	Venmani		Palakurichi	
	Average of income from crop production	Average of estimated crop income	Average of income from crop production	Average of estimated crop income
Landlords and big capitalist farmers	2,79,405	2,80,627	4,44,156	4,76,362
Rich peasants	30,466	42,342	–27,244	16,892
Middle peasants	3,013	17,362	1,997	15,706
Poor peasants	1,264	6,421	–486	5,699
All	7,294	14,067	18,823	28,547

Appendix Table 13.6 *Share of income from crop production in total income, by class, Venmani, 2018–19* in per cent

Class	Venmani		Palakurichi	
	Share of crop income in total income	Share of estimated crop income in total estimated income	Share of crop income in total income	Share of estimated crop income in total estimated income
Landlords and big capitalist farmers	19	19	50	51
Rich peasants	9	13	–18	9
Middle peasants	2	10	1	9
Poor peasants	1	6	–1	6
All	2	4	7	10

Appendix Table 13.7 *Composition of income by socio-economic class, Venmani, 2018–19* in per cent

Socio-economic class	Self-employment in agriculture	Agricultural wage	Self-employment in non-agriculture	Non-agricultural wage	Salaries	Other sources	All
Landlords and big capitalist farmers	21	0	79	0	0	0	100
Rich peasants	21	0	47	16	7	9	100
Middle peasants	12	3	13	18	30	24	100
Poor peasants	7	10	5	44	15	19	100
Wage workers with major income from unskilled, semi-skilled manual work	5	24	1	63	1	6	100
Wage workers with major income from skilled and formal-sector wage work	2	5	3	76	3	11	100
Self-employed in business activity	2	2	78	11	0	7	100
Salaried persons	2	1	1	3	89	4	100
Persons living on pensions, small rents, and remittances	3	4	3	11	1	78	100
All	6	6	19	30	19	20	100

Appendix Table 13.8 *Composition of income by socio-economic class, Palakurichi, 2018–19* in per cent

Socio-economic class	Self-employment in agriculture	Agricultural wage	Self-employment in non-agriculture	Non-agricultural wage	Salaries	Other sources	All
Landlords and big capitalist farmers	56	0	19	0	17	8	100
Rich peasants	1	0	61	7	22	9	100
Middle peasants	7	5	16	46	9	17	100
Poor peasants	3	16	8	52	4	17	100
Wage workers with major income from unskilled, semi-skilled manual work	4	22	1	60	1	12	100
Wage workers with major income from skilled and formal-sector wage work	3	4	3	84	2	4	100
Self-employed in business activity	0	1	89	8	0	2	100
Salaried persons	6	1	3	6	81	3	100
Persons living on pensions, small rents, and remittances	7	3	1	13	0	76	100
All	11	8	14	38	15	14	100

Appendix Table 13.9 *Mean annual household income, by socio-economic class and location of income generation, Venmani and Palakurichi* in rupees

Class	Venmani		Palakurichi	
	Within village or neighbouring villages	Urban	Within village or neighbouring villages	Urban
Landlords and big capitalist farmers	14,56,678		7,69,709	5,10,000
Rich peasants	2,76,907	1,14,000	1,06,265	1,77,000
Middle peasants	98,850	1,10,967	88,131	1,11,103
Poor peasants	48,520	85,958	52,177	77,458
Wage workers with major income from unskilled, semi-skilled manual work	45,862	58,952	47,177	56,459
Wage workers with major income from skilled and formal-sector wage work	56,578	1,63,996	68,497	1,21,694
Self-employed in business activity	1,46,967	1,36,282	1,57,168	69,873
Salaried persons	1,70,004	2,33,266	1,34,786	2,06,254
Persons living on pensions, small rents, and remittances	52,371	1,13,332	45,263	66,011
All	85,267	1,15,998	80,506	95,218

V

Living Standards

14

Education

Fumiko Oshikawa and Sanjukta Chakraborty

HIGHLIGHTS

Tamil Nadu is undoubtedly among the better-achieving States of India in respect of the expansion of literacy and school education. Almost all children of school-going age in the State are enrolled in school, and around half of them continue their school education beyond the secondary level.

This chapter examines progress in the spread of education by looking at data on different age cohorts by caste and gender. There was a visible jump in access to higher education in the age cohort 20–39 years, that is, those born in the 1990s. The spread of higher education began with members of the Backward Classes, and extended later to the Scheduled Castes and Most Backward Classes.

The chapter attempts to relate years of schooling with types of occupation. While most young people have access to diversified non-agricultural occupations, access to white-collar jobs for men improves only with higher education (say, Diplomas or Bachelor's degrees). Expansion of higher education among women is not associated with any major change in likelihood of participation in non-agricultural jobs. Women with ten years of schooling or less remained peasants, agricultural workers, and manual workers.

Lastly, the expansion of private education has brought new issues to the fore that need further study, such as the cost and quality of private education.

Introduction

Tamil Nadu is regarded as one of the most successful States of India in achieving universalisation of primary education. Schemes such as mid-day meals introduced in the 1980s and various other incentives given to poor households have become a standard model of policy package for promoting school education, especially for the rural population, that many other States have followed. Tamil Nadu has also achieved a remarkable expansion of higher education, backed by state policies as well as private investments, over the last couple of decades. Data from two study villages, Venmani and Palakurichi, located in the lower Cauvery delta, confirm these trends. Almost all children of school-going age are enrolled in schools located within these villages, or in nearby villages and towns, and nearly half the young population continued their studies beyond the secondary level. Education, thus, has reached both the villages.

However, the process of expansion of education also entails increasing diversification and disparity in education. The fact that the academic ability of most students in government schools of rural Tamil Nadu, especially at the primary level, is far from satisfactory has been pointed out repeatedly in the NGO Pratham's *Annual Survey of Education Report* (ASER).[1] The spread of private schools in rural Tamil Nadu should be understood in this context. During the PARI survey of the villages of Venmani and Palakurichi, we found that a substantial number of children of school-going age in Venmani are now enrolled in a newly set up private school located in a nearby town, whereas private schooling is still limited in the more isolated Palakurichi village. It is very likely that disparity in education based on class, caste, and gender will be widened further with the spread of private schools. We should pay attention not merely to the statistics of "enrolment," but to the realities of ongoing transformation of education in rural Tamil Nadu.

Institutions of higher education have also diversified over the last few decades. Corresponding to the expanding educational demand in rural areas, many new colleges and institutions offering various diplomas have been set up in smaller cities and towns. Nagapattinam is one such town where a number of colleges and polytechnics with wide variations in terms of courses, academic standards, management, and affiliation have sprung up. While these institutions give access to education to many rural youth without them having to migrate to big cities, it is also obvious that not all of them provide

[1] For a brief summary of the trend in 2010s, see the website of ASER. http://img.asercentre.org/docs/ASER%202021/ASER%20TOT%202012-18/tamilnadu.pdf

"good" or "useful" knowledge and training for the students to develop their own thinking and the ability to adapt to varied jobs in later years. In short, education has become a "must" but not "enough" of a qualification for many youth today, especially when they seek employment other than in agriculture. This is reflected in the PARI survey data.

Literacy and Schooling Years: General Trends

Literacy

According to the PARI survey data, in Venmani, among the population aged seven and above, 73 per cent of females and 88 per cent of males were literate; in Palakurichi, 65 per cent of females and 81 per cent of males were counted as literate (Table 14.1). The Census report of 2011 shows higher literacy rates for the rural population of Nagapattinam district: 76 per cent of females and

Table 14.1 *Proportion of literate persons aged 7 and above, including migrants, by religion and social group, in Venmani and Palakurichi villages, 2019* in per cent

		Venmani			Palakurichi		
		Females	Males	Persons	Females	Males	Persons
Religion	Hindu	73	88	80	65	81	73
	Christian	44	67	53	–	–	–
Social group	Scheduled Castes	72	85	78	58	76	67
	Backward Classes	74	94	84	77	91	84
	Most Backward Classes	71	82	77	74	88	81
	Other	80	100	90	76	92	83
All		72	88	80	65	81	73

Source: PARI survey data.

Table 14.2 *Literacy rates for persons aged 7 and above, Venmani and Palakurichi, Census of India 2011*

Location	Females	Males	Persons	Gender gap
India	65.5	82.1	74.0	16.7
Tamil Nadu	73.9	86.8	80.3	13.0
Tamil Nadu (Rural)	65.5	82.1	73.8	16.6
Nagapattinam	78.0	90.4	84.1	12.4
Nagapattinam (Rural)	76.0	89.3	82.5	13.4

Source: Census of India 2011.

89 per cent of males (Table 14.2). Literacy rates in Nagapattinam district were higher than the corresponding rates in rural Tamil Nadu. A simple comparison between the Census and the PARI survey may not be appropriate because of differences in survey methods and the time gap, but it is perhaps safe to presume that literacy rates in the two villages are approximately at the level of the State average and slightly below the Nagapattinam average. As we will discuss later, school education has expanded rapidly in both villages over the last couple of decades, and literacy levels of the younger generations have reached almost 100 per cent.

At the same time, we have to make the following observations about the literacy rates. First, there is a gap between the two villages. The precise reasons for this difference are not clear from the PARI survey data, but geographical location and the historical experience of development of school education may be among the reasons. This inter-village gap suggests that even as the State-level average of literacy improves there is a good possibility of "backward pockets," especially in the process of rapid development. Secondly, there is a gender gap. The data show a consistent gender gap in all categories, though the gaps are relatively moderate if compared to that in the States of northern India. In the two villages we surveyed, the gender gap was wide among all the caste groups.

Years of Schooling

Similar observations emerge from data on years of schooling for different groups in the two villages (Appendix Tables 14.1 and 14.2). As far as median years of schooling are concerned, all social groups in the two villages have achieved almost the same level of schooling: around 10 years for males and 8–9 years for females. Years of schooling are longer for males, but the gap between males and females is relatively small.

Although there is not much difference in the median years of schooling, the timing of educational development differed across social groups and socio-economic classes. Figures 14.1 to 14.2 show the age-wise average years of schooling in the two villages, and Figures 14.3 to 14.8 give the same information for different social groups.

As Figures 14.1 and 14.2 clearly show, there was a jump in the expansion of higher education, that is, education beyond 12 years of schooling, in the age group 20–39 years, namely, among those who were born in the 1990s. This jump is very visible in Venmani, where more than 60 per cent of males and 50 per cent of females in the age group 20–39 years were educated beyond the secondary level. At the same time, a substantial proportion of this age group,

Figure 14.1 *Years of schooling by age group, males and females, Venmani*

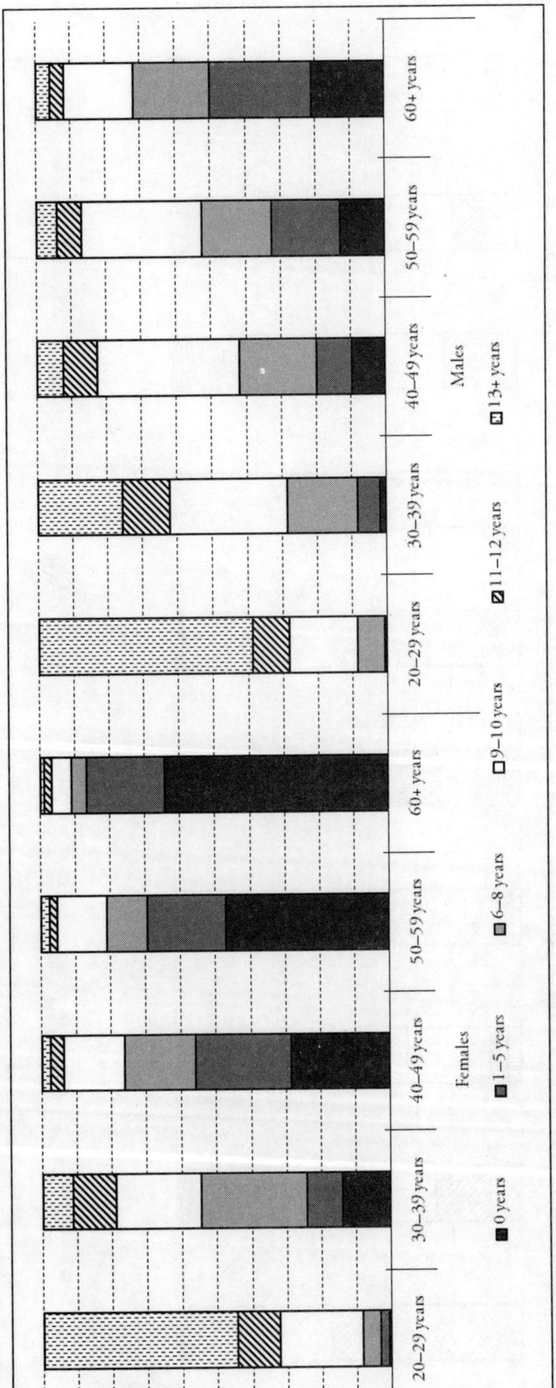

Source: PARI survey data.

Figure 14.2 *Years of schooling by age group, males and females, Palakurichi*

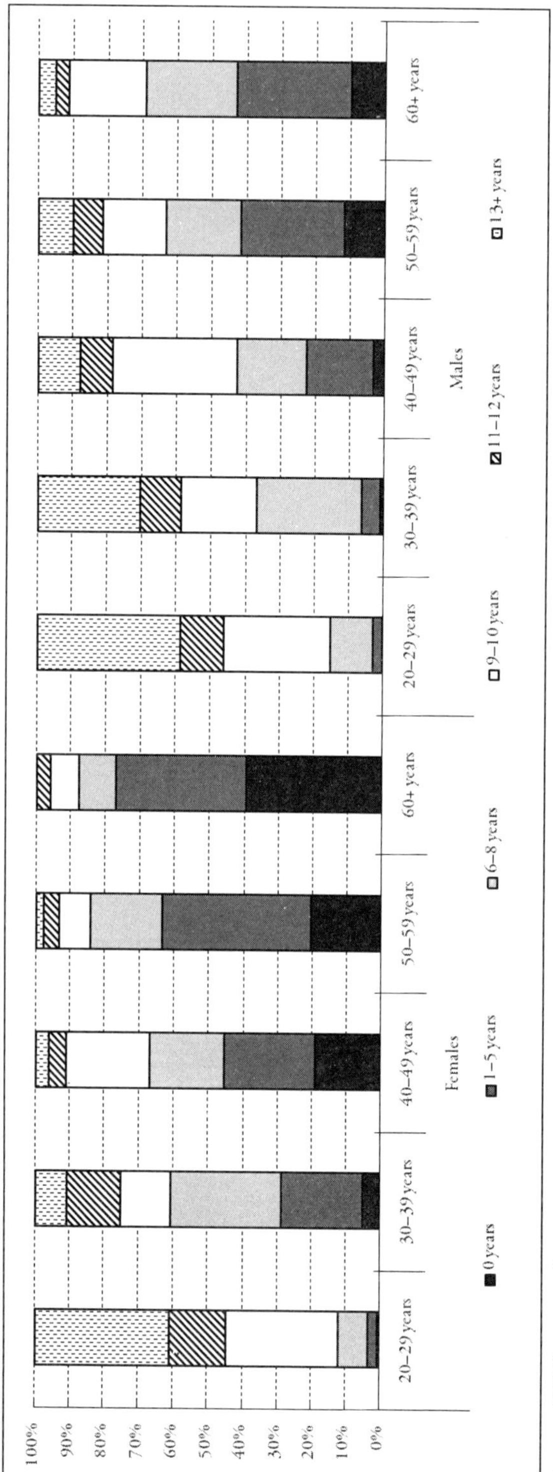

Source: PARI survey data.

around 30 per cent in Venmani and 40 per cent in Palakurichi, left school without proceeding to further education.

The jump in expansion of higher education also brought a new dimension of disparity to school education in the villages. Figures 14.3 to 14.8 show age-wise years of schooling according to social group. In both study villages, the Backward Classes started to gain higher education earlier than the Scheduled Castes and Most Backward Classes: around 30 per cent of those in the age group 30–39 years had more than 12 years of education; this proportion rose to 80 per cent for those in the age group 20–29 years, both males and females. The speed of this change was faster for females than for males, and the gender disparity had almost disappeared at the time of the PARI survey. On the other hand, the process of change differed between Scheduled Castes and Most Backward Classes, and between the two villages. In Venmani, the spread of higher education was much more visible among Scheduled Castes than among Most Backward Classes, while Most Backward Classes seemed to be at an advantage in Palakurichi. Among the Scheduled Castes, there were greater changes in Venmani, especially in respect of females, than in Palakurichi. The expansion of education was a remarkable feature of all social groups in the two villages including social groups that have been virtually excluded from higher education for a long time. At the same time, it is worth noting that the youth of the villages did not experience this change equally. Youth in Venmani had an advantage over youth in Palakurichi, and youth from socially better-off groups enjoyed better chances even though the gap has narrowed. It should also be noted that educational disparity has widened within social groups that were once excluded from higher education.

Children's Activities

The data on schooling can be verified by data on children's activities. These were collected in the survey.

As Tables 14.3 and 14.4 show, 100 per cent of children aged 6–9 years and around 95 per cent of those in the age group 10–14 years old were students without any reported secondary activity. The number of children whose primary activity was other than student was rather limited: only two children in Palakurichi and none in Venmani. We also checked whether the grades/standards in which the children were studying corresponded to the prescribed ages defined by the State government. Here again, more than 95 per cent of children were enrolled in the age-appropriate grade. We can conclude that the notion of compulsory schooling has been well settled in the two villages, at least as far as enrolment is concerned.

Figure 14.3 *Years of schooling by age group, Scheduled Caste males and females, Venmani*

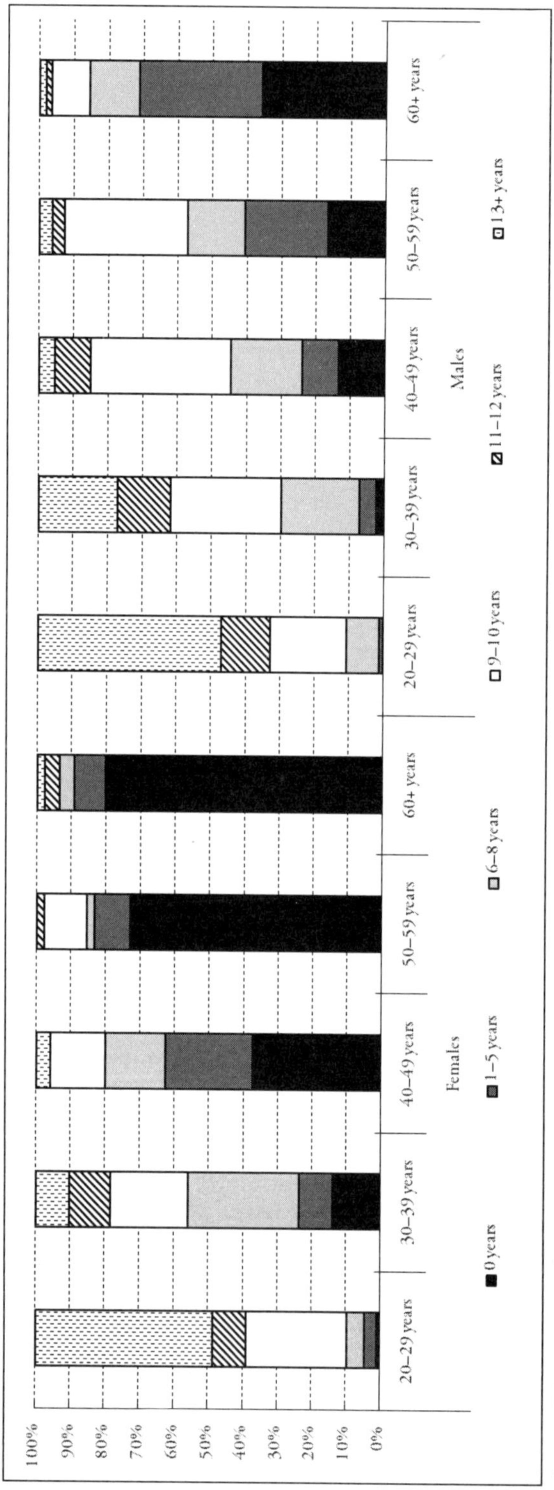

Source: PARI survey data.

Figure 14.4 *Years of schooling by age group, Most Backward Classes males and females, Venmani*

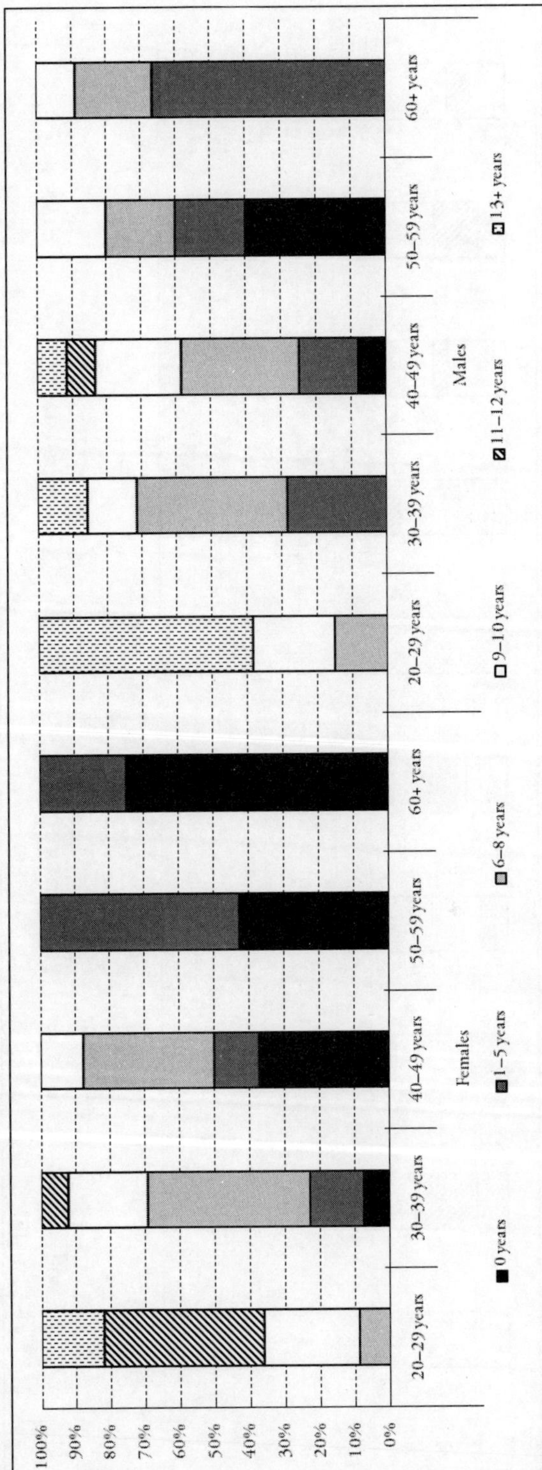

Source: PARI survey data.

Figure 14.5 *Years of schooling by age group, Backward Classes males and females, Venmani*

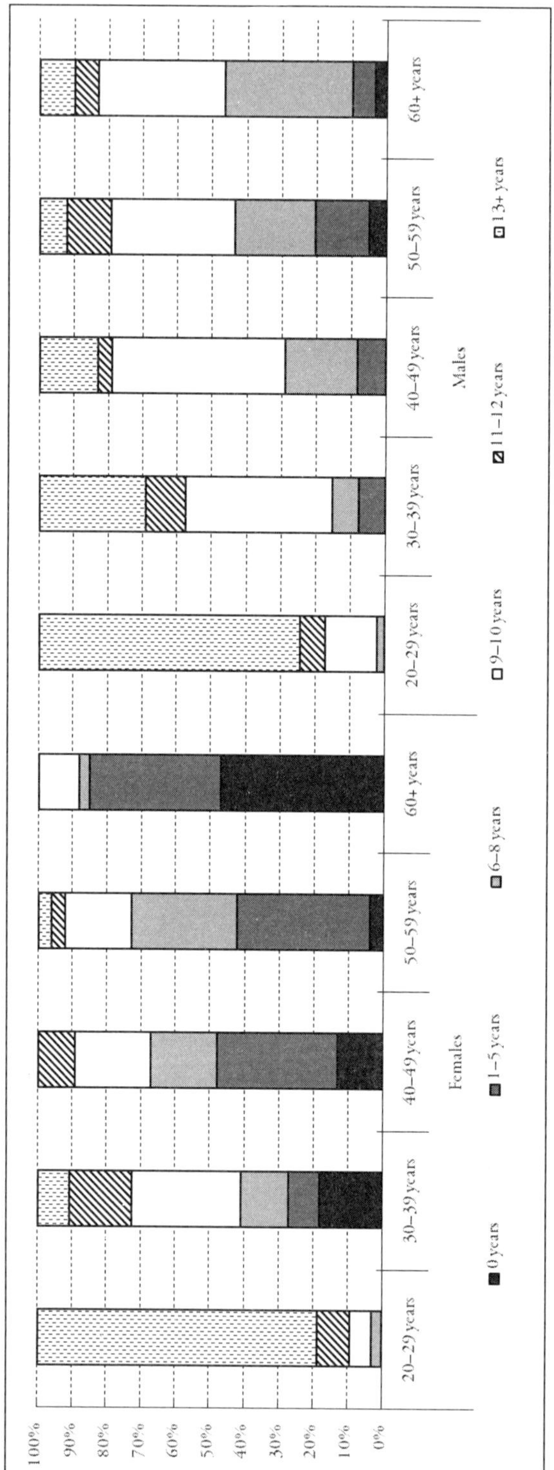

Source: PARI survey data.

Figure 14.6 *Years of schooling by age group, Scheduled Caste males and females, Palakurichi*

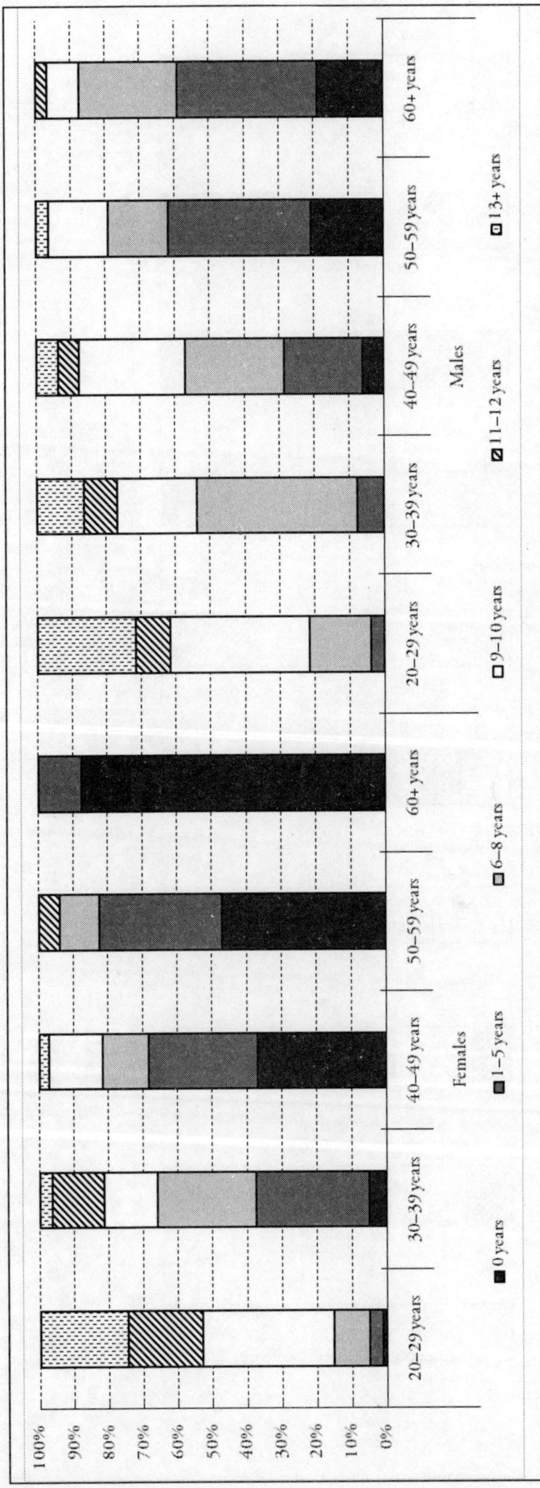

Source: PARI survey data.

Figure 14.7 *Years of schooling by age group, Most Backward Classes males and females, Palakurichi*

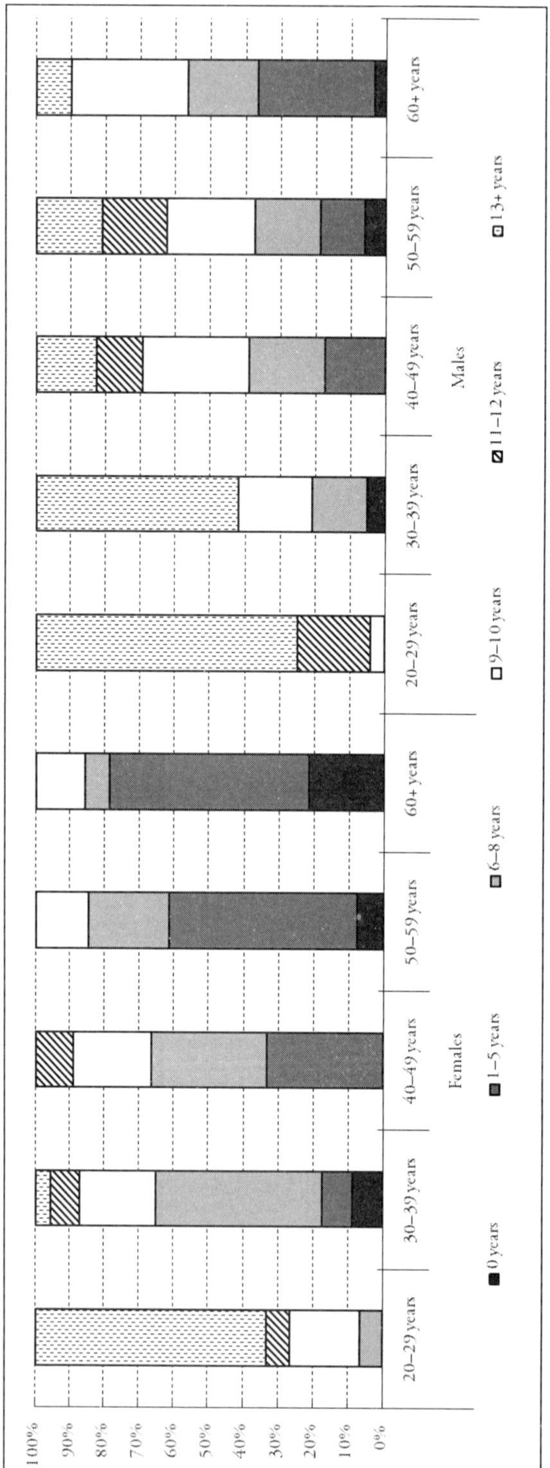

Source: PARI survey data.

Figure 14.8 *Years of schooling by age group, Backward Classes males and females, Palakurichi*

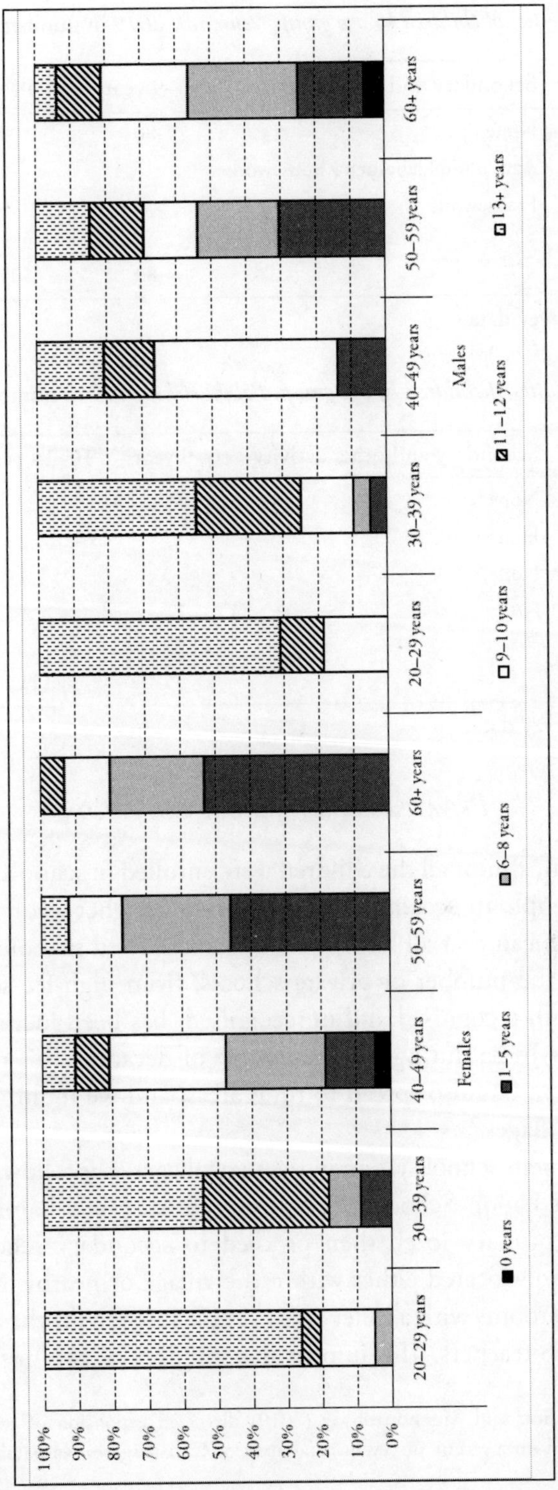

Source: PARI survey data.

Table 14.3 *Activities of children by age group, Venmani, 2019* in number

Primary activity	Secondary and other activity	6–9 years	10–14 years	6–14 years
Student	None	80	99	179
Student	Agricultural labourer + housework	–	1	1
Student	Housework	–	5	5
Total number of children		80	105	185

Source: PARI survey data.

Table 14.4 *Activities of children by age group, Palakurichi, 2019* in number

Primary activity	Secondary and other activity	6–9 years	10–14 years	6–14 years
Student	None	55	107	162
Student	Housework	–	2	2
Manual work	None	–	1	1
Others	None	–	1	1
Total number of children		55	111	166

Source: PARI survey data.

Privatisation of School Education

As we have seen, almost all the children were enrolled in schools, and more and more young people are seeking to proceed beyond higher secondary schooling. This does not mean that all have equal or standardised schooling. It has been observed that the number of private schools, from high-fee schools to low-fee schools, both recognised and unrecognised, has been increasing in urban centres all over India during the last couple of decades. This privatisation of school education has also spread to rural areas, and we found this to be true in the survey villages.[2]

The government school system in the two villages is as follows. The children join Panchayat Union Schools (PUSs) located in several hamlets within the village at the primary level, then proceed to secondary schools or higher secondary schools located either within the village or nearby. Most PUSs are small (two classrooms with a toilet and a simple kitchen for the mid-day meal) with one or two teachers. This implies that children of two or three grades sit

[2] For example, Lahoti and Mukhopadhyay (2019) discussed expansion of private schools and school choice based on a recent survey in rural areas of Chhattisgarh, Karnataka, Rajasthan, and Uttarakhand.

together and are taught by a single teacher. PUSs have enabled the children of the villages, even among households at a disadvantaged position, to study in schools within walking distance from their homes, with schoolmates familiar to them since birth. Mid-day meals cooked and served at the school are an attractive incentive. However, for parents who expect "better" schooling with a scope for higher education, PUSs are no longer the "only" option to place their children.

In the vicinity of the villages surveyed, a private mission school for boys, pre-school to 10th standard, was set up by a Catholic organisation in a town adjacent to Venmani. It claims "good" English-medium education, a "100 per cent pass-ratio" in Secondary School Certificate (SSC) exams, and a link with a higher secondary school run by a sister organisation. Well-established within a decade of being set up, the school attracts students not only from the town itself but also surrounding villages.

Table 14.5 *Children attending school, by age group, type and location of school, Venmani* in number

Type of school and location	6–9 years	10–14 years	15–16 years	17 years and above
Government school, within village	32	10		
Government school, within district	23	53	24	17
Government school, within Tamil Nadu	2	5		1
Government-aided private school, within district	1	12	5	1
Private school, within district	13	21	11	10
Private school, within Tamil Nadu	2			1

Source: PARI survey data.

Table 14.6 *Children attending school, by age group, type and location of school, Palakurichi* in number

Type of school and location	6–9 years	10–14 years	15–16 years	17 years and above
Government school, within village	41	91	30	26
Government school, within district	1	2	1	
Government school, within Tamil Nadu	1	1		
Government-aided private school, within district	3			
Private school, within district	4	6	1	
Private school, within Tamil Nadu		3		1

Source: PARI survey data.

Tables 14.5 and 14.6 show the schools in which children and youth are enrolled in the study villages.

Most of the children of Venmani and Palakurichi are enrolled in government schools and government-aided schools within their village or nearby. However, about 20 per cent of children in the age group 6–14 years in Venmani go to private schools.

Tables 14.7 and 14.8 show the socio-economic backgrounds of the children who are attending private schools. Interestingly, while in Venmani, children belonging to the Scheduled Castes are well represented in this group, they are less so in Palakurichi. Children from different socio-economic classes, especially middle peasants, are well represented among children going to

Table 14.7 *Social group of children attending private schools, Venmani and Palakurichi* in number

Social group	Venmani	Palakurichi
Scheduled Caste	18	2
Most Backward Class	5	1
Backward Class and Others	13	10
All	36	13

Source: PARI survey data.

Table 14.8 *Socio-economic class of children attending private schools, Venmani and Palakurichi* in number

Class	Venmani	Palakurichi
Landlords and big capitalist farmers	NA	2
Rich peasants	2	0
Middle peasants	10	5
Poor peasants	3	2
Wage workers with major income from unskilled, semi-skilled and manual work	4	0
Wage workers with major income from skilled and formal sector wage work	6	1
Self-employed in business activity	2	2
Salaried persons	5	0
Persons living on pensions small rents, and remittances	4	1
All	36	13

Note: NA – not available.
Source: PARI survey data.

private schools, but not exclusively so. We are not in a position to assess whether government schools or private schools are better for the development of children, but the data show that a large section of the rural population recognises the importance of education and is willing to pay fees for the same.

Education and Occupation

We observed increased aspiration for education in the study villages. Most inhabitants of the two villages, irrespective of class and caste, accept that children should be enrolled in school when they are six years old, continue their studies till at least the secondary level, and if possible, beyond that. Apart from the intrinsic value of education and the joy of learning with friends, or the social prestige attached to education, it is obvious that economic concerns are also a driving force behind the growing aspiration for education. Education is now deemed as one of the major preconditions to get stable employment in both the public and private sectors, or to join business activities, even if it does not ensure these.

To what extent has education changed occupational patterns in the study villages? Evaluating the role of education in transforming occupational patterns requires a long time period and elaborate research. There are obviously many other factors that decide the range and scope of occupations, and the choices available. Here, we simply try to show the occupational patterns of two age groups in the study villages, namely, those aged 20–39 years, and 40 years and more. The reason for this separation is that persons aged 20–39 years in the survey year (those who were born in the 1990s) experienced a big jump in higher education.

Tables 14.9 and 14.10 show the occupations of non-migrant males in the two villages. Differences are visible between persons in the age groups 20–39 years, and 40 years and more, although it is likely that the older generation returned to agriculture and related work when their sons and daughters started to work. The occupations of the younger generation have diversified beyond agriculture. In the age group 20–39 years, the proportion of skilled workers is high among those with secondary school and ITI (Industrial Training Institute) education; and white-collar jobs and business occupations are higher among Diploma and Bachelor's degree holders as compared to persons with secondary school education in the older age group. This observation was common to both villages, though the extent of change is more visible in Venmani.

The pattern is more visible in the case of migrants, who work in an environment of more diverse employment and economic activities, as shown in Table 14.11. Those who have Bachelor's degrees and more seem to have more

Table 14.9 *Occupational patterns of non-migrant males, by years of schooling, Venmani, 2019*

Years of schooling	20–39 years (Males)									
	Peasant	Agricultural labourer	Artisan	Manual work	Factory worker	Skilled worker	Student	White-collar job	Business/ shop owner	Others
0–5 years	2	4		1		4				
6–8 years	2	13		4	1	5			3	
9–10 years	3	7		12	3	19		1	1	
11–12 years	1	1		2	1	12	1	1	1	1
ITI	2	2				12		3	2	3
Diploma or Bachelor's degree	1		1	1		12	5	10	5	9
Master's degree and beyond				1			1	3		

Years of schooling	40 years and above (Males)										
	Peasant	Agricultural labourer	Animal husbandry	Manual work	Skilled worker	White-collar job	Artisan	Factory worker	Business/ shop owner	Housework	Others
0–5 years	28	28	1	28	1				9		9
6–8 years	27	15	1	6	1	1	1	1	2		7
9–10 years	38	12		10	9	5	1		11	2	2
11–12 years	6	1		3	3	2		1			3
ITI	1				1	1					
Diploma or Bachelor's degree	4								2		3
Master's degree and beyond						3					1

Source: PARI survey data.

Table 14.10 *Occupational pattern of non-migrant males, by years of schooling, Palakurichi, 2019*

	20–39 years (Males)									
Years of schooling	Peasant	Agricultural labourer	Artisan	Manual work	Factory worker	Skilled worker	Student	White-collar job	Business/	Others
0–5 years	1	5		3						
6–8 years	7	10		15	1	7				1
9–10 years	4	5	2	19	2	17			1	1
11–12 years	2	3	1	6		10		2		2
ITI		2		9		8		2	1	1
Diploma or Bachelor's degree			1	2	3	3	7	7	2	3
Master's degree and beyond	1			1				2		

	40 years and above (Males)									
Years of schooling	Peasant	Agricultural labourer	Animal husbandry	Artisan	Manual work	Skilled worker	White-collar job	Business/ shop owner	Housework	Others
0–5 years	30	13	2		24	2		4	1	6
6–8 years	22	8		1	9	6		3		3
9–10 years	23	4		1	10	8	3	8		5
11–12 years	5	1		1	1	3	2	1		
ITI	1				1	2	1	1		
Diploma or Bachelor's degree	8					1	1	1		1
Master's degree and beyond	1						2			

Source: PARI survey data.

Table 14.11 *Occupational patterns of migrant males, by years of schooling, age group 20 years and above, Venmani and Palakurichi, 2019*

	20–39 years (Males)									
Years of schooling	Agricultural labourer	Manual work	Factory worker	Skilled worker	Student	White-collar job	Professional work	Business/ shop owner	Housework	Others
6–8 years		2		8						
9–10 years	1	5	6	21				2	2	1
11–12 years		1		9		3			2	
ITI				5		5				
Diploma or Bachelor's degree			2	9	6	25	1	1	3	1
Master's degree and beyond					2	2		1		

	40 years and above (Males)							
Years of schooling	Peasant	Manual work	Factory worker	Skilled worker	Student	White-collar job	Housework	Others
0–5 years				1				
6–8 years		4		3			1	
9–10 years		1	7	13			1	1
11–12 years		3	3	1		2		
ITI		1	2	6		2		
Diploma or Bachelor's degree	2			6	3	14	1	
Master's degree and beyond					1	2	2	

Source: PARI survey data.

Table 14.12 *Occupational patterns of non-migrant females, by years of schooling and age group, Venmani*

Years of schooling	20–39 years (Females)										
	Peasant	Agricultural labourer	Animal husbandry	Manual work	Factory worker	Skilled worker	Student	White-collar job	Business/ shop owner	Housework	Others
0–5 years	5	18		7						6	
6–8 years	5	18		12		1		1	1	9	
9–10 years	5	16		12		4	1	2	2	22	
11–12 years	2	3		5		1	1	1		19	
ITI				1						3	1
Diploma or Bachelor's degree		2	1	4	1	3	19	6		22	1
Master's degree and beyond							2	9		5	1

Years of schooling	40 years and above (Females)								
	Peasant	Agricultural labourer	Animal husbandry	Manual work	Skilled worker	White-collar job	Business/ shop owner	Housework	Others
0–5 years	22	50	4	61	1		4	50	18
6–8 years	6	7	2	11			1	13	
9–10 years	8	4	1	13			1	12	
11–12 years	1			1	1	1		5	
ITI									
Diploma or Bachelor's degree	1					1		3	
Master's degree and beyond						1			

Source: PARI survey data.

Table 14.13 *Occupational patterns of non-migrant females, by years of schooling and age group, Palakurichi*

Years of schooling	20–39 years (Females)								
	Peasant	Agricultural labourer	Manual work	Skilled worker	Student	White-collar job	Business/ shop owner	Housework	Others
0–5 years	5	13	7	1				5	1
6–8 years	5	17	10	1		1	1	5	
9–10 years	4	8	11	2		1		19	
11–12 years	3	7	8		1	1	1	10	
ITI								1	
Diploma or Bachelor's degree	1		4	1	2	6	1	18	1
Master's degree and beyond					5	4		3	

Years of schooling	40 and above (Females)							
	Peasant	Agricultural labourer	Animal husbandry	Manual work	White-collar job	Business/ shop owner	Housework	Others
0–5 years	17	22		32		2	17	11
6–8 years	2	4	1	12		1	11	
9–10 years	5	3	1	2	2	1	12	1
11–12 years	1		1			2	4	
Diploma or Bachelor's degree					1			
Master's degree and beyond								1

Source: PARI survey data.

chances of securing white-collar jobs, and among male migrants who had less than 10 years of schooling, more than half worked as either "skilled worker" or "factory worker." Unfortunately, we do not have enough information on the conditions and status of work, or the mode of recruitment of "skilled worker"/"factory worker," and so we have to be cautious about drawing any conclusions regarding a correlation between educational qualification and occupation from the data on the two villages. However, we note that those having higher educational qualifications tend to have wider choices when they migrate, as compared to those in their age group who remain in the village.

Finally, Tables 14.12 and 14.13 show the occupational patterns of females in the two different age groups and with different levels of education. As noted earlier, the gender gap in education, even at higher levels of education, has narrowed remarkably over the last couple of decades, and women are now getting much longer years of schooling than earlier.

However, the expansion of female education does not necessarily lead to higher female work participation. While 10–15 per cent of women who obtained a Bachelor's degree or higher educational qualifications worked at "white collar" jobs, nearly half of them were engaged in "housework." In Venmani, of the younger generation of women who studied up to the higher secondary school level, more than half reported their main activity as "housework." On the other hand, among those who left school in Class 10 or below, we observed an occupational pattern similar to that of their mother's and grandmother's generations. These women were peasants, agricultural and manual labourers, and engaged in housework. While education certainly enlarges the occupational scope, such as employment in "white collar" job, for highly educated females, the current situation is rather unclear.

Concluding Remarks

One of the most striking findings from the PARI survey of the two villages in the lower Cauvery delta is the rapid expansion of higher education in the last few decades. There are several factors that account for this. The policies of the government including incentives at the school level such as free mid-day meals, a relatively well-managed school system, and encouragement of private investment in educational institutions are among them. The most crucial factor is the expectation on the part of inhabitants of the villages that higher education is almost the sole step towards securing an income that could be an alternative to agriculture and related work. The empowerment and aspiration brought about by long-term social/political movements, and the commitments of various organizations, are also important, especially in the case of Venmani.

It could be argued that occupational diversification, at least to a certain extent, is related to the expansion of education. Confirmation of this relationship requires data for a much longer time period and a more nuanced story. One relevant observation here is that the privileged sections have better chances in the employment market because of their advantageous social networks and social capital, especially under conditions of job-less growth.

The rapid expansion of education in recent years has changed the rural scene tremendously. Within a social group or among households with similar productive resources, the access to income brought by educated members significantly differentiates the economic position of particular households. It is true that education is by nature class-reproductive, namely, those who have better resources tend to enjoy better access to education, but this link is not exclusive. Although a discussion of these is beyond the scope of this chapter, education must have a tremendous impact on various aspects of the everyday lives of people in the village, such as family relationships, marriage alliances, migration, and consumption, besides its direct impact on occupational and economic activities. We would like to conclude by making the point that education has become one of the crucial factors to understand the dynamics of rural society today.

Appendix

Appendix Table 14.1 *Median years of schooling by social group, including migrants, Venmani*

Social group	Females	Males	Persons
Scheduled Castes	9	10	9
Backward Classes	8	10	10
Most Backward Classes	8	9	8
Other	8	11	10

Source: PARI survey data.

Appendix Table 14.2 *Median years of schooling by social group, including migrants, Palakurichi*

Social group	Females	Males	Persons
Scheduled Castes	9	9	9
Backward Classes	10	12	10
Most Backward Classes	8	10	10
Other	10	9	10

Source: PARI survey data.

15

Housing

R. Gopinath

HIGHLIGHTS

The Government of Tamil Nadu has a better record than many other State governments in providing housing and other basic amenities (toilets, water, electricity, and LPG) to the rural population. In 1983, S. Guhan noted that 84 per cent of all houses in Palakurichi were thatched huts. In 2019, 40 per cent of the houses were fully *pucca* and another 38 per cent were semi-*pucca* (with tiled roofs). Four out of five *pucca* houses that are owned by Scheduled Caste households today were constructed with aid from government schemes. Many households, however, had to borrow funds to complete house construction, as allocations from the government were not adequate.

A substantial number of households in the study villages of Palakurichi and Venmani continue to live in poor-quality *kutcha* houses. The proportion of households with *kutcha* houses was higher among wage workers with income from unskilled and semi-skilled jobs than any other class (32 out of 46 houses of unskilled wage workers in Venmani were *kutcha* houses).

Almost all the households had access to electricity. Drinking water was available either within the homestead or within 200 metres of the homestead for the large majority of households in Venmani. In Palakurichi, many Scheduled Caste households had to travel up to 1 kilometre to get drinking water. Nagapattinam district had been declared "open defecation free," but about one-half of the households in our survey lacked access to toilets. Most of these were Scheduled Caste households.

Caste-based residential segregation persists. Cramped conditions of houses in low-lying Dalit settlements means less area (homestead land) available for better housing, for the construction of toilets and more rooms, and for the drainage of water.

Introduction

Shelter is a basic need, along with food and clothing, for human subsistence. The last three-and-a-half decades were important in terms of implementation of social security schemes in Tamil Nadu. Government agencies played a strong supporting role in improving the conditions of housing and related amenities. This chapter analyses changes that took place in two villages, Venmani and Palakurichi, in Nagapattinam district of Tamil Nadu. A comparison of housing and related amenities was done over two time periods wherever possible, using the study by S. Guhan (1983). The analysis found that all sections of residents of the two villages, particularly the Scheduled Castes, reported an improvement in living standards. However, stark differences were noted between the economically affluent classes and the other classes, as also between the Scheduled Castes and Most Backward Classes, and persons of other social groups.

Conditions of Housing

The quality of housing structure depends on the materials used for the construction of roof, wall, and floor. While the Census of India and the National Sample Survey (NSS) consider materials used for the roof and wall, our analysis includes the material used for the floor as well.[1] Therefore, in this chapter, a *pucca* structure refers to a house that used *pucca* materials for roof, wall, and roof. Semi-*pucca* structures are those that used *pucca* materials for roof or wall or floor, or any two of these but not all three.

Guhan observed in 1983 that 84 per cent of the houses in Palakurichi were thatched and only eight houses were terraced. Since then, however, there have been significant improvements in housing conditions and amenities in the village. At the time of our survey in 2019, two-fifths of the houses in Palakurichi, or 156 out of 390 dwellings (40 per cent), were *pucca* houses; and in Venmani, more than half the houses (213 out of 415) were *pucca* in structure (Appendix Table 15.1). Semi-*pucca* houses, mostly with tiled roof, were significant in number in both the villages: 144 houses (35 per cent) in Venmani and 149 houses (38 per cent) in Palakurichi.

[1] The NSS and the Census define a *pucca* structure as one where roof and walls are constructed using materials such as cement, concrete, overburnt bricks, hollow cement/ash bricks, stone, stone blocks, jack boards (cement-plastered reeds), iron, zinc or other metal sheets, timber, tiles, slate, corrugated iron, asbestos cement sheet, veneer, plywood, artificial wood of synthetic material, and polyvinyl chloride material.

Figure 15.1 *Proportion of pucca houses constructed with government support, by social group, Venmani and Palakurichi, 2019* in per cent

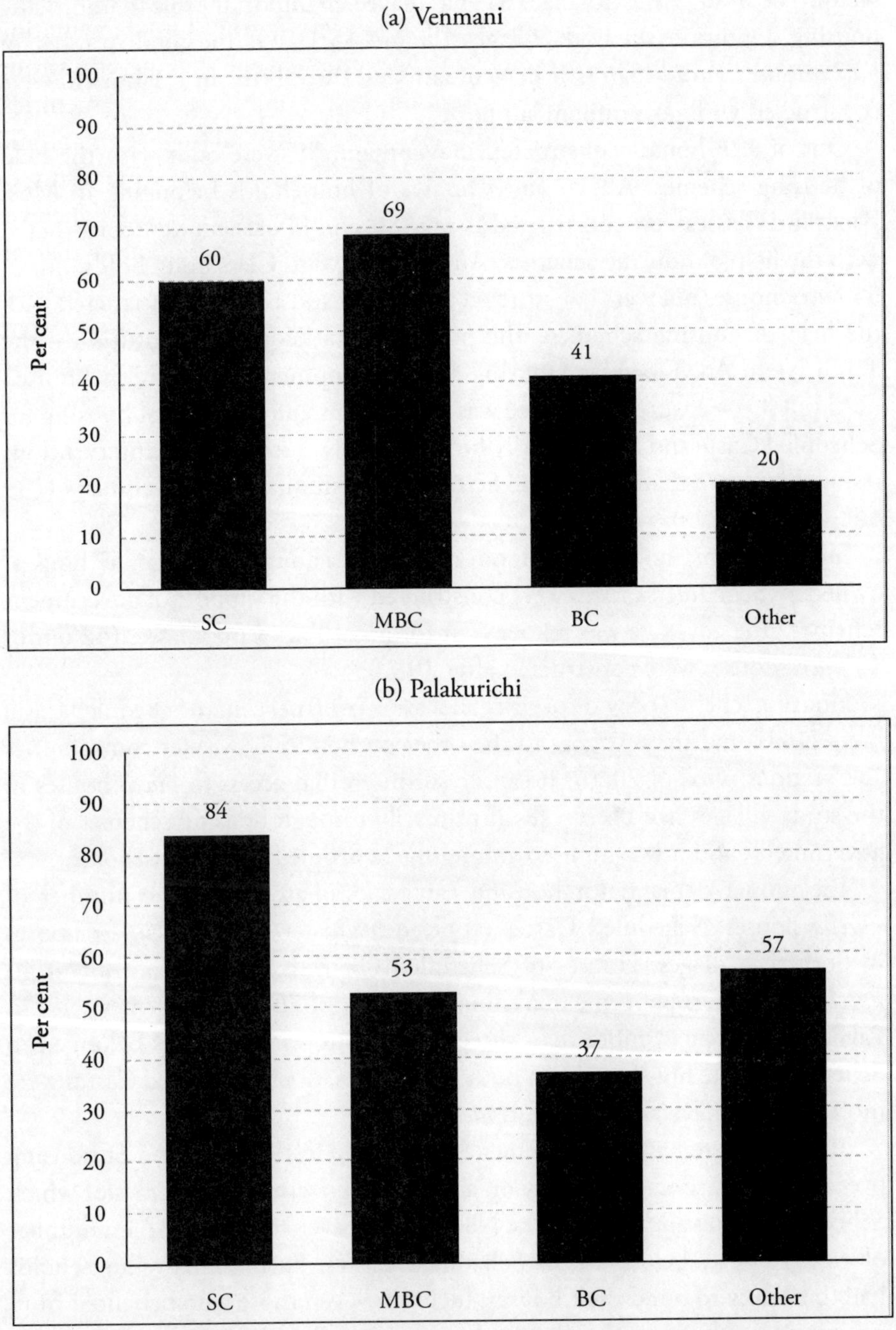

Note: SC – Scheduled Caste, MBC – Most Backward Class, BC – Backward Class.

Tamil Nadu started housing schemes for the poor much earlier than the national housing schemes, and there were sizeable investments in the housing sector. The Indira Awas Yojana (IAY) has played an important role in improving housing conditions in both villages (Figure 15.1). Of the total number of *pucca* houses, more than half in Venmani and three-fifths in Palakurichi were constructed with government support.

Out of 128 houses constructed in Venmani, 79 were built with the help of housing schemes. All 16 *pucca* houses of households belonging to Most Backward Classes were constructed after 1980, and 11 of them were constructed with the help of housing schemes. Among Backward Class households, out of 55 *pucca* houses, 44 were constructed after 1980 and 18 were constructed with the help of housing schemes. The presence of a dedicated institution – the Tamil Nadu Adi Dravidar Housing and Development Corporation Limited (TAHDCO) – ensured that there was better focus and coverage of housing for Scheduled Caste and Scheduled Tribe households. Such targeted interventions resulted in more than half of the Scheduled Castes having *pucca* houses (139 out of 263 houses).

In Palakurichi, more than four out of five *pucca* houses (48 out of 57 houses) owned by Scheduled Castes were constructed with the support of government schemes. The coverage was 53 per cent for Most Backward Classes (42 out of 49 *pucca* houses were constructed after 1980).

Housing schemes provide priority allocation of 60 per cent to Scheduled Caste households, and the rest goes to the other economically weaker communities and sections (GoTN 2020). It can be surmised that access to *pucca* houses in the study villages had been realised primarily through housing schemes of the government, and it was more so among the Scheduled Caste households.

The unmet demand for housing can be estimated from the number of *kutcha* houses. Scheduled Castes reported a greater share of *kutcha* houses in both the villages. Houses of Scheduled Castes constituted 35 out of 46 *kutcha* houses (75 per cent) in Venmani, and 59 of 76 houses (77 per cent) in Palakurichi. That is, more than three out of four *kutcha* houses belonged to Scheduled Caste households. In both the villages, non- Scheduled Castes were more likely to have *pucca* or semi-*pucca* houses.

In short, there has been a tremendous change in the condition of housing over the last few decades, largely on account of government schemes of which Scheduled Castes are beneficiaries. Nevertheless, even today, the largest number of *kutcha* houses belong to the Scheduled Castes. Further, many households had to borrow to build their houses, including even those who benefited from government schemes. The allocated amount of Rs 1,70,000 per house was often not sufficient to complete construction according to the beneficiaries,

Figure 15.2 *Proportion of households that reported outstanding debt to build or repair houses, by social group, Venmani and Palakurichi, 2019* in per cent

(a) Venmani

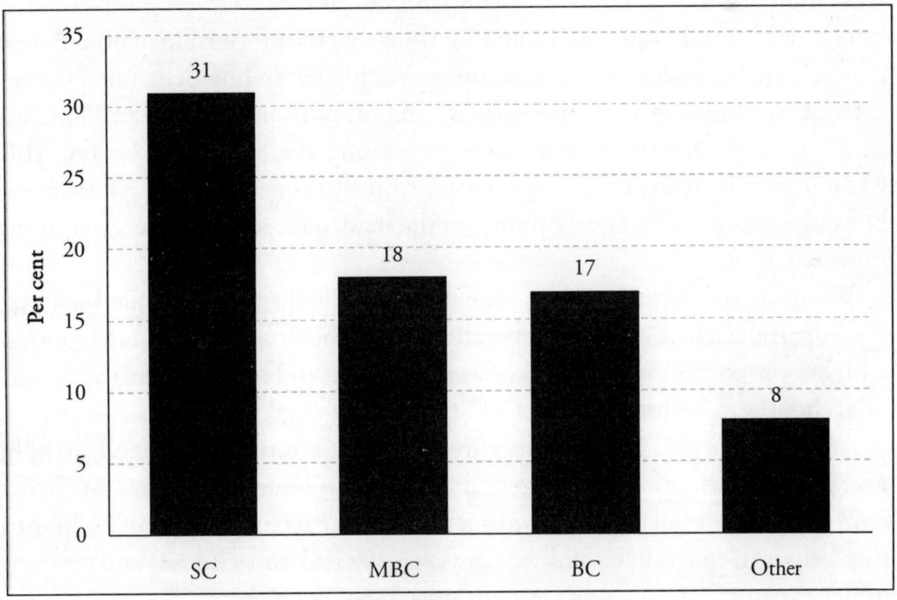

(b) Palakurichi

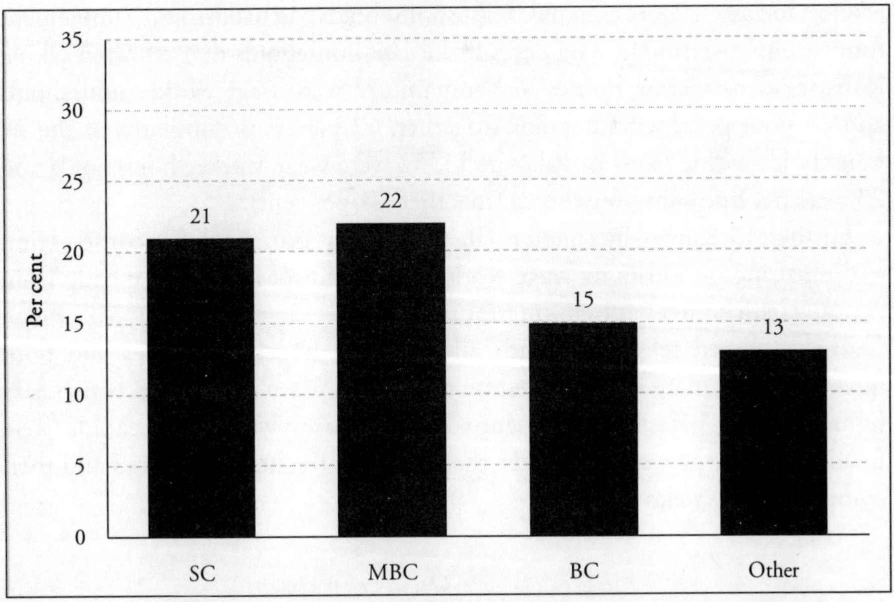

Note: SC – Scheduled Caste, MBC – Most Backward Class, BC – Backward Class.

resulting in borrowing from various sources for completion. In chapter 10 in this volume, Swaminathan and Dutta show that around 30 per cent of the principal borrowed in Venmani and Palakurichi was for house construction and house repair.

Figure 15.2 and Appendix Table 15.2 show that the proportion of households that incurred debt for housing purposes was higher among Scheduled Castes than other groups in both the villages. The proportion was high in Venmani where more *pucca* houses were reported among the Scheduled Castes. This was followed by Most Backward Classes, who also benefited from government housing schemes. This clearly points to the inadequacy of funds received from these schemes.

Wage workers with major income from unskilled and semi-skilled manual work, particularly agricultural operations, and construction workers reported a higher proportion than others of *kutcha* houses in both the villages (32 out of 46 houses in Venmani; 53 out of 76 houses in Palakurichi).

All landlords and rich peasants in Venmani, except one, resided in fully *pucca* houses. Out of 13 landlord and rich peasant households, only one had a semi-*pucca* house; all others had *pucca* houses. In Palakurichi, out of 16 houses that belonged to landlord and rich peasants, 15 had *pucca* houses and one was under construction.

Meanwhile, the construction of new houses was ongoing across socio-economic classes. Poor Scheduled Caste households had to borrow to supplement funds from government schemes. Of the 107 households that reported taking loans for constructing houses in Venmani, 52 were wage worker households and 14 poor peasant households (together, 62 per cent). Similarly, of the 78 households taking loans in Palakurichi, 32 were wage worker households and 23 were poor peasant households (together, 71 per cent).

Further, as shown in chapter 10, the money borrowed for construction and repairing of houses by wage workers and poor peasants was mostly from private credit sources at high interest rates.

The staggered release of funds allocated for housing schemes and poor quality of raw materials supplied as tied funds often forced the beneficiary households to invest by incurring debt. In cases where households were unable to raise the required funds, the quality of the houses suffered and their completion was delayed.

Availability of Homestead Land

Availability of homestead land points to stark differences between castes and classes. The mean extent of homestead land of the Scheduled Castes was less

Table 15.1 *Descriptive statistics on extent of homestead land, by social group, study villages, 2019* in square feet

Social group	Venmani				Palakurichi			
	Mean	Median	Min.	Max.	Mean	Median	Min.	Max.
Scheduled Castes	5,181	2,309	131	58,065	4,343	2,614	131	29,011
Most Backward Classes	6,076	4,247	218	36,155	7,546	3,485	44	1,08,900*
Backward Classes	7,318	4,356	196	87,120	6,191	3,920	566	43,560
Other	9,513	9,148	261	25,395	18,818	8,146	1,307	76,230
All	5,970	3,049	131	87,120	5,682	2,919	44	1,08,900

Note: * One house that belongs to a Most Backward Class (Vanniyar) household was a house constructed in the middle of orchards, in Palakurichi.
Source: Survey data, 2019.

than that of all other caste groups (Table 15.1). Further, non-Scheduled Caste households had larger homestead area even if their house was of semi-*pucca* type. Traditional houses, particularly among Naidus and other Backward Classes, were maintained with tiled roofs in many instances in both the villages. These tiled-roof houses were different from the semi-*pucca* tiled houses owned by the Scheduled Castes (though both are counted as semi-*pucca*).

Scheduled Caste houses, though *pucca* thanks to government schemes, lacked the necessary extra land around the house for drainage of water, drying of clothes, and other activities. The settlements and streets on which Scheduled Caste houses stood were cramped: houses without any gap between them was a common feature in both villages, particularly in Venmani.

The homestead land of houses belonging to wage workers was not even one-fourth the corresponding average of houses of landlords and rich peasants in Venmani and less than one-third in Palakurichi (Appendix Table 15.3). Historically, Scheduled Caste households had limited access to homestead land. They acquired land over a period through various struggles led by political parties (Ramakrishnan 2014). Land redistribution was one of the recommendations of the Ganapathia Pillai Commission that was appointed by the State government to inquire into agrarian labour problems in East Thanjavur in the year 1969 (GoTN 1969). The Tamil Nadu Occupants of Kudiyiruppu (Conferment of Ownership) Act, 1971 passed by the Dravida Munnetra Kazhagam (DMK) government supported the demand for homesites by vulnerable groups, particularly Scheduled Castes. It was struggles such as these and organised movements that facilitated the acquiring of land for building *pucca* houses.

Caste continues to be an important form of organisation of space in rural Tamil Nadu, and continues to be manifested in residential segregation. Caste-based colony houses given under different schemes is a testament to this – arising from overlapping factors such as a sense of security and group solidarity, unaffordability and social prejudices, and exclusive clustering of privileged groups.

Living Space

According to ILO standards, two persons per room is an acceptable norm for decent housing (ILO 1961). The average size of a household was 3.9 in Venmani and 3.7 in Palakurichi. As Appendix Table 15.4 indicates, a high proportion of Scheduled Caste households in both the villages exceeded the norm of two persons per room. Of the 261 houses that had more than two persons per room in Venmani, 163 belonged to Scheduled Castes; in Palakurichi, this number was 161 out of 270 houses.

Importantly, even among those with semi-*pucca* houses, there is a visible difference between Scheduled Caste houses and non-Scheduled Caste houses. While non-Scheduled Caste houses were bigger in size, Scheduled Caste houses were small and congested.

Houses built by the government for the Scheduled Castes, termed locally as "colony houses," lacked more than one room, but usually the single room was divided to make space for a kitchen by means of a half-built wall. Residents were forced to use the single room for multiple purposes. They used the same limited space to store their materials, food articles, provisions, and all other household items, apart from living in it. During the rainy season, they often ended up drying their clothes in the same room where they ate and slept. Children studied in the room while their parents watched TV or were engaged in other activities. The situation was especially deplorable for households with adolescent girls.

A Separate Kitchen

A separate kitchen is important for good health. According to NSSO (2019), 29.5 per cent of houses in rural Tamil Nadu do not have separate kitchens, lower than the rural all-India average of 47.6 per cent.

Overall, more than one-third of the houses in Venmani and more than half of the houses in Palakurichi did not have separate kitchens (Figure 15.3). In Palakurichi, the proportion of houses not having separate kitchens was

Figure 15.3 *Proportion of households without separate kitchen, by social group, study villages, 2019* in per cent

(a) Venmani

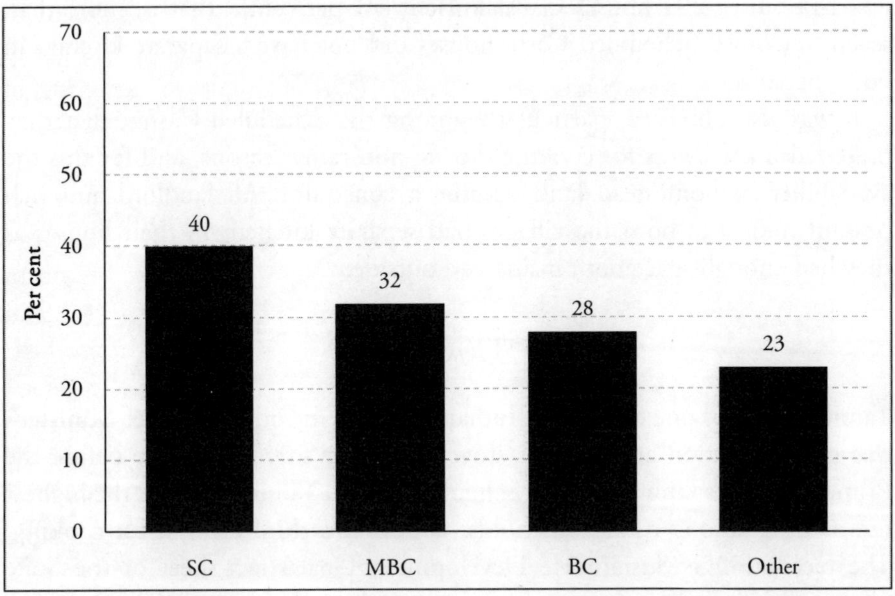

(b) Palakurichi

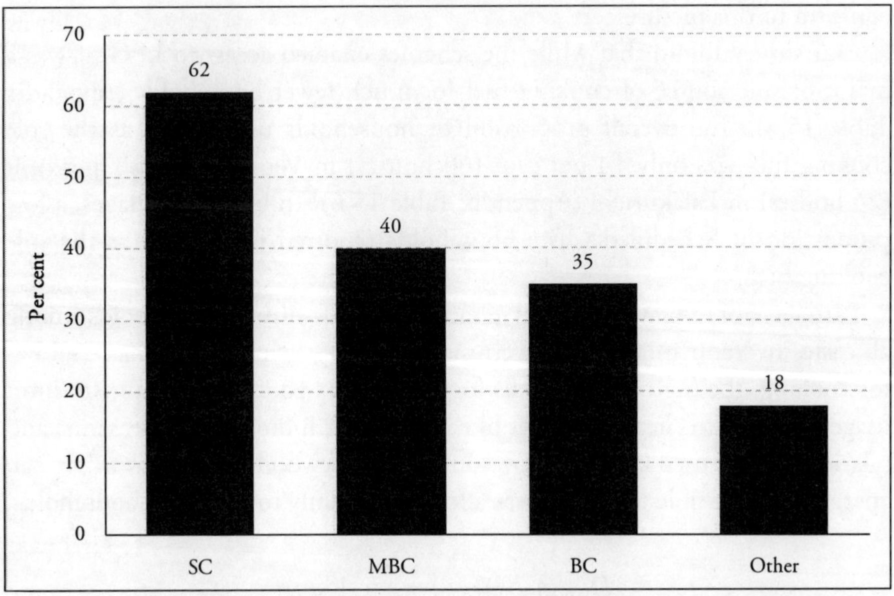

Note: SC – Scheduled Caste, MBC – Most Backward Class, BC – Backward Class.

particularly high among the Scheduled Castes as compared to other caste groups. Out of 149 households in Venmani that reported no separate kitchen in their houses, 106 were Scheduled Caste houses (71 per cent); the number was 145 out of 201 houses in Palakurichi (71 per cent). That is, more than seven out of 10 Scheduled Caste houses did not have a separate kitchen in both the villages.

It was also observed, particularly among the Scheduled Castes, that they preferred open spaces for cooking during non-rainy seasons, and for this the availability of homestead land became a constraint. All landlord and rich peasant houses in both the villages had separate kitchens in their houses as they had enough space both inside and outside.

Cooking Fuel

Tamil Nadu was one of the first Indian States to introduce a Chief Minister's free gas connection and free gas stove scheme in 2006, a decade before the Prime Minister's Ujjwala Yojana Scheme of 2016. Tamil Nadu has the highest use of LPG among rural households, with over a third using it for cooking. The recent SDG (Sustainable Development Goals) fact-sheet of the State government indicates that 99.4 per cent of households in Tamil Nadu use clean cooking fuel. However, the usage in Venmani and Palakurichi does not conform to this picture.

Our survey found that while the schemes enabled access to LPG, it was a major or sole source of cooking fuel for much fewer households (Appendix Table 15.5). The overall proportion of households using LPG as the sole cooking fuel was only 14 per cent (60 houses) in Venmani and six per cent (24 houses) in Palakurichi (Appendix Table 15.6). In both the villages, a low proportion of Scheduled Caste households reported using LPG as the sole cooking fuel.

Partial use of LPG was reported in more than four-fifths of households among all castes in Venmani. While government schemes helped people access LPG for cooking, the high cost of refills forced workers and poor peasants to limit usage and shift to cheaper sources like firewood. Landlords, rich peasants, and salaried persons used kerosene stoves instead of firewood. In other words, clean energy was accessible to all, but was affordable mainly to better-off households.

Durable Household Assets

Ownership of household assets such as electrical and electronic goods is widespread due to free distribution of such items by the State government for more than a decade. A free colour TV scheme was implemented in 2006, and a free mixer-grinder, fan, and rice-grinder scheme from 2011. The free colour TV scheme was stopped in 2011. This was an important reason for 50 (out of 263) Scheduled Caste households in Venmani and 69 (of 235) in Palakurichi not having a TV. It is common to see a thatched house with one room in the Scheduled Caste settlement having a TV, mixer-grinder, fan, and rice-grinder.

In Tamil Nadu, over the last one decade and more, successive governments have spent nearly 2 billion dollars (Rs 11,561 crore) on three schemes – providing colour television sets, laptops, and household appliances.[2] The State has invested significantly in creating these private assets for poorer households. However, the reach of laptops was negligible in the two study villages.

Another asset which people considered as "essential" was a two-wheeler. The increase in non-farm employment outside the village necessitated two-wheelers for easier mobility (Appendix Table 15.7). In more than one-third of wage worker households (72 out of 163 in Venmani and 68 out of 139 in Palakurichi), the major source of income was unskilled and semi-skilled manual work which required a two-wheeler to commute to nearby places hassle-free and on time. Therefore, people from all socio-economic groups perceived the two-wheeler as an essential item, despite the presence of public transport.

Other home appliances such as refrigerators were far from accessible to the economically weaker sections. While more than one-fifth of households in both villages (92 of 415 in Venmani and 86 of 390 in Palakurichi) had refrigerators, the proportion was 16 per cent (42 out of 263 houses) among Scheduled Castes in Venmani and just nine per cent (21 out of 235 houses) in Palakurichi.

Access to Electricity, Drinking Water, and Sanitation

Electricity

According to Guhan (1983), 40 per cent houses in Palakurichi were electrified during his survey in 1983. Among Scheduled Caste houses, 30 per cent had electricity. The sustained intervention in this sphere along with the free electricity to thatched houses scheme introduced in the 1980s (popularly known as the single light scheme) helped the poor gain access to electricity. Almost all households in both the villages had electricity during our survey period. Even in newly built houses, one of the non-negotiable components was an electricity connection.

[2] https://www.thehindu.com/news/national/tamil-nadu/tamil-nadu-the-ultimate-freebie-state/article7046314.ece

Water Supply

Ensuring that the population has adequate drinking water is an important prerequisite for hygiene. The task of providing safe drinking water and sanitation facilities to rural areas in the State of Tamil Nadu is the responsibility of the Department of Rural Development and Panchayat Raj and the Tamil Nadu Water Supply and Drainage Board (TWAD). As per official records, 76,704 habitations (78.13 per cent) were fully covered and 21,475 habitations (21.87 per cent) were partially covered (Chitra and Kanta 2017).

The water supply in Palakurichi improved from the late 1970s and early 1980s, after digging of wells and construction of a water tank (Guhan 1983). However, people had to fetch water by cycle and this was possible only for those who owned a cycle (*ibid.*). The situation had improved significantly by 2019. In Palakurichi, more than three-fifths of the houses (253 out of 390 houses) had access to drinking water within the homestead or within 200 metres. In Venmani, 374 out of 415 houses (90 per cent) had access to water within the homestead or within 200 metres.

According to NSSO, 91 per cent of rural houses in Tamil Nadu had drinking water within the homestead or within 200 meters. While Venmani was close to the State average (with 90 per cent), Palakurichi (64 per cent) still had scope for improvement.

Among social groups, there were differences in the incidence of drinking water within the homestead (Figure 15.4). Not even one-fifth of Scheduled Caste houses (45 out of 263 houses) in Venmani and one-tenth of Scheduled Caste houses (14 out of 235 houses) in Palakurichi had access to drinking water within the homestead. Among houses belonging to the Backward Classes and Most Backward Classes, more than 30 per cent had drinking water within the homestead. In Palakurichi, 58 households, of which 39 were Scheduled Caste households, said they had to travel more than one kilometre to get drinking water (Appendix Table 15.8). Further, 32 households, of which 24 were Scheduled Caste households, had to travel between half a kilometre and one kilometre to fetch drinking water.

Gram panchayats provide individual water connections to houses based on requests and a minimum deposit of Rs 3,000 to Rs 5,000 per connection. Economically better-off households got these connections whereas Scheduled Caste households were not able to access them.

In terms of public facilities, the number of houses per water outlet (street pipe/common water tank) was lower among the Backward Classes and Most Backward Classes, and higher among the Scheduled Castes as their settlements were congested and densely populated. Therefore, Scheduled Caste households

Figure 15.4 *Proportion of houses having access to drinking water with location, by social group, 2019* in number and per cent

(a) Venmani

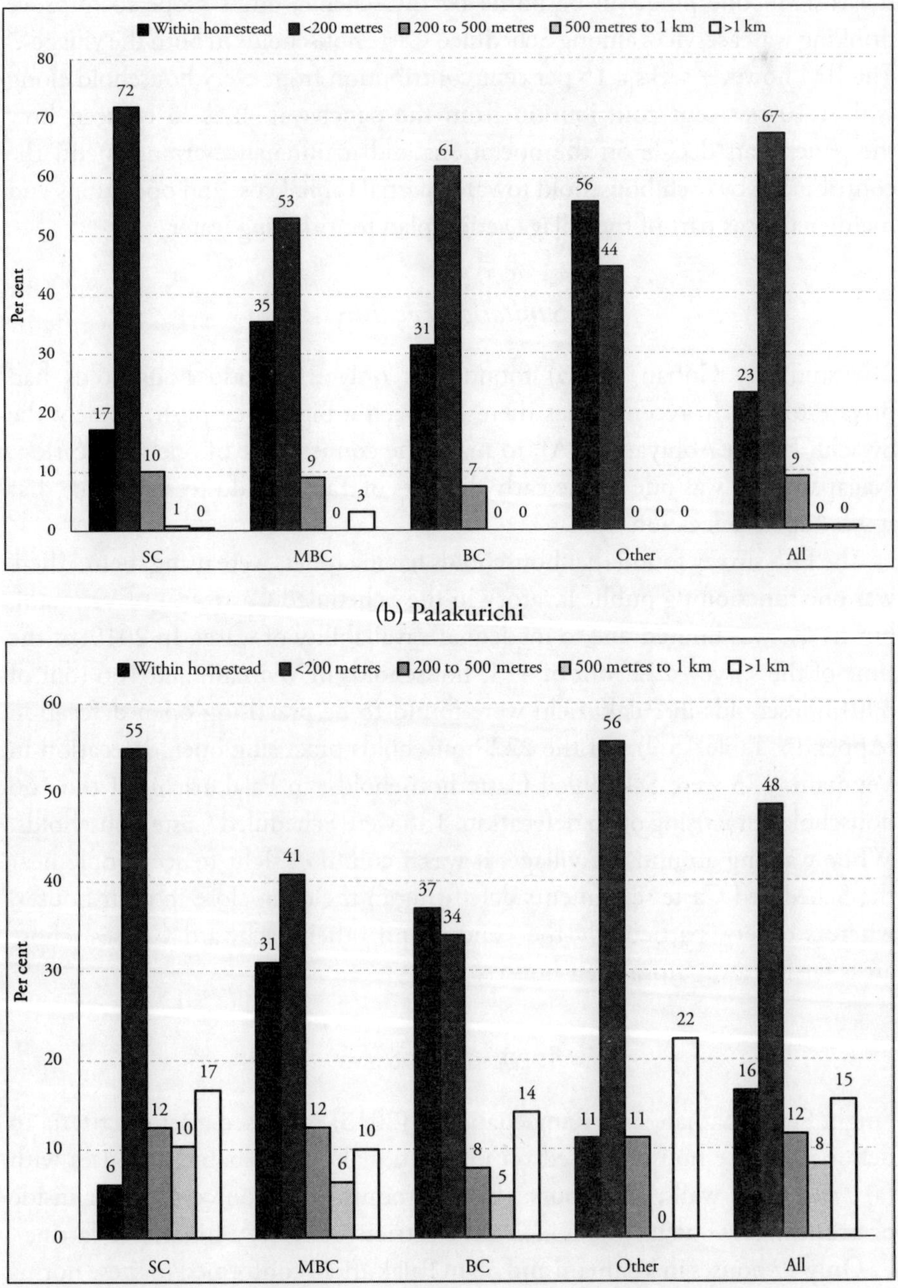

(b) Palakurichi

Note: SC – Scheduled Caste, MBC – Most Backward Class, BC – Backward Class.

spent more time on collection of water than others. The objective of the current Jal Jeevan Mission (JJM) of moving to fixed household tap connections at the household level, whereby up to three pipes will be provided per house of which the costs of one pipe will be borne by the scheme, offers scope to improve drinking water services among Scheduled Caste households in both the villages.[3] The JJM however seeks a 15 per cent contribution from every household along with a 10 per cent contribution from the panchayat. It is to be seen how the panchayats decide on the operations and maintenance arrangement, the contribution by each household towards partial capital cost and operations and maintenance as part of the village action plan for drinking water.

Sanitation Facilities

The study by Guhan (1983) found that only 21 Naidu households had private toilets. In recent times there has been a big policy push, namely the Swachh Bharat Abhiyan (SBA), to make the country free of open defecation. Nagapattinam was one of the early districts of Tamil Nadu to announce that it was "open defecation free."

The FAS survey found that households having toilets were using them. There was one functioning public lavatory in the Scheduled Caste area of Venmani, but its use was limited due to inadequate availability of water. In 2019, at the time of the survey, 222 (out of 415) households in Venmani and 166 (out of 390) households in Palakurichi were found to be practising open defecation (Appendix Table 15.9). Of the 222 households practising open defecation in Venmani, 173 were Scheduled Caste households; in Palakurichi, of the 166 households practising open defecation, 138 were Scheduled Caste households. While walking around the village, it was a common sight to see people near the Scheduled Caste settlements defecating in the open close to their houses, whereas others, particularly the Naidus and other Backward Classes, chose areas farther away from their houses.

Adequate Housing

Singh, Swaminathan, and Ramachandran (2013) proposed a set of criteria to define adequate housing based on international norms, namely, houses with (a) *pucca* roof, walls, and floors; (b) two rooms; (c) a source of water inside or immediately outside the house; (d) electricity; and (e) a functional latrine.

Only 37 houses in Venmani and 38 in Palakurichi conformed to these norms

[3] https://jalshakti-ddws.gov.in/sites/default/files/JJM_note.pdf

Figure 15.5 *Proportion of households with adequate housing, Venmani and Palakurichi, 2019* in per cent

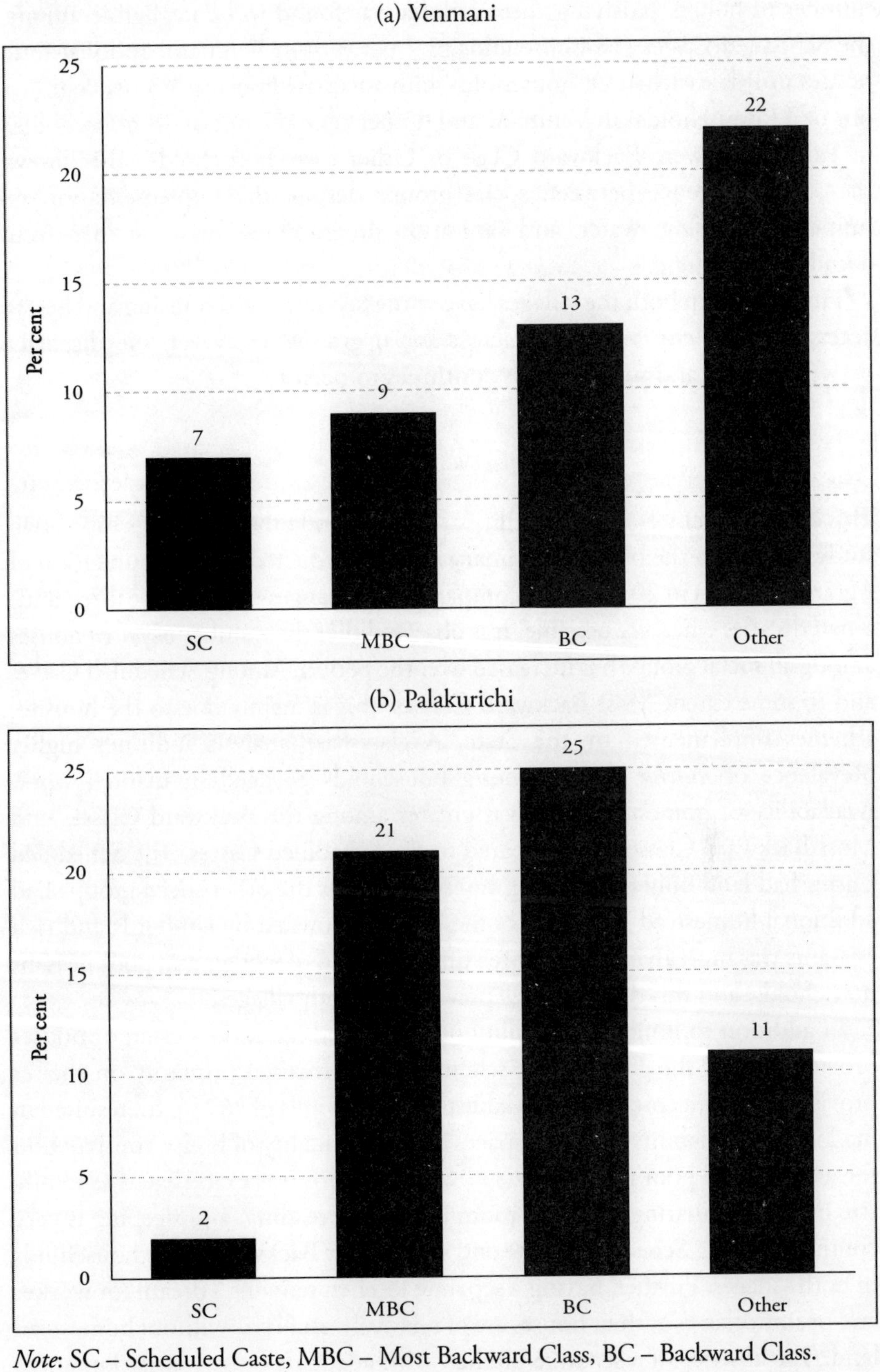

Note: SC – Scheduled Caste, MBC – Most Backward Class, BC – Backward Class.

of adequate housing. In other words, hardly one out of ten households fulfilled all criteria proposed under this integrated view of housing (Figure 15.5). The number of houses satisfying these criteria was found to be negligible among the Schedued Castes (18 households or 7 per cent in Venmani, and just four houses in Palakurichi). Of households with adequate housing, 43 per cent (16 out of 37 households) in Venmani and 45 per cent (17 out of 38 households) in Palakurichi were Backward Class or Other caste households. This shows the stark difference between social groups despite the implementation of numerous housing, water, and sanitation programmes for more than four decades in the State.

Households in both the villages have witnessed improved housing and better access to electricity and water across social groups. However, the disparity between classes and social groups continues to persist.

Conclusion

This chapter discusses the availability of housing and other amenities in the two study villages on the basis of a primary survey conducted by the Foundation of Agrarian Studies in 2019 with a comparison of changes over the last three-and-a-half decades wherever possible. It is observed that the number of *pucca* houses among all social groups has increased over the period. Among Scheduled Castes and to some extent Most Backward Classes, this is mainly due to the housing schemes implemented by the State. A class-wise analysis indicates higher prevalence of *kutcha* houses among households engaged in manual work. Availability of homestead land was greater among the Backward Classes and Most Backward Classes, as compared to the Scheduled Castes. The Scheduled Castes had land only for building houses, whereas the other social groups had additional homestead land. The homestead land owned by landlords and rich peasants was more than at least three times the land of worker and poor peasant households, and this disparity was prevalent in both villages.

In addition to limited availability of homestead land, the design of houses provided under the government scheme, which focused primarily on shelter provision at a unit cost of Rs 1.70 lakh and a plinth area of 269 sq. ft., resulted in inadequate availability of living spaces and poor quality of house construction for workers and poor peasant classes, which in turn was exacerbated as family size increased. Sharing the same room for eating, reading, and sleeping is very common among Scheduled Caste and some Most Backward Class households in both villages. Further, having a separate kitchen remains a dream for worker and peasant classes as their houses are of relatively small size without homestead land. The absence of a separate kitchen with adequate cross-ventilation and a toilet adjacent to the house is inconsistent with the provision of minimum human needs that would help to classify such houses as "liveable" dwellings.

The design of houses under government schemes are ill-conceived, focusing only on offering shelter as opposed to improving living conditions, and executed without sufficient thought given to many inter-related issues. Building houses without considering the size of the family or new additions to it often resulted in congested homes. An average floor space of 38 sq. ft. per individual in rural areas, not including the space taken by livestock and agricultural requirements, results in a very unhealthy and uncomfortable indoor environment.

It is important to note that while the government has been facilitating the building of new houses for all social groups, the availability of credit at lower interest rates is critical as the incidence of borrowing is very high. The inadequacy of money allotted under the government schemes and the desire to expand houses over and above the approved design led to borrowing of money from other sources; and this could be addressed by improved credit availability from banks and housing finance companies at reasonable interest rates or interest subventions.

Most government schemes are narrowly focused on replacing thatched huts with cemented houses at the same location. It would be a better strategy to develop new residences at an alternate location by properly laying out the entire housing area. These new developments may incorporate facilities for sharing water, sewage processing, and biogas production, as well as fruit and vegetable gardens and small shops. Shared resources could lead to improving lives and health conditions, thereby increasing overall productivity. The United Nations Committee on Economic, Social and Cultural Rights, General Comment No. 4 (1991) on the Right to Adequate Housing states that

> The rights to housing should not be interpreted in a narrow or restrictive sense, which equates it with, for example, the shelter provided by merely having a roof over one's head, or views shelter exclusively as a commodity. Rather it should be seen as the right to live somewhere in security, peace and dignity. (UNESCR 1991)

It would augur well for the government, before investing more funds towards public housing, to reconsider its approach by formulating a new strategy where planners focus on inter-related goals of providing basic amenities, preventing disease, and assuring social integration. The approach must shift from offering shelter to developing healthy and integrated communities in an inclusive manner, that considers the size of the family and the normative requirements of the household rather than a one-shoe-fits-all approach. Apart from the

Scheduled Castes and Most Backward Classes who are eligible, those belonging to Backward Classes and other castes should not be denied assistance if they have low incomes. Mixed-income housing programmes have been successfully implemented in Tamil Nadu to bring about integration across caste and class, and such models should be promoted to achieve social equality. This kind of development, though more capital-intensive than building shelters, has the long-term benefit of creating healthy and sustainable societies.

APPENDIX

Appendix Table 15.1 *Distribution of households with housing type, by social group, Venmani and Palakurichi, 2019* in number

Social group	Venmani				
	Fully *kutcha*	Semi-*pucca*	Fully *pucca*	Unspecified	Total
Scheduled Castes	35	82	139	7	263
Most Backward Classes	3	15	16	0	34
Backward Classes	8	43	53	5	109
Other	0	4	5	0	9
All	46	144	213	12	415
Social group	**Palakurichi**				
	Fully *kutcha*	Semi-*pucca*	Fully *pucca*	Unspecified	Total
Scheduled Castes	59	115	57	4	235
Most Backward Classes	11	20	48	2	81
Backward Classes	5	13	44	3	65
Other	1	1	7	0	9
All	76	149	156	9	390

Source: Survey data, 2019.

Appendix Table 15.2 *Distribution of households which reported outstanding debt to build or repair houses, by social group, Venmani and Palakurichi, 2019* in number

Social group	Venmani		Palakurichi	
	Number	Total	Number	Total
Scheduled Castes	82	263	49	235
Most Backward Classes	6	34	18	81
Backward Classes	19	109	10	65
Other	0	9	1	9
All	107	415	78	390

Source: Survey data, 2019.

Appendix Table 15.3 *Descriptive statistics on homestead land, by socio-economic class, Venmani and Palakurichi, 2019* in square feet

Sl. No.	Socio-economic class	Venmani			Palakurichi		
		Average	Median	Max	Average	Median	Max
1	Landlords and big capitalist farmers	16,887	16,117	25,395	21,225	9,366	1,08,900
2	Rich peasants	15,272	7,994	44,736	11,783	6,599	43,560
3	Middle peasants	12,276	7,928	87,120	7,032	3,920	37,723
4	Poor peasants	4,905	3,267	21,780	4,471	2,919	29,011
5	Wage workers with major income from unskilled, semi-skilled manual work	4,819	2,178	58,065	3,235	2,178	21,780
	Wage workers with major income from skilled and formal-sector wage work	4,337	2,919	14,505	5,558	3,920	23,522
6	Self-employed in business activity	4,430	2,919	21,780	3,743	1,960	10,454
7	Salaried persons	4,550	2,614	17,424	9,198	4,356	43,560
8	Persons living on pensions, small rents, and remittances	5,089	2,767	36,460	7,423	2,178	76,230
	All	5,970	3,049	87,120	5,682	2,919	1,08,900

Source: Survey data, 2019.

Appendix Table 15.4 *Distribution of households with more than two persons per room, by social group, Venmani and Palakurichi, 2019* in number

Social group	Venmani		Palakurichi	
	Number	Total	Number	Total
Scheduled Castes	163	263	161	235
Most Backward Classes	22	34	57	81
Backward Classes	72	109	46	65
Other	4	9	6	9
All	261	415	270	390

Source: Survey data, 2019.

Appendix Table 15.5 *Distribution of households that use LPG at least partially for cooking, by social group, Venmani and Palakurichi, 2019* in number

Social group	Venmani		Palakurichi	
	Number	Total	Number	Total
Scheduled Castes	214	263	164	235
Most Backward Classes	28	34	69	81
Backward Classes	97	109	59	65
Other	9	9	8	9
All	348	415	300	390

Source: Survey data, 2019.

Appendix Table 15.6 *Distribution of households that use clean energy for cooking, by social group, Venmani and Palakurichi, 2019* in number

Social group	Venmani		Palakurichi	
	Number	Total	Number	Total
Scheduled Castes	31	263	9	235
Most Backward Classes	5	34	2	81
Backward Classes	20	109	12	65
Other	4	9	1	9
All	60	415	24	390

Source: Survey data, 2019.

Appendix Table 15.7 *Distribution of households by ownership of consumer goods and social group, Venmani and Palakurichi, 2019* in number

(a) Venmani

Social group	Total number of households	Two-wheeler	Mobile phone	TV	Other
Scheduled Castes	263	137	227	213	69
Most Backward Classes	34	22	29	30	9
Backward Classes	109	70	99	101	64
Other	9	4	8	8	8
All	415	233	363	352	151

(b) Palakurichi

Social group	Total number of households	Two-wheeler	Mobile phone	TV	Other
Scheduled Castes	235	118	187	166	27
Most Backward Classes	81	52	68	68	38
Backward Classes	65	46	59	55	43
Other	9	3	9	9	7
All	390	219	323	298	115

Source: Survey data, 2019.

Appendix Table 15.8 *Distribution of households by access to drinking water and social group, Venmani and Palakurichi, 2019* in number

(a) Venmani

Social group	Total	Within homestead	<200 metres	200 to 500 metres	500 metres to 1 km	>1 km	Unspecified
Scheduled Castes	263	45	189	26	2	0	1
Most Backward Classes	34	12	18	3	0	1	0
Backward Classes	109	34	67	8	0	0	0
Other	9	5	4	0	0	0	0
All	415	96	278	37	2	1	1

(b) Palakurichi

Social group	Total	Within homestead	<200 metres	200 to 500 metres	500 metres to 1 km	>1 km	Unspecified
Scheduled Castes	235	14	129	29	24	39	0
Most Backward Classes	81	25	33	10	5	8	0
Backward Classes	65	24	22	5	3	9	2
Other	9	1	5	1	0	2	0
All	390	64	189	45	32	58	2

Source: Survey data, 2019.

Appendix Table 15.9 *Distribution of households by availability of sanitary facilities and social group, Venmani and Palakurichi, 2019* in number

(a) Venmani

Social group	Total	Toilet within homestead	Public lavatory	Open defecation	Unspecified
Scheduled Castes	263	77	8	173	5
Most Backward Classes	34	10	0	22	2
Backward Classes	109	77	5	27	0
Other	9	9	0	0	0
All	415	173	13	222	7

(b) Palakurichi

Social group	Total	Within homestead	Open defecation	Unspecified
Scheduled Castes	235	95	138	2
Most Backward Classes	81	60	20	1
Backward Classes	65	58	7	0
Other	9	8	1	0
All	390	221	166	3

Source: Survey data, 2019.

16

Cyclone Gaja

T. P. Harshan

HIGHLIGHTS

During the last decade, there have been multiple cyclonic storms of varying severity in the lower Cauvery delta. Cyclone Gaja hit Tamil Nadu in November 2018, causing extensive damage in eight districts including Nagapattinam. Using data from the FAS household survey, we estimated the impact of Cyclone Gaja on household assets and incomes.

The major damage was to houses, cattle-sheds, and other structures. The damage was very high for landless households living in poor-quality housing. Landless households also suffered the loss of goats (that went missing or died). The main damage experienced by richer, landowning households was to standing crops.

While the economic value of the damage or loss per household on account of the cyclone was highest for those with large landholdings, the burden of damage, measured by the ratio of value of damage to assets owned, was highest for landless households. The total damages amounted to 12 per cent of the value of assets owned by landless households in the village of Venmani, and 11 per cent in Palakurichi village.

The Government of Tamil Nadu was prompt in providing immediate relief as well as in announcing compensation. However, village-level data show that not all households that suffered damage received compensation, particularly for crop damage. The compensation that most households received was less than the estimated value of the damage. The impact of Cyclone Gaja and the Covid-19 pandemic on incomes and assets of households in the region is likely to be felt in the coming years.

Introduction

This chapter examines the impact of Cyclone Gaja of 2018 on households in the villages of Palakurichi and Venmani in Nagapattinam district of the State of Tamil Nadu.[1] Tamil Nadu is susceptible to multiple natural hazards – both regularly occurring hazards such as drought, floods, cyclones, and landslides, as well as hazards that are less frequent but of higher magnitude, such as a tsunami. The Cauvery delta region, to which these two villages belong, has experienced multiple disasters over the last decade. The PARI survey of the Foundation of Agrarian Studies conducted in the summer of 2019 was able to capture some of the effects of Cyclone Gaja on livelihoods and assets of households in the two villages.

Measuring Damage and Loss

Assessing the loss and damage incurred due to frequent as well as lower magnitude disasters is a complicated process. One problem with measuring damage is that while the damage caused by individual disasters can be relatively small, the cumulative effect of disasters over years can turn out to be large. There is also the indirect impact of disasters on various economic sectors. Measuring the impact and effect of disasters on society and the economy is an imperative exercise across the globe.

The severity of a disaster depends upon three factors: the magnitude of the disaster, the number of people exposed to the event, and the vulnerability of the population (Strömberg 2007). According to Emergency Events Database (EM-DAT), since 1970, the number of people killed and the number of people affected per disaster has been decreasing; on the other hand, the cost of damage per disaster has been increasing over the years (Kellenberg and Mobarak 2011).[2] This pattern shows that rather than casualties, the most worrying part of a disaster is the damage to properties and income losses. Therefore, it is critical in disaster studies to conduct more empirical studies which directly measure damage and losses in a disaster-affected region.

The impact of a disaster varies across regions and socio-economic groups, based on vulnerability. The economic conditions of an affected region are a significant factor in determining vulnerability. Low-income countries are more vulnerable to natural disasters because of the location of people's residences

[1] *Gaja* means a mighty elephant in Sanskrit. The cyclone was formally named by Sri Lanka.

[2] EM-DAT has data on the occurrence and effects of over 22,000 disasters in the world from 1900. The database is collated from different sources such as UN agencies, NGOs (non-governmental organisations), insurance companies, research institutes, and the press.

in high disaster-risk zones, poor housing conditions, inadequately developed early warning systems, insufficient assets, and ineffective and low social security measures that help people to cope with disaster. Within low-income countries, poor households are more vulnerable because they do not have sufficient income and assets to prepare and cope with disasters, and they have disproportionally higher losses and damages due to disasters (Fothergill and Peek 2004).

The Food and Agriculture Organization (FAO) of the United Nations reviewed the Post-Disaster Need Assessment (PDNA) reports of the United Nations Development Programme (UNDP), in order to compare the impact of disaster across various sectors. The FAO reviewed 74 PDNA reports among 53 developing countries from 2006 to 2016. This study showed that crops, livestock, fisheries, aquaculture, and forestry activities accounted for 23 per cent of all damages and losses caused by medium-scale and large-scale disasters. Agriculture was the sector most severely affected by disasters in the developing countries (FAO 2018). Disasters have a direct as well as an indirect impact on agriculture. The direct impact is the damage to crops, livestock, trees, farm buildings, machinery, and irrigation facilities. The indirect damage stems from a decline in production due to disruption in the transportation of goods and services, increased costs of production, and loss of production capacity. These indirect effects result in lower incomes and decreased production (Das 2003).

Disaster Profile of Tamil Nadu

Tamil Nadu has been subjected to multiple hazards. It is projected that the State will experience a drought once every two-and-a-half years. The major cause of drought is low rainfall due to uncertainty of the monsoon combined with scarcity of ground water and reservoir resources. Out of 38 districts in the State, 23 are classified as drought-prone districts (Balaganesh *et al.* 2020).

Floods are another major disaster in the State, which are caused mainly by cyclones and heavy rainfall. The coastal districts (Chennai, Tiruvallur, Kanchipuram, Cuddalore, Nagapattinam, and Kanyakumari) and north-western districts (Salem and Dharmapuri) of Tamil Nadu are flood-prone. According to the State Disaster Management Authority, 0.45 million hectares of land (3 per cent of the total geographical area of the State) is vulnerable to floods. Landslides are also a regular feature of Nilgiri district, which belongs to the category of severe to very severe landslide-prone areas (TNSDMA 2019).

The Bay of Bengal is a part of six major cyclone-prone regions of the world. During October to December, India's eastern coastline is affected by one or two cyclonic events on average, especially during the period of the north-east monsoon. Between 1891 and 1990, 292 cyclones landed on the east coast of

Table 16.1 *Disaster events in Tamil Nadu, 2010–18*

Year	Name	Category of disaster	Extent of damage
2010	Jal	Severe cyclonic storm	5 human lives lost; 100 houses damaged
		Floods and heavy rain *	181 human lives lost; 29,000 houses damaged; 1. 65 lakh hectares of cropland affected
2011	Thane	Very severe cyclonic storm	46 human lives lost; 1,67,925 houses damaged
		Floods and heavy rain	74 human lives lost; 10,500 acres of cropland affected
2012	Nilam	Severe cyclonic storm	17 human lives lost; 3,520 houses damaged; 4,646 hectares of cropland affected
		Floods and heavy rain	3,859 houses damaged; 9,656 hectares of cropland affected
2013	Madi	Very severe cyclonic storm	Beneficial rain for Tamil Nadu with minimal damage
		Floods and heavy rain**	113 human lives lost; 185 houses damaged; 2,428 hectares of cropland affected
2014		Floods and heavy rain ***	11 human lives lost; 12 houses damaged
2015		Floods and heavy rain ****	232 human live lost; 9,517 houses damaged; 25,973 hectares of cropland affected
2016	Vardha	Floods and heavy rain	5 human lives lost
		Very severe cyclonic storm	33 human lives lost; 46;546 hectares of cropland affected
2017	Okhi	Floods and heavy rain	29 human lives lost
		Very severe cyclonic storm	27 human lives lost; 6,363 houses damaged; 6,625 hectares of cropland affected
2018	Gaja	Floods and heavy rain	58 human lives lost; 9 houses damaged
		Very severe cyclonic storm	63 human lives lost; 4 lakh houses damaged; 1.2 lakh hectares of cropland affected

Notes: *13 heavy rain incidents; **6 heavy rain and flood incidents; ***5 heavy rain and flood incidents; ****15 heavy rain and flood incidents.
Source: Data from Indian Meteorological Department's publication, *Annual Disaster Weather Report, 2010 to 2018.*

the country; of these, 92 were severe cyclones. In the same period, 33 cyclones hit the west coast and 19 of these were severe (NDMA 2004). The coastal districts (southern and central districts) of Tamil Nadu are prone to cyclones (Kuppuswamy and Rajarathnam 2009). The SDMA has identified 591 villages (8 per cent of all villages) in the State as vulnerable to cyclones.[3]

[3] The India Meteorological Department has a classification of cyclones based on associated wind speed: cyclonic storm (60–90 km/hour), severe cyclonic storm (90–119 km/hour), very severe cyclonic storm (119–220 km/hour), and super cyclonic storm (220 km/hour).

Table 16.1 lists the major hydro-meteorological disasters (floods, heavy rainfall events, and cyclones) that have affected Tamil Nadu in the last decade, clearly indicating that the region is prone to frequent cyclones and floods. These natural disasters have caused significant economic damage (damage to houses and crops). In most cases, the disasters occurred in the Cauvery delta region, which is the study area of this chapter.

Cyclone Gaja

Gaja was the fifth cyclone in the north Indian Ocean in 2018, after cyclones Sagar, Mekunu, Luban, and Titli. A low pressure system formed over the Gulf of Thailand which crossed to southern Thailand and the Malay Peninsula, and intensified into a depression over the Bay of Bengal on November 10 and further intensified to a cyclonic storm on November 11. Cyclone Gaja lasted till November 21, 2018. When the cyclone hit Tamil Nadu on November 15, its wind speed was 100–120 kmph. The highest speed was recorded in Thanjavur district at 165 kmph. Cyclone Gaja affected eight districts of Tamil Nadu: Nagapattinam, Thanjavur, Thiruvarur, Pudukottai, Karaikal, Cuddalore, Trichy, and Ramanathapuram. Extremely heavy rainfall of 89.54 mm was observed along the cyclone-hit districts (NIDM 2019).

The damage caused by the cyclone was extensive and widespread. Storm surge was the major reason for the loss of lives and properties. Water rose 1.8 metres above MSL and extended to 2 kilometres from the sea shore. Sixty-three persons lost their lives and 259 persons were injured. The total number of people who were directly affected by the cyclone was 5.6 lakh. It is estimated that 6.04 lakh huts were completely damaged due to speedy winds, and that 1.2 lakh hectares of croplands were damaged (with more than 33 per cent of crop damage). Coconut trees spread over 69,000 hectares were uprooted due to the heavy wind. The number of livestock that died was 14,239. Government buildings numbering 2,168 and 284 culverts were also damaged. Damage in the power sector was huge: 3.3 lakh electricity poles, 1,655 distribution transformers, and 31,824 kilometres of conductors were affected.[4]

Extent of Damage

This section describes the damage caused by Cyclone Gaja in the two villages of Palakurichi and Venmani. The estimate is based on a household survey that provides an overview of village-level production, production systems, and

[4] GoI (2019).

livelihoods, as well as the socio-economic characteristics of different strata. The survey questionnaire included questions regarding the type and value of damage, as well as compensation received from the government.

We have specifically estimated the damage to crops, livestock, trees, houses and buildings, and other assets, to understand the impact of the cyclone on the local economy. Compensation received by various households is also assessed in order to give an idea of the effectiveness of the state's response after the disaster.

For this analysis, we grouped households on the basis of size of operational landholding. We began with an assessment of the total damage, and the following sections discuss each type of damage. The data are based on self-reporting by households.

The major damage in Venmani was to houses, cattle-sheds, and other structures. However, the extent of damage varied from household to household. It was estimated that 86 per cent of all damages among landless households was to buildings, whereas 63 per cent of damages suffered by large landholders was on account of crop damage.

The extent of damage to buildings among landless and poor households reflects disparities in the quality of housing. In contrast to concrete houses owned by the largest landowners in the village, many of the landless households resided in *kutcha* houses which were more susceptible to cyclones (chapter 15). The damage to crops, however, was most severe for the largest landowners. Damage to livestock was minimal for most households. Damage to trees was also significant.

The burden of damage can be gauged from the ratio of total value of damage to total value of assets owned. This ratio was 12 per cent for landless

Table 16. 2 *Total damage caused by Cyclone Gaja and ratio of damages to assets in Venmani* in '000 rupees

Size-class of operational landholding	Number of households	Value of asset per household (000)	Total damage (000)	Ratio of damages to assets
Landless	229	359	4,625	12.88
0.1–2 acres	127	630	3,783	6.00
2.1–4 acres	37	1,223	1,000	0.82
4.1–10 acres	16	3,959	937	0.24
More than 10 acres	6	16,709	501	0.03
All	415	911	10,846	11.9

Source: Survey data, 2019.

Table 16.3 *Total damages caused by Cyclone Gaja and composition of damage by size-class of landholding in Venmani* in '000 rupees and per cent

Size-class of operational landholding	Number of households	Specific damage as ratio of total damage					Total damage (000)	Damage per household (000)
		Buildings	Livestock	Trees	Assets	Crops		
Landless	229	80	4	12	4	–	4,625	20
0.1–2 acres	127	44	2	43	1	10	3,783	30
2.1–4 acres	37	26	3	35	2	34	1,000	27
4.1–10 acres	16	28	5	14	–	52	937	59
More than 10 acres	6	26	3	25	–	63	501	84
All	415	56	3	25	2	14	10,846	26

Source: Survey data, 2019.

Table 16.4 *Total damages caused by Cyclone Gaja and composition of damage by size-class of landholding in Palakurichi* in '000 rupees and per cent

Size-class of operational landholding	Number of households	Specific damage as ratio of total damages					Total damage (000)	Damage per household (000)
		Buildings	Livestock	Trees	Assets	Crops		
Landless	201	82	0.4	11	6	–	4,602	23
0.1–2 acres	133	67	2	9	5	18	3,752	28
2.1–4 acres	29	35	1	17	11	36	886	31
4.1–10 acres	13	40	2	13	4	40	777	60
More than 10 acres	14	20	1	4	1	62	1,175	84
All	390	64	1	11	5	18	11,192	29

Source: Survey data, 2019.

households and much less for all others. For landowners with large holdings, the damage was a negligible fraction of total assets.

Turning to Palakurichi village, again, damage to houses and other structures was the biggest component of total damages on account of Cyclone Gaja (64 per cent). The extent and type of damage varied across households categorised by size of landholding. Damage to houses accounted for 82 per cent of total damages of landless households, but only 20 per cent for households with large landholdings. Crop damage was the major contributor to damages suffered by households with large landholdings.

Table 16.5 *Total damages caused by Cyclone Gaja and ratio of damages to assets in Palakurichi* in '000 rupees and per cent

Size-class of operational landholding	Number of households	Value of assets per household (000)	Total damages (000)	Ratio of damage to asset
Landless	201	416	4,602	11
0.1–2 acres	133	564	3,752	7
2.1–4 acres	29	1,064	886	1
4.1–10 acres	13	2,209	777	0.4
More than 10 acres	14	6,523	1,175	0.2
All	390	801	11,192	13.9

Source: Survey data, 2019.

Another interesting factor to note is the ratio of total damages to total assets. In terms of total damages to assets, landless households suffered damages that amounted to 11 per cent of the value of their assets, which is a large blow to a poor household. This ratio was less than one per cent among large landholder households.

Damage to Buildings

Table 16.6 gives an estimate of damage to buildings in Venmani. Houses, cattle-sheds, and other farm buildings are included here. The value of damage to buildings was Rs 60 lakh. Large landholder families had the highest per unit damage (Rs 21,500 per household). There was no clear relation between size of landholding and extent of damage. However, in terms of the number of structures affected, it can be seen that the damage was very high among the landless. Similarly, taking the value of damage in relation to value of total assets, the ratio was more than 10 per cent among landless households but 0.01 per cent among the largest landholders. Thus, the severity of the impact was felt more by households with poorer conditions of housing.

Palakurichi had more damaged structures (272 houses, cattle-sheds, and toilets) than Venmani. In Palakurichi, out of 273 houses affected by the cyclone, 66 were totally destroyed, whereas in Venmani, 40 houses were completely damaged. Accordingly, the value of damages to buildings in Palakurichi was higher than in Venmani.

In Palakurichi, the damage per household was highest for those with 4–10 acres of land. Landless and small peasants suffered more damage as compared to landlords in the village. The widespread damage to houses reflects the fact that many buildings in the village were of a "non-engineered" type, with

Table 16.6 *Number and volume of damaged buildings by size of landholding, Venmani*

Size-class of operational landholding	Number of households	Number of damaged structures		Value of damage (Rs)	Damage per household (Rs)	Damage–asset ratio
		Houses	Cattle-sheds			
Landless	229	153	6	37,01,640	16,164	10.32
0.1–2 acres	127	87	8	16,66,200	13,017	2.65
2.1–4 acres	37	19	4	2,64,240	7,142	0.22
4.1–10 acres	16	9	1	2,64,000	16,500	0.07
10.1–40 acres	6	4	0	1,29,000	21,500	0.01
All	415	272	19	60,25,080	14,483	0 .02

Source: Survey data, 2019.

Table 16.7 *Number and value of damaged buildings by size of landholding, Palakurichi*

Size-class of operational landholding	Total households	Number of damaged structures		Value of damage (Rs)	Average damage per household (Rs)	Damage–asset ratio
		Houses	Other buildings			
Landless	201	157	11	37,85,000	18,831	9.11
0.1–2 acres	133	100	5	24,98,500	18,786	4.43
2.1–4 acres	29	22	2	3,07,500	10,603	0.29
4.1–10 acres	13	10	5	3,13,000	24,077	0.14
Above 10 acres	14	9	2	2,38,000	17,000	0.04
All	390	298	25	71,42,000	18,313	0.03

Source: Survey data, 2019.

thatched or tiled roofs (see chapter 15 in this volume). These structures could not resist the heavy wind during the cyclone. In Palakurichi, 76 per cent of the houses were damaged either partially or fully. The corresponding proportion was 65 per cent in Venmani. The ratio of value of damage to value of assets was 9.1 for landless households; this ratio was smaller for those with bigger size of landholdings.

Damage to Crops

Cyclone Gaja hit the area on November 16, 2018, causing heavy rains and strong winds. It affected standing crops in their initial stage of growth. As a

Table 16.8 *Number of households reporting crop damage and extent of crop damage in Venmani*

Size-class of operational landholding (in hectares)	Total number of households	Number of households that reported damage to crops	Share of households that reported crop damage in total number of households (%)	Crop income (Rs)	Value of damage (Rs)	Damage per household (Rs)
0.1–1	129	57	44	-1,760	3,83,280	11420
1.01–2	34	23	68	-8,102	3,82,930	27,352
2.01–4	9	6	67	-27,417	3,39,450	67,890
4.01–10	7	6	86	60,060	12,93,000	43,000
10.01–20	2	2	100	3,57,498	2,85,000	1,42,500
All	181	94	51	6,640	15,24,660	42,352

Note: Only households with operational holdings are included. 23 households, 9 households, 1 household, 3 households from size-class of 0.1–1 hectare, 1.01–2 hectares, 2.01–4 hectares, 4.01–10 hectares, respectively, did not report any value of damage.
Source: Survey data, 2019.

result, crop yields have been lower than they would have been during a normal season.[5]

Table 16.8 gives data on crop damage due to Cyclone Gaja by size of landholding. Cultivators in Venmani reported a total damage of Rs 15 lakhs due to the cyclone. The damage is estimated based on self-reporting by households. A little more than half (51 per cent) of all households with operational holdings in the village faced crop damage. Although the damage per household was more among large landowners, their total income remained significantly higher than that of all other cultivating households in the village. Extensive crop damage occurred among the large landholders (83 per cent), with the damage per household amounting to around Rs 63,000. Additionally, the negative incomes and lower incomes of small farmers are an indication of their vulnerability in the event of disruptions in production processes and natural calamities.

The damage was greater in Palakurichi village as compared to Venmani. In Palakurichi, 62 per cent of total cultivating households suffered crop damage due to Cyclone Gaja, compared to 51 per cent in Venmani. The proportion varied across land size: it was 59 per cent among small landholding households and

[5] As shown in Manah (2022), based on data on cyclones in the lower Cauvery delta over a long period, 1891–2019, "the peak sowing or harvesting time coincides with the seasonal frequency peak of cyclonic storms and severe cyclonic storms." See also, Box 6 in chapter 6.

Table 16.9 *Number of households reporting crop damage and extent of crop damage in Palakurichi*

Size-class of operational landholding (in hectares)	Total number of households	Number of households that reported damage to crops	Share of households that reported crop damage in total number of households (%)	Crop income (Rs)	Value of damage (Rs)	Damage per household (Rs)
0.1–1	131	88	67	–4,143	7,06,990	16,067
1.01–2	30	22	73	–1,665	4,17,587	3,79,624
2.01–4	7	4	57	–59,936	1,86,300	62,100
4.01–10	11	8	72	37,203	4,17,265	83,453
10.01–20	4	3	75	–1,38,437	2,50,000	2,50,000
>20	2	2	100	11,15,198	88,200	88,200
All	189	127	68	3,012	20,66,342	31,789

Note: Only households with operational holdings are included. A total 62 households did not report any value of crop damage: 0.1–1 hectare = 44 households, 1.01–2 hectares = 11 households, 2.01–4 hectares = 1 household, 4–10 hectares = 3 households, 10–20 hectares = 2 households, >20 hectares = 1 household.
Source: Survey data, 2019.

79 per cent among the largest landholding households in the village. Damage per household was higher among all landholding classes in Palakurichi as compared to Venmani. Due to its location near the tail end of the Cauvery river delta, Palakurichi village is more susceptible to floods than Venmani village.

Damage to Livestock

Another sector that was severely affected was livestock. Heavy precipitation and wind led to the collapse of cattle-sheds and households were unable to shelter their livestock during the crisis. Livestock resources were also affected by the spread of infectious diseases immediately after the disaster.

The total damage to livestock in the village of Venmani was Rs 3 lakhs (Table 16.10). Landless households were the most affected, accounting for more than one-half of the total damage to livestock in the village. The damage was highest among goats, a major source of income for landless households (chapter 8).

In Palakurichi, the total damage to livestock was less than in Venmani (Table 16.11). The major component of livestock damage was on account of goats dying or going missing. Among landholding categories, those who suffered the most were households with less than 2 acres. The two villages showed different patterns in respect of damage to livestock.

Table 16.10 *Loss from damage to livestock by type of animal and size-class of landholding in Venmani* in rupees

Size-class of operational holding	Chicken			Cows			Goats			All animals
	Number of households	Total loss from livestock	Loss per household	Number of households	Total loss from livestock	Loss per household	Number of households	Total loss from livestock	Loss per household	
Landless households	10	37,210	3,721	1	1,000	1,000	13	1,34,950	10,381	1,73,160
Landed households	2	4,050	–	1	10,000	10,000	7	1,21,400	51,533	1,35,450
Total	12	41,260	3,438	2	11,000	5,500	20	2,56,350	12,818	3,08,610

Source: Survey data, 2019.

Table 16.11 *Loss from damage to livestock by type of animal and size-class of landholding, Palakurichi* in rupees

Size-class of operational land holding	Chicken			Cows			Goats			All animals
	Number of households	Total loss from livestock	Loss per household	Number of households	Total loss from livestock	Loss per household	Number of households	Total loss from livestock	Loss per household	
Landless households	1	600	600	–	–	–	5	16,200	3,240	16,800
Landed households	1	300	300	2	38,000	19,000	9	50,500	5,611	88,800
Total	2	900	900	2	38,000	19,000	14	66,700	4,764	1,05,600

Source: Survey data, 2019.

Damage to Trees

Trees, including trees on farm land, home gardens, and orchards, are an important asset for rural households. Trees are used for the fruit they bear (in orchards) and also for firewood. The major species are tamarind, banana, guava, lemon, mango, coconut, and banyan. Strong and severe wind storms during Cyclone Gaja caused widespread uprooting of trees across the State.

The total damage to trees reported in Venmani was Rs 27 lakhs. All the landholding categories were affected by the damage. A pattern of differential damage according to size of landholding was not seen in the village (Table 16.12). In Palakurichi, the total damage reported was Rs 12 lakhs. Landlords in Palakurichi were more affected by the damage as compared to other landholding categories (Table 16.13).

Table 16.12 *Total value and per household value of damage to trees in Venmani* in rupees

Size-class of operational land holding (hectares)	Number of households	Total value of damage (Rs)	Value of damage per household (Rs)
Landless	120	5,59,929	4,666
0.1–2	84	16,25,200	19,348
2.1–4	31	3,46,123	11,165
4.1–10	14	1,33,100	9,507
10.1–40	5	56,530	11,306
Total	254	27,20,882	10,712

Note: Number of households refers to households reporting damage.
Source: Survey data, 2019.

Table 16.13 *Total value and per household value of damage to trees in Palakurichi* in rupees

Size-class of operational land holding (hectares)	Number of households	Total value of damage (Rs)	Value of damage per household (Rs)
Landless	57	5,21,800	9,154
0.1–2	61	3,27,350	5,366
2.1–4	16	1,53,600	9,600
4.1–10	9	1,04,000	11,556
10.1–40	7	1,65,000	23,571
Total	150	12,71,750	8,478

Note: Number of households refers to households reporting damage.
Source: Survey data, 2019.

Damage to Household Durable Goods

The damage to houses was widespread, and durable goods inside houses were also affected by strong winds and inundation. The official damage assessment does not include such items, but households require resources to regain the amenities damaged during the disaster.

The total value of damage on account of damage to consumer goods in Venmani was Rs 2.6 lakhs (Table 16.14). Landless households were more affected in this village, as compared to landholding households. The value of damage to durable consumer goods in Palakurichi was Rs 6 lakhs (Table 16.15).

Table 16.14 *Total value and per household value of damage to consumer durable goods, Venmani* in rupees

Size-class of operational landholding (in hectares)	Number of households	Total value of damage (Rs)	Value of damage per household (Rs)
Landless	29	1,89,950	6,550
0.1–2	17	50,300	2,959
2.1–4	6	24,700	4,117
Total	52	2,64,950	5,095

Note: Number of households refer to households reporting damage.
Source: Survey data, 2019.

Table 16.15 *Total value and per household value of damage to consumer durable goods in Palakurichi* in rupees

Size-class of operational landholding (in hectares)	Number of households	Total value of damage (Rs)	Value of damage per household (Rs)
Landless	48	2,78,000	5,792
0.1–2	39	1,79,200	4,595
2.1–4	9	95,000	10,556
4.1–10	5	32,800	6,560
above 10	3	17,000	5,667
Total	104	6,02,000	5,788

Note: Number of households refers to households reporting damage.
Source: Survey data, 2019.

Compensation

Adequate compensation is an important indicator of the success of state intervention after a disaster. State governments have the responsibility to implement essential relief measures after natural calamities, using the State Disaster Response Fund (SDRF). Additional financial assistance can be sought from the Central National Disaster Response Fund (NDRF). This is given based on a memorandum submitted by the State government to the Central government. The Government of Tamil Nadu sought Rs 14,910 crores as Central assistance from the NDRF. In response, the Government of India sanctioned Rs 1,146.12 crores or less than 10 per cent of the amount requested, of which Rs 353.7 crores were released as interim relief immediately after the disaster.

The Government of Tamil Nadu announced Rs 10 lakhs as compensation to families that had lost lives on account of the cyclone, Rs 1 lakh as compensation for people with serious injuries, and Rs 25,000 for those who suffered minor injuries. For crop loss, the compensation rates announced were: Rs 600 for each uprooted coconut tree, and Rs 13,500 per hectare for crop loss of paddy, sugarcane, banana, vegetables, and flowers (Inter Agency Group 2018).

Turning to the village-level data, I examined the information on compensation received by households for damage to houses and crops. The data show discrepancies between damage and compensation. First and foremost, all households that suffered damage did not receive compensation.

Secondly, the data show that the extent of assistance given for damaged houses varied across households within a village, as well as across the two villages. According to official reports, there is a fixed or uniform compensation for houses as per the SDRF norms (Table 16.16).

In Venmani, only 14 households reported that the value of compensation received was equal to the damage. There were 176 households that received compensation lower than the value of damage, and 52 households received compensation higher than the estimated damage. In Palakurichi, the

Table 16.16 *Compensation package as per State Disaster Relief Fund* in rupees

Type of damage	*Pucca* houses	*Kutcha* houses
Full damage	95,100	17,600
Severe damage	12,600	3,800
Partial damage	3,800	2,300

Source: State Disaster Response Fund, 2018.

compensation value was less than the damage value for 230 households, whereas 60 households received higher compensation than the damage value and nine households received compensation equal to the damage value. These data show that the compensation was less than the estimated value of damage for a majority of households in both villages (Tables 16.17 and 16.18).

The situation was worse in respect of compensation for crop loss. First, very few households (9 per cent) received compensation for crop damage in Venmani. In Palakurichi, only one household received compensation. As per NDRF norms, Rs 13,500 per hectare was the rate of compensation, which was received by only two households (Tables 16.19 and 16.20).

Table 16.17 *Compensation received and value of damage to houses by size-class of landholding in Venmani* in rupees

Size-class of operational landholding (hectares)	Total number of households	Number of households that received compensation	Per cent of households that received compensation	Value of damage (Rs)	Compen-sation (Rs)	Compen-sation per household (Rs)
Landless	188	133	71	39,55,640	8,63,900	6,495
0.1–2	99	83	84	16,25,200	5,09,900	6,143
2.1–4	23	18	78	2,54,240	98,800	5,489
4.1–10	12	5	42	2,64,000	25,000	5,000
10.1–40	4	3	75	1,29,000	15,000	5,000
All	326	242	74	62,28,080	6,48,700	2,681

Source: Survey data, 2019.

Table 16.18 *Compensation received and value of damage to houses by size-class of landholding in Palakurichi* in rupees

Size-class of operational landholding (hectares)	Total number of households	Number of households that received compensation	Per cent of households that received compensation	Value of damage (Rs)	Compen-sation (Rs)	Compens-ation per household (Rs)
Landless	161	153	95	37,85,000	18,11,500	11,840
0.1–2	111	104	94	32,05,400	12,13,300	11,666
2.1–4	24	23	96	3,07,500	2,80,200	12,183
4.1–10	12	10	83	3,13,000	95,000	9,500
above 10	11	9	82	5,16,000	45,400	5,044
All	319	299	94	81,26,900	16,33,900	5,465

Source: Survey data, 2019.

Table 16.19 *Compensation for crop loss and actual crop loss in Venmani* in rupees

Size-class of operational landholding (hectares)	Number of households that reported crop damage	Number of households that received compensation	Per cent of households that received compensation	Value of crop loss (Rs)	Compen-sation (Rs)	Compen-sation per household
0.1–2	55	6	11	3,83,280	28,500	4,750
2.1–4	23	1	4	3,37,930	14,000	14,000
4.1–10	11	1	9	4,88,450	48,000	48,000
10.1–40	5	0	0	3,15,000	0	0
Total	94	8	9	15,24,660	90,500	11,312

Source: Survey data, 2019.

Table 16.20 *Compensation for crop loss and actual crop loss in Palakurichi* in rupees

Size-class of operational landholding (hectares)	Number of households that reported crop damage	Number of households that received compensation	Per cent of households that received compensation	Value of crop loss (Rs)	Compen-sation (Rs)	Compen-sation per household
0.1–2	78	0	0	6,88,590	0	0
2.1–4	21	1	5	3,17,587	12,000	12,000
4.1–10	7	0	0	3,11,300	0	0
10.1–40	11	0	0	7,30,465	0	0
Total	117	1	1	20,47,942	12,000	12,000

Source: Survey data, 2019.

Concluding Remarks

Drawing on data from the PARI household survey of the Foundation for Agrarian Studies, this chapter estimates the extent of damage from Cyclone Gaja in the two study villages of Venmani and Palakurichi. It estimates the damage to buildings, crops, trees, livestock, and household durables. The total damage in each village was substantial: Rs 1.08 crores in Venmani and Rs 1.1 crores in Palakurichi. As calculated by EM-DAT (International Disaster Database),[6] the overall damage from Cyclone Gaja was Rs 5,686 crores. While the damage incurred by large landholding households was greater than that

[6] The EM-DAT database combines information from different sources including agencies of the United Nations, non-profit organisations, insurance companies, research institutes, and press agencies.

suffered by small landholders, their damage ratio (loss as compared to total assets) was minimal.

Over 50 per cent of the total damage was on account of damage to houses and other buildings. The next in scale of damage was that due to crop loss. Households in the two villages did not receive adequate compensation from the State. Given the scale of loss and inadequate compensation, it is likely that the impact of Cyclone Gaja will carry over to the future, and be reflected in the incomes and assets of households. The impact of the Covid-19 pandemic in the immediately following years is of great concern. To conclude, it is important to study economic conditions and living conditions at regular intervals in areas prone to frequent disasters, such as this region, so as to capture the real impact of disasters on households and livelihoods.

17

Covid-19

C. A. Sethu and Tapas Singh Modak

HIGHLIGHTS

Residents of villages of the lower Cauvery delta are dependent on non-agricultural employment and wages for their livelihood, a good part of this being employment generated in urban and semi-urban areas. The lockdowns in response to the Covid-19 pandemic closed all avenues of non-agricultural employment and access to jobs outside the village.

We conducted three rounds of telephone surveys with households in the two study villages during the pandemic. We found that the sole source of employment during the first pandemic lockdown (April–May 2020) and immediately after was the Mahatma Gandhi National Rural Employment Guarantee Scheme (MGNREGS). Non-agricultural employment had not recovered even a year later (mid-2021). The lack of jobs outside agriculture meant a sharp fall in household incomes.

On account of the effectiveness of the public distribution system in Tamil Nadu, all households were enrolled in the public distribution system (PDS) and received free rice, and pulses, oil, and sugar at subsidised rates, every month during the pandemic. This provision was a key to survival for many households. Many households reported that they had gone into further debt because they had to borrow money to meet their immediate requirements of cash.

The pandemic affected Dalit households in compounding ways (as they are over-represented among those who suffered employment losses, those who had no access to online learning, and were indebted to high-cost microfinance lenders), and exacerbated the marginalisation of people belonging to the Scheduled Castes.

Introduction

The Covid-19 pandemic led to unprecedented disruptions in every aspect of the rural economy, including agriculture and allied activities, employment opportunities, household incomes, and consumption patterns (Dev and Sengupta 2020; Modak *et al.* 2020; Ramakumar 2020; Ramakumar and Kanitkar 2020; Srivastava 2020; Afridi, Sangwan, and Mahajan 2021; Kesar *et al.* 2021). Notably, the pandemic and subsequent lockdowns in 2020 and 2021 led to a total collapse of employment in the non-agricultural sector. Households in the villages of Venmani and Palakurichi are heavily dependent on employment outside agriculture and outside the village (see chapters 12 and 13 in this volume), and were therefore severely affected.

The data used in this chapter come from three rounds of telephonic surveys conducted by the Foundation for Agrarian Studies (FAS). Venmani and Palakurichi were a part of the larger surveys conducted by the Pandemic Studies Unit (PSU) of FAS.[1] The first round of surveys was conducted in April 2020, immediately after the announcement of a nationwide lockdown. It was designed as a rapid assessment study covering informants from different strata of the population in select villages. The second round of surveys was conducted in September–October 2020, with the objective of studying the effect of the pandemic on the kharif production cycle of 2020–21. These households belonged to different socioeconomic classes in the study villages. The third round of surveys was conducted in August–September 2021, with a focus on the rabi production cycle of 2020–21. A majority of these households were selected from the previous survey round, thereby creating a panel of households to examine the long-term effect of the pandemic on rural households. Here, we have used information from interviews conducted with six informants in April 2020, 18 informants in September 2020, and 17 informants in September 2021, from Venmani and Palakurichi. The informants are from different socioeconomic classes and social groups (Appendix Tables 1 and 2). The reference census-type household surveys of May–June 2019 provide an important baseline for the year before the pandemic.

The two study villages of Venmani and Palakurichi are located in the same agro-ecological region, and have similar features in terms of demography, agricultural production, livelihoods, and socioeconomic characteristics of the population. First, Dalit households constitute a majority of the population in both villages, and they can be characterised as poor peasant and wage worker households. Landlords in the two villages are mainly Naidus, and they own

[1] See https://fas.org.in/research/research-projects/pandemic-studies-unit/

around one-fifth of all the assets in each village, including land. Secondly, as a consequence of aridification of the lower Cauvery delta region and problems of water availability, agricultural production and incomes are low and declining. Thirdly, as a corollary of the last point, the share of non-agricultural sources of income is significant and rising for all sections of society. The widespread disbursal of tertiary education among the young and the presence of towns and cities at a commutable distance provide opportunities for semi-skilled and skilled wage workers such as carpenters, electricians, ITI workers, and painters. Households whose major income comes from such non-agricultural wage work formed more than one-third the population of the villages of Venmani and Palakurichi. Fourthly, the villages are characterised by significant indebtedness, especially among wage workers and poor peasants. A large part of this indebtedness is in the form of microfinance loans from non-banking financial institutions that are active in the region. The majority of these loans are used for consumption rather than production.

Agriculture

A single crop of paddy is usually grown in the two villages. At the survey of 2019, close to one-half of all households (44 per cent in Venmani and 47 per cent in Palakurichi) were engaged in crop production, but crop incomes were low as this was not a "normal" year for agriculture (see chapter 11 in this volume).

Our telephonic surveys indicated that agricultural operations proceeded unimpeded during the pandemic. Unseasonal heavy rains in December 2020, a month before the harvest, reduced crop productivity. A landlord who operated 60 acres of land said that paddy production was lower by a third as compared to his expectation. Our respondents reported a rise in the costs of production. Additional machine labour was required due to the rains and damaged crops. Machine labour costs and irrigation costs also rose on account of rising diesel prices. On the sale front, however, cultivators sold most of their produce to the government's direct procurement centre in the village. This helped the cultivators as transport services were affected by the pandemic. Prices offered, however, changed marginally, from Rs 1,800 per quintal in 2018–19 to Rs 1,918 per quintal in 2020–21.

The main takeaway here is that in a year when agricultural incomes became crucial, net incomes were not much higher on account of the rise in costs with no corresponding rise in procurement prices.

Employment and Earnings

In 2018–19, we found that wage employment constituted a critical component of household incomes in Venmani and Palakurichi. Both villages had only one round of paddy cultivation, which began in August and ended in January. Therefore, days of employment available in agriculture were limited. The most important source of earnings was non-agricultural casual labour employment, which constituted about 30 per cent of total income in Venmani and 38 per cent in Palakurichi (see chapter 13). Many workers commuted to nearby urban centres, and were employed as drivers, loading and unloading workers, masons and other construction labourers, carpenters, electricians, welders, sales persons, etc. The lockdowns induced by the pandemic resulted in a halt to all these economic activities, and the impact of this collapse was most severely felt by households which depended on non-agricultural labour earnings.

In our rapid assessment survey conducted in April 2020, NT, a respondent from Palakurichi, reported a complete shutdown of non-agricultural activities in and around the village:

> There is work available in construction and brick kiln sector during summer period each year. But after the lockdown was announced, everything was closed. No one could go for any work outside because of the fear of spread of Covid-19. In many places, roads were blocked by putting thorns and sand on the road. I work in a hotel nearby. The lockdowns stalled my earnings. I was trying to finish my house construction, but it is stopped now.

From March to May 2020, during the first lockdown period, only employment under the Mahatma Gandhi National Rural Employment Guarantee Scheme (MGNREGS) was available in the village, but for a limited number of days. Only six of the 18 households interviewed received employment from MGNREGS in this period. Not a single person obtained work outside the village.

Remittances were an important source of income for about one-fourth of all households in both villages. People from the villages migrated to distant urban locations such as Chennai, Coimbatore, Tiruchirappalli, Tirupur, and Bengaluru for work. Most of this out-migration happened in the summer months, when there were no agricultural activities. This movement was brought to a complete halt under the lockdown of March–May 2020. Migrant workers returned to their villages. As VB, a wage worker, reported,

> I returned to the village from Chennai by bus after the lockdown announcement. I received work under MGNREGA. But apart from this, there was no work at all for us in or outside the village.

In the post-lockdown period, from June to August 2020, the survey showed a rise in the days of employment. However, this was mainly due to increased work under MGNREGS. Among the 18 households from Palakurichi and Venmani surveyed in September 2020, 11 households reported being engaged in MGNREGS work for an average of 65 days between June and August 2020. Workers who lost their jobs in the non-agricultural sector during the lockdown period did not recover these jobs after the lockdown was lifted. Only two households reported any non-agricultural work other than MGNREGS work. In one case, the head of the household worked as a mason for ten days and his wife worked for 30 days as a coir worker. The head of this household stated that "the number of labour days definitely decreased during the lockdown and there was no way to go for work outside the village." The head of the second household worked as a painter in Nagapattinam for ten days.

In the second year of the pandemic, from December 2020 to June 2021, our survey did not find any sign of recovery in non-agricultural employment outside MGNREGS. Among 17 surveyed households, 13 households received work under MGNREGS with an average of 38 days of employment. Only one household reported non-agricultural employment other than MGNREGS. The head of this household reported 15 days of coir work within the village. Between December 2020 and June 2021, her husband worked as a salesman in a bakery in Tiruvarur district for 30 days.

In sum, non-agricultural employment had not recovered even by mid-2021. This had a severe impact on households of manual workers and poor peasants who earned a significant share of their income from employment outside the village economy.

Coping Strategies

Coping strategies are ways of mitigating the consequences of an adverse event. In the telephonic surveys, we asked the respondents whether they had to borrow new loans during the lockdowns and if there was any impact on their food consumption during the pandemic, as compared with the situation before the lockdown.

Indebtedness

Incidence of indebtedness was very high in both the study villages in 2018–19, with microfinance loans for consumption being predominant among manual worker and poor peasant households (see chapter 10). A critical aspect of this type of loan is that repayment is dependent on the flow of regular income to a household. The pandemic led households into a double jeopardy. They were forced to take fresh loans to meet regular expenses at the same time as they had lower incomes to repay these loans. Sixteen out of 18 households in 2020, and 14 out of 17 households in 2021, took new loans during the pandemic, including by pledging gold jewellery. GM, a woman from a Dalit manual worker household in Venmani, said:

> I pledged a lot of gold during the pandemic periodically for meeting day-to-day expenses. I have pledged and repledged in local pawn shops at least five times since this January [2021] alone. We have three children studying. It is very difficult.

SJ, another Dalit woman respondent, said,

> Our outstanding microfinance loans are for more than one lakh rupees in total. We had to pledge gold three items, for Rs 5,000, Rs 5,000, and Rs 20,000. We also took loans of Rs 5,000 and Rs 15,000 from [a local] moneylender which is being repaid daily and every week respectively.

During the lockdowns in 2020, there was a moratorium for repayment of microfinance loans only for three months.[2] Thereafter, borrowers had to repay loan instalments even in the absence of earnings and employment.

Food Security

The State of Tamil Nadu is known for a universal and effective system of public distribution. There is no differentiation in the quantity and price of commodities made available to beneficiaries through fair price shops, based on an income criterion.

In the 2018–19 census survey, all households in Venmani and Palakurichi were enrolled in the public distribution system. The households received, on average per card, 22 kg rice (free of cost), 1.6 kg sugar (at Rs 24 per kg on average), 1 kg pulses (at Rs 29 per kg on average), 1 litre cooking oil (at Rs 25 per litre on average), and 1 litre of kerosene (at Rs 16 per litre on average), in the month immediately before being surveyed in 2019. This was not significantly different from the scale of supply and issue price provided by the state.[3] In the telephonic surveys during the pandemic, we found that all households had received rice and other commodities at the same subsidised rates. In addition to this, they received extra quantities of rice free of cost.

[2] See RBI notification, available at https://www.rbi.org.in/Scripts/NotificationUser.aspx?Id=11835, which permits lending institutions to grant a moratorium from March 1 to May 31, 2020.

[3] See https://tnpds.gov.in/pages/staticPages/family-cards.xhtml for details.

The robust public distribution system in the State ensured a baseline level of food security for all households. In 2020, however, seven households (six of which were Dalit households) reported an overall decline in food intake during the pandemic as compared to the situation before the lockdown, particularly in terms of consumption of vegetables, meat, and milk.

A case study by Niyati and Vijayamba (2021) describes the situation on the ground:

> AD is a manual wage worker from Tamil Nadu's Palakurichi village (Nagapattinam district). His job is that of a contract worker at a circuit board manufacturing factory in Coimbatore. Between April and June 2020, when he had no work, his household members could manage only two meals in a day. His wife is a casual wage worker in the village, and they have two school-going children. After August, he returned to Coimbatore for work. Between September and October, his wife got 14 days of employment for weeding paddy, at a daily wage of Rs 200. The household received 25 kg of rice, 2 kg of pulses, 1.5 kg of sugar, and 1 litre of cooking oil from the PDS every month. AD's two children received 5 kg of rice, 1 kg of pulses, and 10 eggs per month per child, in lieu of the mid-day meal they would have got in school. They managed to eat at least two meals a day because of access to PDS, despite an overall reduction in food intake.

Condition of Scheduled Caste Households

Dalits constitute 60 per cent of all households in the study villages. The FAS pandemic surveys show that the Scheduled Caste population faced multiple pandemic-induced pressures in disproportionately compounding ways, particularly in Palakurichi and Venmani (Sethu and Thangaraj 2022). A majority of the Dalit households depended on non-agricultural semi-skilled and unskilled employment. So the collapse of non-agricultural employment outside the village led to severe income losses during the first lockdown, with no clear sign of a full recovery as of mid-2021.

Dalit households reported a very high incidence of indebtedness (89 per cent) in Palakurichi and Venmani in 2018–19. Most of the loans they took were for consumption (see Chapter 10). After the pandemic-induced lockdowns, they were forced on account of distress to take fresh loans, to meet regular expenses and to repay existing loans.

The pandemic led to a situation where regular schooling was disrupted and alternative arrangements had to be resorted to in order to continue schooling. Dalit households were particularly affected by disruptions in schooling caused by the pandemic. In 2020, for instance, among 16 Dalit children surveyed, 13 had no educated adults at home, 12 had no access to devices that facilitated alternate schooling, and 10 were not engaged in alternatives in lieu of regular school (*ibid.*). In short, Dalit children had few opportunities for home-based learning.

As argued in Sethu and Thangaraj (2022), the pandemic affected Dalit households in compounding ways: they were over-represented among those who suffered the most from loss of non-agricultural casual labour earnings; they were over-represented among those who were susceptible to a debt trap; they were over-represented among those who faced challenges to food security; and they were over-represented among those for whom education was disrupted. The pandemic exacerbated the marginalisation of the Scheduled Castes.

Concluding Remarks

In this chapter, we have examined the impact of the Covid-19 pandemic on households in the two study villages, drawing on telephonic surveys conducted by FAS in 2020 and 2021. The pandemic and subsequent lockdowns acutely affected manual worker and poor peasant households. A large share of the village income comes from non-agricultural employment opportunities outside the village, and the collapse of this sector severely affected earnings and employment opportunities. Receipts from remittances were also halted. Importantly, a majority of Dalit households who were largely dependent on wage earnings suffered. Even in January–June 2021, there was no sign of recovery in employment opportunities and MGNREGS work continued to be the main source of non-agricultural incomes in the villages. With reduced incomes, most households depended on loans to cope with the situation. Although the public distribution system played an important role in ensuring basic food security, consumption of vegetables, meat, and milk fell.

Appendix

Appendix Table 17.1 *Distribution of households by socioeconomic class and social group in Palakurichi and Venmani, Pandemic survey, 2020* in number

Village	Social groups	Landlord/ capitalist farmer	Rich/ Middle peasant	Poor peasant	Manual worker	Others	Total
Palakurichi	SC			2	2	2	6
	MBC/BC	2	2			1	5
	All	2	2	2	2	3	11
Venmani	SC		1	1	2	2	6
	BC		1				1
	All		2	1	2	2	7

Note: SC – Scheduled Castes; MBC – Most Backward Classes; BC – Backward Classes.
Source: Telephonic survey data.

Appendix Table 17.2 *Distribution of households by socioeconomic class and social group in Palakurichi and Venmani, Pandemic survey, 2021* in number

Village	Social groups	Landlord/ capitalist farmer	Rich/ Middle peasant	Poor peasant	Manual worker	Other	Total
Palakurichi	SC			2	1	1	4
	BC	1	1			1	3
	All	1	1	2	1	2	7
Venmani	SC		1	2	3	4	10
	BC						–
	All	0	1	2	3	4	10

Note: SC – Scheduled Castes; MBC – Most Backward Classes; BC – Backward Classes.
Source: FAS PSU data, 2021.

Bibliography

Abatzoglou, J. T., Dobrowski, S. Z., Parks, S. A., and Hegewisch, K. C. (2018), "TerraClimate, A High-Resolution Global Dataset of Monthly Climate and Climatic Water Balance from 1958–2015," *Scientific Data*, vol. 5, no. 170191, January 9, available at https://doi.org/10.1038/sdata.2017.191, viewed on February 20, 2023.

Abraham, R., Basole, A., and Kesar, S. (2022), "Down and out? The Gendered Impact of the Covid-19 Pandemic on India's Labour Market," *Economia Politica*, vol. 39, April, pp. 101–28.

Afridi, F., Mahajan, K., and Sangwan, N. (2021), "Employment Guaranteed? Social Protection During a Pandemic," IZA Institute of Labour Economics discussion paper no. 14099, available at https://docs.iza.org/dp14099.pdf, viewed on February 20, 2023.

Agarwal, B., Anthwal, P., and Mahesh, M. (2021) "How Many and Which Women Own Land in India? Inter-Gender and Intra-Gender Gaps," *The Journal of Development Studies*, vol. 57, no. 11, April 8, pp. 1807–29.

Agricultural Economics Research Centre (AERC) (1961), *Economics of Irrigation and Water-Rates under Cauvery Mettur Project*, University of Madras, Chennai.

Alexander, K. C. (1975), *Agrarian Tension in Thanjavur*, National Institute of Community Development, Hyderabad.

Ali, J. (2007), "Livestock Sector Development and Implications for Rural Poverty Alleviation in India," *Livestock Research for Rural Development*, vol. 19, no. 2.

Ambedkar, B. R. (1947/1979), "States and Minorities: What are Their Rights and How to Secure Them in the Constitution of Free India," in *Dr. Babasaheb Ambedkar: Writings and Speeches*, vol. 1, Dr Babasaheb Ambedkar Source Material Publication Committee, Government of Maharashtra, Mumbai, pp. 396–97.

Ambedkar, B. R. (1997), "Small Holdings in India and Their Remedies," in Ambedkar, B. R., *Writings and Speeches, Journal of Indian Economic Society*, vol. 15, Education Department, Government of Maharashtra, Mumbai.

Ambedkar, B. R. (1982), "On Small Holders' Relief Bill: 1," in *Dr. Babasaheb Ambedkar: Writings and Speeches*, vol. 2, Dr. Babasaheb Ambedkar Source Material Publication Committee, Government of Maharashtra, Mumbai.

Azim Premji University (2021), *State of Working India 2021: One Year of Covid-19*, Centre for Sustainable Employment, Azim Premji University, Bengaluru.

Bakshi, A., and Modak, T. S. (2017), "Incomes of Small Farmer Households," in Swaminathan, M., and Baksi, S. (eds.), *How Do Small Farmers Fare: Evidence from Village Studies in India*, Tulika Books, New Delhi, pp. 126–70.

Bakshi, A., and Modak, T. S. (2021), "Income Diversification in West Bengal Villages," in Bakshi, A., and Modak, T. S. (eds.), *Socio-economic Surveys of Three Villages in West Bengal: A Study of Agrarian Relations*, Tulika Books, New Delhi, pp. 399–436.

Balaganesh, G., Malhotra, R., Sendhil, R., Sirohi, S., Maiti, S., Ponnusamy, K., and Sharma, A. K. (2020), "Development of Composite Vulnerability Index and District Level Mapping of Climate Change Induced Drought in Tamil Nadu, India," *Ecological Indicators*, vol. 113, no. 106197, available at https://doi.org/10.1016/j.ecolind.2020.106197, viewed on February 20, 2023.

Bandyopadhyay, D. (1986), "Land Reforms in India: An Analysis," *Economic and Political Weekly*, vol. 21, nos. 25 and 26, June 21–28, pp. A50–A56.

Barber, C. G. (1940), *History of Cauvery-Mettur Project*, Central Board of Irrigation and Power, New Delhi.

Beteille, A. (1974), *Studies in Agrarian Social Structure*, Oxford University Press, New Delhi.

Birthal, P. S., Joshi, P. K., and Gulati, A. (2005), "Vertical Coordination in High-Value Commodities: Implications for Smallholders," International Food Policy Research Institute MTID discussion paper, Washington.

Birthal, P. S., and Negi, D. S. (2012), "Livestock for Higher, Sustainable and Inclusive Agricultural Growth," *Economic and Political Weekly*, vol. 47, nos. 26–27, pp. 89–99.

Birthal, P. S., and Taneja, V. K. (2012), "Operationalizing the Pro-Poor Potential of Livestock: Issues and Strategies," *The Indian Journal of Animal Sciences*, vol. 82, no. 5, pp. 441–47.

Bouton, M. M. (1985), *Agrarian Radicalism in South India*, Princeton University Press, Princeton.

Brown, D. D. (1971), *Agricultural Development in India's Districts*, Harvard University Press, Cambridge.

Census of India (1961), *District Census Handbook, Thanjavur*, available at https://censusindia.gov.in/nada/index.php/catalog/31249/download/34430/22139_1961_THA.pdf, viewed on March 9, 2022.

Census of India (1971), *District Census Handbook, Thanjavur*, available at https://censusindia.gov.in/nada/index.php/catalog/29959/download/33140/24789_1971_THA.pdf, viewed on March 9, 2022.

Census of India (1981), *District Census Handbook, Thanjavur*, available at https://censusindia.gov.in/nada/index.php/catalog/29958/download/33139/52949_1981_THA.pdf, viewed on March 9, 2022.

Census of India (1991), *District Census Handbook, Thanjavur*, available at http://lsi.gov.in:8081/jspui/bitstream/123456789/6731/1/35978_THA_1991.pdf, viewed on March 9, 2022.

Census of India (2001), *District Census Handbook, Nagapattinam*, available at https://censusindia.gov.in/DigitalLibrary/data/Census_2001/Publication/Tamil%20Nadu/33_2001_NAG.pdf, viewed on March 9, 2022.

Census of India (2011), *District Census Handbook, Nagapattinam*, available at https://censusindia.gov.in/2011census/dchb/3317_PART_B_DCHB_NAGAPATTINAM.pdf, viewed on March 9, 2022.

Central Statistical Organisation (CSO) (2008), "Manual on Cost of Cultivation Surveys," Ministry of Statistics and Programme Implementation, Government of India, New Delhi.

Chitra, M., and Kanta, L. B. (2017), "An Analysis on Supply of Water in Tamil Nadu," *Shanlax International Journal of Economics*, vol. 5, no. 3, pp. 48–54.

Das, A., and Swaminathan, M. (2017), "Cropping Pattern, Crop Productivity, and

Incomes from Crop Production," in Swaminathan, M., and Baksi, S. (eds.), *How Do Small Farmers Fare? Evidence from Village Studies in India*, Tulika Books, New Delhi.

Das, H. P. (2003), "Introduction," in *Agrometeorology Related to Extreme Events*, WMO no. 943, Technical Note no. 201, World Meteorological Organization, Switzerland.

Deshpande, R. S. (2003), "Current Land Policy Issues in India," in Groppo, P. (ed.), *Land Reform*, 2003/3, Special Edition, Land Settlement and Cooperatives, Food and Agriculture Organization.

Dev, M. S., and Sengupta, R. (2020), "Covid-19: Impact on the Indian Economy," Indira Gandhi Institute of Development Research working paper no. 13, available at http://www.igidr.ac.in/pdf/publication/WP-2020-013.pdf, viewed on February 20, 2023.

Dhar, N. S. (2012), "On Days of Employment of Rural Labour Households," *Review of Agrarian Studies*, vol. 2, no. 2, pp. 106–15.

Fernando, A. (2018), "Fifty Years After Caste Violence, Keezhvenmani Village Waiting for Daylight," *The New Indian Express*, December 23, available at https://www.newindianexpress.com/states/tamil-nadu/2018/dec/23/fifty-years-on-keezhvenmani-waiting-for-daylight-1915275.html, viewed on February 20, 2023.

Food and Agriculture Organization (FAO) (1998), "Crop Evapotranspiration, Irrigation and Drainage," Paper no. 56, FAO, Rome.

Food and Agriculture Organization (FAO) (2017), *The Impact of Disasters and Crises on Agriculture and Food Security*, FAO, Rome, available at https://www.fsinplatform.org/sites/default/files/resources/files/i8656en.pdf, viewed on February 20, 2023.

FAO, IFAD, UNICEF, WFP, and WHO (2020), *The State of Food Security and Nutrition in the World 2020: Transforming Food Systems for Affordable Healthy Diets*, FAO, Rome.

Fothergill, A. and Peek, L. A. (2004), "Poverty and Disasters in the United States: A Review of Recent Sociological Findings," *Natural Hazards*, vol. 32, no. 1, pp. 89–110.

Foundation for Agrarian Studies (FAS) (2015), "Calculation of Household Incomes: A Note on Methodology," available at https://fas.org.in/wp-content/uploads/2021/10/Calculation-of-Household-Incomes-A-Note-on-Methodology.pdf, viewed on August 24, 2020.

Frankel, F. R. (1971), *India's Green Revolution: Economic Gains and Political Costs*, Princeton University Press, Princeton.

Gough, K. (1978), "Agrarian Relations in Southeast India, 1750–1976," *Review (Fernand Braudel Center)*, vol. 2, no. 1, pp. 25–53, available at www.jstor.org/stable/40240788, viewed on October 29, 2022.

Gough, K. (1981), *Rural Society in Southeast India*, Cambridge University Press, Cambridge.

Gough, K. (1989), *Rural Change in Southeast India: 1950s to 1980s*, Oxford University Press, New Delhi.

Government of India (GoI) (2011), *Report of the Working Group on Rural Housing: XII Five Year Plan*, Ministry of Rural Development, New Delhi.

Government of India (GoI) (2015), *All India Report on Agriculture Census 2010–11*, Agriculture Census Division, Department of Agriculture, Cooperation and Farmers' Welfare, New Delhi.

Government of India (GoI) (2017), *Report of the Committee on Doubling Farmers' Income Volume I: Structural Reforms and Governance Framework*, Department of Agriculture, Cooperation and Farmers' Welfare, Ministry of Agriculture and Farmers' Welfare, New Delhi.

Government of India (GoI) (2018), *Report of the Committee on Doubling Farmers' Income Volume XIII: Structural Reforms and Governance Framework*, Department of Agriculture, Cooperation and Farmers' Welfare, Ministry of Agriculture and Farmers' Welfare, New Delhi.

Government of India (GoI) (2019), Lok Sabha unstarred question no. 4906 on July 23, 2019, National Institute of Disaster Management, Ministry of Home Affairs, New Delhi.

Government of India (GoI) (2020), *All India Report of Agricultural Census, 2015–16*, Department of Agriculture, Cooperation and Farmers' Welfare, Ministry of Agriculture and Farmers' Welfare, New Delhi.

Government of India (GoI) (2022), *Wage Rates in Rural India*, Ministry of Labour and Employment, Labour Bureau, available at https://labourbureau.gov.in/wage-rates-in-rural-india, viewed on September 13, 2022.

Government of Tamil Nadu (GoTN) (1969), *Report of the Commission of Inquiry on the Agrarian Labour Problems of East Thanjavur District* (Ganapathia Pillai Commission), Department of Revenue, Chennai.

Government of Tamil Nadu (GoTN) (n.d.), *Agriculture*, Chapter IV, available at https://www. tn.gov.in/dear/Agriculture.pdf

Government of Tamil Nadu (GoTN) (2019), *Minimum Wages Act, 1948: Revision of Minimum Rates of Wages for Employment in Aerated Water Manufactory*, Labour and Employment Department, Chennai.

Government of Tamil Nadu (GoTN) (2020), *Indira Awaas Yojana*, Department of Rural Development and Panchayati Raj, Chennai.

Guhan, S. (1983) "Palakurichi: A Resurvey," MIDS working paper no. 42, Madras Institute of Development Studies, Chennai.

Guhan, S. (1993), *The Cauvery River Dispute: Towards Conciliation*, a *Frontline* Publication, Chennai.

Guhathakurta, P., Khedikar, S., Menon, P., Prasad, A. K., Sable, S. T., and Advani, S. C. (2020), "Observed Rainfall Variability and Changes over Maharashtra State," *Met Monograph*, no. ESSO/IMD/HS/Rainfall Variability/16(2020)/40, Climate Research and Services, India Meteorological Department, Pune.

Harriss, J. (2022), "The Politics of Dignity and Development: The Tamil Nadu Story," *Economic and Political Weekly*, vol. 57, no. 17, April 23, 2022.

Harriss, J. and Jeyaranjan, J. (2016), "Rural Tamil Nadu in the Liberalization Era: What Do We Learn from Village Studies?" in Himanshu, Jha, P., and Rodgers, G. (eds.), *The Changing Village in India: Insights from Longitudinal Research*, Oxford University Press, United Kingdom.

Haswell, M. R. (1967), *Economics of Development in Village India*, Allied Publishers, Bombay.

Heyer, J. (2013), "Integration into a Global Production Network: Impacts on Labour in Tiruppur's Rural Hinterlands," *Oxford Development Studies*, vol. 41, no. 3, pp. 307–21.

Heyer, J. (2022), "Inclusivity and Growth Under the 'Dravidian Model': Controversial Omissions and Claims," *Economic and Political Weekly*, vol. 57, no. 8, February 19, 2022.

Inter Agency Group Tamil Nadu (2018), *Cyclone Gaja Assessment Report*, available at https://sphereindiablog.files.wordpress.com/2018/12/iag-tn-cyclone-gaja-assessment-report-alligned-f-novemebr-2018.pdf, viewed on February 21, 2023.

International Labour Organisation (ILO) (1961), "Workers' Housing Recommendation, 1961," no.115, Geneva.

Jagannathan, S. (2003), "Land for Tiller's Freedom: A Humane Approach to the Land Problem," in Thangaraj, M. (ed.), *Land Reforms in India – Tamil Nadu: An Unfinished Task,* vol. 9, Sage Publications, New Delhi.

Kalaiyarasan, A., and Vijayabaskar, M. (2021), *The Dravidian Model: Interpreting the Political Economy of Tamil Nadu,* Cambridge University Press, Cambridge.

Kellenberg, D., and Mobarak, A. M. (2011), "The Economics of Natural Disasters," *Annual Review of Resource Economics,* vol. 3, pp. 297–312.

Kesar, S., Abraham, R., Lahoti, R., Nath, P., and Basole, A. (2021), "Pandemic, Informality, and Vulnerability: Impact of Covid-19 on Livelihoods in India," *Canadian Journal of Development,* vol. 42, nos. 1–2, pp. 145–64.

Krishnan, A. (1988), "Delineation of Soil Climatic Zones of India and Its Application in Agriculture," *Fertilizer News,* vol. 33, no. 4, pp. 11–19.

Kumar, A., Parappurathu, S., Shinoj, P., and Jee, S. (2013), "Do Dairy Co-operatives Enhance Milk Production, Productivity and Quality? Evidences from the Indo-Gangetic Plain of India," *Indian Journal of Agricultural Economics,* vol. 68, no. 3, pp. 457–68.

Kumar, A., Staal, S. J., and Singh, D. K. (2011), "Smallholder Dairy Farmers' Access to Modern Milk Marketing Supply Chain in India," *Agricultural Economics Research Review,* vol. 24, no. 2, pp. 243–53.

Kumarappa, J. C., (1949), *Report of the Congress Agrarian Reforms Committee,* All India Congress Committee, New Delhi.

Kuppuswamy, S., and Rajarathnam, S. (2009), "Women, Information Technology and Disaster Management: Tsunami Affected Districts of Tamil Nadu," *International Journal of Innovation and Sustainable Development,* vol. 4, nos. 2 and 3, pp. 206–15, available at https://doi.org/10.1504/ijisd.2009.028074, viewed on February 21, 2023.

Kurien, C. T. (1980), "Dynamics of Rural Transformation: A Case Study of Tamil Nadu," *Economic and Political Weekly,* vol.15, no. 5, February.

Kurien, C. T. (1981), *Dynamics of Rural Transformation: A Study of Tamil Nadu, 1950–75,* Orient Longman, New Delhi.

Kurien, C. T. (1987), "Planning and the Institutional Transformation of the Indian Economy," *Social Scientist,* vol. 15, no. 7, July.

Lahoti, R., and Mukhopadhyay, R. (2019), "School Choice in Rural India: Perceptions and Realities in Four States," *Economic and Political Weekly,* vol. 54, no. 49.

Lakshmanan and Sethuraman (2023), "Elusive Justice to Dalits in the 'Land of Social Justice'," *Economic and Political Weekly,* vol. 58, no. 23, available at https://www.epw.in/journal/2023/23/commentary/elusive-justice-dalits-%E2%80%98land-social-justice%E2%80%99.html, viewed on September 13, 2023.

Lindberg, S., Athreya, V. B., Djurfeldt, G., Rajagopal, A., and Vidyasagar, R. (2014), "Progress over the Long Haul: Dynamics of Agrarian Change in Kaveri Delta," in Gooptu, N., and Parry, J. (eds.), *Persistence of Poverty in India,* Social Science Press, New Delhi.

Manah, I. (2022), "Tropical Cyclones in the North Indian Ocean Affecting the Lower Cauvery Delta," unpublished manuscript, M. S. Swaminathan Research Foundation (MSSRF), Chennai.

Mazumdar, I., and Neetha, N. (2011), "Gender Dimensions: Employment Trends in India, 1993–94 to 2009–10," *Economic and Political Weekly*, vol. 46, no. 43, October.

Mishra, A. K., and Singh, V. P. (2010), "A Review of Drought Concepts," *Journal of Hydrology*, vol. 391, nos. 1–2, pp. 202–16, available at https://www.sciencedirect.com/science/article/abs/pii/S0022169410004257, viewed on February 21, 2023.

Mishra, S. N., and Sharma, R. K. (1990), *Livestock Development in India: An Appraisal*, Vikas Publishing House, New Delhi.

Menon, P. (1986), "The Agrarian Economy of the Carnatic in the 17th and 18th Centuries," unpublished PhD thesis, Aligarh Muslim University, Aligarh.

Menon, S. (1983), "Social Characteristic of Land Control in Thanjavur District During the Nineteenth Century: A Sociological Study," unpublished PhD thesis, Jawaharlal Nehru University, New Delhi.

Modak, T. S., and Swaminathan, M. (2019), "Income Levels and Variations in Three Villages of Tripura," in Swaminathan, M., and Basu, R. (eds.), *Socio-economic Surveys of Three Villages in Tripura: A Study of Agrarian Relations*, Tulika Books, New Delhi, pp. 225–57.

Nagaraj, K. (2007), "Structure of Asset Ownership among Households in the Villages," paper presented at workshop on "Dalit Households in Village Economies," Sociological Research Unit, Indian Statistical Institute, Kolkata, February 22–23.

Nair, G. G. K., Shankaranarayana, L., and Ram, K. (2015), "Agriculture Gold Loans: Issues and Concerns," NABARD occasional paper no. 62, Mumbai.

Nancharaiah, G. (1988), *Land and Caste*, Himalaya Publishing House, New Delhi.

National Disaster Management Authority (NDMA) (2004), "Cyclones," available at https://ndma.gov.in/Natural-Hazards/Cyclone, viewed on February 21, 2023.

National Institute of Disaster Management (NIDM) (2019), *Study Report on Gaja Cyclone 2018*, available at https://reliefweb.int/report/india/study-report-gaja-cyclone-2018, viewed on February 21, 2023.

National Sample Survey Office (NSSO) (2019), "Drinking Water, Sanitation, Hygiene and Housing Condition in India," Report no. 584, Ministry of Statistics and Programme Implementation, New Delhi.

National Sample Survey Office NSSO (2021), "Situation Assessment of Agricultural Households and Landholdings of Households in Rural India," NSS 77th Round, Ministry of Statistics and Programme Implementation, Government of India, New Delhi.

National Statistical Office (NSO) (2019), *Annual Report, Periodic Labour Force Survey (PLFS), 2017–18*, Ministry of Statistics and Programme Implementation, Government of India, New Delhi.

National Statistical Office (NSO) (2020), *Annual Report, Periodic Labour Force Survey (PLFS), 2018–19*, Ministry of Statistics and Programme Implementation, Government of India, New Delhi.

NITI Aayog (2016), *Report of the Expert Committee on Land Leasing*, Government of India, New Delhi.

NITI Aayog (2021), *India: National Multidimensional Poverty Index – Baseline Report*, Government of India, New Delhi, available at https://www.niti.gov.in/sites/default/

files/2021-11/National_MPI_India-11242021.pdf, viewed on February 21, 2023.

Niyati, S., and Vijayamba, R. (2021), "Impact of the Covid-19 Pandemic on Food Security and Indebtedness in Rural India," *Review of Agrarian Studies*, vol. 11, no. 1, pp. 107–23.

Rajalu, K. S. (1918), "Tanjore District: Palakurichi Village," in Slater, G. (ed.), *Economic Studies, Volume 1: Some South Indian Villages*, University of Madras and Oxford University Press, Madras.

Rajasekaran, Ilangovan (2023), "Caste Atrocity: Pudukkottai Incident Leaves Tamil Nadu Outraged," *Frontline*, January 6, 2023, available at https://frontline.thehindu.com/news/caste-atrocity-pudukkottai-incident-leaves-tamil-nadu-outraged/article66345618.ece, viewed on September 13, 2023.

Raju, B. M. K., Rao, K. V., Venkateswarlu, B., Rao, A. V. M. S., Rama Rao, C. A., Rao, V. U. M., Bapuji Rao, B., Ravi Kumar, N., Dhakar, R., Swapna, N., and Latha, P. (2013), "Revisiting Climatic Classification in India: A District-Level Analysis," *Current Science*, vol. 105, no. 4, pp. 492–95.

Ramachandran, V. K. (1990), *Wage Labour and Unfreedom in Agriculture: An Indian Case Study*, Clarendon Press, Oxford.

Ramachandran, V. K. (2011), "The State of Agrarian Relations in India Today," *The Marxist*, vol. 27, nos. 1–2, January–June, pp. 51–89.

Ramachandran, V. K. (2015), "Agrarian Issues, Local and National: Extracts from Conversations with P. Ramamurti," *Review of Agrarian Studies*, vol. 4, no. 2, available at http://www.ras.org.in/agrarian_issues_local_and_national_extracts_from_conversations_with_p_ramamurti

Ramachandran, V. K. (2017), "Socio-Economic Classes in the Three Villages," in Swaminathan, M., and Das, A. (eds.), *Socio-economic Surveys of Three Villages in Karnataka: A Study of Agrarian Relations*, Tulika Books, New Delhi, pp. 69–85.

Ramachandran, V. K., and Swaminathan, M. (eds.) (2014), *Dalit Households in Village Economies*, Tulika Books, New Delhi.

Ramakrishnan, G. (2014), "The Peasant Movement and Dalit Rights in East Thanjavur, Tamil Nadu," in Ramachandran, V. K., and Swaminathan, M. (eds.), *Dalit Households in Village Economies*, Tulika Books, New Delhi, pp. 85–110.

Ramakumar, R. (2013), "India's Agricultural Debt Waiver Scheme, 2008," *Review of Agrarian Studies*, vol. 3, no. 1, available at http://ras.org.in/indias_agricultural_debt_waiver_scheme_2008, viewed on February 2, 2023.

Ramakumar, R. (2019), "Agricultural Credit and Financial Liberalization in India," in Narayanamoorthy, A., Bhavani, R. V., and Sujatha, R. (eds.), *Whither Rural India? Political Economy of Agrarian Transformation in Contemporary India*, Tulika Books, New Delhi, pp. 94–119.

Ramakumar, R. (2020), "Agriculture and the Covid-19 Pandemic: An Analysis with Special Reference to India," *Review of Agrarian Studies*, vol. 10, no. 1, pp. 72–110.

Ramakumar, R., and Kanitkar, T. (2020), "Impact of Covid-19 Pandemic on the Indian Economy: A Critical Assessment," NIAS working paper no. 18, available at http://eprints.nias.res.in/2002/1/2020-WP-18-Tejal-Kanitkar-Final.pdf, viewed on February 21, 2023.

Ramaswami, B., Birthal, P. S., and Joshi, P. K. (2006), "Efficiency and Distribution in Contract Farming: The Case of Indian Poultry Growers," MTID discussion paper no.

91, available at https://ebrary.ifpri.org/utils/getfile/collection/p15738coll2/id/125238/filename/125239.pdf, viewed on February 21, 2023.

Ramiah, K. (1937), *Rice in Madras: A Popular Handbook*, Government Press, Madras.

Rao, V. M., and Hanumappa, H. G., (1999), "Marginalisation Process in Agriculture: Indicators, Outlook and Policy Implications," *Economic and Political Weekly*, vol. 34, no. 52, Dec 25–31, pp. A133–138.

Rawal, V. (2014), "On Identification of Rural Labour Households in NSS Surveys," Statistics on Indian Economy and Society, available at https://www.indianstatistics.org/2014/04/02/rural-labour-households.html, viewed on February 21, 2023.

Reserve Bank of India (RBI) (2014), *Guidelines for Licensing of Small Finance Banks in the Private Sector*, Reserve Bank of India, Mumbai.

Rigby, A. (1987), "LAFTI Making Offers the Landowners Cannot Refuse," *Community Development Journal*, vol. 22, no. 4, October, pp. 310–21.

Rukmani, R. (1994), "Urbanisation and Socio-Economic Change in Tamil Nadu, 1901–91," *Economic and Political Weekly*, vol. 29, nos. 51–52, pp. 3263–72.

Saravanan, V. S. (2017), "Kaṇṇu muṉṉāṭi 44 pērai ericcik koṉṉāṅka!" Kīḻveṇmaṇi koṭūram collum kāvalkārar #Venmani ["They Burnt 44 People Alive in Front of My Eyes!" A Policeman Recalls the Cruelty of Kilavenmani, #Venmani], *Vikatan*, December 25, available at https://www.vikatan.com/literature/arts/111787-44-people-were-burned-alive-infront-of-my-eyes-a-police-officer-recalls-keezhvenmani-massacre, viewed on February 21, 2023.

Schendel, V. W. (1991), *Three Deltas: Accumulation and Poverty in Rural Burma, Bengal and South India*, Sage Publications, New Delhi.

Seema (2021), "Aspects of Female Labour Force Participation in India: With Case Studies from Haryana," unpublished PhD thesis, Indian Institute of Technology Delhi, Delhi.

Sethu, C. A., and Thangaraj, M. (2021), "The COVID-19 Pandemic and Rural Dalit Households: Observations from Two Villages in Tamil Nadu," *Review of Agrarian Studies*, vol. 11, no. 2, pp. 153—63.

Shrivastav, Urvi (2020), "Land Fragmentation: The Core Issue in Agriculture," *Business World*, December 16, available at https://www.businessworld.in/article/Land-Fragmentation-The-Core-Issue-In-Agriculture/16-12-2020-354418/, viewed on February 21, 2023.

Singh, S., Swaminathan, M., and Ramachandran, V. K. (2013), "Housing Shortages in Rural India," *Review of Agrarian Studies*, vol. 3, no. 2, pp. 54–75.

Singh, V. K., Suresh, A., Gupta, D. C., and Jakhmola, R. C. (2005), "Common Property Resources, Rural Livelihood and Small Ruminants in India: A Review," *Indian Journal of Animal Sciences*, vol. 75, no. 8, pp. 1027–36.

Sivaraman, M. (1973), "Thanjavur: Rumblings of Class Struggle in Tamil Nadu," in Gough, K., and Sharma, H. P. (eds.), *Imperialism and Revolution in South Asia*, Monthly Review Press, New York.

Slater, G. (ed.) (1918), *Economic Studies, Volume 1, Some South Indian Villages*, Oxford University Press, London.

Srivastava, R. (2020), "Covid-19 and Circular Migration in India," *Review of Agrarian Studies*, vol. 10, no. 1, pp. 164–80.

Strömberg, D. (2007), "Natural Disasters, Economic Development, and Humanitarian Aid," *The Journal of Economic Perspectives*, vol. 21, no. 3, pp. 199–222.

Study Group on Agrarian Classes (2016), "Report of the Study Group on Agrarian Classes,"

The Marxist, vol. 32, no. 2, April–June, available at http://cpim.org/sites/default/files/marxist/201602-marxist-studynotes-agrarian-classes.pdf, viewed on October 24, 2022.

Suresh, A., and Chaudhary, K. R. (2015), "Intervention Points for Small Ruminant Development in India: Insights from a Field Level Survey," *Indian Journal of Animal Sciences*, vol. 85, no. 12.

Suresh, A., Gupta, D. C., Mann, J. S., and Singh, V. K. (2008), "Effect of Socio-Economic and Agro-Ecological Factors on Structure and Ownership of Livestock: Evidence from Rajasthan," *Indian Journal of Agricultural Economics*, vol. 63, no. 2, pp. 244–64.

Surjit, V. (2004), "Tenancy and Distress in Thanjavur Region, Tamil Nadu: A Case Study of Palakurichi Village," in Ramachandran, V. K., and Swaminathan, M. (eds.), *Dalit Households in Village Economies*, Tulika Books, New Delhi.

Surjit, V. (2008), "Farm Business Income in India: A Study of Two Rice Growing Villages of Thanjavur Region, Tamil Nadu," unpublished PhD thesis, University of Calcutta, Kolkata.

Surjit, V. (2011), "Cropping Pattern and Farming Practices in Palakurichi Village, 1918–2004," *Review of Agrarian Studies*, vol. 1, no. 1, available at http://www.ras.org.in/3_1_1, viewed on February 21, 2023.

Swaminathan, M. (2020), "Contemporary Features of Rural Workers in India with a Focus on Gender and Caste," *Indian Journal of Labour Economics*, vol. 63, no. 1, pp. 67–79.

Swaminathan, M. (2020), "The Majority Cannot Afford a Balanced Diet," *The Hindu*, July 28, available at https://www.thehindu.com/opinion/op-ed/the-majority-cannot-afford-a-balanced-diet/article32206439.ece, viewed on September 30, 2022.

Swaminathan, M. (forthcoming 2023), "The Costs of Financial Inclusion," in Damodaran, S., Gupta, S., Mitra, S., and Sinha, D. (eds.), *Development, Transformations and the Human Condition*, Routledge, India.

Swenson, C. J. (1973), "The Effect of Increases in Rice Production on Employment and Income Distribution in Thanjavur District, South India," unpublished PhD thesis, Michigan State University, Michigan.

Taneja, V. K., and Birthal, P. S. (2004), "Role of Buffalo in Food Security in Asia," *Asian Buffalo Magazine*, vol. 1, no. 1, pp. 4–13.

Tamil Nadu Agricultural University (TNAU) (1985), *Techno-Economic Survey of Thanjavur District*, Centre for Agricultural and Rural Development Studies, Coimbatore.

Tamil Nadu State Disaster Management Authority (TNSDMA) (2019), *State Disaster Management Perspective Plan 2018–2030*, Chennai, available at https://tnsdma.tn.gov.in/app/webroot/img/document/SDMP-29-08.pdf, viewed on February 21, 2023.

Tirumalai, S. (1940), "Palakurichi," in Thomas, P. J., and Ramakrishnan, K. C. (eds.), *Some South Indian Villages: A Resurvey with Analysis and Observations*, University of Madras, Madras.

Thangaraj, M. (1995), "Trends in Fragmentation of Operational Holdings in India: An Exploratory Analysis," *Indian Journal of Agricultural Economics*, vol. 50, no. 2, April–June, pp. 176–84.

Thangaraj, M. (2003), "Land and Castes in Tamil Nadu," in Thangaraj, M. (ed.), *Land Reforms in India – Tamil Nadu: An Unfinished Task*, vol. 9, Sage Publications, New Delhi.

The Hindu (2021), "Teacher Held for Kicking Dalit Boy in Classroom," October 15, available at https://www.thehindu.com/news/national/tamil-nadu/teacher-held-for-kicking-dalit-boy-in-classroom/article37004798.ece, viewed on September 13, 2023.

Thornthwaite, C. W., and Mather, J. R. (1955), "The Water Balance," *Publications in Climatology*, vol. 8, no. 1, Laboratory of Climatology, Drexel Institute of Technology, Centerton.

Thomas, J. J. (2012), "India's Labour Market during the 2000s: Surveying the Changes," *Economic and Political Weekly*, vol. 47, no. 51, pp. 39–51.

Thomas, J. J. (2020a), "Labour Market Changes in India, 2005–18: Missing the Demographic Window of Opportunity," *Economic and Political Weekly*, vol. 55, no. 34, pp. 57–63.

Thomas, J. J. (2020b), "Sectoral Shifts and Declining Labour Participation Rate of Women," in Ramachandran, V. K., Swaminathan, M., and Nagbhushan, S. (eds.), *Women's Work in Rural India*, Tulika Books, New Delhi.

Thomas, J. J. and Satheesha, B. (2021), "Agriculture and Rural Labour Markets in India," in Raj, S. N. R., and Singha, K. (eds.), *The Routledge Handbook of Post-Reform Indian Economy*, Routledge, New Delhi, pp. 15–34.

Thomas, J. J. (2021), "Realizing the Demographic Dividend: Demographic Transition and Labour Market Changes across Indian States, 2005–2018," unpublished policy paper, United Nations Population Fund (UNFPA), New Delhi.

Thomas, J. J. and Satheesha, B. (2021), "Agriculture and Rural Labour Markets in India," in Rajesh Raj, S. N., and Singha, K. (eds.), *The Routledge Handbook of Post-Reform Indian Economy*, Routledge, New Delhi.

Thomas, P. J. and Ramakrishnan, K. C. (eds.) (1940), *Some South Indian Villages: A Resurvey with Analysis and Observations*, Madras: University of Madras, Madras.

United Nations Committee on Economic, Social and Cultural Rights (UNCESCR) (1991), *General Comment No. 4: The Right to Adequate Housing (Art. 11 (1) of the Covenant)*, no. E/1992/23, December 13, available at https://www.refworld.org/docid/47a7079a1.html, viewed on May 31, 2023

United Nations Development Programme (UNDP) (2011), *Disaster Management of India: A Status Report, 2014*, Natural Disaster Management Division, Ministry of Home Affairs, Government of India, New Delhi.

Usami, Y., Patra, S., and Kapoor, A. (2018), "Measuring Female Work Participation in Rural India: What do the Primary and Secondary Data Show?" *Review of Agrarian Studies*, vol. 8, no. 2, available at http://ras.org.in/86c3e748cd7c8263a1f762aa12c3e37e, viewed on February 2, 2023.

Vaidyanathan, A. (1988), *Bovine Economy of India*, Centre for Development Studies Monographs Series, Oxford and IBH Publishing Company, New Delhi.

Venkataraman, S., and Krishnan, A. (1992), *Crops and Weather*, Publications and Information Division, Indian Council of Agricultural Research, New Delhi.

Vijayamba, R. (2022), "Women in Livestock Economy," unpublished PhD thesis, Indian Statistical Institute, Bengaluru.

Viswanathan, S. (2008), "The Fall of a Wall," *Frontline*, vol. 25, no. 11, available at https://frontline.thehindu.com/social-issues/article30196334.ece, viewed on September 13, 2023.

Yadu, C. R., and Satheesha, B. (2016), "Agrarian Question in India: Indications from NSSO's 70th Round," *Economic and Political Weekly*, vol. 51, no. 16, pp. 20–23.

Yitzhaki, S. (1994), "Economic Distance and Overlapping of Distributions," *Journal of Econometrics*, vol. 61, no. 1, pp. 147–59.

Contributors

Sanjukta Chakraborty, independent researcher; former Senior Data Analyst, Foundation for Agrarian Studies, Bengaluru

Arindam Das, Joint Director, Foundation for Agrarian Studies, Bengaluru

Charu Chandra Devshali, Research Associate, M. S. Swaminathan Research Foundation, Chennai

Ritam Dutta, Research Scholar, Economic Analysis Unit, Indian Statistical Institute, Bengaluru

R. Gopinath, Principal Scientist, M. S. Swaminathan Research Foundation, Chennai

T. P. Harshan, Private Secretary to Vice Chairperson, Kerala State Planning Board, Thiruvananthapuram

Isaac M., PhD candidate, University of Sussex

T. Jayaraman, Senior Fellow Climate Change, M. S. Swaminathan Research Foundation, Chennai

Rakesh Kumar Mahato, Senior Data Analyst, Foundation for Agrarian Studies, Bengaluru; PhD scholar, Birla Institute of Technology and Science – Pilani (Hyderabad campus)

Nelson Mandela S., Assistant Professor, Department of Economics, School of Humanities and Social Sciences, GITAM University, Hyderabad

Parvathi Menon, journalist (retired), The Hindu Group

Tapas Singh Modak, Associate Fellow, Foundation for Agrarian Studies, Bengaluru

Fumiko Oshikawa, Emeritus Professor, Kyoto University, Kyoto

V. K. Ramachandran, Vice Chairperson, Kerala State Planning Board, Thiruvananthapuram

B. Satheesha, Research Scholar, Department of Humanities and Social Sciences, Indian Institute of Technology Delhi

Sethu C. A., Senior Research Assistant, Foundation for Agrarian Studies, Bengaluru

A. Suresh, Principal Scientist (Agricultural Economics), ICAR – Central Institute of Fisheries Technology, Kochi

V. Surjit, Associate Professor and Head, Centre for Agrarian Studies, National Institute of Rural Development and Panchayati Raj, Hyderabad

Madhura Swaminathan, Professor and Head, Economic Analysis Unit, Indian Statistical Institute, Bengaluru

M. Thangaraj, Visiting Professor, Department of Economics, Raiganj University, Raiganj; former Professor and Head, Department of Economics, University of Madras

Jayan Jose Thomas, Professor (Economics), Department of Humanities and Social Sciences, Indian Institute of Technology Delhi

Index